The United States and the
European Alliance since 1945

The United States and the European Alliance since 1945

Edited by
Kathleen Burk
and
Melvyn Stokes

BERG

Oxford • New York

First published in 1999 by
Berg
Editorial offices:
150 Cowley Road, Oxford, OX4 1JJ, UK
70 Washington Square South, New York, NY 10012, USA

Berg is the imprint of Oxford International Publishers Ltd.

Library of Congress Cataloging-in-Publication Data

A catalogue record for this book is available from the Library of Congress.

British Library Cataloguing-in-Publication Data

A catalogue record for this book is available from the British Library.

ISBN 1 85973 277 1 (Cloth)

Typeset by JS Typesetting, Wellingborough, Northants.
Printed and bound in Great Britain by Biddles Ltd, Guildford and King's Lynn

Contents

Acknowledgements

Early versions of the chapters in this book were presented as papers at the Commonwealth Fund Conference in American History at University College London in February 1996. They have been revised, in part in response to points made in discussions at that conference. Without financial assistance – which is gratefully acknowledged – from the Commonwealth Fund and Graduate School of University College London, the British Academy, the Royal Historical Society, the War Studies Department of Kings College London, the History Faculty of Cambridge University, the London University Institute of United States Studies, and the *Journal of American Studies*, the conference itself could not have taken place. This book has been published with the help of a grant from the late Miss Isobel Thornley's bequest to the University of London.

Introduction
Kathleen Burk

Relations between the United States and its European allies in the post-war period have for the past decades been a lively field for research. The original question was, how did the Cold War originate and develop, and how did the United States and the Western European states organize themselves for their defense against the perceived threat presented by the Soviet Union? Interest then moved on to the period after 1955: during that year the Federal Republic of Germany gained full sovereignty and joined NATO and, weeks later, the Soviet Union set up the Warsaw Pact; thereafter, with two organised blocs facing each other, there were long periods of stability, and interest could turn to inter-alliance relations. This period came to an end with the proclamation of the end of the Cold War in 1989, and, aided by the opening of the archives year by year, politics is now being turned into written history.

In this book, we look at the relationship from different angles, from that of Europe as well as that of the United States, and at personal and economic relationships as well as those focusing on defense. We look at the language of power, and at the very concept of a special relationship. Although we do not look specifically at the relationship of the alliance with the Soviet Union, which would be another topic entirely, its threatening presence can be assumed throughout the book. It is also worth noting that since the contributors come from six different countries, the book is not dominated by the assumptions arising from just one historical context but benefits from the different points of departure of historians from both big and small states.

The first chapter, which sets the scene for all those that follow, was written by a Norwegian historian of American and European foreign policy, Geir Lundestad. In it, he argues that the United States differed from other imperial powers: rather than follow the approach of divide and rule, it protected its superior position by encouraging the integration of its European allies. Europe was not to be a third force, but rather to be integrated into an organization with an Atlanticist perspective. The United States expected to dominate but not to rule, and this left scope for European self-organization and for European maneuvers.

The American passion for European integration varied over time, the U.S. Government strongly supporting it during the 1940s, 1950s, and 1960s, but more weakly thereafter, as European scope for independent action increased. Lundestad argues that the United States had five motives: it wanted to push the American system as a model to follow; it wanted a more rational and efficient Europe; it wanted to reduce the American defense burden; it wanted the containment of the Soviet Union; and it wanted the containment of Germany, the last-named especially to reassure the French, and especially during the period of the late 1940s and early 1950s, the formative years of European integration and of American support for it. In general, Washington promoted European integration by explicitly pushing the Europeans in that direction. From the European point of view, the United States was the ultimate balancer in Europe: if it was eventually to withdraw, it would be best to have the structure of European integration in place.

There is no doubt that, within the basic alliance relationship, ferocious battles were fought between the Europeans and the Americans over economic interests. The next two chapters look at two areas of conflict, civil aviation and oil, both of which were seen as important, and the latter as vital, to individual national interests. Alan Dobson, in chapter 2, argues that the desire for a freer air market has generally been the hallmark of American policy towards Europe, a goal which has been resisted by most European countries to a greater or lesser extent. The United States wanted liberal access to European markets, especially to those of Germany and the United Kingdom, and especially the right to pick up passengers in another country and carry them to a third-party destination. The United States would not, however, agree in return to compensate the Europeans by allowing them multiple access into the U.S. market as of right.

The United Kingdom was the focus of much American attention in this context for two reasons: the British empire provided numerous areas where U.S. airlines wanted landing rights; and, much more important in the long term, the United Kingdom controlled the landing slots at Heathrow, the most desirable of negotiating currencies, since Heathrow is the most important "hub" airport in the world. Indeed, the latter point, when combined with the fact that Britain had a unified policy and very tough negotiators and negotiating tactics, meant that the United States had less leverage over the United Kingdom than over other countries. Therefore, Britain fought off American attempts in the mid-1970s to change the rules of the game in the American favour. By the 1980s and 1990s, the United States was fearful that a Fortress Europe, arising from the European Union, would curtail rather than enlarge American aviation rights. Not for the first time, the United States had to contemplate the implications of the European integration which it had earlier so assiduously fostered.

The same combination of national interests plus increasing European consciousness and the growing desire of European countries to coordinate policies if possible was also seen in the 1973–1974 OPEC (Organization of Petroleum Exporting Countries) oil crisis. Fiona Venn, in chapter 3, argues that, until the late 1960s, there was a stable petroleum regime because of surplus productive capacity and the control of the large exporting oilfields by an interlocking group of multinational oil companies. After the 1967 Arab–Israeli War, however, the European Community recognized that some joint policies with regard to the supply of oil should be accepted; finally, in May 1973, the Council of Ministers of the European Economic Community agreed on joint action if there was a supply crisis. This decision did not, however, include the United States. A month earlier, the United States had proclaimed that 1973 was to be the "Year of Europe," which the Europeans found patronising and some – such as France – even found alarming, since the United States appeared to expect the subordination of European interests to its own in a new Atlantic Charter. (The United States tended to perceive American interests as identical with those of the alliance.) The stage was set for a conflict of interests in oil matters.

Matters came to a head with the 1973–1974 OPEC oil crisis. The U.S. Secretary of State, Henry Kissinger, moved to establish a permanent consumers' organization, the International Energy Agency (IEA), as a counterbalance to OPEC, and called an Energy Conference in Washington for February 1974. The United States tried to link defence and economic matters by threatening American isolationism as a response to European unilateralism in energy matters. Germany caved in, since it was very susceptible to arguments based upon this linkage, but France refused to cooperate. In the end, the IEA was established as an adjunct to the Organization for Economic Co-operation and Development, but this was the result, not of genuine negotiations, but of American domination and threats. Therefore, the IEA actually reinforced the divisions between member states and it became an agency in which governments acted to defend their national interests rather than to develop a common energy consumers' policy. At the end of chapter 3, Venn emphasizes the growing self-confidence of the European Community, which led increasingly to clashes with the United States, in particular over the implicit, if not explicit, American claim to unchallengeable leadership of the Western alliance.

In chapter 4, Frank Costigliola looks at the language used by American officials to describe their position within the alliance. He argues that U.S. foreign policy officials used "tropes of gender," i.e. the language of sex and gender, to conceptualize the relationship between a dominant United States and a subordinate Europe: American officials talked the language of co-operation but exercised a sophisticated control.

Costigliola demonstrates that U.S. officials often responded to an ally's resistance to American policy with language that depoliticized and trivialized the difference of opinion. Allied opposite numbers would be characterized as less than a healthy male – as a sick patient, an hysterical woman, an emasculated man. Such images of the needy inspired altruistic language, and helped to transform American control into (self-perceived) American caring. George Kennan, in his Long Telegram, utilized the image of the Soviet Union as a rapist which the United States had to contain, while later discussions over NATO saw American officials referring to that organization as something which would make the European allies feel better; the point of the latter, according to Costigliola, was to manipulate the allies rather than to deal with them as fully capable actors.

Costigliola looks at the cases of France, Germany, and the United Kingdom. France is particularly interesting because the contempt with which the Americans viewed the Fourth Republic in due course gave way to admiration of the de Gaulle of the Fifth Republic: he was so obviously tall and masculine that he could hardly be relegated to the position of a flighty woman. Costigliola also points out that this was an approach that was not restricted to one country: Britain certainly characterized the Americans as naive and inexperienced in 1945–46, when they anticipated guiding their American cousins in foreign affairs, and British officials were not shy of expressing their felt superiority over the French.

James Miller also looks at the alliance from the view of a weaker power confronting the United States, in this case Italy. In chapter 5, Miller grounds the ambivalence felt in Italy about the United States in the main currents of Catholic thought. He emphasizes the distaste felt by the Catholic Church in Italy for the United States, especially for mass popular American culture, for the domination of Protestantism, and for its wide acceptance of contraception and abortion. On the other hand, the Church was drawn to the United States because of a shared anti-communism, since communism was both totalitarian and anti-religious.

There were parallel efforts against the Communist Party by the Vatican and the American government during the 1948 Italian general election, efforts which were powerfully reinforced by the victory of the Christian Democratic Party (DC) over the Communist Party (PCI). During the following few years, both the Church and the U.S. government expressed uncompromising anti-communism, but this began to change in the early 1950s. The DC feared civil conflict if the political temperature of the country was not lowered, and the end of the Korean War and the death of Stalin, leading to changes in the international climate, facilitated the working-out of a domestic *modus vivendi:* the PCI would remain in permanent opposition but within the official structures of Italian democracy. The left wing of the DC, in fact, provided a strong push towards this rapprochement with the Italian left: they believed that democracy in Italy required a strong welfare state, which would include economic planning and attempts to modify Italy's vast inequality, and for this the unified support of the left was required.

Giorgio La Pira, the mayor of Florence, was at the forefront of this effort to create a centre–left coalition at both the local and national level. He was very ambivalent about the United States' assumption of the leadership of the Christian West, rejecting both the consumerism and the secularism central to the "American way of life." At first, he enjoyed some support from American officials, but the American government eventually decided that this ambivalence about America and his readiness to seek allies on the left meant that he had embraced communism. In truth, La Pira did not know how to deal with America.

La Pira, however, still enjoyed some support from the Vatican. His bungled attempt to mediate between North Vietnam and the United States, along with a foolish newspaper interview in 1965, ironically marked a turning point in U.S.–Vatican relations. The U.S. administration had rebuffed the Vatican over Vietnam and this led to a fundamental re-evaluation by the Vatican of its relations with the United States. By 1967, it was criticizing American-style economic and political liberalism and free trade; later, it attacked the American rapprochement with China. The DC moved cautiously in the same direction: the European Community was by now an alternative pillar of support, and Italy began to pursue a more independent line. It disassociated itself from the United States over the United Nations and Israel, it took a softer line than the U.S. towards the Soviet Union, and it expanded trade with Eastern Europe and with the radical states of the Middle East.

These changes in policy by the DC were taken account of by the PCI, and by the mid-1970s there came the DC's opening to the left, "the Historic Compromise," led by Aldo Moro. The common thread in all of this, the result of growing scepticism about the desirability of all of America's policies, was the ambivalence felt about the United States, grounded in cultural, if not always religious, Catholicism.

The following two chapters turn from culture to the most fundamental link between the United States and its allies, that of defense. In chapter 6, Beatrice Heuser makes the point that, while solidarity within NATO during the Cold War derived from the recognition of the interdependence of West European–North American security interests, this solidarity was weakened by a structural asymmetry: while the United States dominated because of its nuclear might, the Europeans were more likely than the Americans to suffer nuclear war on their territory. They were also likely to suffer a loss of sovereignty over their own territory during peacetime, as a result of American deployment of nuclear weapons on their soil. The larger countries – the United Kingdom, France, Canada, and Germany – tried to redress the balance in different ways. However, the inescapable fact that the United States was more essential yet less vulnerable than its allies as a counterbalance to the Soviet Union led to structural strains within NATO.

Heuser focuses on the reactions of Canada, the United Kingdom, France, and Germany to the problems arising from the stationing of American forces – and particularly nuclear weapons – on their soil. There was concern about the bases, but of much greater importance was the reluctance of the United States to inform, let alone to consult, its allies about the ways in which it might use these weapons. Canada knew that its geographical location was its only asset in negotiations with the United States and, therefore, did not want to give the U.S. Government *carte blanche* (the base at Goose Bay, Labrador was important to the U.S. Strategic Air Command (SAC) because planes stationed there could reach 75–100 per cent of all Soviet strategic targets in the Urals, the Moscow–Leningrad area, and the Don Basin). The jettisoning of a payload by a plane *en route* from Goose Bay to Arizona in November 1950 underlined for the Canadians their need to know in advance of any movement of nuclear weapons on or over their territory. Therefore, in May 1951, the Canadians told the Americans that they wanted the right to approve or veto any use of Goose Bay by SAC – in other words, to retain sovereign control in peacetime. However, they also emphasized that if there was a surprise Soviet attack against continental North America, they would support immediate retaliation by SAC without any need for prior consultation. In short, because North America was seen as indivisible by both the United States and Canada, ultimate command remained in the hands of the former, the concession Canada paid for the security of solidarity with its southern neighbor.

American nuclear-capable bombers, used both for NATO and non-NATO missions, have been stationed in Britain from the period of the

Berlin blockade in 1948 until the present. From the beginning of nuclear co-operation, the United Kingdom pushed to be consulted on the basis of equality by the United States on any use of nuclear weapons and, particularly, if the bases in Britain were to be utilized. There were no U.S. concessions until January 1952, when it was agreed that there had to be explicit British agreement before the United States utilized nuclear weapons from British bases. It was, however, a communiqué, not a treaty, and therefore the U.S. government took the position that it was not necessarily binding on future American presidents – and certainly not during an emergency – although the British government has always interpreted it as binding. In any case, from the early 1950s, Britain was informed of American nuclear strategy in much greater detail than was any other European power, and there gradually built up far-reaching Anglo-American cooperation on nuclear strategy and targetting.

France developed into the most important bridgehead for American forces, providing the ports for supplies, the pipeline for fuel to the central front area, and the headquarters for NATO. Not surprisingly, France was increasingly vexed to be excluded from nuclear planning, in spite of being part of NATO's tripartite emergency executive, the "Standing Group." In March 1957, France announced that it would only accept nuclear weapons on its soil if the French government had full national control over them, a view confirmed by de Gaulle in mid-1958. However, there is evidence that they were deployed and that the French government was not told; indeed, when de Gaulle asked the American commander whether this was the case, the information was refused. In September 1958, de Gaulle proposed a concertation mechanism involving the United States, the United Kingdom, and France which would go beyond the Standing Group to concert strategic nuclear planning, including areas outside of Europe. The United States said no, and de Gaulle then began withdrawing parts of the French armed forces from the integrated military command.

By 1960, France was a nuclear power and, with the successful production of the Mirage IV aircraft in 1964, it had a nuclear delivery system which was fully operational from the end of 1965. The country now had an independent nuclear deterrent. In March 1966, therefore, France sent a memorandum to the United States requesting the withdrawal of all foreign forces from French soil: for France, national sovereignty was more important than alliance solidarity.

Germany, Heuser argues, had even less knowledge than France of American nuclear strategy. The country was led to believe that its manpower was important to balance Warsaw Pact conventional forces: the German government had no knowledge that the U.S. Government had moved to a strategy of massive nuclear retaliation with the concomitant downplaying of on-the-ground fighting. Furthermore, American nuclear strategy kept changing from 1955 onwards and Germany was unable to make sense of it. This was particularly worrying, as German territory was the focal point for any nuclear war. Eventually, a range of nuclear missiles were given or sold to European NATO allies, including Germany, but the warheads remained in U.S. custody. But it meant, at the very least, that Germany and others could exercise militarily with them and knew roughly how they would be used.

Yet Germany, like France, wanted more input into nuclear decision-making. The Athens Guidelines of May 1962 laid down that consultation would take place – but only if U.S. decision-makers thought there was time to do so. Germany wanted a veto over the release of nuclear weapons from Federal Republic territory as well as a veto over targets in the German Democratic Republic. Many of these aims were attained, thanks to the French withdrawal from NATO's integrated military structure in 1966. The United States was brought to realize that the allies were entirely serious when they demanded more say, and Germany was included in the Nuclear Planning Group established in 1967 to determine the general principles which should guide nuclear use.

In sum, as Heuser argues, during the first half of NATO's history the United States refused to tell its allies how many nuclear weapons were stationed on their soil or where they were or how they were to be used. During the second half, after the French withdrawal, there was much more mutual consultation and consequently more alliance solidarity.

Lawrence Freedman and John Gearson, in chapter 7, argue that the British decision whether to order Polaris or Skybolt was the outcome of the balance of bureaucratic interests on both sides of the Atlantic, but that the way it was done – a decision by the political leaders – reflected the need for Prime Minister Macmillan to circumvent those who opposed either Polaris itself or the whole concept of a British nuclear force.

The late 1950s and early 1960s saw fundamental problems in the management of British defense policy. The policy-making area was dominated by the three services, who were organizationally independent, with mutually contradictory doctrines, and led by career officers who gave priority to the interests of their own services. In the late 1950s, the cost of defense led the Conservatives (and the Republicans in the United States) to give priority to nuclear retaliation, which was cheaper than maintaining huge armies. By the end of the 1950s, however, many writers on strategic doctrine were arguing for a move away from an overreliance on nuclear forces; this was complicated by the beginning of the missile age, which threatened bombers both as weapons-carriers and on the ground. The argument moved towards a submarine-based force, which swung the priority towards the navy and away from the air force. The air force objected, but so did admirals, who preferred aircraft-carrier groups to submarine forces. This was common in both the United States and the United Kingdom.

There was considerable discussion over the pros and cons of Skybolt and Polaris on both sides of the Atlantic. The problem for the United Kingdom was the delivery system; the United States wanted to help the British because it was concerned to avert further cuts in Britain's conventional forces and hoped to draw the United Kingdom into a multilateral nuclear force. The British government had a serious lack of analytical capability in the Ministry of Defense, and assumed that the United States would take the cheapest, rather than the best, option. They did not think through the problems. If they had, they would have realized that Polaris was the best option and would have requested it. On the other hand, Secretary of Defense Robert McNamara and other American officials did not fully appreciate the problems that cancellation of Skybolt would cause the British. Furthermore, McNamara did not like independent nuclear deterrents, preferring total American control.

Macmillan, as Freedman and Gearson argue, did not initially request Polaris for domestic political as well as foreign policy reasons. The Cabinet was split, with some members disliking the political and financial price which Britain would have to pay to maintain an independent capability. This was a view also shared by a number of civil servants, such as the Secretary to the Cabinet, Norman Brook. Thus, the issue in 1962 for the Cabinet was not in fact Skybolt versus Polaris, but whether or not Britain should have a nuclear strike force at all. A formal request for Polaris, Macmillan knew, would have required a Cabinet debate and allowed the "no deterrent" option to gain adherents. He needed to see President Kennedy, gain Polaris, and present the Cabinet with a *fait accompli*. He was also aware that revealing his hand in advance would allow U.S. opposition to such a deal to build up.

Macmillan argued that the United States had a moral commitment to supply the United Kingdom with a viable nuclear force, and Kennedy, McNamara, and Secretary of State Dean Rusk agreed that Eisenhower had probably made such a commitment in 1960. In fact, Kennedy had essentially agreed to supply Britain with Polaris even before the meeting at Nassau. Had the United States not done so, it would have uncoupled the nuclear relationship, making U.S. command and control of all of the nuclear forces of the alliance more difficult. Also, the U.S. State

Department pro-Europeans depended on the Tory moderates around Macmillan for their European policy, and bringing Macmillan down – the outcome if he had not secured Polaris – would have brought in either the nationalistic Tory right wing or the deeply ambiguous Labour Party, neither of which would have supported a pro-European policy. The summit by the politicians lifted the decision above the level of bureaucratic politics, and their political decision, Freedman and Gearson conclude, also turned out to be the correct strategic decision.

It was for some time argued that the decision at Nassau turned on the personalities of Macmillan and Kennedy. Freedman and Gearson demonstrate that this was not wholly the case, but it is true that in certain situations personalities do make a difference. The next two chapters consider this point explicitly. Pascaline Winand in chapter 8, focuses on Jean Monnet and Max Kohnstamm, his adviser, and their American connections. Informal contacts amongst Monnet's network of Europeanists, Winand argues, played a central role in shaping American policy towards European integration in specific cases. Some of the policies he inspired, however, had mixed results.

One example was the Pleven Plan for the European Defence Community (EDC). Monnet inspired it, Winand argues, and worked to get the United States to support it, since otherwise it would certainly not be accepted by the European powers. The Americans did indeed support it, but this did not prevent its being defeated in France. Again, with regard to the European Economic Community (EEC), it took some time for American support to crystallize, since there was a lack of agreement between the State Department and American representatives abroad on what was meant by "European unity." However, the United States eventually decided to back a supranational, six-nation approach as the one most likely to lead to political integration, the approach backed by Monnet as the only way to channel German energies into European integration.

The Americans, from the sidelines, exerted considerable influence on the EEC and Euratom negotiations. Monnet tended to place Euratom before the EEC because he believed that it would capture the public imagination. It was accorded the same priority by Secretary of State John Foster Dulles and President Eisenhower. Strong opposition, however, came from Lewis Strauss and his Atomic Energy Commission. However, nuclear power gained in importance as Suez demonstrated the need to lessen Western dependence on Middle Eastern oil, and the road to joint U.S.–Euratom progress was facilitated by the success of Sputnik, launched by the Soviet Union in 1957. Monnet's policy, Winand concludes, was accepted and enshrined in the joint Euratom–U.S. Agreement, but because of a lack of leadership in its first year, and a lack of strong governmental commitment, it was not very successfully implemented.

Klaus Schwabe, in chapter 9, begins by asking whether or not there was an American elite which had a specific impact on the execution of U.S. foreign policy. Deciding that there was, he looks at the links which held it together. There was no common background to this network. Some of its members came from old families, others did not. But all went to private schools and Ivy League universities, they all worked in corporate or international law or on Wall Street (or both), and few were career diplomats. They all shared personal integrity, a belief in the importance of integrating Germany into Europe along with apprehension about the Soviet Union, and the belief that the future of Europe was the primary challenge to U.S. diplomacy.

Schwabe then looks at five case studies to determine the extent of this elite's contribution to European policies from 1947 to 1957, including the extent to which individual responsibility for success or failure can be fixed. Firstly, he looks at the Marshall Plan and concludes that, except for the Administrator of the Plan, Paul Hoffman, most responsible Marshall Plan officials belonged to this Washington network. Secondly, he examines the question of supranational (rather than intergovernmental) structures as a starting point for long-term cooperation, a question given urgency by the establishment of the Federal Republic of Germany in 1949. This underlined the need to harness Germany economically and politically to the West. Britain was the impediment, and this split the network. George Kennan, in the summer of 1949, developed the idea of decoupling Britain from continental European integration, a policy rejected by American diplomats in Europe in October 1949 but backed by Dean Acheson, the Secretary of State, who decided that France should be encouraged to assume the leadership of Europe in place of Britain. This policy, though originally a minority view within the elite, was upheld through the early 1960s and was effectively the beginning of the "triple alliance" of the United States, France, and Germany in developing policy for Europe.

The third example is the European Coal and Steel Community (ECSC), dreamt up by Monnet and Robert Schuman to ensure continuing control of Germany's heavy industry without discrimination against the Federal Republic. The Washington network wholeheartedly supported the pro-posal – John J. McCloy in Bonn, David K. E. Bruce in Paris, and Acheson in Washington. The network became crucial in the last stages of the negotiations in January to March 1950, when the opposition by Ruhr heavy industry to deconcentration was at its height. The opposition was broken by linking German agreement to the ECSC to the restoration of sovereignty and rearmament.

The fourth case study is the EDC. Schwabe argues that McCloy and the network won a victory in ensuring the commitment of the United States to the EDC as the capstone of European integration. At first, Acheson was doubtful about and the Pentagon was against the whole idea of the EDC, but Monnet convinced NATO's Supreme Allied Commander, Europe, Eisenhower, of its importance in June 1951, and this was the breakthrough: the conclusion Eisenhower came to was that this was the only way to get a German defense contribution, and he would have to accept the primacy of political over military considerations. Acheson was then persuaded, he in turn persuaded President Truman, and the network fell into line to sell the policy. However, it met a resounding defeat in 1954 at the hands of the French National Assembly.

Finally, Schwabe looks at the case of Euratom, which, while backed by Monnet, had only lukewarm support from a number of powers. France was not keen if it meant renouncing nuclear weapons; Germany preferred its existing bilateral relationship with the United States, and agreed to pursue Euratom only if negotiations also pursued the setting-up of a common market; Britain preferred to deal with atomic developments within the framework of the Organization for European Economic Cooperation. In July 1955, the State Department decided to support the Euratom project as a way of reviving the integration movement and forging a new link between Germany and the West. This was opposed, as Winand also emphasized, by the AEC, which preferred bilateral agreements. Monnet requested American backing as a way of overcoming German resistance, and in this he was finally successful.

Schwabe's conclusion is that there was an elite, which was Atlanticist, committed to preventing European hegemony by one power, whether Germany or the Soviet Union, and to preventing conflict. Their panacea was integration along supranational lines, and it was this outlook which held them together. Schwabe points out that most members of this elite developed close ties with their opposite numbers in France, especially with Monnet, and to a lesser extent in the Federal Republic, particularly with Adenauer and Walter Hallstein. There was so strong a commitment to European integration that it became a basic assumption of American foreign policy, and changes in advisers in due course made no difference. Yet individuals do stand out, Schwabe argues: personalities make a difference.

The final two chapters try to go beyond individual relationships to look at the question of special relationships between governments. Alex

Danchev, in chapter 10, looks primarily but not exclusively at whether there is an Anglo-American special relationship and, particularly, at what this might mean. He argues that this whole concept is undertheorized and a sham. The point of reference for all those who claim the existence of such a relationship was the Grand Alliance of the Second World War, whose evangelist was Winston Churchill. For the past two decades, Danchev claims, the dominant mode was the functional, in which the relationship depended not on a common past but on common enemies. With the fall of the Soviet Union from the position of chief enemy, there has been a shift to what he calls the terminal mode, signifying the end of the Anglo-American relationship.

Danchev proposes ten criteria by which the importance of such a relationship can be ascertained. The most significant of these are what he terms transparency and mythicality. These are purely qualitative: specialness is a term of art. After looking briefly at the German–Israeli and the U.S.–Israeli special relationships in search of a good theory, he concludes that specialness is "a process of interaction laced with expectations."

The final chapter is by Gottfried Niedhart. Niedhart's theme is the German attempts to secure American support for Ostpolitik, the development of a new relationship based on détente with the Soviet Union, primarily between 1969, when the Brandt government took office, and 1971, when the agreement on Berlin was signed by the four occupying powers. Henry Kissinger, President Nixon's National Security Advisor, and Washington generally were especially worried by the independence and self-consciousness of the German government when formulating the guidelines of Ostpolitik. Since Germany's membership of NATO was not in question, American perceptions of this policy were influenced primarily by the legacy of German nationalism and by the confident way in which it was implemented. Could Germany resist if the Soviets offered reunification in exchange for neutralism? Kissinger did not believe that Brandt had either the intellectual capacity or the stamina to manage the forces which he had unleashed.

One problem was that the American Government was informed by Bonn, not consulted. One of Brandt's close advisers met with Kissinger in Washington, in October 1969, and they discussed three issues: the desire for greater independence for the Federal Republic, in that it wished to think for itself; the willingness of Bonn to sign the Nuclear Non-Proliferation Treaty, although desiring some minor Soviet clarifications; and the wish of the Federal Republic to emphasize the essential continuity of German foreign policy and the renunciation of force in German–Soviet relations. Kissinger advised the Germans to begin negotiations with the Soviet Union as soon as possible, although there is no doubt that he was more skeptical than the Germans about the whole process, fearing a Soviet policy of selective *détente* which would improve relations with European countries while remaining tough towards the United States. Kissinger also feared that Ostpolitik could weaken NATO. Kissinger's doubts were shared by the French President, Georges Pompidou, although British leaders endorsed Ostpolitik.

The first result was the Treaty of Moscow, signed in August 1970. Thereafter, an attempt was made to do something about adverse pockets of American public opinion: trade union leaders and the Jewish community in particular were highly pessimistic about Ostpolitik. It was decided that a new "German claque" had to be built up in the United States, since the old one, led by McCloy and General Lucius Clay, was no longer very influential. Contacts in the United States had to be intensified, since the Germans had failed to understand the anti-communist stance of both American business and labor. December 1970 saw considerable unhappiness in the United States over the spread of Ostpolitik, but Kissinger and the German representatives could agree that security and détente went hand in hand. In the final resort, Ostpolitik was perceived as it had always been in truth: as an integral part of Western détente. When Brandt and Nixon met in June 1971, Ostpolitik was no longer on the agenda; at the time of their next meeting, in December 1971, Nixon stressed the interrelationship of Ostpolitik, the Four-Power Agreement over Berlin of September 1971, and the breakthrough in U.S.–Soviet relations. Ostpolitik had smoothed the way.

Post-Ostpolitik, Niedhart argues, Germany continued to rely on the United States for security, but increasingly shifted to a more independent foreign policy. American resources were clearly limited, and this meant that there was a vital German interest in improving the European security system. Germany supported a European security conference as proposed by the Soviet Union, but this was inconceivable without the participation of the United States. Kissinger regarded such a conference as superfluous, but Bonn wanted it as a confidence-building move: American forces were not necessarily going to be in Europe at their present strength forever, and a continuing policy of détente seemed vital to Bonn. In due course, the conference was held.

Niedhart concludes that the accommodation to realities was a characteristic feature of international relations during the 1970s and 1980s. The Federal Republic accepted the territorial status quo. The superpowers accepted that their resources were limited and that the days of a bipolar world were gone. The United States had to accept that Europe was integrating, as it had encouraged it to do, and that this was changing the U.S.–European power relationship; and the United States also acknowledged that having American troops in Europe was in the American, as well as the Western European, interest. Moscow would attempt to overcome economic problems by a reduction in arms and by economic cooperation with the West. Western aid was, in fact, dependent on Moscow's accepting realities in Europe, especially integration, the links between the Federal Republic and Berlin, and the presence of American troops. Ostpolitik was intended to foster both the Federal Republic's reconciliation with the Soviet Union and a change in the postwar order. Détente and its implications – better East–West communications, more trade relations – might transform the Warsaw Pact: more trade might lead to more friction within the communist communities and this might lead to change. It did.

And with these changes – the transformation first of the domestic political order within the former Warsaw Pact states, then of the relationship between these states and the Soviet Union, and then of these states plus the Soviet Union with the West – an epoch in international relations came to an end. During this epoch most attention was paid to the U.S.–Soviet relationship, the only one, of course, which threatened annihilation. But the interrelationships of other states were equally interesting, and in particular those of the Western European states with their main ally, the United States. In this book we attempt to chart some of those relationships.

–1–

"Empire" by Integration:
The United States and European
Integration, 1945–1996[1]

Geir Lundestad

Throughout history empires have been ruled from an imperial center. This imperial center has almost always tried to guard its special position and if there was one development it feared, it was the emergence of anything that looked even remotely like an alternative center. Divide and rule was an important part of imperial techniques in keeping the imperial subjects calm. Among modern empires, this description can be applied to relatively loose empires such as the Austrian and the British ones, and to more centralized ones such as the French and, particularly, the Soviet empires. For Vienna, London, Paris, and Moscow it was out of the question to promote an alternative center, since this could come to weaken the position of the imperial capital.

Whether the American role after 1945 was so dominant that we should call the areas where the United States made its influence the most strongly felt an "empire" or simply "a sphere of influence" may be debated.[2] Most of the countries under some sort of American influence were independent, but at the same time there could be little doubt about the predominant role of the United States. In the looser sense of the term, the American sphere of influence could well be called an "empire."

Yet, the United States clearly organized its "empire" differently than other great powers did. The United States *promoted* the integration of the most important region within this sphere, namely Western Europe. Washington actually favored the creation of a supranational Europe with its own political bodies and, accordingly, at least the possible development of an alternative political center.

As the "father" of European integration Jean Monnet put it, the American insistence on European integration "is the first time in history that a great power, instead of basing its policy on ruling by dividing, has

– 17 –

consistently and resolutely backed the creation of a large Community uniting peoples previously apart."[3]

Yet, this argument can easily be taken too far. Two reservations are particularly important. First, while the United States was indeed different from other great powers, it did not pursue its pro-integrationist policy for the sake of the West Europeans primarily. Washington thought its policy best also for them, but naturally it had its own motives for supporting an integrated Europe. These motives will be discussed shortly.

Second, while the United States supported an integrated Western Europe, this was not to be an independent Europe in the sense of the "third force" often discussed, particularly on the European left. In the American perspective, the integrated Europe was always to be fitted into a wider Atlantic context. Through this context, the United States would presumably be able to protect its leading role within the Western world, although this could not be *guaranteed* once a supranational Europe had been established.

The United States, as other great powers, protected its interests. Its domination was, however, based on American values, in the way other powers had exercised domination based on theirs. On the American side, these values left a remarkably wide scope for European self-organization. Thus, while the United States certainly protected its superior role, it did so in a rather different way than other great powers. Perhaps we could call this policy hegemony, or even "empire" by integration.

This is the overall argument and structure of the present chapter. I shall, however, discuss one additional point, namely the impact the American policy had on the development of European integration. As we shall see, this is both a most relevant and a highly controversial point. In conclusion, I shall offer some words not only on where the American–European relationship stands today, but even on where it might be headed in the future.

Most of the historians who have written about the United States and European integration have indeed stressed the American support for such integration.[4] I would agree with this analysis. The United States supported the integration of Western Europe, very strongly in the 1950s and 1960s, rather more weakly later. More and more, U.S. support had to be balanced with other American objectives, particularly the explicit protection of the NATO framework, but also of U.S. economic interests.

Obviously such a deep-seated attitude flowed from many different sources. Yet, without simplifying matters too much, these sources, or motives, may be arranged in five different clusters which we may refer to respectively as the American model, a more rational and efficient

Europe, a reduced American burden, the containment of the Soviet Union, and, finally, the containment also of Germany.

I believe this list puts the five elements in an ascending order of importance, with the last two being particularly important and closely linked. The "double containment" of the Soviet Union and of Germany represented the answer to immediate American security problems while the first three clusters of motives represented longer-term interests. As almost always happens in politics, the short term is more important than the long one, but all five clusters worked in favor of the United States strongly supporting European integration.

In a brief chapter it is impossible for me to deal with all five of these motives. If I were to stress *one* of them, it would have to be the need to integrate Germany with Western Europe in general and with France in particular. This motive was especially strong in the period from the late 1940s until the early 1960s, i.e. in the formative years both of European integration and of American support for it. Statements about Germany's crucial role abound in the sources and the urgency of these statements is quite striking.

In the combination of Germany's need for equality and of Europe's need to contain Germany lay probably the deepest roots of European integration. In October 1949, Washington instructed the French that they had to take the lead on European integration, since the British had so clearly demonstrated their unwillingness to do so. In May 1950, rather amazingly, the French responded, in the form of the proposal for the European Coal and Steel Community (the Schuman plan).[5]

Secretary of State Dean Acheson informed U.S. embassies in Europe that the "US attaches greatest importance [to the] Schuman principles as [a] contribution [to] French–German *rapprochement*."[6] John Foster Dulles proclaimed that "the conception is brilliantly creative and could go far to solve the most dangerous problem of our time, namely the relationship of Germany's industrial power to France and the West."[7]

In the discussions about the European Defence Community (EDC), President Dwight D. Eisenhower could become quite alarmist about Germany's future. In his talks with British Prime Minister Winston Churchill in July 1954, before the French vote on the EDC, he emphasized that "we could not afford to lose Germany even though we were to lose France." He raised the question "as to the point at which action to preserve Germany would be required on our part."[8]

In May 1961, President John F. Kennedy told British Prime Minister Harold Macmillan that, in the EEC question, "Our central interest here, as I am sure you know, is political. We believe that only with growing political coherence in Western Europe can we look to a stable solution of the place of Germany."[9] Two weeks later, Kennedy told French President Charles de Gaulle that, in addition to the economic and political strengthening of Europe, "There is also another reason why we favor the Community. It is because it contributes to tie West Germany to Europe. It is not clear what will happen in Germany after Adenauer and, therefore, every tie which links Germany to Europe should be welcome."[10]

In the period of maximum concern with Germany, the ultimate fear was that Germany would side with the Soviet Union. Again and again, members of the Eisenhower administration returned to this horror among other horror scenarios. After the French national assembly in August 1954 had rejected the EDC, Secretary of State Dulles thus told the National Security Council that

> The heart of the matter was whether or not we should be able to preserve NATO. The Soviets successfully used Mendès-France to kill, or at least to maim, EDC. Will they now try to destroy NATO? . . . There is no use talking about the U.S. proceeding unilaterally to arm Germany. In such a situation Germany may well choose not to rearm. There would certainly be heavy pressure in these circumstances for Germany to accommodate to the Soviet Union. The latter could dangle the possibility of unification of Germany, rectification of the Polish frontier, and economic advantages.[11]

The Soviets held strong cards, and if they played them well, the consuming fear was that the Germans would be tempted by the siren songs of neutrality. Chancellor Konrad Adenauer held them in place. He rejected Soviet overtures, in the form of Soviet proposals for unification, particularly the one in 1952, but, again, what would happen after him?

In the preparations for Kennedy's visit to Europe in June–July 1963, Under Secretary of State George Ball, the person largely responsible for European integration in the Kennedy administration, pointed out that

> Up to this point, the Germans have largely been tractable because of their fear of the Soviet Union and the knowledge that we alone can provide an effective defense. But a process of shifts and changes is under way on both sides of the Iron Curtain, and the possibility of some Soviet overture to a post-Adenauer Germany must not be overlooked . . . *In those changed circumstances a Germany not tied closely and institutionally to the West can be a source of great hazard. Embittered by a deepening sense of discrimination and bedeviled by irredentism, a Germany at large can be like a cannon on shipboard in a high sea* [italics in the original text].[12]

While Eisenhower–Dulles had a very close relationship with Adenauer, the Kennedy administration increasingly came to feel that the German chancellor was just too rigid on East–West matters, including the status of Berlin and even of East Germany.[13] Despite this, as the Ball quotation clearly indicates, the Kennedy administration too was concerned about Germany as a possible loose cannon. Washington's drawn-out support for the Multilateral Force (MLF) in NATO illustrated the fear that if the Germans were discriminated against, they could come to respond in dangerously nationalistic ways.

As Germany proved a loyal supporter of European integration, even after Adenauer had retired and German political life stabilized in the political center, the overriding fear about Germany's position gradually abated. Yet, the process was rather slow. Alarmist analyses and statements were still made. De Gaulle's independence, in fact, gave them new life. His policies allegedly represented a threat not only to the United States, but also to Germany. As President Johnson told Prime Minister Harold Wilson in May 1966,

> there is grave danger that the Germans will over time feel that they have been cast adrift. A growing sense of uncertainty and insecurity on their part could lead to a fragmentation of European and Atlantic relations which would be tragic for all of us. On our part, we cannot risk the danger of a rudderless Germany in the heart of Europe.[14]

Germany's position remained an important consideration even with later administrations. In Nixon–Kissinger's guarded response to Chancellor Willy Brandt's *Ostpolitik*, a lingering fear of Germany's political reliability could still be detected, although less dramatic now than before.[15] With Germany's unification in 1990, the concern came back in a different form. Thus, the Clinton administration recently pointed out that one of the reasons why it encouraged the European Union (EU) was because "it provides a home for Germany to act out its future in an integrated Europe and not independent of it."[16]

In two world wars, the United States had intervened to stop European integration in the form of German domination. In the Cold War, it intervened to stop Soviet domination and to contain German influence. Thus, the American support for European integration was clearly premised on certain conditions being fulfilled. By far the most important of the conditions attached to European integration was that the more united Europe had to be fitted into a wider Atlantic framework. The Atlantic framework was established through, first, the Marshall Plan and the

Organization for European Economic Cooperation (OEEC) and, then, even more importantly, through NATO. To a large extent this "Atlantic framework" was a code phrase for overall American leadership. There was never any real doubt that Western Europe belonged to the American "empire."

In the early years, the Atlantic framework was rarely explicitly formulated. The main reason for this was quite simply that at this early stage it was more or less taken for granted that the United States and Europe had the most basic interests in common. These interests definitely included the Atlantic framework and American leadership.

In historical perspective, the Eisenhower administration was remarkable not for its implicit emphasis on the framework, but rather for the strong and direct support it gave to European integration. The British kept pushing for unambiguously Atlantic solutions, whether in the form of German rearmament in NATO, an OEEC approach to cooperation in atomic energy, an Atlantic free trade area to "dilute" the EEC, or even putting all the European institutions – the European Coal and Steel Community (ECSC), Euratom, and the Common Market – into some sort of Atlantic setting. All these efforts were, however, *opposed* in Washington. While there should definitely be a wider Atlantic framework for European integration, the United States, unlike Britain, insisted – in Dulles's words – that the "six should increasingly act as a unit within [the] Atlantic organization, and that integrity of developing institutions of [the] six-country Community should be safeguarded."[17]

The coming to power of de Gaulle and the EEC's economic challenge to the United States were to strengthen Washington's emphasis on the Atlantic framework. While this framework had been largely implicit until 1959–60, thereafter it became a constant and explicit part of U.S. policy. The fact that John Foster Dulles – who combined strong support for both European and Atlantic integration – became ill and had to leave office in April 1959, being replaced by the more Atlantic-oriented Christian Herter, helped smooth this transition.

With this kind of Atlantic framework, rather implicit at first, then more explicit, it was evident that Washington did not really see Western Europe as an independent actor. Europe might occasionally come to have positions different from those of the United States, but the assumption was that the two sides of the Atlantic would continue to share the most basic interests.

True, before the founding of NATO, Washington, in the words of John D. Hickerson, head of the State Department's Office of European Affairs, "had envisaged the creation of a third force which was not merely the extension of US influence but a real European organization strong enough to say `no' both to the Soviet Union and the United States, if our actions should seem so to require." With an Atlantic defense organization being created, a development to which Hickerson himself contributed so much, the "third force" quickly became aligned with the United States.[18]

In the 1950s and 1960s, there were still many American references to an integrated Europe representing such a "third force." Most of these references, however, simply meant that a united Europe would be a third important actor in international politics, after the United States and the Soviet Union. The implication was almost never that it would be an independent unit standing in the middle between the two existing super-powers; it was just an additional one. The expectation was almost always that it would be standing rather close to the United States.

Eisenhower repeatedly talked about Western Europe as a "third force," but always in this context of a united Europe cooperating with the United States. Thus, in November 1954 he told French Premier Pierre Mendès-France that Western Europe "should be the third great force in the world . . . [the] US was related by culture and blood to countries of Western Europe and in this sense was a product of Western Europe. For this reason we favor a strong Western Europe."[19] In February 1956, Eisenhower referred to the industrial capacity of a united Europe and then expressed his belief that "such a `third force' *working with the rest of the free world* [my italics] would change the whole complexion of present circumstances and insure peace."[20] Earlier, he had even talked about "developing in Western Europe a third great power bloc, after which development the United States would be permitted to sit back and relax somewhat."[21]

The Kennedy and later administrations rarely used the expression "third force." This was probably because General de Gaulle was now the spokesman of a truly independent Europe. Washington certainly did not want to express support for his kind of "third force." Instead, the Atlantic framework was to be emphasized more explicitly than ever. Thus, George Ball, in referring to a united Europe, stated that while in de Gaulle's view such a Europe should be independent from the United States, the United States, on the other hand, wanted "to insure that a united Europe works with us ever more closely in the framework of an Atlantic alliance for ensuring our common security and a close partnership for carrying out our common responsibilities in Asia, Africa, and Latin America."[22] And, in the very same speech in which President Lyndon B. Johnson proclaimed Washington's strong support for European integration, he also affirmed that "It remains our conviction that an integrated Atlantic defense is the first necessity and not the last result of the building of unity in Western Europe, for expanding partnership across the Atlantic, and for reconciling differences with the East."[23]

European integration flowed from many different sources, certainly including some that had little or nothing to do with the American role.[24] With many forces pulling in the same direction, it is difficult to isolate the American influence. Nevertheless, the combined facts that a more or less continuous deepening and widening of European integration has taken place and that the United States supported this process have led most historians to assume there was a close connection between these two things. For what we may call "traditionalists," the American impulse was definitely an important driving force, for a few of the traditionalists even *the* most important force behind European integration.[25]

Traditionalist viewpoints of one kind or another dominate most general accounts of European integration. Van der Beugel and Ellwood offer clear-cut examples of traditionalism, while more moderate versions are found with Vaughan, Urwin, and even Loth.[26] Among specialized studies of the United States and European integration, as reflected in accounts of specific periods or American relations with specific countries, Camps, Rappaport, Melandri, Bossuat, Hogan, Wall, Gillingham, Schwartz, Winand, and Schwabe may all be categorized as traditionalists of one kind or another.[27]

The traditionalist interpretation has received strong support on both sides of the Atlantic. What we may call the "revisionist" case can be seen as a partial European reaction to the traditionalist focus on the role of the United States.[28] European revisionism has been presented with the greatest vigor by Alan S. Milward. Milward sees the American influence as relatively unimportant both for European reconstruction, which is at the focus of attention in his *The Reconstruction of Western Europe 1945–51*, and for European integration. European integration as it actually developed was based not on American ideas, not even on the influence of the European "saints" (Monnet, Schuman, Adenauer, Spaak, etc.), but on practical, largely economic considerations in the various European nation states: "the process of integration was a Western European solution to a Western European problem." The objective of this European process was not at all to replace the nation state but, as the title of Milward's second major work in this field makes clear, rather *The European Rescue of the Nation-State.*

Still, Milward believes, the United States had *some* influence, if only because the Europeans had to develop their own ideas in response to American pressure: "without the drive of the United States to impose integration to suit its own strategic goals Western Europe would perhaps not have discovered its own different route to a settlement." His down-playing of the American influence seems more pronounced in *The Reconstruction of Western Europe 1945–51* than in *The European Rescue of the Nation-State*.[29] Although Milward is definitely in a minority among historians, his interpretation has received some support.[30]

My own position is in the middle, although definitely closer to that of the traditionalists than to that of Milward and the revisionists. However, I will not for the most part emphasize the effects of the American position on integration as such, important as that was at least through most of the 1950s. Rather, I shall stress the great influence that flowed from the more general position of the United States in Europe.

It is easy to demonstrate the limits of American influence. The EDC was defeated, despite the strong American threats to France. Initially at least, Washington was pushing for Euratom while providing less leadership on the much more important and far more successful EEC. The United States was not able to bring Britain into the Community until after de Gaulle had left the scene. The widening and deepening of European integration that took place in the 1980s and 1990s happened in a period when U.S. support for European integration had declined substantially. In the end, Europeans decided the forms European integration was to take, although the United States could, of course, encourage some Europeans over others.

Yet, the American position in the world after 1945 was probably stronger than that of any earlier great power had ever been. Naturally, this position was particularly strong within the American "empire", which certainly included Western Europe. With the kind of preeminent position the United States had in several European countries, including a crucial Germany at least through the 1950s, it is difficult to believe that European integration could actually have taken place without American backing.[31]

In general, Washington promoted European integration by explicitly pushing the Europeans in that direction. The American influence was greatly enhanced by the fact that strong forces in most of continental Europe shared the U.S. objective. Occasionally, the American influence could also be negative, in the sense that some Europeans wanted to strengthen Europe also *vis-à-vis* the United States. In 1956, the United States humiliated Britain and France, two of its most important allies, in the most striking way over Suez. Particularly in France, the Suez humiliation magnified support for European integration, in part to make it easier for France and Europe to stand up to the United States.[32]

The effects of the American policy on German reconstruction probably meant even more for European integration than the formal American position on integration as such. Washington insisted that Germany had to be reconstructed. It clearly indicated that European integration was the way in which to do this, but still left it to Paris to decide exactly how this was to be accomplished. Paris took the "plunge" in the form of the ECSC.

The fact that the French in the end did make the "plunge" brings up the question of why they now felt that they could do so. The French hand was certainly forced by the events in Germany and by the pressure from Washington. Yet, without the risk being manageable in some way, Paris might still not have agreed to the full reconstruction of Germany, much less taken the crucial first steps on the road to European integration.

When French foreign minister Robert Schuman launched his Coal and Steel initiative, the French still hoped to include the British, but they were clearly prepared to proceed without them.[33] In the EDC, Britain was expected to remain outside, although the British forces in Germany could help in the control function toward Germany. Nevertheless, the French did proceed, admittedly rather hesitantly, but proceed they did. In a deeper sense, it may be argued that the French "plunge" represented a shift in the French focus, away from the United Kingdom and towards the United States.

With the strong American role in Europe, which was similar to the role the French had wanted the United States to play even after the First World War, and with NATO not only in place, but also becoming an integrated organization after the outbreak of the Korean War, the United States was clearly the ultimate balancer, in case anything should go wrong with the integration of Germany.[34]

Therefore, Milward's view that the French were the strongest proponents of European integration and the least influenced by the United States, while perhaps superficially convincing, may at least in part represent a misunderstanding of the role of the United States in French policy. Thus, in parts of *The European Rescue of the Nation-State*, even Milward actually appears to recognize the importance of the Atlantic structure for the integration of Germany.[35]

European integrationists usually favored very close ties with the United States. This was most definitely the case with Jean Monnet on the French side and with the Dutch generally. The latter were reluctant to proceed with the ECSC and the EDC without Britain being included and, at least indirectly, the Americans being committed as well. Dutch foreign minister Johan Willem Beyen, who played such a fundamental role in working out the EEC, clearly appreciated the American role of support for European integration, although, after the EDC failure, he too encouraged a lower American profile.[36]

The balancing of Germany in Europe, and of Japan in Asia, was one of America's most important functions within its "empire". In this perspective, of the United States as the ultimate balancer of Germany, Charles de Gaulle again seems to represent a special case. True, de Gaulle was strongly opposed to supranationality, but the paradox in his position is that he favored close European cooperation based on the Paris–Bonn axis, but with a minimum of ties to the United States, Britain, and NATO. How, then, was Germany to be controlled if anything went wrong? Henry Kissinger, with his keen understanding of *Realpolitik*, after listening to the French President develop his views on Europe, responded that "I do not know how the President will keep Germany from dominating the Europe he has just described." De Gaulle simply replied: "Par la guerre" [through war].[37]

Consequently, it would appear that the direct relationship between European integration and the need for the United States to balance Germany can be overstated. De Gaulle's attitude shows, if proof were needed, that it was possible to pursue forms of European integration without basing them on an explicit Atlantic framework.

Yet, even de Gaulle, rhetoric notwithstanding, did not actually want to push the United States out of Europe. While in his opinion supranationality and American domination were wrong, there was nothing wrong with the American military association with Europe, in the form of the NATO guarantee as such and American atomic weapons and troops on European, although not on French, soil. The American role in Europe represented a form of hegemony, but even de Gaulle called it a "protective hegemony." When the Soviet threat was most evident, de Gaulle clearly stressed the importance of the American presence in Europe. This had been the case in 1945–1946 and it happened again after the Soviet invasion of Czechoslovakia in 1968.[38]

In the end, therefore, perhaps for de Gaulle as well, the United States *was* the ultimate balancer in Europe. If, on the other hand, the United States should really come to leave Europe, as de Gaulle frequently implied (but probably actually feared), then it would be best to have the European integrative structure in place before that happened. It might be too late to do it after the Americans had left.

The role of the United States as the ultimate balancer remained important long after the American support for integration as such had begun to weaken. The developments related to Germany's unification would seem to bear this out even in the 1990s. Only the United States, among the old occupying powers in Germany, supported Chancellor Helmut Kohl's policy on unification. Both Britain's Margaret Thatcher and France's

François Mitterrand were skeptical, but had no real alternative and therefore had to flow with the dramatic events. Most important in this context, as Elizabeth Pond, among others, has argued, the United States also played a crucial role by reassuring Moscow that its "security interests would not be impaired," reassuring "Germany's neighbors that the United States would be on hand as a counterweight to ascendant German power," and uttering "some hard truths about the need for NATO's continuance that the British and the French, by their resistance to unification, had disqualified themselves from saying."[39]

Germany's unification had some immediate effects on French policy. It was undoubtedly one very important factor behind the Maastricht Treaty. The new unified Germany had to be more closely bound up with Europe than before.[40] More slowly, France also moved closer not only to Britain and to the United States, but has now even in part resumed its place on NATO's Military Committee. These events would have been less likely without Germany's unification. Thus, even today the United States would appear to be the ultimate balancer of European politics.

To return to the comparative note on which I began, the United States, like other great powers, tried to remain dominant, but it did so in its own way. In a comparative context, the most surprising element in this American way remains not the qualifications that gradually developed in the support given to an integrated Western Europe, but rather that so strong support was given for so long to what at least had the potential of becoming an alternative political center.

Why did the United States pursue a course so different from that of other great powers? It is impossible to give definitive answers to such a complex question, but some relevant points may be briefly discussed.

The reasons for the American support of European integration have already been rehearsed. The deeper comparative answer, however, has to come in several parts. First, the United States definitely did not consider itself an imperial power. On the contrary, it viewed itself as anti-imperial. The United States had been created in rebellion against British imperial rule. The whole idea of one center formally controlling other territories was imperial. In a sense, therefore, it was also un-American.

After the Second World War, the United States continued to oppose imperial rule, even by Western European powers, although this opposition was often tempered by various Cold War considerations. And Washington, of course, opposed Soviet domination. It would have been awkward for the United States to pursue policies which could be seen as too much resembling those of more traditional great powers.

Second, European integration represented the European version of

American federalism, democracy, and the free market. Americans considered federalism closely related to the other two concepts, and as one of their most beneficial inventions. It was quite simply the "right" way to run large territorial units. To some Europeans, however, federalism of the American variety seemed probably more closely connected with democracy and open markets than reality justified. The French, in particular, and this certainly included American favorite Jean Monnet, consequently combined integration with heavy doses of state ownership and *dirigisme*.[41]

Integration, democracy, and open markets represented core American values. This is what America exported. Other great powers exported their systems of government, whether it be French centralism, British indirect rule, or Soviet communist direct control.

Of course, American ideals were sometimes corrupted by great-power practices. Leftist democracies (Czechoslovakia in 1946, Guatemala in 1954, Chile in 1973) were undermined; many a right-wing dictatorship was supported. Yet, as Tony Smith has recently argued so powerfully, America's more general mission was to promote democracy.[42] Free trade could be combined with central political control, as the British imperial example clearly showed. Until 1932, Britain was a stronger believer in, and a considerably more consistent executor of, free-trade policies than the United States was ever to become. Democratic rule, however, could hardly, at least not in the long run, be combined with formal control over other peoples. Ultimately, the widening of democracy in the metropolitan country stimulated the dissolution of empire, as the history of the British empire suggests, and as the more recent histories of the Portuguese and Soviet empires so clearly demonstrate.

The informal American "empire" did not sit well with any form of direct control. Not only that, the core American values of federalism, democracy, and open markets probably made the United States much more comfortable with spontaneity and self-organization than earlier great powers had been. Local initiatives were more highly appreciated, particularly when, as in the case of European integration, they fell well within the realm of what Washington wanted anyway.[43]

Similarly, in American eyes, an integrated Europe was not only the most efficient way for Europe to run itself, but it would also result in the smallest expense for the United States. Other great powers presumably also tried to run the areas they controlled, far more directly than did the United States Western Europe, in ways they considered both efficient and inexpensive.[44]

Third, the United States encouraged integration in Europe because this was seen as the most effective way of organizing the containment of the Soviet Union. As we have seen, this motive was underlined time and again by all administrations in Washington, starting with Truman's. America's policy cannot be understood without keeping this factor clearly in mind.

Yet, when viewed in a comparative perspective, this factor becomes more complicated. Other great powers, of course, also had enemies. The effect of the existence of such enemies was sometimes to underline the importance of imperial control. The Soviet Union was particularly vigilant against nationalist deviations during the height of the Cold War; with *détente,* more openness was tolerated. In the short run, the effect of the Second World War on the British empire was to postpone the process of independence in a now-crucial India. No immediate changes were to be brought about since they might disturb the war effort.

In the long run, however, the effect both of the Second World War and of the Cold War was to undermine the control of the traditional imperial powers. The huge significance of the Japanese defeat of the European colonial powers in East Asia is not particularly relevant in this context, but other effects are, such as the promises given to the colonies to encourage their full support and avoid their siding with the enemy, the idealism on which the struggle against the enemy had to be based, the need to draw upon the resources of the various areas as effectively as possible, and so on.[45]

Some of these effects may be compared with the effects of the Cold War on U.S. policies towards Western Europe, but in the latter case they were more immediate than in most of the former. For the United States the direct threat from the Soviet Union became a key argument in favor of integrating Western Europe.

Fourth, the importance of the indirect threat from Germany has been repeatedly underlined in this chapter. With Germany being seen as responsible for two world wars, how could one really trust the Germans? With the Soviets holding such strong cards *vis-à-vis* Germany, how could Washington in the long run prevent a *rapprochement* between the past and the present enemy? Western European integration seemed to be the obvious answer.

When viewed in a comparative perspective, it was something new that the victors in the Second World War not only defeated, but also occupied the entire territory of, the main enemy. Not even Napoleon, who temporarily controlled such a large part of Europe, had in the end been able to defeat and then occupy his main antagonists, Britain and Russia. The completeness of the victory left a problem which earlier victors had not faced. In the short run Germany would be held down, the traditional way of controlling a defeated enemy. But in the long run, this approach was untenable for the United States and at least also for Britain, for obvious reasons, most of which have really been presented in the previous points. Since Germany could not be let loose either, integration was again the answer. The American experience in Germany in a way resembled the North's experience with the South after the American Civil War. First there would be occupation and control, later integration and equality.

Fifth, one is struck by the strength, self-confidence, and success of the American approach. This strength, self-confidence, and success disposed the United States toward European integration as compared with more imperial and more direct ways of rule. It was not only difficult, it was quite unnecessary for the United States to establish any form of direct rule. It could achieve the kind of control it wanted through more indirect, more American, means.

The United States of Truman and Eisenhower was really much stronger in absolute as well as in relative terms than not merely Stalin's Soviet Union, but also Victoria's Britain, Napoleon and Louis XIV's France, Philip II's Spain or Charles V's Hapsburg empire. The United States was stronger than all of them in all categories of power at the same time, military, economic, political, cultural, and structural.[46]

Despite occasional bouts of self-doubt, the United States after 1945 was also remarkably self-confident. American isolationism, especially in the 1930s, had been a reaction to the dangers of Europe. America must not be contaminated by the evils of the Old World. After the Second World War there was little danger of such contamination. Influence seemed to flow all in the other direction, from the New to the Old World.

American policy was also quite successful. Globally, the United States was defeated in the backyard of the Soviet Union, in Eastern Europe, and in the world's most populous country, in China. These were significant defeats, but they should not make us overlook the success the United States had in organizing "the free world," or the American "empire." This "empire," unlike earlier empires, contained most of the key areas of the world. In Western Europe, Washington was able to organize NATO, keep the Communists out of power, and include the region in the American-organized system of freer trade. In comparative perspective, this was an outstanding record. It compared quite well with those of more formal empires.[47]

When, starting in the late 1950s, challenges began to arise to the American position in Western Europe and America's strength and, a little later, its self-confidence began to erode, then Washington's support for European integration became more conditional. The domination only implicit in the NATO structure had to be made explicit and American economic interests had to be protected more directly than before.

Sixth, the United States felt much closer to Western Europe than the Soviet Union did toward Eastern Europe and Britain, France, or other imperial powers had generally done toward their colonial areas. Because of this closeness, moreover, Washington had much to gain and little to lose by promoting European integration. The best parallel here would be the British attitude to the white dominions. There, unlike in other areas of the empire, London was prepared to grant early self-government.

The assumption behind the American policy on European integration was that the United States and Western Europe had the most basic interests in common. They had fought together against Germany; now they stood united against the Soviet Union. The two sides of the Atlantic shared democratic ideals. If the Europeans were to the left of the Americans in their economic policies, this was at least in part not only understandable, but perhaps also desirable under the circumstances prevailing in Europe.[48] In their general culture, as in their degrees of development, the United States and Western Europe were close. Most Americans were of European descent and race.

The Europeans had in fact "invited" the Americans to play the overall role they did in Europe after the Second World War.[49] The Americans, in turn, basically trusted the Europeans. Dulles thus believed it was almost certain that the United States and Western Europe would stay close together "for the very good reason that the Western European nations and the United States were part and parcel of Western civilization, with similar religion, culture, and other fundamental affinities."[50] Or, in McGeorge Bundy's words, "in the end our confidence in Europe rests on deeper and more solid political ground. These peoples are our cousins by history and culture, by language and religion. We are cousins too in our current sense of human and social purpose."[51]

Once again, in other parts of the American "empire" or sphere of influence, where the interests of the United States and the local governments did not coincide to the extent they did in Western Europe, American rule could be more direct. In Central America, much of the Pacific, and East Asia the United States was certainly able to act much more imperially than it did in Western Europe.[52]

Finally, Washington promoted European integration with the expectation that this was a realistic option. It assumed that integration was what the Europeans wanted or at least what they would come to want once they were able to see beyond their small national states (and recognize that Germany could not be kept down indefinitely). The difference with Asia is striking. Because of the widespread hatred of Japan, the liberated colonies' emphasis on national self-determination, and the general complexity of the regional scene, East Asian integration was really out of the question. It was even impossible for Washington to establish one overall defense organization on the pattern of NATO. Instead, a complicated system of regional alliances and bilateral defense treaties was created.[53]

In the British empire, the integration of the far-flung colonies and territories was probably not possible without London's direct control. They had too little in common to make voluntary integration go very far. Integration in the form of, for instance, Joseph Chamberlain's plans for an imperial federation was widely perceived as just another form of colonial domination. Even the white dominions, sentimentally close to Britain, but also with the highest degree of existing autonomy, rejected such a federation. Where the British promoted local federations without direct British participation, as in Central Africa in the 1950s, this was done to strengthen the influence of Britain and/or the white settlers.[54] These efforts, too, collapsed. Almost without exception the colonies came to want national independence.

French and Portuguese attempts at fully integrating the colonies into the mother country and ruling on the basis of a common assimilated culture were always based on the assumption that Paris or Lisbon would ultimately decide. In the Soviet case, the Eastern European states were tied directly to Moscow, and had rather limited contact with each other.[55]

After 1945, the United States acted from a position of unique strength. Today, the European Union (EU) has a population that is substantially larger and an economy that is somewhat larger than that of the United States. The economic strength of the EU is reflected in many ways. Thus, the countries of the EU, not the United States, are now the major contributors of economic assistance, to the countries both of the South and of Eastern Europe.

The EU, however, still has far to go to reach the military strength and the political organization of the United States. As we have seen so clearly in the Gulf War and in former Yugoslavia, only the United States can undertake really large-scale military action. Most likely, there will never be a United States of Europe in any way similar to the United States of America. In that sense the dream of the integrationists on both sides of the Atlantic may well come to naught.

Since President Kennedy's famous speech on Atlantic interdependence on 4 July 1962, ever new statements have been made from both sides of the Atlantic about cooperation between the United States and a new, strong Europe. Yet, as long as the EU is as incomplete a construction as it still is, these statements ring a little hollow. There *is* no politically united Europe. As long as there is an underlying, although well-contained, rivalry among the major powers of the EU, there can be no equality between the United States and Europe. Were a really united EU to emerge, this would be so strong a unit that there would be virtually no need for the EU to draw upon the military and political resources of the United States.

The United States and Western Europe have actually never had a balanced relationship. Under isolationism, the United States feared Europe since it saw itself as weak. When, after the Second World War, it was itself strong, it promoted Europe's integration. Thus, a balanced relationship would represent a new state of affairs. It would also probably create a more challenging state of affairs.

It has been argued that, almost without exception, alliances do not survive the disappearance of the threat against which they were directed.[56] As Lord Ismay quipped, "NATO was founded to keep the Russians out, the Germans down, and the Americans in." Now the Americans are reducing the number of troops in Europe greatly, the Germans, although unified, seem to be in place, and the Soviet threat is gone. NATO is obviously searching for new missions. Economic disputes between the allies are proliferating, particularly between the United States and Japan, but also between the United States and the EU.

Yet, in much modified form, the original rationale for NATO still exists. The Soviet Union is gone, but no one is certain what will happen in the dominant new unit, Russia. Germany remains strongly democratic, but concern is growing about the "renationalization" of European security politics, about the new Germany simply becoming too strong compared to the other powers of the EU. The United States is reducing its military presence in Europe, but although the invitations are more ambiguous now, few Europeans want the Americans to leave entirely. If something should go wrong, it is still useful to have the Americans in place. And, finally, the United States, though strongly interested in reducing the burdens of leadership, is "the only remaining superpower" and clearly expects to remain Number One. That role is much facilitated by a close relationship with Western Europe.

The American–European relationship will be redefined. The redefinition will probably result in the further weakening of the American "empire," although it must be said that recent events in Germany and in former Yugoslavia, as well as the entire process of NATO expansion, have rather underlined the continued role of the United States as the ultimate balancer in Europe. The greater the need of the Europeans for America's services and the closer Washington feels the Europeans are to the United States, the greater the chance of continued American support for European integration. Once the Atlantic context is questioned, however, U.S. support for European integration will falter.

For the historian, it is time to stop. We are good at proclaiming matters "inevitable" once they have happened. We are rather bad at predicting matters *before* they happen.

Notes

1. Many scholars have assisted me during my work on this chapter, which was later expanded into my *"Empire" By Integration. The United States and European Integration, 1945–1997* (Oxford: Oxford University Press, 1998). I want to thank Frode Liland for his highly appreciated research assistance and Tor Egil Førland, John Gaddis, Melvyn Leffler, Rolf Tamnes, and Odd Arne Westad for their useful comments on early drafts of the book.

2. For my own analysis of these terms, see *The American "Empire" and Other Studies of US Foreign Policy in a Comparative Perspective* (Oxford and Oslo: Oxford University Press, 1990), pp. 31–115, particularly 37–39. See also Geir Lundestad, ed., *The Fall of Great Powers: Peace, Stability, and Legitimacy* (Oslo and Oxford: Scandinavian University Press, 1994), particularly pp. 383–402.

3. François Duchêne, *Jean Monnet: The First Statesman of Interdependence* (New York: Norton, 1994), p. 386.

4. Some basic accounts of European integration are Richard Vaughan, *Post-war Integration in Europe* (London: Croom Helm, 1976); Vaughan, *Twentieth-Century Europe: Paths to Unity* (London: Croom Helm, 1979); Walter Lipgens, *A History of European Integration, 1945–47*, vol. 1, *The Formation of the European Unity Movement* (London: Oxford University Press, 1982); Wilfried Loth, *Der Weg nach Europa: Geschichte der europäischen Integration 1939–1957* (Göttingen: Vandenhoeck & Ruprecht, 1982); Derek W. Urwin, *The Community of Europe: A History of European Integration since 1945* (London: Longman, 1991). Two particularly stimulating accounts,

both by Alan S. Milward, are *The Reconstruction of Western Europe 1945–51* (Berkeley: University of California Press, 1984) and *The European Rescue of the Nation-State* (London: Routledge, 1992). For analyses particularly of the American policy on European integration, see Max Beloff, *The United States and the Unity of Europe* (Washington, D.C.: Brookings, 1963); Ernst H. van der Beugel, *From Marshall Aid to Atlantic Partnership: European Integration as a Concern of American Foreign Policy* (Amsterdam: Elsevier, 1966); Michael Hogan, *The Marshall Plan: America, Britain, and the Reconstruction of Western Europe, 1947–1952* (Cambridge: Cambridge University Press, 1987); Pascaline Winand, *Eisenhower, Kennedy, and the United States of Europe* (London: Macmillan, 1993); Klaus Schwabe, "The United States and European Integration: 1947–1957," in Clemens Wurm, ed., *Western Europe and Germany: The Beginnings of European Integration 1945–1960* (Oxford: Berg, 1995); Pierre Melandri, *Les Etats-Unis face à l'unification de l'Europe 1945–1954* (Lille: Université de Lille III, 1979); Gerard Bossuat, *L'Europe Occidentale a l'Heure Americaine 1945–1952* (Paris: Editions Complexe, 1992).

5. The events in 1949–50 are analyzed in detail in my book on the United States and European integration, by the same title as the present chapter.

6. *Foreign Relations of the United States*, hereafter *FRUS*, 1950, Volume 3, Secretary of State to certain diplomatic offices, 8 July 1950, p. 740.

7. *FRUS*, 1950, 3, Acting Secretary of State to the Secretary of State, 10 May 1950, pp. 695–96.

8. *FRUS*, 1952–54, 5:1, Memorandum of conversation Eisenhower–Churchill, 27 June 1954, pp. 985–87.

9. *FRUS*, 1961–63, Telegram from the Department of State to the Embassy in the United Kingdom, 23 May 1961, pp. 20–21.

10. *FRUS*, 1961–63, Memorandum of conversation Kennedy-de Gaulle, 2 June 1961, p. 25.

11. *FRUS*, 1952–54, 5:2, Memorandum of discussion, 215th meeting of the NSC, 24 September 1954, p. 1266.

12. *FRUS*, 1961–63, 13, Memorandum from Ball to President Kennedy, 20 June 1963, p. 209.

13. Thomas Alan Schwartz, "Victories and Defeats in the Long Twilight Struggle: The United States and Western Europe in the 1960s," in Diane B. Kunz, ed., *The Diplomacy of the Crucial Decade: American Foreign Relations during the 1960s* (New York: Columbia University Press, 1994), pp. 122–27.

14. *FRUS*, 1964–68, 13, Telegram from Johnson to Wilson, 21 May 1966, 396. See also *ibid.*, pp. 397–98.

15. Henry A. Kissinger, *Years of Upheaval* (Boston: Little, Brown and Company, 1982), pp. 143–48.

16. United States Information Service (USIS), U.S.–European Summit Discussed, 15 June 1995, p. 2.

17. *FRUS*, 1955–57, 4, Circular Telegram from the Secretary of State, 7 March 1957, pp. 535–36. See also Miriam Camps, *European Unification in the Sixties: From the Veto to the Crisis* (London: Oxford University Press, 1967), particularly pp. 236–57.

18. *FRUS*, 1948, 3, Memorandum of conversation by Hickerson, 21 January 1948, p. 11; Geir Lundestad, *America, Scandinavia, and the Cold War, 1945–1949* (New York: Columbia University Press, 1980), pp. 167–98.

19. *FRUS*, 1952–54, 5:2, Minutes of meeting Eisenhower–Mendès-France, 22 November 1954, p. 1482.

20. *FRUS*, 1955–57, Memorandum of conversation Eisenhower–Mayer, 8 February 1956, p. 409. See also *ibid.*, Memorandum of conference with the president, 6 February 1957, p. 517.

21. *FRUS*, 1955–57, Editorial note (Remarks by President Eisenhower), p. 349.

22. *FRUS*, 1961–63, 13, Scope paper prepared in the Department of State, 11 June 1962, p. 106. See also *ibid.*, Memorandum of conversation Ball–de Murville, 21 May 1962, p. 94.

23. *Public Papers of the Presidents of the U.S.: Lyndon B. Johnson, 1966* (Washington, D.C.), p. 477.

24. See references in n. 4.

25. These "traditionalists" are different from the traditionalists in the debate on the origins of the Cold War. In that debate both traditionalists and revisionists actually see a strong American influence on Western Europe. The first see this influence as largely beneficial; the latter view it much more negatively. For my own analysis of the Cold War debate, see *America, Scandinavia, and the Cold War*, particularly pp. 7–35 and *The American "Empire"*, pp. 11–29.

26. Van der Beugel, *From Marshall Aid to Atlantic Partnership*, passim; David W. Ellwood, *Rebuilding Europe: Western Europe, America and Postwar Reconstruction* (London: Longman, 1992), pp. 168–72, 226–40; Vaughan, *Post-war Integration in Europe*, pp. 1–10; Vaughan, *Twentieth-Century Europe*, pp. 80–81, 152–54; Urwin, *The Community of Europe*, pp. 12–25, 48–49, 60–67, 118–19. In the conclusion of his *Der Weg nach Europa*, Loth plays down the American

influence rather more than his treatment of the American role in the rest of the book would seem to justify. For the conclusion, see p. 140; for his more general treatment of the United States, see particularly pp. 37–43, 60–68, 76–84, 106–10.

27. Camps, *European Unification in the Sixties*, pp. 236–57; Armin Rappaport, "The United States and European Integration: The First Phase," *Diplomatic History*, Spring 1981, 121–49; Melandri, *Les Etats-Unis face à l'unification de l'Europe*, passim; Bossuat, *L'Europe Occidentale a l'Heure Americaine*, particularly pp. 305–16; Irving M. Wall, *The United States and the Making of Postwar France 1945–1954* (Cambridge: Cambridge University Press, 1991), particularly pp. 192–204; John Gillingham, *Coal, Steel, and the Rebirth of Europe, 1945–1955: The Germans and the French from the Ruhr Conflict to Economic Community* (Cambridge: Cambridge University Press, 1991), pp. 228–34, 264–66, 297–300, 340–42, 367–68; John Gillingham, "From Morgenthau Plan to Schuman Plan: America and the Organization of Europe," in Jeffery M. Diefendorf, Axel Frohn, and Hermann-Josef Rupipier, eds., *American Policy and the Reconstruction of West Germany, 1945–1955* (Washington, D.C., German Historical Institute, 1993), pp. 111–33, particularly 132; Thomas Alan Schwartz, *America's Germany: John J. McCloy and the Federal Republic of Germany* (Cambridge, Mass.: Harvard University Press, 1991), particularly pp. 187, 210–34, 298–301; Schwartz, "Victories and Defeats in the Long Twilight Struggle," pp. 115–48, particularly 115–16; Schwabe, "The United States and European Integration: 1947–1957," pp. 115–36.

28. A similar reaction against American-dominated interpretations, whether traditionalist, revisionist, or post-revisionist, can also be found in the debate on the origins of the Cold War. For a collection of European interpretations of this question, see David Reynolds, ed., *The Origins of the Cold War in Europe: International Perspectives* (New Haven: Yale University Press, 1994).

29. Milward, *The Reconstruction of Western Europe 1945–51*; Milward, *The European Rescue of the Nation-State*; Milward, "Conclusions: The Value of History," in Alan S. Milward, Frances M.B. Lynch, Federico Romero, Ruggero Ramieri, and Vibeke Sørensen, *The Frontier of Sovereignty: History and theory 1945–1992* (London: Routledge, 1993). The quotations are from *The Reconstruction of Western Europe 1945–51*, p. 502. See also *ibid.*, pp. 168–72, 320–34, 380–400, 465–77, 491–502.

30. See the other contributions in Milward *et. al.*, *The Frontier of National*

Sovereignty, particularly Romero's; see also Gunther Mai, "American Policy toward Germany and the Integration of Europe, 1945–1955" in Diefendorf, Frohn, and Rupipier, *American Policy and the Reconstruction of West Germany, 1945–1955*, pp. 85–109, particularly 96–98, and even Richard T. Griffiths, "The European Historical Experience," in Keith Middlemas, ed., *Orchestrating Europe: The Informal Politics of European Union 1973–1995* (London: Fontana, 1995), pp. 1–70.

31. Lundestad, *The American "Empire"*, particularly pp. 39–54; Schwartz, *America's Germany*, particularly pp. 298–301.

32. Pierre Guillen, "Europe as a Cure for French Impotence? The Guy Mollet Government and the Negotiation of the Treaties of Rome," in Ennio Di Nolfo, ed., *Power in Europe? II: Great Britain, France, Germany and Italy and the Origins of the EEC, 1952–1957* (Berlin and New York: Walter de Gruyter, 1992), pp. 513–16; John W. Young, *Britain and European Unity, 1945–1992* (London: Macmillan, 1993), pp. 49–56. For a different emphasis, see Milward, *The European Rescue of the Nation-State*, pp. 214–15.

33. Edmund Dell, *The Schuman Plan and the British Abdication of Leadership in Europe* (Oxford: Oxford University Press, 1995), pp. 110–70.

34. Duchêne, *Jean Monnet*, pp. 204–205. See also Josef Joffe, "Europe's American Pacifier," *Foreign Policy*, Spring 1984, 64–82; Uwe Nerlich, "Western Europe's Relations with the United States," *Daedalus*, Winter 1979, 87–111.

35. Milward, *The European Rescue of the Nation-State*, pp. 425–26, 431, 444.

36. *FRUS*, 1955–57, 4, Chargé Durbrow to the Department of State, 17 June 1957, pp. 300–301; *ibid.*, Memorandum of conversation Merchant–van Voorst, 13 December 1955, pp. 364–65. For an analysis of Holland's and Beyen's role in the integration process, see Milward, *The European Rescue of the Nation-State*, pp. 173–96.

37. Henry A. Kissinger, *White House Years* (Boston: Little, Brown and Company, 1979), p. 110.

38. Eckart Conze, "Hegemonie durch Integration? Die amerikanische Europapolitik und de Gaulle," *Vierteljahreshefte fur Zeitgeschichte*, April, 1995, p. 307; Jean Lacouture, *De Gaulle: The Ruler, 1945–1970* (London: Harvill, 1991), pp. 61–63, 363–86, 471–74; Georges-Henri Soutou, "France," in Reynolds, *The Origins of the Cold War in Europe*, pp. 96–120, particularly 98, 100–104.

39. Elizabeth Pond, *Beyond the Wall: Germany's Road to Unification*

(Washington, D.C.: Brookings, 1993), p. 164; Margaret Thatcher, *The Downing Street Years* (New York: Harper Collins, 1993), pp. 792–96. For a similar argument, see Philip Zelikow and Condoleezza Rice, *Germany Unified and Europe Transformed: A Study in Statecraft* (Cambridge: Harvard University Press, 1995).

40. Middlemas, *Orchestrating Europe*, pp. 156–79.

41. Duchêne, *Jean Monnet*, pp. 370–72; Gillingham, *Coal, Steel, and the Rebirth of Europe, 1945–1955*, pp. 229–31.

42. Tony Smith, *America's Mission: The United States and the Worldwide Struggle for Democracy in the Twentieth Century* (Princeton: Princeton University Press, 1994), particularly chapters 2–6. For a similar argument emphasizing the effects of liberalism on cooperation amongst democracies, see Thomas Risse-Kappen, *Cooperation among Democracies: The European Influence on U.S. Foreign Policy* (Princeton: Princeton University Press, 1995), pp. 24–41.

43. On this point, I have particularly benefited from conversations with John Gaddis. A similar argument is found in Smith, *America's Mission*.

44. The literature on the colonial empires is vast. For as good a starting point as any, see D. K. Fieldhouse, *The Colonial Empires: A Comparative Survey from the Eighteenth Century* (London: Macmillan, 1982). This book also contains a good bibliography (pp. 435–58). The costs of empire are further discussed in my *The American "Empire"*, pp. 107–14.

45. A good, short discussion of the effects of the Second World War on the British empire is found in John Darwin, *The End of the British Empire: The Historical Debate* (Oxford: Blackwell, 1991), pp. 43–45, 117–20.

46. Lundestad, *The American "Empire"*, pp. 39–46, 85–87. See also Paul Kennedy, *The Rise and Fall of the Great Powers: Economic Change and Military Conflict from 1500 to 2000* (New York: Random House, 1987); Aaron L. Friedberg, "The End of the Cold War and the Future of American Power," in Lundestad, ed., *The Fall of Great Powers*, pp. 175–96; Joseph S. Nye, *Bound to Lead: The Changing Nature of American Power* (New York: Basic Books, 1990).

47. For elaboration of this argument, see my *The American "Empire"*, pp. 39–85.

48. Lundestad, *America, Scandinavia, and the Cold War, 1945–1949*, pp. 110–18, 154–66; Schwartz, *America's Germany*, pp. 51, 80, 85, 91, 205–208, 298–99.

49. Geir Lundestad, "Empire by Invitation? The United States and

Western Europe, 1945–1952," *Journal of Peace Research*, September 1986, 263–77.

50. Geoffrey Warner, "Eisenhower, Dulles and the unity of Western Europe, 1955–1957," *International Affairs*, 1993, 69:2, 326.

51. Department of State, *Bulletin*, 12 March 1962, p. 423. For the wider issue of race in American foreign policy, see Michael H. Hunt, *Ideology and U.S. Foreign Policy* (New Haven: Yale University Press, 1987).

52. The literature on the United States and the Third World is huge and growing rapidly. For a good, recent review of this literature, see David S. Painter, "Research Note. Explaining U.S. Relations with the Third World," *Diplomatic History*, Summer 1995, 525–48. For a strong, comprehensive attack on U.S. policies, see Gabriel Kolko, *Confronting the Third World: United States Foreign Policy, 1945–1980* (New York: Pantheon Books, 1988).

53. Melvyn P. Leffler, *A Preponderance of Power: National Security, the Truman Administration, and the Cold War* (Stanford: Stanford University Press, 1992), chaps. 9–11. For an account of U.S. policies toward Third World neutralism, see H. W. Brands, *The Specter of Neutralism: The United States and the Emergence of the Third World, 1947–1960* (New York: Columbia University Press, 1989).

54. Prosser Gifford, "Misconceived Dominion: The Creation and Disintegration of Federation in British Central Africa," in Prosser Gifford and Wm. Roger Louis, eds., *The Transfer of Power in Africa: Decolonization, 1940–1960* (New Haven: Yale University Press, 1982), pp. 387–416.

55. For a fine, short study of Stalin's attitude to a Balkan federation, see Leonid Gibianski, "The 1948 Soviet–Yugoslav Conflict and the Formation of the 'Socialist Camp' Model," in Odd Arne Westad, Sven Holtsmark, and Iver B. Neumann, eds., *The Soviet Union in Eastern Europe 1945–89* (London: St. Martin's, 1994), pp. 26–46.

56. This is one of the basic assumptions of the so-called realist school in international relations. The starting point here is Kenneth N. Waltz, *Theory of International Relations* (Reading, Mass.: Addison-Wesley, 1979). For a reference to the likely disintegration of NATO, see John J. Mearsheimer, "Back to the Future: Instability in Europe after the Cold War," *International Security*, Summer 1990, 52.

Part I
Economics and Trade

Economic Leverage: The United States, Civil Aviation, and Europe, 1945–1996
Alan P. Dobson

Aviation is a highly political commercial activity which depends upon governments to negotiate bilateral air service agreements (ASAs) to provide a framework for international operations. For the United States and Europe, this has involved a highly contentious relationship, which this chapter seeks to explore and – in so doing – to show how the United States has attempted to craft a system at three significant points in time: the early postwar years; the mid 1970s; and the 1990s. The chapter will further examine if, in each of these periods, the United States managed to create a system to its own liking and whether it achieved an institutionalized position which enabled it to exploit the system in its own interests. It asks whether the United States was a system hegemon. It also examines the tactics the United States used to pursue its policy goals and how European countries responded. The result is a study which, I hope, should illuminate the overall character of U.S. policies and tactics in the postwar period and shed some general light on economic statecraft.

Before examining the relationship as a whole, however, some preliminary explanations are necessary in order to show why civil aviation is an important matter between the United States and Europe; how international aviation works; and to elucidate the concept of economic statecraft.

Aviation relations between the United States and Europe since 1945 have been extremely important for both sides. Approximately 30 million passengers were carried between Europe and the United States in 1992 and, of that total, 36 per cent or just over eleven million were carried in the U.S.–U.K. market.[1] The north Atlantic is the largest international aviation market in the world and, in 1994, no fewer than nine U.S. airlines operated in it.[2] The economic and political importance of routes into Europe, the political nature of civil aviation, and the need to negotiate ASAs have all meant that aviation has been significant in U.S. economic statecraft. In Europe, much of U.S. policy has been directed primarily at

Britain because of the importance of its market and because of its role in the general relationship between the United States and Europe. In the 1940s, Britain was the main gateway to Europe and a major player in aviation because of its control over a world-wide system of landing grounds in its Empire, Commonwealth, and client states. Britain was also important as an example to others: if the United States could persuade Britain to accept an ASA which reflected its way of thinking, then that could be held up as a model of good practice for others to emulate. By the mid-1970s, however, the situation had changed. Britain no longer controlled a world-wide system of landing grounds and was not so influential in international aviation, but it remained the main destination for U.S. citizens flying beyond the western hemisphere. By the 1990s, in terms of emplanements, Britain retained that lead, although in monetary terms the Japanese market was larger, and it gained a new dimension to its negotiating hand – membership of and an influence in the developing single European aviation market (SEAM).

The European market thus has been of tremendous importance to the United States because of the volume passenger market, because of the impact on the rest of the world that its relations with Europe would have, and because of its overall economic, political, and strategic relationship with its European allies. On more than one occasion, salvaging good relations overrode demands for civil aviation concessions.[3] Of course, many of these considerations were felt reciprocally by the Europeans. International aviation is a prime example of commercial activity where benefits can only be reaped by mutual agreement.

Airline operations have always been highly politicized because of government ownership, the prestige attached to national flag carriers, and because of strategic, research, and development considerations. In the interwar period, the system was plagued by politics, but then in 1944 the United States seemingly tried to change all that by seeking multilateral acceptance of "five freedoms" of the air at the Chicago International Civil Aviation Conference. Such freedoms might have taken a lot of politics out of the industry, but their promotion by the United States was itself politically motivated. The United States was the only country in the world in 1944 with modern airliners that could effectively exploit the potential of the international market. However, before this could happen, there had to be a new regime that would allow market access, which was precisely what the five freedoms were designed to accomplish. These freedoms, or air rights, granted airlines (1) reciprocal rights to innocent passage over national territory; (2) the right to technical stops for repairs or refuelling; (3 and 4) the rights to carry passengers to another country and pick up passengers for the return journey; and (5) the right to pick up passengers in another country and carry them to a third party destination. The unfettered grant of these commercial rights, combined with a free market fare system, could have allowed the United States to dominate the world's airline system, but British opposition foiled the multilateralism of Chicago. In its place, a system developed based upon a liberal model ASA – the Bermuda Agreement – negotiated between the United States and Britain in 1946. It was based upon the bilateral exchange of the five freedoms and a fare regime centred on the workings of the International Air Transport Association (IATA), which was a users' club of the world's major airlines. IATA fixed fares through negotiations, which then had to be ratified by governments.[4]

These matters will be considered again later, but for the moment it is only necessary to note that desire for a freer market has generally been the hallmark of U.S. policy toward Europe. The United States has sought lower fares, freer access, liberal or no controls over frequency and capacity (the number of seats offered on a route), and, more recently, double or multiple designation (when two or more airlines from the same country operate on a route). Such demands have been resisted by most European countries to one degree or another despite American criticisms and demands that the market be allowed to run its course. But to see U.S. policy as neutral commercialism and European policy as political would be inaccurate.[5]

Economic statecraft often works in the guise of trying to depoliticize the market, but opting for a free market is as political as selecting mercantilism. Both are chosen in the national interest and are components of a nation's economic statecraft. When the free market has threatened U.S. interests in aviation, there has been little compunction about allowing political considerations to override its workings. Nevertheless, the story of the United States's relationship with Europe since 1944 has been primarily about pushing for a freer airline market, and many U.S. officials and airline executives have seen these policies as generally beneficial for the airlines of other countries and for the travelling public as well as for the United States.[6] When decisions are taken in one's own interests, this does not necessarily entail damaging other people's. Diplomacy attempts to reconcile the self-interest of states in such a way that aggregate losses are at least outweighed by aggregate gains. In civil aviation, this is complicated by the variety of *bona fide* interests involved: national, airline, and public. Furthermore, interests can extend further than immediate reciprocal benefit to what has been termed diffuse reciprocity, or longer-term benefits, broadly defined.[7]

Thus economic statecraft emerges as a focus of concern and a subset of activity rather than as a self-sufficient model of a type of foreign policy practice and a *sui generis* activity. It is inextricably entwined with non-economic tactics and strategies of statecraft. Thus, economic statecraft here is taken to mean the use of economic or non-economic instruments directed at another party's economic activities in order to damage their interests and/or persuade them to change their policies, or to enhance the power, influence, and status of the party undertaking the action in tangible or intangible ways. Success or failure often depends on the type of message given, the amount of resolve it conveys, and the likelihood of economic sanctions being followed by force if compliance is not forth-coming. In the relationship between the United States and Europe between 1945 and 1996, the threat of force has never entered the diplomatic equation, but other less potent attempts at coercion have been made.[8]

As in other countries, U.S. aviation policy in the early postwar period was influenced by politics. For Americans, the advantages of having efficient airlines and modern equipment made some kind of a competitive free market politically desirable. However, after the Chicago Conference, it was far from certain what form U.S. policy would take. Matters were complicated not only by opposition from foreign countries, but also by domestic pressures for protection and fears about the long-term effect of foreign competition. In the interwar period, U.S. foreign air services had been monopolized by Pan American World Airways (Pan Am) and the political process of changing that continued to have fall-out well into the postwar period. Pan Am's dominant position was eroded during the war as other airlines were drawn into the war effort overseas, and also because of political opposition to the continuation of Pan Am's monopoly from factions within the Roosevelt administration.[9] Nevertheless, Pan Am continued to fight a rearguard action – even after it had lost its monopoly – until 1947, and there were others who did not want U.S. interests, more broadly construed than by Pan Am, undermined by foreign competition. The U.S. military, for example, were sensitive to the strategic importance of aviation. A report by retired admiral R. E. Byrd, a friend of President Roosevelt, commented: "however tough or merciless foreign competition may be; this nation cannot allow its . . . airlines to go bankrupt."[10] The market had to have limits.

On 1 June 1945, Pan Am lost its monopoly when the U.S. regulatory body, the Civil Aeronautics Board (CAB), licensed American Export Lines (later it became American Overseas Airways) and Trans World Airlines (TWA) to operate alongside Pan Am. This looked like a competi-tive scenario but, in fact, each airline had a favored instrument status within a regional route framework. Competition between U.S. airlines was only allowed in an indirect way. The situation changed in 1950 when Pan Am took over the routes of American Overseas Airways and the government insisted that, as part of the price for being allowed to do that, Pan Am had to compete more directly with TWA, the only other remaining U.S. operator on Atlantic routes.[11]

U.S. policy generally favored a freer international market (the domestic market was closely regulated by the CAB), but not at the expense of the general well-being of the U.S. airline industry. There were too many political considerations involved to allow that. In bargaining with Britain and other European states, the United States was in a rather delicate position. It wanted access to routes and markets for its airlines and consequently argued on free-market principles for much of the time. However, the United States strictly controlled the number of gateways it granted to others and, as the postwar situation developed, felt the need both to depart from liberal principles in other ways and to resort to traditional forms of political leverage to secure its goals.

First and foremost, the United States wanted liberal access to the European market. This was particularly so with regard to Britain's, including extensive fifth freedom rights, and to Germany's, where the U.S. military presence added a special dimension and one that would encourage the growth of an important market. Immediately a problem arose from these wants in that there could not be a trade of like for like. In Europe, the United States not only wanted access to individual countries, it also wanted beyond or fifth freedom rights which it believed would be essential if commercial operations were to be viable. For example, Pan Am's round-the-world route needed to fill seats emptied by passengers disembarking at London with fifth freedom traffic. Unfortunately, the United States could not offer any viable fifth freedom rights in return. Even after the development of much longer-range and larger aircraft, this still remained a problem. Furthermore, the Americans would not compensate the Europeans by allowing them multiple routes into the United States as of right, which would have allowed them to exploit the vast U.S. market more effectively. So far as routes were concerned, the U.S. position was consistent: they had to be negotiated bilaterally.[12] There was to be no "open skies" policy regarding routes until the 1990s. The Americans argued that if other countries were given numerous gateways to the vast U.S. market, this would not be a comparable trade for access to such tiny markets as the Dutch or Austrian. The inconsistency between this and their free market principles did not appear to trouble them, though it did the Europeans.

Britain was the main European country from which the United States wanted fifth freedom rights: they would enhance the main gateway to Europe, and provide a vital component of both Pan Am's famous round-the-world service and the route to occupied Germany. Such a liberal agreement would also set a precedent that America hoped others would follow. In effect, the Americans demanded liberal access to the European market, including fifth freedom rights which soon ate into the European regional market,[13] at a time when European countries were not in a position to compete. In return, they offered limited access to their market, which Europeans could not exploit effectively; commercially unviable fifth freedom rights; and the opportunity to buy modern American equipment which some countries were reluctant to do on nationalistic grounds, while others simply lacked the dollars to do so.[14]

Second, the United States sought competition in the airline market. At the Chicago Conference, this had been in terms of fares, frequency, and capacity. In the following months, the American position changed. In 1945, Pan Am unilaterally reduced its one way transatlantic fare by $100, which looked suspiciously like predatory pricing aimed as much, if not more so, at TWA and American Overseas Airways as at European carriers.[15] This suggested to many Americans that price fixing had benefits. Furthermore, a British official explained that "the British Govt. would never permit Panam or any other carrier to fly into England with unlimited frequencies and with unilateral power to set its rates without approval of either IATA or the govt."[16] The Americans realized that they might have to accept IATA fare-setting as part of the price of flying into Britain. In fact, they soon found themselves in the happy position of being able to offer agreement on IATA fare-setting (which they now saw as being in the interests of U.S. airlines in any case) in return for British concessions on capacity, frequency, and fifth freedoms. The American position thus shifted on the fare regime, but it remained committed to competition where it believed its airlines could be effective, that is, through liberal frequency and capacity provisions. So the Americans sought to create a regime that would allow more competition than the prewar system, but it was a qualified form of competition. In addition to their change of attitude on fares, there were also doubts about America's long-term ability to compete in Europe. These fears arose largely from the fact that Europe had cheaper labor than the United States. In fact, from 1945 to 1996, U.S. airlines have operated well below the costs of their European competitors.[17] Nevertheless, fear of low-cost competition from Europe was real and helps to explain why the Americans were so keen to establish a favorable position in the marketplace while they still had the advantages of possessing capable airlines and of ready access to efficient long-range aircraft.

This review of the United States' aims in Europe discloses just how one-sided things were. The Americans were in a strong position and vigorously sought a regime that would provide some element of competition and, most important of all, give them broad access to Europe's market. The Europeans were not in a position to compete and the most important aviation power in Europe, Britain, favored "internationalisation to Americanisation" as one early wartime study had put it,[18] but found that she was unable to achieve this in the face of U.S. opposition.

The Americans had four means of wielding influence and of exerting leverage to get what they wanted: the threat of bypassing states that would not accept liberal ASAs; the ability to withhold the right to buy modern American aircraft; the use of their general prestige and influence, which were clearly going to play a large role in postwar reconstruction and security matters; and, finally, the ability to offer or withhold economic aid. Not all of these weapons were single-edged swords, and even those that were were sometimes rather blunt. For example, the threat of bypassing Britain via Eire could lead to Britain bypassing the United States via Canada, and some Americans believed that in this type of game the advantage lay with Britain. With regard to the supply of modern U.S. airliners, many countries were unwilling to take that road for fear of damaging their own aerospace industry. It was not until the late 1960s that the benefits of buying U.S. equipment overcame the national prejudice in favour of home-made aircraft. This is not to say that countries did not see the competitive advantage for their airlines of buying U.S. aircraft in limited numbers before home-produced aircraft became available, but it was viewed as a stopgap measure and one complicated by lack of dollars.

After the failure of the Chicago Conference to establish the commercial framework for international aviation, both Britain and the United States struggled to gain advantageous positions. The British tried to block U.S. "efforts to gain unrestricted Fifth Freedom traffic into and out of countries such as Greece, Egypt, Iraq and so forth"[19] and required their airlines to buy British planes, but the attempts to restrict U.S. penetration of the market and to resist the temptation of America's superior aircraft could not be sustained by Britain, never mind by other European countries.

America launched a full-scale campaign to penetrate Europe. The first major success (there were others with Denmark, Iceland, Spain, and Sweden) of the campaign came with the negotiation of a liberal ASA with Eire – a deal consummated despite the bitter protests from Prime

Minister Churchill to President Roosevelt.[20] But the Irish deal was conceived as only the first shot in a long campaign, as Acting Secretary of State Grew disclosed in a letter to the U.S. Legation in Dublin: "it [is] desirable to implement without delay our arrangements made at Chicago . . . through bilateral agreements giving us as many gateways to Europe as possible and with no limitations on frequencies."[21] However, the main goal for the United States was liberal access to Britain and much of the reason for pressurizing other states to come to agreement was to push the British into doing the same. In this game, the United States had more economic leverage to wield and better aircraft to offer than Britain. Most important of all, Britain needed U.S. aid to help reconstruct its war-torn, exhausted economy. The Americans knew that as well and, in September 1945, Peter Masefield, the British Civil Aviation Attaché in Washington, was ominously told that the United States saw civil aviation as part of an overall economic understanding to be reached with the British.[22] Part of that understanding involved a U.S. loan of $3.75 billion but, when the British and the Americans met in Bermuda to discuss the terms of their ASA in January 1946, the loan still needed congressional approval. The head of the American delegation, G. P. Baker, later recalled: "I remember that the loan was very much at the back of everybody's mind."[23]

It was a combination of knowing that the Americans were out-manouvering them through bilateral ASA negotiations with other countries, that they had modern airliners and economic assistance to offer which outmatched any British counter-inducements, together with fears of alienating the United States in an uncertain and dangerous world situation and of losing the U.S. loan that led to major British concessions. And with them went most of Europe's ability to restrict U.S. access to its market.

The British had to give way on frequency and capacity and on the contentious fifth freedom. Only on pricing did they appear to win concessions but, as Baker smugly observed, all the U.S. delegation now believed that rate controls were desirable and so the overall arrangements constituted a "real victory," because no *quid pro quo* had been paid by the United States.[24] The head of the British delegation put things in a nutshell: "if the Cabinet felt that the signing of the agreement was of vital importance from the point of view of our general relations with the United States and the consideration of the loan agreement by Congress he was willing that our delegation be authorised to sign."[25]

The Bermuda Agreement was duly signed. It provided for "fair and equal opportunity for the carriers of the two nations to operate on any route between their respective territories." This was to be effected by the mutual exchange of the five freedoms, liberal capacity and frequency provisions, and the fixing of fares through IATA with government approval.[26] The Americans achieved similar results with other European countries and, in some cases, notably West Germany, where it was easy to exert and justify political pressure, more liberal arrangements were made.[27] The United States held Bermuda up as a model for the rest of the world. It looked as if the United States had indeed achieved what it had set out to: an international aviation system conducive to its own interests.

Some scholars have claimed that the U.S. role in the postwar Western economy was tantamount to hegemony, but the meaning of hegemony is not always clear.[28] Here, I have adopted the following definition: the ability of an agent to influence the formulation of rules and the creation of institutions in such a way that they grant it a position of leadership and allow it to exploit the system in its own interests over time. There is no doubt that the aviation system, including relations between the United States and Europe, was greatly influenced by U.S. inputs, but was it hegemonically so? The term hegemon seems rather inapt when the United States itself was not always entirely clear what policy it should adopt. Differences existed within both the airline industry and the Federal government. U.S. policy on a free aviation market changed between 1944 and 1945 and continued to do so in the years that followed. Of the two international organizations that had input into world aviation, the UN International Civil Aviation Organization and IATA, only the latter had any major impact on commercial operations and it was far from being the brainchild of America. Even before the United States attacked IATA's fare-fixing role in 1978, its relationship with IATA was uneasy. At the Chandler Rate Conference in Arizona in 1962, both Pan Am and TWA voted for higher fares, which were then rejected by the CAB, and there followed a serious row between the United States on the one hand and IATA members and their governments on the other.[29] At other times, U.S. officialdom took a different line on fares. In 1973, the CAB vetoed low Advance Purchase Excursion Fares (APEX) proposed by BOAC and Lufthansa, and later opposed Laker's cheap fare Skytrain.

Serious problems also arose for the United States out of the postwar aviation system. There were persistent difficulties over routes, particularly in the Pacific, competitive challenges from Europe such as low-cost charter operations, and sixth freedom rights. This latter problem came mainly from the competitive Dutch carrier KLM, which carried the overwhelming proportion of the passenger traffic between Holland and the United States. The imbalance was partly to do with the ASA giving

KLM access to a much larger market than Holland could provide American airlines, and partly to do with KLM's effective feeder services which reaped passengers from other countries for transatlantic flights – they were referred to as gateway or sixth freedom traffic – and by 1974 they made up 55 per cent of the total traffic KLM carried to the United States. The Americans objected to this. They could not "tolerate the overall imbalance of benefits in the bilateral . . . Agreement"[30] and made it known to the Dutch in strong terms. To the Europeans, this seemed hypocritical. The United States objected to the results of KLM's resourcefulness in generating sixth freedom traffic and condemned it in the regulatory language of balanced benefits. At the same time, therefore, as the United States was protecting its own market by restricting the number of routes a bilateral partner could operate, it was insisting on liberal access to Europe.

Although the United States did effectively gain liberal access to Europe, it was unable to prevent the development there of a highly regulated and anti-competitive airline system. All the major European airlines were government-owned. Bilateral agreements which the Europeans made, except with the United States, were generally more restrictive than the Bermuda model and the aviation system within Europe was characterized by the division of markets between national flag carriers, by capacity and frequency agreements and revenue sharing, by IATA fare-fixing, and by routes restricted to national capitals.[31] For thirty years, such arrangements did not directly damage U.S. interests because the Bermuda model still characterized the way Europe related to the United States, but the more regulatory mind-set in Europe eventually posed a threat, first from individual countries and then later from the SEAM.

The United States failed to create an international organization in the form of IATA that either fully reflected its interests or was subject to straightforward direction from Washington. It also failed to create operating rules that were universally adopted and had to compromise its principles in a number of agreements, amendments, and renegotiations. It can also be seen that the United States fluctuated in its attitude toward what the commercial operating system should actually be. This was partly to do with differences between its airlines, the CAB, and successive U.S. administrations, and the differing approaches needed by different markets. Some of the broad characteristics of the system roughly accorded with U.S. desires, but those desires changed over time, as did the operations of the system, because the rules were subject to interpretation and renegotiation. By the mid-1970s, the United States itself came to the conclusion that the system needed radical change. Simultaneously, other countries came to the same conclusion, but they took actions different from, but no less radical than, those espoused by the Americans.

Four factors affected U.S. aviation policy in ways that brought radical change. First, Americans saw their proportion of the world scheduled airline market diminish from a high of 73 percent of total world domestic and international passenger traffic in 1946 to approximately 39 percent in 1975.[32] This was no more dramatic than the decline of America's percentage of the world's total wealth from 50 percent in the late 1940s to 23 percent in 1988,[33] but many in the United States came to believe that something had gone seriously wrong in the aviation industry. Second, airlines were buffeted by economic hardship caused by the Arab–Israeli Wars, the rise in OPEC fuel prices, and the general world economic recession. Under these circumstances, international carriers which had just re-equipped with costly Boeing 747s found themselves in severe difficulties. Third, newly emerged nations introduced new and heavily subsidized airlines to the market which, along with the operations of charters, added to excess capacity and the tendency toward below-cost fares. In 1974, thirteen carriers operating with "jumbos" on the Atlantic flew the equivalent of one out of two scheduled flights empty. Fourth, there was a change in economic philosophy in the United States away from the postwar Keynesian consensus to a rugged form of economic liberalism which, among other things, advocated deregulation. These new ideas did not achieve immediate success. There was debate, but little action, during the presidencies of Nixon and Ford. Indeed, notwithstanding the right-wing economic philosophy of the Ford administration, it adopted several protectionist and regulatory measures to try to cope with the immediate crisis and salvage the fortunes of its ailing international carriers. However, it also sought to maintain the traditional, long-term U.S. commitment to liberal ASAs and thus took a very dim view when Britain denounced the Bermuda Agreement and demanded regulation similar in kind to that which prevailed in Europe. This happened just before Jimmy Carter became President and, because of his unwavering commitment to deregulation, he proved to be even more troubled by British actions than Ford had been.[34]

By 1976, the British were unhappy with the workings of the Bermuda Agreement. On the Atlantic they had about 44 percent of the traffic to America's 56 percent and overall benefits from the ASA yielded a 70–30 split in favor of the Americans.[35] At a time when Britain was in severe financial difficulties, this situation was unacceptable to Edmund Dell, the Secretary of State for Trade and Industry. In June 1976, he therefore denounced the Agreement with twelve months' notice, as provided for in the ASA, and forced the Americans into negotiations. Dell wanted to lower capacity through controls, single designation, and the withdrawal of fifth freedoms. He also wanted a more equal division of traffic; more gateways to the United States, particularly to the south-west and Seattle; and a change in the fare system (there were a number of other matters, but they do not bear on the main theme of this chapter). The British negotiating team was well led and backed with strong political courage on the part of Dell. The U.S. delegation was more troublesome and leadership lines were not as clearly drawn. The American team used several negotiating strategies to try to salvage a competitive market, but in the end they had only limited success.[36]

The possibility of stopping air services between the two countries was used as a threat repeatedly by the United States, but the British rightly estimated that they would not carry it out. Stopping scheduled flights would have damaged both sides through loss of valuable dollar earnings for Britain, and loss of revenue for the financially troubled U.S. carriers. Suspending services or bypassing Britain would have had severe costs for America. Even in 1992, after a relative decline, the U.S.–U.K. market still accounted for 36 percent of the total traffic between Europe and the United States.[37] Both sides made contingency plans to serve each other through third parties: U.S. airlines would have used Holland and British Airways (BA) Canada, but in the end the United States decided that the cost of stopping services would be too high.

Another tactic which the Americans soon decided upon was to give the talks as high a profile as possible. They felt that by raising the level above the parochialism of air rights and "narrow minded" British bureaucrats they could introduce broad matters which would push the British into making concessions. Thus, Alan Boyd was appointed as a special ambassador to lead the U.S. delegation and there was a similar upgrade on the British side, from Under-Secretary George Rogers to Patrick Shovelton, deputy secretary at the Department of Trade and Industry. The Americans were right. By upgrading the talks, broader considerations did come into play, but ironically they had more impact in Washington than in London. The British prime minister James Callaghan called in Dell on one occasion and asked if the talks were going to fail. Dell said he thought that there would be an agreement and Callaghan therefore left matters in his hands.[38] Issues were never taken to Cabinet for discussion. On the American side, broad issues were more influential and it looks like the "special relationship" had more impact in the United States than in Britain. Boyd confessed later that he was an Anglophile and that, if he had not been, agreement might not have been reached.[39]

As for Carter, he was concerned "to get a fair agreement with the UK in such a way as to prevent political embarrassment to Prime Minister Callaghan."[40] There were also worries among Carter and his immediate advisers that "Failure to reach agreement would have an adverse impact on overall relations and [would] possibly undermine Western cooperation in other economic areas."[41]

A combination of American unwillingness to push the talks into a major crisis, their misjudgement about the benefits of upgrading the talks, and the formidable ability of the British negotiating team, especially when contrasted with the divided U.S. delegation, resulted in the Bermuda 2 Agreement, which was more in tune with British than American thinking. The British failed to get single designation for all routes to the United States, but reduced the number from 8 to 2. The United States lost fifth freedom rights to Vienna, Brussels, Sweden, and the Netherlands; it retained them for Frankfurt and for Pan Am's round-the-world route – later Boyd said "God help us . . . what we paid for that, incredible!"[42] Access to Hong Kong remained restricted. Capacity screening was introduced. More routes to the United States were opened, but no more than would benefit BA and not as many as the United States wanted. There was no agreement on charters and only ineffective provisions for revising the fare regime. The agreement was not all one-sided: fifth freedom rights retained by the United States were important. Under new provisions, their airlines could offer through tickets to the U.S. public even if the flight did not originate from an international gateway and involved a change of aircraft. And there were restrictions on British access to the American south-west which advantaged U.S. airlines.[43] Even so, the agreement was undoubtedly more regulatory than deregulatory. Arguments in Washington about the wisdom of finalizing the agreement continued until the formal signing ceremony. However, weighed against the criticisms were doubts that the capacity provisions would restrict growth, and the belief that nothing else could have been squeezed out of the British on double designation and gateways. Stuart Eizenstat summed things up for Carter on the eve of the signing of Bermuda 2:

> it might be a mistake to postpone signing to give Congress and other critics of the agreement time to generate opposition. Prolonged negotiations and cessation of service to Britain might be able to produce an agreement that is marginally better than this one. But there will be criticism of *any* agreement that does not grant unlimited service to all cities by all carriers at unrestricted prices.[44]

Carter's reply was: "Stu – I'm not going to postpone."[45] On 23 July 1977, Bermuda 2 was duly signed, but the United States never did a Bermuda 2-style agreement with another country and never held it up as a model.

Bermuda 2 was wholly uncharacteristic of the Carter deregulation revolution. In 1978, his administration deregulated the domestic airline market. It issued a new international aviation policy statement and formulated legislation which eventually became the International Air Transportation Competition Act of 1979 (signed into law on 15 February 1980) to help implement the aims of that statement. Moreover, the CAB, under the chairmanship of Alfred Kahn, issued the Show Cause Order (SCO) which required IATA to show reason why its fare agreements did not fall foul of U.S. anti-trust legislation.[46] These measures had a serious effect on world aviation and posed an important challenge to Europe.

The SCO caused a tremendous storm. It did not break IATA's role in setting fares, but it diminished it and shifted the emphasis to airlines in deciding their own fares. By 1980, the United States had started to retreat from its more extreme stance and, in 1982, it agreed to a Memorandum of Understanding on Fares with the European Civil Aviation Conference which reintroduced more stability to fare-setting between the United States and Europe.[47] Over the following months, the SCO faded from sight but there was no denying that more competitive fares were now the order of the day. This was not solely because of the SCO. The State Department, strongly encouraged by Carter, exerted pressure for competitive fares by renegotiating or amending ASAs. The Department negotiated in accordance with the principles set down in the new policy statement:

> The guiding principle of United States aviation negotiating policy will be to trade competitive opportunities, rather than restrictions, with our negotiating partners. We will aggressively pursue our interests in expanding air transportation and reduced prices rather than accept the self-defeating accommodation of protectionism. Our concessions in negotiations will be given in return for progress toward competitive objectives, and those concessions themselves will be of a liberalizing character.[48]

Even the British succumbed and agreed to lower fares when America threatened to reroute traffic through Holland and other countries: there were also fears that the United States might denounce Bermuda 2 if the British did not prove accommodating. By 1982, the State Department, often through the threat of rerouting and the inducement of better access to the United States, had renegotiated or amended twenty-three ASAs, including five with European countries: Holland, West Germany, Belgium, Finland, and Britain. But some were with insignificant countries and not all changes were liberal. The Memorandum of Understanding with Britain, among other things, exchanged double designation for the Boston–London route in return for the right to restrict access to Heathrow airport to TWA and Pan Am or their corporate successors, which would have important consequences in 1990–1991.[49]

U.S. policy toward Europe in the mid-1970s began in an uncertain way. The arguments for and against deregulation in Washington and the financially difficult positions of TWA and Pan Am resulted in contradictory and confused policies until the Carter Administration came out unambiguously for deregulation. However, Carter's policy was compromised by Bermuda 2 and his international policy statement recognized that there would have to be a progressive horse-trade of advantages in the gradual move towards a more competitive market. With regard to Europe, the United States achieved some, but by no means universal, success in achieving liberalization. Its tactic of picking off one country after another worked with some countries more than others. Its pursuit of competitive pricing through the SCO and the renegotiation of ASAs yielded successes, but Laker's Skytrain and other airlines such as Air Florida also helped to open the market, and consumer pleasure with this was so great that it became ever more difficult to reregulate if it meant higher fares.

In summary, once again the Americans had a major impact on how airlines operated between the United States and Europe, but as in the 1940s they neither controlled nor initiated all the new developments. The changes they brought about were piecemeal and varied from bilateral partner to bilateral partner. Their own policy was changeable, though it evolved eventually into a clear demand for a deregulated and competitive international market.

As the 1970s closed, it was unclear what effect new technology and new patterns of practice arising out of some of the systemic changes the United States had either fathered, or encouraged, or which had arisen elsewhere in the system, would have on international aviation. Over the next decade those changes became clearer and influenced aviation between the United States and Europe.

Deregulation in the United States unreined competition by allowing free entry and exit to the marketplace, by abandoning controls over fares, capacity, frequency, and routes, and by encouraging lower labour costs. A volatile period ensued, but gradually there was consolidation with mega-carriers emerging to operate a new hub-and-spoke route configuration, which enabled airlines to reap economies of scale for the first time. Hub-and-spoke is based on as large a throughput of passengers as possible at one or more interconnected hubs. In this imagery, the hub is a major airport and the spokes represent routes fanning out from it: even passengers wishing to travel between two minor airports generally have to do so via hubs where passengers are concentrated onto well-serviced high-density economic routes. The results have been increased efficiency, higher load factors, more emphasis than ever on the need for access to markets and major airports, the growth in importance of very costly computer reservation systems (CRSs) to monitor and run the vast and complex global market, and a shift away from fifth freedom rights in favour of the freedom to "code share" (that is, where tickets for journeys involving a change of aircraft and airline are marketed as a continuous flight with the same code number and the airlines involved share the revenue. Such arrangements are extremely important for feeder services to and from major hubs for international flights.)

The logical outcome toward which these developments inexorably worked was globalization, as spokes fanned out from hubs around the world in their search for an ever-wider passenger market. For the U.S. mega-carriers, such as United Airlines (UA), American Airlines (AA), and Delta, these new market developments posed problems for relations with the European Community/Union (EC/EU) and its more regulatory mind-set. This continued to be the case even though there were changes in the 1980s as the European Commission came forward with proposals for the SEAM, which involved liberalization of the European aviation system. But just as the danger of the regulatory mind-set seemed to be weakening, another danger emerged, namely a uniform European position on ASAs. Even if that position were to prove less regulatory than in the worst of the European ASAs, the United States feared that it would be more regulatory than in the most liberal. U.S. interests would thus lose out in the aggregate. In the late 1980s, Americans became paranoid about the danger of a fortress Europe emerging that would diminish rather than enlarge U.S. aviation rights.[50]

By the late 1980s, there was a feeling of unease in many European countries about the renewal of the U.S. competitive drive. Deregulation in the United States had halted and then reversed the decline in its market share of world aviation, and some of this change had been at the expense of European airlines. When the world airline market slumped in the early 1990s because of economic recession and the effects of the Gulf War, some European countries started to look askance at their ASAs with the United States. In 1992, Germany threatened to denounce its bilateral agreement, but stopped short with a temporary agreement. In May 1992, France more dramatically did denounce its ASA, failed to negotiate a replacement within a year, and thus it and the United States had to resort to comity and reciprocity to keep air services going.[51] Of all the European states, Britain maintained the most regulatory ASA with the United States, and appeared to thrive on it. In talks with the Americans in 1990–91, in order to replace TWA and Pan Am at Heathrow with UA and AA, the Americans were forced to pay a price for the British waiver of the corporate succession clause in the 1980 agreement. The United States gave Britain unlimited code-sharing rights as part of the deal. When BA proceeded to exploit that to the full through a deal with U.S. Air to develop feeder services in the United States for its transatlantic services, the Americans lamented that they had not fully understood the implications of what they had given away and asserted that restrictions on access to Britain were intolerable. In talks which followed, Americans considered the possibility of denouncing Bermuda 2.[52]

While these unsettling developments were happening, the European Commission completed its third and final package of proposals for the creation of the SEAM. The package came into operation on 1 January 1993.[53] The intention of liberalisation was to create a level playing field for the airlines of the member states. Competition was facilitated by easy and equal entry rights into the marketplace and by allowing competitive fares. However, if the SEAM is to be an effective reality, its airlines must compete within the same framework not only within the EU, but outside it as well. The importance of the external dimension is demonstrated by the facts that European airlines fly six times as many revenue passenger kilometers on long haul international routes as they do on domestic ones and that BA in 1990 made £3 million profit in Europe and £249 million on the north Atlantic.[54] Members of the SEAM thus need a model ASA so that they all give and receive the same external rights. Only then would there be a level playing field for all member states. That prospect is not palatable to the United States for a range of reasons. It fears that the SEAM will be less liberal in practice than in theory, and Commission approval of $10.3 billion of subsidies for state-owned airlines between 1991 and 1994 is seen as proof of this. Second, even if the operations of the SEAM match the rhetoric of the Commission, it would probably not grant open-skies access to U.S. airlines throughout the EU, or the kind of code-sharing and fare regimes it can negotiate with individual European countries, at least not without a more costly *quid pro quo*. Third, the Directorate General for Transportation, DG7, has only a handful of people in its aviation section. It lacks the personnel and the expertise to conduct negotiations on behalf of the EU and, even if it were charged with that responsibility, the Americans believe that it would be a long, if not interminable, process during which U.S. airlines would continue to lose opportunities because of "artificial constraints" on their ability to exploit the market.

What, then, has all this led to in terms of U.S. policy? The United States has tried to use the lure of better access to its enormous market to get liberal ASAs. The drawback to this is that with small countries, such as Holland and Austria, the trade of opportunities is disproportionately in favor of the smaller country. With countries like Germany, France, and Britain, the opportunity for fifth freedom rights and code-sharing deals would make the trade of benefits more balanced but, apart from a four-year deal struck with Germany in September 1993, the Americans have made little headway with the larger states. For Britain, the lure of more gateways does not exist: BA has all it wants. There are no more (or at best only one or two) which it could operate profitably and code-share agreements give it the feeder services it needs to exploit the U.S. domestic market effectively. The Americans have little leverage left on Britain at the moment.

With the smaller European states, the United States has had more success. In 1992, the Bush Administration negotiated an open skies ASA with Holland: "This removed all the traditional bilateral restrictions, enabling [their] . . . airlines to operate freely, all third, fourth and fifth freedom services."[55] Subsequently, some Americans doubted the wisdom of this ASA, which gave KLM far more market opportunities than U.S. airlines received in return, even after the alliance between KLM and Northwest Airlines is taken into account. But the deal was supposed to send a signal to the rest of Europe about what was on offer in terms of access to the United States if they would agree to liberal ASAs. The United States was prepared to absorb immediate costs for future gains, but the situation in the early 1990s made it look as if those gains were going to be a long time in coming.

After the Dutch and German deals, the United States pulled back from seeking further open-skies agreements. The German agreement had a number of regulatory aspects to it in any case and was not truly open-skies. In Washington, the new Democratic Administration of Bill Clinton was unsure of itself and policy development was engulfed by internal debates, undermined by lack of leadership, and complicated by divisions among U.S. airlines. Of all the major U.S. carriers, only Delta wanted to push ahead with liberal ASAs with small countries, which were the only ones willing to talk open-skies with the United States at the time.[56]

However, by 1994–95, things again began to change and another campaign was launched to negotiate as many liberal ASAs as possible. By June 1995, preliminary open-skies deals had been struck with Austria, Belgium, Denmark, Finland, Luxembourg, and Sweden. The United States hoped that it could establish liberal air rights that could not be overturned even if a uniform policy on ASAs were decided upon and implemented by the European Commission. In other words, in the event of the SEAM turning out to be protectionist *vis-à-vis* the rest of the world, the United States would have liberal "grandfather rights" of entry to the EU market. It also hoped that open-skies agreements would, in combination with code-sharing agreements, give it such extensive access to the EU market that the large European states would see less point in resisting U.S. penetration and be tempted into open-skies ASAs themselves.

So far, Britain has been in the forefront of resisting those temptations, but there has also been a violent response from the Commission to U.S. tactics. The Transport Commissioner, Karel van Miert, had strong words about the U.S.–Dutch open-skies agreement, but they looked anodyne compared with the reaction of his successor, Neil Kinnock, to the open-skies deals that took shape in 1995. Kinnock was furious, commenting that the open skies deals "could put in peril the whole of European deregulation."[57] The situation was seen as so dangerous that the transport ministers of the EU tentatively agreed to the idea of transferring the power to negotiate ASAs on behalf of the member states to the Commission. The United States, by trying to circumvent what it saw as the potential danger of a common EU policy on ASAs, may have accelerated the creation of that very thing.

Since the Second World War, American experience with Europe in civil aviation has been rather one-sided, in the sense that the United States has often held the advantage in negotiations and been able to conclude ASAs of great benefit to her airlines. However, it has never been able to dictate to Europe. It has never achieved all that it wanted, even in the 1940s. From the Bermuda 2 Agreement onwards, it has felt aggrieved about its rights in Europe, its largest market. And with the SEAM, it fears the development of regional protectionism that would damage the interests of its airlines. These facts place the one-sidedness – and the economic strategies employed by Americans over these issues – into a clearer context.

In the 1940s, the U.S. strategy of divide and rule garnered a rich harvest of air rights in Europe. It was effective because of money, planes, prestige, and the threat of being bypassed. America played upon countries' self-interest when states in Europe were vulnerable and lacked a unified sense of purpose. The ASA with Eire was struck because the Irish saw opportunities to develop Shannon airport as a major European gateway. The deal undoubtedly served Eire well, but it was only a pawn in America's European game, the main aim of which was to extract liberal aviation rights from Britain. The combination of being outmaneuvered like this, the need for economic help, and Britain's determination to keep a "special relationship" with the United States drove Britain into the concessions embodied in the Bermuda 1 Agreement. However, although the United States extracted a series of ASAs from European countries that gave her liberal access to the market, it failed to mould the character of civil aviation between other countries, was often uncertain about what policy would best serve its interests, and experienced difficulties over fares and routes during the 1950s and 1960s.

By the 1970s, the effectiveness of some of America's means of leverage had diminished. The negative impact of Vietnam, the breakdown of the Bretton Woods regime, Watergate, and a growing sense that American capabilities were overstretched in relation to the United States' world role undermined its prestige and influence and made the need for allies seem more important. At the same time, Europe had grown in strength and capability since the 1940s. In particular, it had effective airlines and the idea of denying them American equipment was now not an option. The threat of bypassing states still had some potency, but in the case of the large U.S.–U.K. market it was unclear which side would be damaged worse by such action. All these factors conspired to limit the effectiveness of the initiatives the United States took to liberalize the market in the 1970s. The limits to its influence were most clearly demonstrated in the Bermuda 2 Agreement.

In the 1990s, the main weapons left in the U.S. armory were the efficiency and competitiveness of its airlines and the lure of the American market. Deregulation in the United States produced a renewed competitive drive among U.S. airlines which did much to bring innovations to the market, such as the hub-and-spoke route configuration, designed to reap maximum economies of scale, and CRSs. U.S. airlines tried to carry these new features of the market to Europe, but to get maximum advantage they needed freer access. To try to achieve that they again deployed the tactic of divide and rule, but it has only yielded limited results. The carrot on offer is more access to the U.S. market: the implied stick is a loss of market share to those countries that refuse to welcome open-skies agreements. Britain has firmly resisted these pressures, largely because BA has achieved a satisfactory market position in the United States. Some other states in Europe have complied with U.S. requests for open-skies agreements, but DG7 is seeking to control things and prevent the United States from gaining incremental advantages through individual deals with member states at the cost of the interests of the EU as a whole.

From the Chicago Conference of 1944 to the open-skies ASAs of 1995, the United States has attempted to mould the international aviation system, and in particular its relationship with Europe, to its own interests, but it has had varying results. America, while having had more influence on aviation than any other state, has either had to compromise with bilateral partners, or acknowledge that its influence ran short of being decisive. The failure of multilateralism in 1944 meant that there would be a fragmented arrangement for international aviation. This arrangement had some coherence because of IATA, even if what IATA did was often unpalatable to the United States, and it had some uniformity because of the Bermuda model, although the model disguised a wide variety of ASAs.

Thus, in some ways it is not easy to see international aviation as a system at all, at least not one that is subject to policy influences that result in crafted, uniform systemic change. International aviation takes place within a commercial setting determined by a vast number of bilateral ASAs, the multilateral agreements of the SEAM, and the workings of IATA, to which not all airlines belong and whose decisions have always been subject to national approval or disapproval. For air services to take place between the United States and Europe, there have to be bilateral ASAs. For each of them to come into being, both parties have got to perceive the provisions as being in their own interests. For all these reasons, the "system" is not susceptible to moulding by a single state. The U.S. aviation relationship with Europe defies easy generalizations. We might say that the United States had more influence on relations between itself and Europe in the 1940s than in either the 1970s or 1990s, but even then it is difficult to see how that could be characterized as hegemonical. Since the 1940s, U.S. influence on Europe has fluctuated over the years, but appears to have diminished overall and looks set to decline further if the SEAM provides a uniform policy on how the airlines of member states operate with non-members. A uniform policy would produce a more symmetrical bargaining situation and would undermine the effectiveness of the U.S. tactic of playing off the interests of one European state against another in order to reap advantages for itself. Thus, even the one-sidedness that has existed may soon disappear.

Notes

1. *The House of Commons Transport Committee Report, The Future of Air Services Between the United Kingdom and the United States of America*, vol. 1 (London: HMSO, 1994), p. xiv.
2. *UK Civil Aviation Authority, Airline Competition on European Long Haul Routes* (London: CAA, 1994).
3. Alan P. Dobson, "Regulation or Competition? Negotiating the Anglo-American Air Service Agreement of 1977," *Journal of Transport History*, 15 (1994), 144–65.
4. Alan P. Dobson, *Peaceful Air Warfare: the United States, Britain, and the Politics of International Aviation* (Oxford: Clarendon Press, 1991); D. McKenzie, "The Bermuda Conference and Anglo-American Aviation Relations at the End of the Second World War," *Journal of Transport History*, 12 (1991), 61–74; M. Dierikx, "Shaping World Aviation: Anglo-American Civil Aviation Relations 1944–46," *Journal of Air Law and Commerce*, 57 (1992), 795–840; Richard Y. Chuang, *The International Air Transport Association* (Leiden: Sijthoff, 1972).
5. Alan P. Dobson, *Flying in the Face of Competition: The Policies and Diplomacy of Airline Regulatory Reform in Britain, the USA and Europe 1968–94* (Andover: Avebury, 1995), chaps. 8–10; Alan P. Dobson, "Developing a Single European Aviation Market," in R. Bideleux and J. Bradbury, eds., *The Development of the European Union: Policy Integration in the 1990s* (London: Macmillan, 2000).
6. Interviews conducted by the author with: Cyril Murphy, Vice President for International Affairs, UA, 1 July 1991; Alan Boyd sometime CAB Chairman, US Secretary of Transportation, and Special Ambassador, 9 April 1991; Jeffrey Shane, US Assistant Secretary of Transportation for Policy and International Affairs, 5 April 1991.
7. Diffuse reciprocity is a term developed in the work of Robert Keohane.
8. These ideas are developed in the opening chapters of my forthcoming book, *Economic Statecraft: US Policies of Economic Warfare and Embargo with Special Reference to Communist States* (London: Routledge).
9. Dobson, *Peaceful Air Warfare*, chaps. 5 and 6.
10. F.D. Roosevelt Library, Map Room, box 162, folder: 5 sect. A4-2, Air Routes, Byrd to Roosevelt, 14 April 1994; ibid., box 207, "Senior Members' Review of Byrd Report"; D. J. Mrozeck, "The Truman Administration and the Enlistment of the Aviation Industry in Postwar Defence," *Business History Review*, 48 (1974), 75–94.
11. Dobson, *Peaceful Air Warfare*, pp. 188–89.

12. D. McKenzie, *Canada and International Civil Aviation 1932–1948* (Toronto: Toronto University Press, 1989), pp. 239–41.

13. Dobson, *Peaceful Air Warfare*, p. 207.

14. To appreciate how Britain agonized over buying American planes see *ibid.*, pp. 199–203.

15. *Ibid.*, pp. 188–90.

16. US State Department decimal file 711.4127/11-2445, Winant to Secretary of State reporting on views of Sir William Hildred, UK Director of Civil Aviation, 24 Nov. 1945.

17. Comité des Sages, *Expanding Horizons* (Brussels: Director General for Transportation, 1994), p. 51.

18. Cabinet Papers (PRO, CAB) 87/2, RP(42)48, "Internationalisation of Civil Aviation after the War," 15 Dec. 1942, Public Record Office, London.

19. House of Lords Record Office, Beaverbrook Papers, D/370, comments on WP(45)21B.

20. W. F. Kimball, ed., *Churchill and Roosevelt: the Complete Correspondence, 3 vols.* (Princeton, Princeton University Press, 1984), vol. 3, pp. 519–20, 566–67, Churchill to Roosevelt, 27 Jan. and 6 March 1945, and Roosevelt to Churchill 15 March 1945.

21. State Department decimal file 811.79641D/1-2945, Grew to US Legation, Dublin, 29 Jan. 1945.

22. *Ibid.*, 711.4127/9-1045, memo of conversation between S. Morgan and P. Masefield, 10 Sept. 1945.

23. Harry S. Truman Library, G.P. Baker Oral History, 22–23.

24. *Ibid.*

25. PRO, CAB 128/5, 11(46)8, 4 Feb. 1946, CP37(46) memo by Winster.

26. Cmd. 6747, 1946, "US, UK Civil Air Services Agreement, Bermuda."

27. Interview by the author with Paul Wisgerhof, Director of Aviation Negotiations, US State Department, 4 Apr. 1991.

28. There is a large and varied literature on hegemony theory, see David P. Calleo, *Beyond American Hegemony: The Future of the Western Alliance* (New York: Basic Books, 1987); Duncan Snidal, "The Limits of Hegemonic Stability Theory," *International Organization*, 39 (1985), 579–614; R. Keohane, *After Hegemony: Cooperation and Discord in the World Political Economy* (Princeton: Princeton University Press, 1984).

29. Dobson, *Peaceful Air Warfare*, pp. 242–44; Boyd interview.

30. Gerald Ford Library, Papers of William Seidman, box 113, folder: Airlines 9/74-7/75, CIEP memo. "US–Dutch Negotiations on Airline Capacity," Oct. 1974.

31. Dobson, "Developing a Single European Aviation Market."
32. Quoted from B.R. Nayar, "Regimes, Power, and International Aviation," *International Organization*, 49 (1995), 139–71, using International Civil Aviation Organization (ICAO) statistics.
33. Joseph P. Nye, "Understanding US Strength," *Foreign Affairs*, 72 (1988), 105–29.
34. Dobson, *Flying in the Face of Competition*, chaps. 3–5.
35. Nayar, "Aviation," 166, quoting US DOT statistics; Dobson, "Regulation or Competition?" 150–51.
36. The analysis of the Bermuda 2 negotiations is taken from Dobson, "Regulation or Competition?"
37. Transport Committee, *Future of Air Services*, p. xiv, quoting European Civil Aviation Conference (ECAC) statistics.
38. Interview by the author with Edmund Dell, U.K. Secretary of State for Trade and Industry, 1976–78, 8 Dec. 1989.
39. Boyd interview.
40. Jimmy Carter Library, WHCF, Subject File, box CA1 folder: 10/1/77-8/31/78, Eizenstat and McIntyre to Carter, 18 May 1978.
41. *Ibid.*, box 64, folder: CO 167, 3/1/77-3/31/77, Brzezinski to Hormats, 29 March 1977.
42. Boyd interview.
43. Cmd. 7016, 1977, "Agreement Concerning Air Services [Bermuda 2]."
44. Carter Library, Staff Offices, Domestic Policy Staff, Eizenstat, box 299, folder: US–UK Civil Aviation Negotiations 1, Eizenstat and Johnston to Carter, 22 July 1977.
45. *Ibid.*, Carter's response was written in longhand on the above.
46. Dobson, *Flying in the Face of Competition*, chap. 7; C. Jonsson, *International Aviation and the Politics of Regime Change* (London: Pinter, 1987); P.P.C. Haanappel, *Pricing and Capacity Determination in International Air Transport: A Legal Analysis* (Deventer: Kluwer, 1984); H.A. Wassenberg, *Aspects of Air Law and Civil Air Policy in the Seventies* (The Hague: Nijhoff, 1970); James A. Atwood, "How Much Competition and How?," *Stanford Law Review*, 32 (1980), 1061–74.
47. Haanappel, *Pricing*, appendix 4, "U.S. ECAC Memorandum of Understanding on North Atlantic Air Tariffs," signed May 1982, and came into effect Aug. 1982.
48. Carter Library, WHCF, Subject File, box CA 1, folder: 9/1/78-12/31/78, "US Policy for the Conduct of International Air Transportation Negotiations."

49. *Air Services Agreement Between the Government of the United States of America and the Government of the United Kingdom and Northern Ireland including Amendments thru 1980* (Washington: US DOT, 1981).

50. Interview by the author with Michael Colvin, MP, Chairman of the Conservative Backbench Aviation Committee, 7 Dec. 1989; speech by Robert Crandall, President and Chairman of AA, Duke University North Carolina, 28 March 1991, text by courtesy of AA.

51. CAA, *Long Haul Routes*, pp. 35–36.

52. Alan P. Dobson, "Aspects of Anglo-American Aviation Diplomacy 1976–93," *Diplomacy and Statecraft*, 4 (1993), 235–55; interviews conducted by the author with: Brendan Hanniffy, Civil Aviation Attaché, US Embassy London, 26 May 1994; Patrick V. Murphy, Acting Assistant Secretary for Aviation and International Affairs, US DOT, 3 Aug. 1994; and Paul L. Gretch, Director Office of International Aviation, US DOT, 4 Aug. 1994.

53. OJ L 240 of 24/8/92 and "Completion of Civil Aviation Policy in the European Communities Toward Single Market Conditions," proposals for Council regulations COM(91)255; for further details see Dobson, "Developing a Single European Aviation Market."

54. CAA, *Long Haul Routes*; *British Airways Report and Accounts 1990–91*, p. 37.

55. CAA, *Long Haul Routes*, p. 37.

56. Interview by the author with an employee of the airline industry, Washington, 4 Aug. 1994.

57. *Flight International*, 16 (7 June 1995).

— 3 —

International Co-operation versus National Self-Interest: The United States and Europe during the 1973–1974 Oil Crisis

Fiona Venn

In 1973–74 the repercussions of the two major crises of Autumn 1973 (the Arab–Israeli War and the OPEC-sponsored oil price rise) led to a number of strains within the international system, particularly affecting the newly enlarged European Community (EC) and its relationship with the United States. For the United Kingdom, the need to prove itself a "good citizen" of the EC, which it had so recently joined, conflicted both with its potential position as a major oil producer and with its traditional relationship with the United States on matters relating to the Middle East, defense, and their joint role as parent governments to the world's most powerful oil companies. French pro-Arab leanings and traditional distrust of the United States militated against policies of international co-operation based on American-sponsored initiatives such as the International Energy Agency. For West Germany, as for the other countries of the EC, national policies had to be weighed against calls for a common response to the crises and their consequences. For the United States, in its self-proclaimed "Year Of Europe," the need to develop relationships with a united Europe and the desire to negotiate a new Atlantic Charter interacted with its desire to take the lead in responding both to the Arab-Israeli War and to the energy crisis. For all the countries of the developed, industrialized world, highly dependent upon petroleum-fuelled energy production and transportation, there was a clear conflict between an agenda of global conservation on the one hand and national economic interest on the other. These problems, sharply presented in 1973–1974, were to come to the fore again in the late 1970s and particularly during the energy crisis at the time of the Iranian Revolution. In this chapter, I propose to examine the dynamics of conflicting interests in the countries of the EC, as they sought to evolve a common energy policy that would reconcile conservation with economic growth. This raised issues of crucial importance to the development of European integration, and its consequent impact upon relations between the United States and the EC.

In October 1973, two crises intersected: an economic crisis triggered by the decision of the Organization of Petroleum Exporting Countries (OPEC) unilaterally to assume responsibility for oil price levels, in the face of mounting world inflation and the instability of the dollar; and the political crisis caused by the outbreak of the Yom Kippur War in the Middle East. Whilst the first prompted all states in OPEC to enforce a sudden, substantial price increase for crude oil, the latter persuaded a small number of Arab oil producers to restrict production and impose an embargo upon states defined as friendly to Israel. In the consequent upheaval, prices soared from $2.59 a barrel in January 1973 to over $11 by the end of the year.[1] Panic swept the industrialized nations, as they recognized their vulnerability to the policies of a small group of Third World petroleum producers. The continuing high price levels for petroleum undermined the industrialized world's expectations of cheap energy and transportation, and added the immediate threat of soaring costs and potential shortages to the always present (but rarely acknowledged) awareness of the long-term scarcity of petroleum resources. It seemed desirable, therefore, that the major consumers of petroleum should try to act in concert: to husband available resources, particularly those not susceptible to OPEC policies; to plan ways of preventing future shortage scares, which would have an immediate disruptive impact upon the industrialized economies of the world; and to reduce demand for petroleum, thus, under the normal rules of supply and demand, helping to prevent future massive price hikes and economic disruption.

What was required, therefore, was a policy of cooperation between industrialized consumers, including, if possible, those which were also petroleum producers (i.e. the United States and the North Sea producers such as the United Kingdom and Norway). There were a number of different forums in which such discussions might logically be based. The United Nations offered the possibility of discussions encompassing not only the industrialized oil consumers, but also those in the developing world, as well as the producers themselves. The Organization of Economic Cooperation and Development (OECD) offered the opportunity for consultation for North America, Europe, and Japan. Within Europe itself, there was the European Community, recently (January 1973) enlarged from six members to nine. Finally, there was the possibility of special negotiations, such as the Washington talks of February 1974. In short, there existed mechanisms for concerted action, in line with a common perception that the united action of the oil-producing host governments called for united responses from consumers. The evolution of a common energy policy seemed a logical step for the newly enlarged European Community to take, as did negotiations and united action by the Atlantic community. However, despite many attempts to reach such a common policy, none succeeded. The reasons for that failure shed much light on the central preoccupation of this book: the relationship between the United States and the Western Alliance since 1945.

The issues of resource security and resource scarcity are by no means new concerns in the history of the oil industry. Petroleum is, along with the other significant fossil fuel, coal, the ultimate non-renewable, depletable resource. In the twentieth century, and in particular during the years since 1945, petroleum has come to play a crucial and central role in the modern world. Whilst it has rivals in energy generation, for example wood, coal, and nuclear power, these cannot so easily provide the motive power associated with petroleum, and are certainly not so readily transported. Its fluid nature distinguishes it from coal, and its mobility distinguishes it from other alternative sources of energy such as solar, water, and wind power. Its very centrality to the world economy, therefore, would appear to dictate a united policy of avoiding waste and promoting efficient use.[2] However, from an early stage the structure of the oil industry largely prevented a coherent international policy of conservation. Until the late 1960s, there was a stable petroleum regime guaranteed by, on the one hand, the surplus production capacity in the world, and, on the other, a careful control of the large exporting oilfields of the Middle East, Venezuela, and North Africa by an interlocking group of multinational companies. These companies took key decisions on production levels, prices, and supply patterns; their pursuit of profit often militated against the efficient and non-wasteful exploitation of petroleum reserves in a given producer state.[3] Also significant is the fact that, for much of the twentieth century, the main consumers of petroleum have not been its main producers. The United States is a key exception to this, but even here the creation of a clear petroleum policy has been difficult, since U.S. subsoil rights rest with the landowner rather than the state.[4] The interests of consumers are radically different from those of the main producers, particularly the low-consumption producers of the Third World, who essentially desire high revenues, careful management of oilfields to maximize yield, and control by the host government over such value-enhancing operations as refining and distribution.[5] Particularly since 1945, the industrialized world's demand for low cost, high-quantity petroleum production has substantially been met at the cost of the producing nations.

This is not to say that there had been no interest in the goal of conservation. The First World War demonstrated the crucial importance of oil as a strategic resource in wartime. A number of leading national consumers, therefore, took active steps towards the implementation of conservation policies, directed at any oil reserves that lay within their own territory or imperial possessions. However, the motive was entirely one of national security. In the United States, still the world's largest producer, the law continued to promote excessively wasteful practices in domestic fields, and it was only in the federally owned oilfields that any idea of efficient exploitation was pursued. Similarly, in its imperial possessions, the British Government was not particularly concerned about methods of exploitation in peacetime, as long as the right of pre-emption remained in time of war. When the United States Geological Survey warned, in both 1919 and during the Second World War, that American supplies of oil reserves were running low, the immediate response was to foster a policy of exploitation abroad in order to conserve domestic supplies.[6]

During the massive economic boom of the immediate post-1945 years, the priority was that the price of petroleum should be as low as possible. Encouraged by the United States, Western Europe increasingly switched towards petroleum, particularly from the newly developed areas of the Middle East and North Africa, for its energy. Whilst in 1950, coal accounted for 75 percent of Europe's energy, by 1966 it provided only 38 percent. Over the same period, the use of oil had soared from 10 percent of total energy generation to 45 percent.[7] However, as Japan, the United States, and Western Europe became ever more dependent upon imported fuel, some doubts were expressed about the future implications. By the late 1960s, with the demand for petroleum roughly doubling every decade, it was estimated that world production would reach its maximum in the year 2000, or thereabouts, and that supplies of petroleum would only last for another 70–80 years. This coincided with a broader awareness of the problems faced by the world, as overpopulation, the depletion of raw materials, and rising pollution appeared to threaten dire consequences, including economic collapse and widespread starvation.[8] Moreover, as oil supplies for the industrialized world increasingly came from the developing world, fears grew about the implications of dependence upon militant producers.

The producers represented in OPEC had also raised the conservation principle, notably in the Declaration of Principles in 1968.[9] By advocating conservation, host governments were able to argue on apparently altruistic grounds for the policies that they espoused for other reasons as well – for example, higher prices, careful production to maximize yield, and proper planning. Conservation justified high prices, as these would force the profligate West into a more thoughtful use of oil resources. However, for both producers and consumers, the cause of conservation was perceived entirely in terms of national self-interest, driven by the economic imperative of current oil prices and the supply/demand balance. Moreover, whilst the producers spoke of conservation, the need to preserve irreplaceable resources and exploit these more carefully, the consumers addressed the problem as one of resource scarcity.

These concerns underpinned a number of discussions taking place, within both the United States and the European Community, even before the oil crisis of 1973–74. Whilst the 1960s had been a period of relatively cheap petroleum prices, which in turn had provided cheap energy and transportation costs for the affluent states of the industrialized world, by 1970 the supply/demand position was changing. Oil had replaced coal as the most important source of energy in every nation in Western Europe with the one exception of the United Kingdom. The United States, itself a major producer, increasingly came to rely upon petroleum imports to supplement its domestic production. By 1973, it was importing roughly 35 percent of its petroleum needs.[10] There were powerful, domestic reasons for American dependence upon oil imports: environmental pressure groups prevented the rapid expansion of nuclear power and considerably delayed the exploitation of Alaska and the building of the Alaskan pipeline. Even as late as 1971, the Texan Railroad Commission which, despite its name, determined the level of all American domestic petroleum production, had seen as its main function the retention of high domestic prices through control of supply and had set the level of domestic production below capacity. By 1973, however, that was no longer the case, as the United States was producing to the maximum of its current capacity.[11]

The potential seriousness of this position in the long run had been recognised by the Nixon administration, not least because of the implications for national security. The Cabinet Task Force on Oil Import Control had reported as early as February 1970. But despite the early recognition of the problem, little was done to address it. Whereas the Task Force had assumed that by 1980 oil imports might have reached a total of five million barrels per day (mbd), already by 1973 imports had exceeded six mbd.[12] Indeed, in April 1973 the United States Government lifted its mandatory oil import quotas, as part of a wide-ranging energy initiative by President Nixon.[13] However, the problem was perceived predominantly in domestic terms, as necessitating a reduction of dependency upon oil imports in the medium term. Collective action was seen in defensive terms: a consumer cartel to confront the producer cartel of OPEC.

Thus, when the U.S. Government raised the issue of collective action in OECD discussions, as it did in the autumn of 1969 and again in May 1970, it was envisaged as a response to host government militancy.[14] This eventually did persuade the OECD that some form of consumer organization, to mirror the producer organization, was necessary. Already at such an early stage, however, differences were emerging within the industrialized nations. The French, in particular, were sceptical about the motives and utility of such an organization. When H. Simonet, the vice-president of the European Commission with responsibility for energy matters, proposed discussions with the United States in May 1973, the French objected, arguing that there was little point in holding such international discussions before the European Community had itself agreed upon a common energy policy.[15] The insistence upon reaching a common European policy first, before engagement in broader international discussions, proved a frequent theme in French reactions to energy matters. It should be stressed that there were two distinct elements in any shared energy policy for the Community: an external policy addressing, in particular, the questions of relationships with the producer states and of cooperation with the United States; and an internal energy policy regulating the Community's own energy market. The United Kingdom was an advocate of a common external policy, but when the French government insisted upon agreement on an internal policy as an essential prerequisite, not only the British but also West Germany and the Netherlands expressed opposition.[16] Thus, although M. Simonet did visit the United States at the end of May 1973 to discuss matters of common interest, the lack of agreement among the nine member states of the EC meant that no immediate outcome transpired.[17]

As this suggests, the EC was also slowly recognizing that some form of collective action might be required, particularly in the form of a common energy policy. In some respects, this was structurally difficult for the EC, as for so long its energy policies had been split among the three main communities.[18] Yet even with the uniting of the communities in 1967, energy policy and particularly oil policy tended to remain within the domain of the separate national governments. In 1968, the Commission published a memorandum to the European Council of Ministers, entitled "First Guidelines for a Common Energy Policy," that was approved in principle by the Council in 1969. This suggested that there should be a number of policies adopted, of which the main ones relating to oil were: a common oil supply programme aimed at the diversification of sources of imports; a periodic forecasting of demand for each energy source; and the stockpiling of 65 days' supplies of petroleum products (later raised to 90 days) as a buffer in the event of crisis.[19] After the United Kingdom joined the EC in January 1973, it pressed for a common external energy policy. In April 1973, the Commission again approached the Council with a major recommendation on energy policy, this time calling for cooperation amongst the major energy-importing areas – the EC, Japan, and the US. At their meeting on 22 and 23 May 1973, the Council of Ministers agreed to a crisis-management directive proposed by the Commission which suggested joint action in the case of a supply crisis, and called upon each of the Nine to have in place by June 1974 the necessary legal powers to introduce petrol rationing and price controls, as well as stressing the importance of maintaining ninety days of petroleum supplies.[20] As outlined above, however, although the Commission also emphasized the desirability of collective action with other major consumers, this foundered in the face of French opposition. So, despite warning signs – such as OPEC's success in persuading the oil companies to negotiate with them collectively rather than by individual country, the fact that the United States was no longer able to act as a producer of last resort,[21] and the instability within the world economy caused by American fiscal policy – the West took little action to address the worsening oil situation.

What is also apparent is the constraints – mainly political constraints – upon the evolution of such a joint policy. Thus, for example, discussions within the EC about a common policy had to take account of a number of factors, not least the growing tendency towards intergovernmentalism rather than supranationalism.[22] However much the Commission might recognize the importance of a common energy policy, the national governments responsible for setting targets and agreeing priorities had their own agendas, in which the availability of indigenous energy supplies, political relationships with major oil-producers, and overall economic policies were all highly significant. The United Kingdom was a particularly important state in this regard. Poised to become a major oil-producer in its own right, the United Kingdom also was a significant parent government to two of the "seven sisters" (British Petroleum and the Shell interest in Royal Dutch-Shell). As a new entrant to the European Community, the British Government also faced substantial domestic opposition to European membership. Moreover, an added complication for the evolution of a common policy related to the relationship of the EC with the United States, again particularly complicated for the United Kingdom by virtue of its traditional emphasis upon the Atlantic partnership.

This issue came to the fore when, in April 1973, Henry Kissinger, Assistant to the President for National Security Affairs, made a powerful speech calling for the United States to have a "Year of Europe," and as part of this to negotiate a new Atlantic Charter. This reflected a wish, in the light of the changed situation in Indo China and developments in the superpower relationship, to revitalise and restructure American relations with its European allies. There were, however, a number of other considerations underpinning the initiative. Although the United States had traditionally welcomed progress towards European integration, its own economic difficulties, which had encouraged many groups in the United States to call for protectionism, made them look warily at a powerful economic bloc with common tariff policies.[23] The United States was perturbed at the impact upon American trade of European policy on standards, subsidies, specifications, public procurement regulations, and quotas. Moreover, American domestic economic problems intersected with unease at the high level of defense commitments around the globe. In calling for the negotiation of a new Atlantic Charter, Kissinger implied that the United States had global responsibilities, whilst those of the EC were purely regional, and, in effect, called for the Europeans to subordinate their own policies to the Americans' wider responsibilities. Linkages between American defence commitments and a willingness by those so protected to meet American economic and political desiderata were stressed, and it was also made clear that the United States would look to Western Europe to assume more of its own defence burden in future.[24] Such a line was in general accord with the thrust behind the Nixon Doctrine,[25] but it brought to the fore the whole question of the transatlantic relationship, in the context of an approach which many Europeans, notably the French, found unsettling, if not downright threatening. In effect, the United States wished to ensure that the EC should not be in a position to challenge it either economically or politically. The response to this within Europe was to strengthen the tendency toward an independent line, consistently advocated by the French, but now encouraged by the British Prime Minister, Edward Heath, who was at pains to avoid any implications of a "special relationship" with the United States.[26] Rather than discussing a comprehensive Atlantic Charter, Europe was able to secure a dual negotiation, within NATO on defense matters and with the EC on economic and political matters. Determined efforts by the United States to link the two were powerfully resisted, and this resistance was to be reinforced by both the Middle Eastern crisis and subsequent negotiations on a common energy strategy.[27]

Despite some initial steps toward a common approach to energy issues, therefore, neither the United States nor the European Community had taken concrete steps towards the implementation of a full energy policy before October 1973. This reflected, in part, an assumption that although prices were rising and demand growing, the problems lay mainly in the medium term. This complacency was rudely shattered by the events of 1973. In early October 1973, the countries of OPEC, meeting in Vienna, decided unilaterally to increase oil prices, in the case of the Gulf states to $5.12 a barrel. At roughly the same time as the Vienna meeting, on 6 October 1973, Egypt and Syria launched a joint attack against Israel. It soon became apparent that this war, unlike that of 1967, would not be over in six days and as the Israeli armed forces sustained heavy damage, the provision of military supplies became crucial.[28] The United States Government, presenting the crisis as a Cold War conflict, acted rapidly to implement a programme of emergency arms shipments to Israel. Requests by King Faisal of Saudi Arabia to the United States to halt these shipments fell on deaf ears and, on 17 October, the Arab oil producers decided to impose production cutbacks and destination restrictions.[29] Two days later, President Nixon – by now fighting for his political future as the Watergate crisis reached new heights – asked Congress to appropriate $2.2 billion for assistance to Israel.[30] On 22 October, the United Nations adopted Security Council Resolution 338, calling for a cease-fire but this was apparently ignored by the Israelis. President Sadat of Egypt requested Soviet and American troops to separate the two sides. When the United States refused, the Soviet Union threatened to send in troops unilaterally, thus threatening to turn the Middle Eastern crisis into a superpower confrontation.[31] On 24 October, American troops world-wide (including in Europe) were put on red alert, but the crisis was averted when the two powers agreed upon a joint initiative calling for a cease-fire. However, the threatened Arab oil boycott continued, in an attempt to force the West to pressure Israel into withdrawing from the Occupied Territories. The United States – or more exactly Henry Kissinger – engaged in an intensive period of shuttle diplomacy in order to mediate between the two sides.[32]

Although clearly interlinked, the economic and political aspects of the October 1973 oil crisis had very different causes. Similarly, although Western reactions to events in the Middle East were shaped in part by the question of Arab oil, it is crucial to distinguish between political and economic dimensions, although the Nixon administration consistently interlinked them. At the most immediate, political level, the handling by the United States of the Middle Eastern crisis did little to advance the cause of European–American cooperation. The countries of Western Europe were far more reliant upon Middle Eastern oil than was the United

States, and were from the beginning correspondingly conscious of the importance of continued supplies of petroleum.[33] However, it was not just a concern for secure oil supplies that prompted their response. Conscious of the delicacy of Middle Eastern issues in domestic American politics, and aware of the need for President Nixon to avert attention from domestic crises to foreign affairs, the governments of Europe were considerably perturbed by the United States' lack of consultation, not least in putting its forces on a state of high alert.[34] This immediately demonstrated the extent to which even apparently localized conflicts could spill over into superpower confrontation, and raised real fears that Europe might find itself embroiled in nuclear war without any say in the matter. It reflected concerns also felt at the time of the Nixon–Brezhnev Agreement of 22 June 1973 on the Prevention of Nuclear War, when key allies were only informed (not consulted) a few days before.[35] Moreover, controversy soon surrounded American attempts to resupply Israel, as several European governments, including Britain, refused refuelling facilities for cargoes en route to Israel. In the short term, supplies from American depots in Europe, particularly in West Germany, were sent to the Middle East from German and Dutch ports. When, eventually, the West German Government requested the United States to cease using American bases as part of the supply route, the Nixon administration challenged the extent of West German sovereignty over the bases.[36] This, in turn, raised the whole issue of whether American troops in Europe were there solely to defend NATO against Soviet aggression, or also formed a powerful base for American activities elsewhere in the world.

The immediate American response to the crisis, consequently, reinforced European resentment and concern at the tendency of the United States to act unilaterally and without consultation, even when its NATO allies were indirectly involved. Moreover, the European countries, and indeed the EC acting collectively, had already departed from the American line toward events in the Middle East. West Germany was seeking a more neutral stance, rather than simply supporting the Israeli state; the British traditionally adopted a more pro-Arab line; and the French had already entered into a number of bilateral deals with major Arab producers.[37] The Netherlands, on the other hand, continued with a pro-Israeli line.

Despite these very real differences, however, the EC was able to adopt a common approach in some respects. The six original members of the EC had, as early as May 1971, called for an Israeli withdrawal from the Occupied Territories. On 6 November 1973, the Nine issued a declaration, again calling for withdrawal from occupied territories, and the recognition of the legitimate rights of the Palestinians.[38] Although there was a strong element of continuity, the Americans, and particularly Secretary of State Kissinger, were quick to condemn European attitudes as giving in to Arab pressure for the sake of continued access to OPEC oil.[39] Thus, the immediate impact of the crisis was to weaken, rather than strengthen, Euro-American relations.

An added complication was the continuing impact of the economic dimension of the crisis. On 20 October, the Saudi Arabian government announced cutbacks of 10 percent in production, whilst an embargo was announced on oil shipments to the United States and later the Netherlands. Whilst not all Arab producers followed the Saudi line, it was made clear that countries would be rewarded or penalized according to their policy towards Israel. Countries that had taken a pro-Arab line, such as the United Kingdom, France, and Spain, were given preferential treatment; countries that had modified their policies to adopt a more pro-Arab line were defined as friendly, and supplies were maintained at the pre-boycott level (this included Belgium and Japan). Neutral countries saw their supplies reduced, first by 25 percent in November and then by a further 5 percent in December. Hostile countries, such as the United States, the Netherlands, Portugal, South Africa, and Rhodesia, suffered a total embargo. To reinforce the embargo, in November 1973 Arab oil ministers agreed to a general reduction of 25 percent on the September level of production, to be increased by a further 5 percent in December.[40] The boycott remained in place until March 1974 (when it was temporarily lifted). The impact of these actions was potentially very serious indeed. The United States had been importing 1.2 million barrels of Arab oil a day, which by February 1974 had fallen to only 18,000 barrels a day. The Netherlands depended upon Arab sources for over 70 percent of its oil.[41]

In fact, the effect of the boycott was less serious than anticipated. Not all countries joined in the production cutbacks. Consequently, with some careful planning and co-operation, oil companies were able to ensure that needs continued, for the most part, to be met. It took time, however, for this to become clear and, in the meantime, affected countries had to plan their response. One immediate problem faced by the EC was the extent to which, in the absence of a previously agreed common energy policy, their response should be a coordinated one. There was an immediate conflict of interest between a feeling of solidarity with the Netherlands, which asked other EC members for support, and those governments which were either parent governments, with oil companies to which they hoped to look for preferential treatment (notably France and the United Kingdom) or indeed were potential producers, such as the U.K.[42] For the latter reason, the British were particularly opposed to any proposal that included the pooling of European fossil fuels. So, although the Benelux countries, stimulated by the Netherlands, called for a common policy, the French and the British (both regarded as friendly by the Arab states) were particularly opposed. In the face of such disarray, there was little chance of a decisive European strategy.[43]

Nonetheless, members of the European Commission, particularly Simonet, saw the October crisis as offering an ideal opportunity to move rapidly ahead with the implementation of an effective Community policy on energy more generally, and oil in particular. Pointing to the very rapid rise in the consumption of oil products, the rising production costs, and the increasing dependence upon outside sources of energy, Simonet identified a number of key priorities. In a speech to the European Parliament in November 1973, he outlined these priorities as being: the need to stabilise consumption, if not reduce it; the full development of any alternative source of energy, particularly nuclear power; the encouragement of any indigenous energy sources, including the coal industry and North Sea oil; and the importance of concerted action, not only between oil-consuming nations but also with oil-producing nations.[44] By June the following year, the Commission had further refined these policies, as well as substantially revising their predicted forecasts of energy requirements for the year 1985. The Commission called for a slowing down of the demand for oil, an increased emphasis upon nuclear energy and natural gas (which between them should account for 50 percent or more of energy needs by the turn of the century), and the growth of a more competitive coal industry. Oil, which had originally been predicted to account for 60 percent of the overall oil supply by 1985, should, it was argued, account for no more than 40 percent, whilst dependence on outside sources for oil should be reduced from the 98 percent of 1973 to 75 percent. Prospecting for oil in the Community should, therefore, be encouraged along with a Community-level organization of the market.[45]

However, as Simonet himself recognized in the speech, the Community was split: between those who felt that the emphasis should be on long-term measures, as against those emphasising the short-term; between those who thought politics should take priority against those who saw the main imperative as an economic one; and between those who stressed the national approach against the Community one. The Netherlands wanted an intra-Community allocation system that would share out available oil equally, a policy rejected by the EC. Countries with nationally directed oil companies sought preferential deals (albeit without success). The United Kingdom was conscious, in the short term, of the ongoing dispute with the National Union of Miners and, in the long term, of its potential wealth from North Sea oil. West Germany wished to continue its traditional policy of stressing the primacy of exports, and thus sought to increase trade with the major oil producers, whilst encouraging individual firms to increase energy efficiency. The French, who had already sought to develop their oil policy through oil companies such as Elf-ERAP (owned by the state) and CFP (partly owned by the state), continued with a policy based on the encouragement of favoured oil companies, the possibility of diversification of supply by increasing refinery capacity within France, the development of nuclear energy, and bilateral deals with key Arab producers. France was particularly eager to resist any attempts by the United States to assume leadership of the West's response to the energy crisis.[46]

Thus, steps towards any common Community policy had to work within the constraints imposed by national priorities, as witnessed at the Copenhagen summit in December 1973. This offered a real opportunity to devise a common energy policy, yet once again the United Kingdom's role as a potential oil producer proved a stumbling block. By now Prime Minister Heath was facing a major domestic crisis, as the miners' overtime ban coincided with the oil crisis. A general election was clearly in the offing (it was eventually to be held in February 1974) and it was inevitable that the questions of energy and the Community itself would be important issues in the campaign. To placate British public opinion on the issue of "our" oil, Heath opposed German proposals for a pooling of Community energy resources. He also pressed hard for the creation and adequate funding of a Regional Development Fund, which would ensure that more Community funds found their way to the United Kingdom. Despite the prevailing atmosphere of crisis, and the forthcoming Washington talks, no substantial agreement on a common energy policy proved possible, whilst Heath's efforts to link the two issues of a common energy policy and the Regional Development Fund foundered in the face of German opposition.[47]

This tendency toward a much more independent national line was strengthened by the fact that between November 1973 and March 1974, five of the Community members saw a change in government. Following the election of Giscard d'Estaing to the Presidency, French policy became slightly more Atlanticist, but it still retained strong nationalist views.[48] One of those new governments, the Labour Government which came to power in Britain in February 1974, was pledged to renegotiate the terms of the United Kingdom's membership of the EC.[49] Moreover, it took office as a minority government, in the midst of a major energy crisis, and facing the inevitability of an imminent second general election. The Labour Party, and indeed the Cabinet, was split on Europe and, according to its Paymaster General, Edmund Dell, the members of the government had had little discussion of economic policy in the period before their election victory.[50] Therefore, rather than seek a collective response to the problem, countries in Western Europe followed a mainly independent line, including efforts to obtain bilateral agreements with the oil exporters. In short, a European policy, as such, did not exist, as each European nation sought to address the particular national problems posed by the boycott. Neither did members of the EC agree a common policy towards American initiatives. So whilst at home the individual governments sought greater control over the domestic operations of oil majors, and tried to increase the functions of their state and marketing corporations, abroad they directed their energies to the conclusion of bilateral agreements with the oil exporters.

Thus, the task of trying to evolve a common European energy policy came at a difficult stage in the evolution of the Community. It was fundamental to the ongoing conflict between those who held to the principle of intergovernmentalism – i.e. those who believed that the Community essentially comprised the pooling of a distinct set of national goals, and that Community policy should continue to be set by representatives of individual governments, such as heads of government and foreign ministers, in accordance with perceived national interests – and those who believed in a Community interest which transcended the sum of the national parts, and which was best addressed by a policy-making process centered on the Commission, and European bureaucrats who would not be driven by purely national priorities.[51] The concept of a common energy policy was at the very centre of this debate; for whilst, on the one hand, the immediate crisis prompted rapid and decisive action, it also raised crucial national interests relating to national security and economic growth. To surrender control over energy policy to the Community was a considerable step to be taken. Yet in many ways it was fundamental to the idea of a Community, as represented by the early stages of integration in the Coal and Steel Community, which had recognised energy as an obvious area of shared concern, offering great potential for common, Europe-wide policies.

However, it was not just Europe that was affected by the oil boycott and its omens for crises in the future. As we have seen, the United States was already conscious of its vulnerability when it came to imported oil. Steps were taken internally to cope with the possible energy shortage; on 16 November 1973, the long-delayed Alaska pipeline bill was signed by the President and measures were taken to cut speed limits as well as appeals made for conservation.[52] Meanwhile, the pressure upon the beleaguered Nixon administration to bring about a major foreign policy victory – for example, by assuring the lifting of the embargo – was very considerable.[53] Hence the high profile given to Secretary Kissinger's shuttle diplomacy. However, the United States was also eager to take steps to counter the collective action of the producers, by returning to the idea, already floated before October 1973, of setting up a consumers' organization.

To accomplish this, however, it was necessary to convince the other main industrialized nations, including Japan and, in particular, the states of Western Europe. The Nixon administration became ever clearer about its policy of linkage between economic and political policies on the one hand, and security and defence priorities on the other. In so doing, it was to exacerbate European, and particularly French, concerns articulated throughout the "Year of Europe." One of the most fundamental of these was that whilst the countries of Europe were far more vulnerable economically to a boycott, by virtue of their high dependence upon imported oil, it was widely assumed that the United States (far less dependent upon imported energy and even petroleum) was more likely to trigger a politically motivated boycott. A further, less direct reason was related to the wider issue of transatlantic relationships, and the nature of the role to be played in these by the United States. Fears grew that American initiatives directed towards a new consumers' organization also had a political agenda, similar to that presented in the "Year of Europe" and the goal of a new Atlantic Charter. France, in particular, which had always resented attempts by the United States to dictate Western policy, was keen to assert its independence.[54] Thus, whilst ostensibly the "Year of Europe" initiative should have made the setting up of a collective consumer organization easier, if anything it undermined the likelihood of success. Moreover, European nations had resented the speed with which the Middle Eastern crisis had been defined as a Cold War crisis, with the United States taking unilateral action on this premise. The coincidental heightening of President Nixon's domestic difficulties, in the form of Watergate, reinforced fears that his administration was pursuing its own agenda, in which domestic considerations played a crucial part, to the possible detriment of its European allies.

These concerns were reinforced by Kissinger's most powerful call for a collective energy policy and a new consumers' organization, as presented in his speech at the annual Pilgrims Dinner in December 1973. In this, he linked energy issues very strongly to political and economic issues as well as the overriding concern with security. Proposing an energy action group drawn from North America, Europe, and Japan, Kissinger warned "This is a challenge which the United States could solve alone with great difficulty and that Europe cannot solve in isolation at all. We strongly prefer and Europe requires a common enterprise." By reinforcing this linkage, Kissinger emphasised the interaction between economic and political crisis, and further increased European fears and frustration.[55]

Attempts, therefore, to set up a common consumers' organization had to encompass not only strains within the European Community, but also strains within the Atlantic partnership. Nowhere was this more apparent than in the Washington Energy Conference held in the U.S. capital in February 1974 at the invitation of the Nixon administration. One key aim was to set up a permanent consumer organization, which might be able to balance OPEC. Following the Pilgrims Dinner speech, the Europeans had given careful consideration to the strategy to be followed at Washington. Before attending the talks, the European countries agreed that they would resist any attempt to set up a special international organization; the discussions should simply address possible strategies, which might then be referred to existing international bodies. Meeting first at Copenhagen in December 1973, they agreed to give a cautious welcome to the proposed American initiative, although France was deeply concerned at the possibility of linkage, particularly as the United States proposed that the economic and financial consequences of the oil crisis should be included on the agenda. Thus, although the EC decided its delegation would attend the Washington talks, so too would each individual member state. Financial ministers would not attend, thus emphasizing a belief that mechanisms already existed to address economic consequences (in the form of the OECD and the IMF).[56] It is noticeable that the French opposed even the idea of such a conference, arguing instead that the most appropriate policy was one of bilateral discussions with the oil producers, of the kind that they had already conducted with Saudi Arabia, Kuwait, and Iraq. Rather than seeing a consumer-only forum, which was likely to be dominated by the United States, France proposed a United Nations conference to include developing consumers and producers as well as the industrialized West, and only agreed to attend the Washington Conference to avoid unnecessary strains within the EC.

French suspicions were reinforced by President Nixon's speech at the conference, which argued that the forces of isolationism in post-Vietnam America were likely to be strengthened by European unilateralism in energy matters. Both the president and his secretary of state emphasised, in public and in private, the linkage of energy matters with political and security matters.[57] Given German concern in particular at vociferous demands by, *inter alia*, Senator Mansfield for a radical reduction in the numbers of American troops overseas and a greater contribution to the costs of such troops by European nations, such a reminder served only to highlight the strains within the Atlantic alliance.[58] However, despite France's desire to assert European (and particularly French) independence from the United States, particularly in Middle Eastern policy, the force of opinion in Europe was still sufficient to ensure that eight members of the EC threw their support behind the formation of a new consumer organization. This was largely due to the influence of West Germany, which was more susceptible than the rest of Europe to the Nixon administration's emphasis upon "linkage," and in particular the presence in Washington of the German finance minister, Helmut Schmidt.[59]

As a result of the conference, the International Energy Agency (IEA) was created in November 1974 as an adjunct to the OECD, comprising the United States and fifteen other nations (but not the French) with the aim of planning consumer counter-attacks against OPEC and if necessary the sharing of oil supplies should there be another embargo (the trigger point would be if overall supplies fell by 7 percent). However, its creation had apparently been secured by American threats and domination, rather than genuine negotiation. France's refusal to join demonstrated forcibly the lack of any European energy policy. Some participants expressed doubts over whether domestic supplies of oil should be included in the pooling arrangements (although the United States agreed to this). The Americans' attempts to gain their ends by threat rather than negotiation, the waving of the isolationist menace (a very real fear to Europe, particularly West Germany), and their refusal to negotiate or consult on their own Middle Eastern policy did little to promote the goals set out in the rhetoric of the "Year of Europe." Thus, whilst both the OECD and OPEC were riven by internal divisions, OPEC had successfully surmounted the problems of posing an effective collective action, whilst the OECD, although seeking to erect a facade of unity, still remained deeply divided as to the best policy to adopt.

The early years of the IEA were to reinforce the divisions between the main industrialized nations. Some common agreements were made, resulting in the establishment of an elaborate emergency programme for implementation in the case of a future embargo, and attention was given to long-term planning. The IEA declared its intention to promote the long-term goals of conservation, whilst seeking to accumulate more information on the oil industry and oil companies, including issues of price. This was at the insistence of non-parent governments, many of whom were convinced that parent governments got preferential deals from their oil companies.[60] The implementation of emergency pooling agreements and the creation of an agency and a reporting structure, including frequent reporting of factual information on the industry, demonstrated the efficacy of leaving the complex details of oil-sharing to the technocrats rather than the politicians.[61] However, the differences in interest were still apparent. A particular cause of dispute was the attempt, led by the United States and the United Kingdom, to set a minimum price for oil. Although justified on the basis that if the price of imported oil fell too low, this would adversely affect the development of alternative sources of energy, it was clearly no coincidence that its two main supporters were themselves major oil producers. Thus, the interests of consumers who were also producers came into sharp conflict with those who did not possess indigenous oil reserves, such as West Germany. West Germany insisted that the price should be set at as low a level as possible, and was indeed deeply reluctant to see any such agreement reached, agreeing only in order to preserve apparent unity. After months of difficult negotiations, the price was set at a level already well below the prevailing market price.[62] In short, the IEA was very much an agency in which individual governments acted to defend their own perceived national interest, rather than developing a common consumer policy. Moreover, it had carefully avoided any of the economic and strategic linkages sought by the United States – one reason, perhaps, for its moderate success.

The acrimonious splits within the Atlantic relationship continued, despite such apparent successes. In March 1974, a month after the conference at Washington, the Nixon administration reacted angrily to the plans for a forthcoming conference between the EC and Arab oil producers. Furious at the lack of consultation, attention was markedly drawn to Congressional unease at the costs of supporting American troops in Europe.[63] In some ways, this was an unnecessary concern. There was not enough of a united European policy to make such talks truly significant, and in the event the discussions did not cover energy problems, but matters of development, consultation, and technological co-operation. At the end of May 1974, the EC and the United States reached agreement on a number of economic issues, including compensation to the United States under Article 24/6 of GATT.[64] Thereafter, the United States withdrew its objections to the European-Arab meetings. However, the misunderstanding and distrust revealed during the previous twelve months had considerably soured the transatlantic relationship.

The West's concern over energy matters related purely to self-interest in terms of conservation to reduce prices and avoiding the possibility of blackmail. Nowhere is this more noticeable than in the attempt by the oil producers and other developing nations to set up a North–South dialogue on the structure of the world economy, with the idea of setting up a new world economic order in which problems of development would be tackled internationally.[65] Although the idea of such a broad-based forum had long been advocated by the French government, the United States was slow to agree. However, eventually the Conference on International Economic Co-operation opened in Paris in December 1975. Here, again, the lack of unity within Europe became clearly apparent. Although originally conceived as an oil producer–consumer dialogue, the agenda widened to include broader issues of, *inter alia*, development, aid, and technological transfer. Originally, the industrialized oil consumer countries were allocated three seats at the conference, which the French proposed should be allocated to the United States, Japan, and the EC. This presupposed, however, that the EC could speak with one voice, a claim rejected by the British government, which pointed to its status as the only major oil producer within the EC. The Labour Government, therefore, demanded separate representation at the conference, a claim opposed by other members of the Community. Although a compromise was eventually reached, in his speech to the conference Prime Minister James Callaghan emphasized the lack of a common European energy policy, whilst failing to point out that this omission was in no small measure due to the British themselves.[66]

The so-called "North–South Dialogue" never successfully reconciled the differing interests of the developed and developing nations.[67] By 1975, the immediate fears of shortage were past; Western consumers were quick to return to old, wasteful habits of consumption, and any collective planning was confined to immediate responses to short-term crises.[68] This was particularly marked at the time of the Iranian Revolution, when again responses to the problem centred on the immediate problem of escalating prices. As the real cost of petroleum and petroleum products fell after 1983, and as the power of OPEC was undermined by the opening up of vast new areas of production in the North Sea, Mexico, and Alaska, the West again returned to a policy of pursuing self-interest and ignoring any wider, more long-term policies.

Throughout debates on energy policies, a consistent theme was the resentment felt by many countries of the West at American attempts to assume leadership of the oil consumers. Yet, ironically, at the same time the United States was failing in any attempt to reduce American dependence upon imported oil by cutting consumption. Combined public inertia and Congressional hostility kept American domestic prices comparatively low, and hence consumption remained high. Despite the recession, which contributed to a decline in consumption elsewhere, by 1975 the United

States was still importing over 6 million barrels per day, or over 35 percent of its requirements, a proportion that had actually risen to nearly 50 percent by the end of 1978. Any success in Europe at cutting consumption, therefore, was undone by the lethargy and unwillingness to change of American consumers.[69] Insofar as consumption declined, it did so more as a consequence of the world depression. Six years after the 1973 crisis, when the Iranian Revolution triggered yet another oil crisis, the United States had abdicated any claim that it might have had to be the leader of Western energy policy. In such a situation, attempts by the American Government to oppose, for security reasons, plans for a natural gas pipeline from Siberia to the West of Europe simply triggered resentment.[70]

Meanwhile, the EC had failed to reach any common energy policy, a problem exacerbated when the United Kingdom became a major producer in its own right. The British Government's policy towards its oil continued to be more that of a *rentier*, keen to maximize revenue rather than increase control over the commercial decisions of the oil companies. Although by the end of 1978 the North Sea provided 75 percent of British home consumption, 60 percent of North Sea oil from the British sector was controlled by foreign companies, many of them American. In its desire to remain identified with the OECD consumers, the British Government was eager to eschew any tactics akin to those of OPEC, and rather than seeking to ensure control over major decisions such as production levels, exploration programmes, or even maximising income, it appeared most concerned to ensure that in any emergency, British oil would not be diverted to more profitable markets, a scheme achieved by the use of the British National Oil Corporation.[71] The legacies of disunity were all too clearly apparent in the aftermath of the 1979 oil crisis: the French failed in their attempt to persuade all European countries to abstain from high bidding on the spot market, whilst the British refused offers by the Germans to provide industrial investment in return for a share of North Sea oil. Indeed, the British have resisted any attempt on the part of the EC to introduce energy pooling. During 1979, Iraq offered France increased oil supplies at a stable price, in return for major arms supplies and confirmation that the experimental nuclear reactor that France was constructing in Iraq would be supplied with at least an initial charge of highly enriched, weapons-grade uranium, thus reinforcing France's bilateral diplomacy.[72] Even the plans of the IEA were of little significance, since they had been geared to ensuring adequate supplies, rather than tackling the problem of rapidly escalating prices. The emergency pooling arrangements were meant to be triggered by a shortfall in supplies, and in particular the declaration of a boycott. Although supplies were hit, by far the most acute problem was the panic-stricken rise in prices, against which the IEA had no emergency plans.[73] At the Tokyo summit of the seven leading industrialized nations in 1979, the simple response to economic and energy problems was to point to OPEC as being primarily responsible for the world's economic problems.[74]

In examining attempts to reach a consensus on appropriate international action to protect the interests of oil consumers against the growing militancy of the oil producers represented in OPEC, it is clearly apparent that attempts to create an international regime fell foul of international politics and national self-interest. Despite attempts before the oil crisis to adopt common energy policies within the EC, and to seek common ground between the major industrialized oil consumers, the disarray so prominent in the immediate aftermath of October 1973 continued largely unabated. Although, in the temporary period of hegemony enjoyed by the United States after the crisis, a consumer organization was set up, it failed to prevent another crisis in 1979, nor did it succeed in encouraging widespread policies of conservation. Most of the attention given to energy in the West centred on disputes: disputes about the role of the United States and the extent of its global leadership; internal dissension within the EC; and above all the inability to escape the pressure of national self-interest. Moreover, although in the short term the oil crisis appeared to strengthen American hegemony, allowing the United States to take the lead role in responding to the Middle Eastern crisis and creating the IEA, in the long term it, and the "Year of Europe" initiative, reinforced the United States' decline in influence.[75] Japan, for the first time, departed from the American line on foreign policy. West Germany, although still very conscious of its reliance on the United States for defence, had challenged it on the use of its bases. As the EC became more confident and assertive, it increasingly clashed with the United States on matters of mutual concern, and challenged the American claim to leadership in the Western Alliance.

Despite the growing interdependence of the modern economy, the reaction of the industrialized world to the oil crisis revealed the very wide divergence between national strategies adopted to address the problem, reflecting different domestic priorities and structures. Yet, this was a golden opportunity to acknowledge the true level of interdependence when it comes to energy matters, and particularly petroleum. However, the political agenda of both the Atlantic relationship and European integration predominated, despite an awareness that policies of conservation and a reduction of energy needs would not only address short-term needs – such as the power of OPEC – but also husband irreplaceable natural resources. The different nation states adopted their own, diverse strategies, putting national self-interest in the short term before international cooperation in an interdependent system. In looking to the current debates about sustainable development, environmental action, and conservation, there is a salutary lesson to be learnt from the events of the 1970s and the aftermath of the oil crisis of 1973–74.

Notes

1. Ian Seymour, *OPEC: Instrument of Change* (London: Macmillan, 1980), pp. 123-25. Raymond Vernon, ed., *The Oil Crisis* (New York: W. W. Norton and Co., 1976) provides a useful survey of the 1973 crisis from the contemporary perspective.
2. For general information, see Fiona Venn, *Oil Diplomacy in the Twentieth Century* (London: Macmillan, 1986), especially pp. 1–13.
3. There are a number of books on the multinational oil industry. See, for example, Anthony Sampson, *The Seven Sisters: The Great Oil Companies and the World They Made* (London: Hodder and Stoughton, 1975) and Daniel Yergin, *The Prize: The Epic Quest for Oil, Money and Power* (New York: Simon and Schuster, 1991).
4. Gerald D. Nash, *United States Oil Policy 1890–1964* (Pittsburgh: University of Pittsburgh Press, 1968).
5. Peter Odell, *Oil and World Power* (London: Penguin, 6th edn., 1981), pp. 77–116 and Seymour, *OPEC*, pp. 29–31.
6. On Britain, see Geoffrey Jones, *The State and the Emergence of the British Oil Industry* (London: Macmillan, 1981) and Colonial Office, Model Oil Mining Ordinances, 14 January 1916, Confidential Print, Miscellaneous No. 319, Public Record Office, London, Colonial Office Records, C.O. 885/24. On the United States, see Nash, *United States Oil Policy*; John DeNovo, "Movement for an Aggressive American Oil Policy Abroad, 1918–1920," *American Historical Review*, 61 (1955–56), 854–76 and Michael B. Stoff, *Oil, War and American Security: The Search for a National Policy on Foreign Oil 1941–1947* (New Haven: Yale University Press, 1980).
7. John Neilson, "Europe's Energy: Why Joint Action is Needed," *European Community*, (Mar. 1973), 8–11.

8. See, for example, Committee on Resources and Man, *Resources and Man: A Study and Recommendations* (San Francisco: W. H. Freeman, 1969) and Richard J. Barnet, *The Lean Years: Politics in the Age of Scarcity* (New York: Abacus, 1980).

9. Seymour, *OPEC*, pp. 63–65 and Dankwart A. Rustow and John F. Mugno, *OPEC: Success and Prospects* (London: Martin Robertson, 1976), pp. 8–9.

10. United States production and imports of petroleum: US Bureau of the Census, *Statistical Abstract of the United States 1982–3* (Washington D.C.: U.S. Government Printing Office, 1982), p. 724.

11. Whereas just prior to the Second World War the United States had produced 62 percent of the world's oil, by 1972 this figure was down to 21 percent. Vernon, *Oil Crisis*, pp. 27–32.

12. The concern that this caused, even before the October 1973 oil crisis, was expressed in an article written by the Department of State's oil expert: James A. Akins, "The Oil Crisis: This Time the Wolf is Here," *Foreign Affairs*, 51 (1973), 462–90.

13. Special Message to the Congress on Energy Policy, 18 April 1973, *Public Papers of the Presidents of the United States: Richard Nixon. 1973* (Washington, D.C.: U.S. Government Printing Office, 1975), particularly pp. 302 and 313.

14. Akins, "Oil Crisis." By this time, the oil companies had accepted OPEC's demand that negotiations should be conducted with the organization, rather than on a country-by-country basis.

15. H. Simonet, "Energy and the Future of Europe," *Foreign Affairs*, 53 (1974–75), 450–63. For the American position, see statement by Under-Secretary of State to the OECD meeting, 26 May 1972, in, *American Foreign Relations: A Documentary Record* (1972), 519–21. See also Louis Turner, "The Politics of the Energy Crisis," *International Affairs*, 50 (1974), 404–15.

16. Stephen George, *An Awkward Partner: Britain in the European Community* (Oxford: Oxford University Press, 1990), pp. 42–70.

17. Simonet, "Energy," 450–51.

18. European Coal and Steel Community for coal, Euratom for nuclear energy, and the European Economic Community for all the rest.

19. Neilson, "Europe's energy," 9.

20. *Bulletin of the European Communities*, 6 (1973), supplement 6/73 and *The European Community*, 7/8 (July/August 1973), 8.

21. This, in effect, meant that the United States had traditionally produced oil at less than full capacity. Therefore it could expand production to compensate for an excess of demand over supply.

22. Paul Taylor, "Intergovernmentalism in the European Communities in the 1970s: Patterns and Perspectives," *International Organization*, 36 (1982), 744–57 and Derek W. Urwin, *Western Europe since 1945: A Political History* (London: Longman, 4th edn., 1989), pp. 367–69.

23. Stephen D. Krasner, "United States Commercial and Monetary Policy: Unravelling the Paradox of External Strength and Internal Weakness," in Peter J. Katzenstein, ed., *Between Power and Plenty: Foreign Economic Policies of Advanced Industrial States* (Madison, Wisc.: University of Wisconsin Press, 1978) and Michael Smith, *Western Europe and the United States: The Uncertain Alliance* (London: Allen and Unwin, 1984), pp. 75–79 and 107.

24. Henry Kissinger, "Year of Europe" speech, 23 April 1973, *American Foreign Relations: A Documentary Record* (1973), 181–89. Also see Karl Kaiser, "Europe and America: A Critical Phase," *Foreign Affairs*, 52 (1973–74), 725–41.

25. The Nixon Doctrine essentially stated that whilst the United States would keep its treaty commitments and provide military and economic assistance to allies and countries vital to its own security, "we shall look to the nation directly threatened to assume the primary responsibility of providing the manpower for its defense." Address to the Nation on the war in Vietnam, 3 November 1969, *Public Papers of the Presidents of the United States: Richard Nixon. 1969* (Washington, D.C.: U.S. Government Printing Office, 1971), pp. 901–909, especially pp. 905–906.

26. Henry Kissinger, *The White House Years* (London: Weidenfeld and Nicolson, 1979), pp. 933–35.

27. Roger Morgan, *The United States and West Germany 1945–1973: A Study in Alliance Politics* (London: Oxford University Press, 1974), pp. 225–26; Michael M. Harrison, *The Reluctant Ally: France and Atlantic Security* (Baltimore: Johns Hopkins University Press, 1981), pp. 165–85.

28. William L. Cleveland, *A History of the Modern Middle East* (Boulder, Colorado: Westview University Press, 1994), pp. 336–38.

29. Seymour, *OPEC*, pp. 118–21.

30. Special Message to the Congress Requesting Emergency Security Assistance Funding for Israel and Cambodia, 19 Oct. 1973, *Public Papers of the Presidents of the United States: Richard Nixon. 1973* (Washington, D.C.: U.S. Government Printing Office, 1975), pp. 884–86.

31. M. E. Yapp, *The Near East Since the First World War* (New York: Longman, 1991), p. 422.

32. On the Geneva Conference and "shuttle diplomacy," see Henry Kissinger, *Years of Upheaval* (London: Weidenfeld and Nicolson, 1982).

33. For detailed figures, see United Nations Statistical Office, *World Energy Supplies: 1973–1978* (New York: United Nations, 1979), pp. 134–45.

34. Harrison, *Reluctant Ally*, p. 178; Morgan, *United States and West Germany*, p. 243; and Smith, *Western Europe and the United States*, p. 68.

35. Smith, *Western Europe and the United States*, p. 105.

36. Morgan, *United States and West Germany*, pp. 243–44.

37. G. John Ikenberry, "The Irony of State Strength: Comparative Responses to the Oil Shocks in the 1970s," *International Organization*, 40 (1986), 105–37.

38. Stephen J. Artner, "The Middle East: A Chance for Europe," *International Affairs*, 56 (1980), 420–42.

39. Kissinger, *Years of Upheaval*, pp. 874ff.

40. Despite this cutback in production, the overall supply was little affected, as countries not participating in the boycott increased production and the oil companies redistributed the available oil. It was panic, rather than severe shortage, which caused the upward pressure on prices.

41. Vernon, *Oil Crisis*, pp. 191–95.

42. Both the United Kingdom and France requested preferential treatment from the companies in which the respective governments held equity, BP and the CFP and Elf-ERAP – but without success. Louis Turner, *Oil Companies in the International System* (London: Allen and Unwin, 3rd edn., 1983) p. 145 and Vernon, *Oil Crisis*, pp. 189–91.

43. For French and British opposition to a general policy, see Vernon, *Oil Crisis*, pp. 97–98 and 106–108.

44. *The European Community* (December 1973), 3; *Bulletin of the European Communities*, 6 (1973), no. 11, 62–63, and no. 10, 54–55.

45. *The European Community* (June 1974), 14–15 and *Bulletin of the European Communities*, 7 (1974) supplements 4/74 and 5/74.

46. On West Germany, see Michael Kreile, "West Germany: The Dynamics of Expansion," pp. 191–224 and, on France, see John Zysman, "The French State in the International Economy," pp. 255–93, both in Katzenstein, *Between Power and Plenty*.

47. John Campbell, *Edward Heath: A Biography* (London: Jonathan Cape, 1993), pp. 559–60; George, *Awkward Partner*, p. 68; and *The Economist*, 22 December 1973.

48. Robert J. Lieber, *The Oil Decade: Conflict and Co-operation in the West* (New York: Praeger, 1983), pp. 82–89.

49. Taylor, "Intergovernmentalism in the European Communities in the 1970s."

50. See Edmund Dell, *A Hard Pounding: Political and Economic Crisis 1974–1976* (Oxford: Oxford University Press, 1991), especially pp. 12–13. For an expression of anti-European sentiment within the Cabinet, see Tony Benn, *Against the Tide: Diaries 1973–76* (London: Hutchinson, 1989). For the renegotiations, see Harold Wilson, *Final Term: The Labour Government 1974–1976* (London: Weidenfeld and Nicolson, 1979), pp. 86–109.

51. The various official publications of the European Communities reflect the continuing – abortive – attempts by the Commission, and particularly Henri Simonet, to put into place a common energy policy. See, in particular, *Bulletin of the European Communities*, 6–8 (1973–75).

52. "Remarks on signing a bill authorising the Trans-Alaska Oil Pipeline, 16 November 1973" and "Special Message to Congress proposing Emergency Energy Legislation, 8 November 1973," *Public Papers of the Presidents of the United States: Richard Nixon. 1973* (Washington, D.C.: U.S. Government Printing Office, 1975), pp. 922–26 and 941–46.

53. In October 1973, Attorney-General Elliott Richardson resigned in protest at President Nixon's dismissal of Watergate special prosecutor Archibald Cox. In the same month, Vice President Spiro Agnew was forced to resign. For energy-Watergate linkage, see Kissinger, *Years of Upheaval*, pp. 873–75.

54. Harrison, *Reluctant Ally*, pp. 165ff.

55. Henry Kissinger, Pilgrim's Society Dinner speech, 12 December 1973, *American Foreign Relations: A Documentary Record* (1973), 566–75.

56. Louis Turner, "The Politics of the Energy Crisis," *International Affairs*, 50 (1974), 404–15 and Ann-Margaret Walton, "Atlantic Relations: Policy Coordination and Conflict: Atlantic Bargaining Over Energy," *International Affairs*, 52 (1976), 180–96.

57. Richard Nixon, "Remarks at a Working Dinner of the Washington Energy Conference, 11 February 1974" and "Statement at the Conclusion of the Washington Energy Conference, 13 February 1974," *Public Papers of the Presidents of the United States: Richard Nixon. 1974* (Washington, D.C.: U.S. Government Printing Office, 1975), pp. 150–56 and 165.

58. Morgan, *United States and West Germany*, pp. 229–35.
59. On French reservations, see Henri Simonet, "Energy"; for final communiqué, and extracts from the final agreement, see *American Foreign Relations: A Documentary Record* (1974), 44–49 and 466–90. See also *The Economist*, 16 February 1974. For Schmidt's general views, see Helmut Schmidt, *A Grand Strategy for the West: The Anachronism of National Strategies in an Interdependent World* (New Haven: Yale University Press, 1985).
60. The goals of the International Energy Agency are set out at the beginning of many of its publications. See, for example, International Energy Agency, Organisation for Economic Co-operation and Development, *Energy Statistics 1974/76* (Paris: OECD, 1978). See also Robert O. Keohane, "The International Energy Agency: State Influence and Transgovernmental Politics," *International Organization*, 32 (1978), 929–51, especially 937–38.
61. Walton, "Atlantic Relations."
62. Keohane, "International Energy Agency," 939–40.
63. *The Times*, 16 March 1974.
64. *The European Community* (June 1974), 3 and Artner, "The Middle East."
65. OAPEC Report on Aid to the Underdeveloped World, in Mohammed W. Khouja, ed., *The Challenge of Energy: Politics in the Making* (London: Longman, 1981).
66. George, *Awkward Partner*, pp. 100–104.
67. On Western perceptions of the North–South Dialogue, see John H. Lichtblam, in United States Congress, Joint Economic Committee, Subcommittee on Energy, *Energy Independence or Interdependence: The Agenda with OPEC* (Washington, D.C.: U.S. Government Printing Office, 1977), p. 32. For the report itself, see *North–South: A Programme for Survival*, Report of the Independent Commission on International Development Issues under the Chairmanship of Willy Brandt (London: Pan, 1980).
68. The IEA was involved in drawing up careful emergency planning procedures, but otherwise its main activities centered on the collection and dissemination of information.
69. In the period 1973–78, U.S. oil consumption had risen by 1.5 mbd, whilst that of other industrialized nations had fallen by roughly the same amount, thus cancelling out any gains. Indeed, for OECD countries consumption by 1978 was over the 1973 level. See Daniel Yergin and Robert Stobough, "Energy: An Emergency Telescoped," *Foreign Affairs*, 58 (1979–80), 563–95, especially 572–73

and International Energy Agency, OECD, IEA Statistics, *World Energy Statistics and Balances 1971–1987* (Paris: OECD, 1989), pp. 2–5.

70. Arthur Jay Klinghoffer, *The Soviet Union and International Oil Politics* (New York: Columbia University Press, 1977), pp. 223–25.
71. Fred Atkinson and Stephen Hall, *Oil and the British Economy* (London: Croom Helm, 1983).
72. Ikenberry, "Irony of State Strength."
73. Turner, *Oil Companies*, pp. 209–11.
74. For a discussion of OPEC and OECD responsibility for the economic crisis, see Denis Healey, "Oil, Money and Recession," *Foreign Affairs*, 58 (1979–80), 217–30.
75. See Alan P. Dobson in chapter 2 of this book for a discussion of declining American leadership and means of leverage in the field of civil aviation.

Part II
Who Commands?

–4–

Language and Power in the Western Alliance*
Frank Costigliola

In February 1995, I was at NATO's political headquarters outside Brussels, conducting an interview with an American Foreign Service officer assigned to the NATO international staff. This person compared the relationship within the alliance to the relationship in the new partnership for peace. "NATO is a marriage," the official declared, that involves "living together with intimate relations" and even the "exchange of bodily fluids, in terms of shedding blood together." In contrast, "partnership for peace is living in sin." The officer continued that the ex-Soviet bloc "countries just got divorced; they are on the rebound, looking to get married immediately – and to someone who is as big and powerful as their previous husband." Although invited to join the partnership, the Russians "don't fit; they are the wrong sex – another masculine power." At another point in the interview, the same official made the point that the United States, when it wanted to, could exercise strong leadership in the alliance because it was like a "macho stud" while the European allies were "saying, come ravish me."[1] We should underscore here the obvious but significant casting in this family drama: the United States as husband or "macho stud," the European nations as marriage partners or ravishee, and Russia as America's masculine competitor who doesn't "fit."

The sexual analogies in this interview fit a pattern in which officials engaged in foreign policy often employ tropes explicitly or implicitly associated with gender to naturalize relationships of unequal power. In reply to a question as to why these particular analogies, the NATO official explained to me that metaphors of sex and of the family "were shorthand; they make it easier to conceptualize complex, nuanced relationships."[2] A major point of this chapter is that such "shorthand" – and language in

*A version of this essay was first published in *Diplomatic History*, vol. 21 (Spring 1997), pp. 163–83 and appears here by permission of The Editor.

general – is neither value-free nor transparent. Language is not just a vehicle through which "ideas," which pre-exist it, "get across." We all know that how you express things matters – there is a difference, for example, between "I disagree" and "I find your ideas childish and crude." I do not, however, subscribe to a reductive linguistic determinism. That is to say, I do not make language the sole *cause* of an attitude or event.

Rather, I argue that figures of speech clarify – and thereby often oversimplify – the meanings of relationships and events that are otherwise complex, contradictory, and confusing. By shaping the patterns of perception through which people categorize and make sense out of events, tropes direct attention to certain aspects of those events while making it more difficult to consider other aspects.[3] Language, particularly language that evokes emotion, can freeze perception and conception, thus facilitating the acceptance of some assumptions – such as that the Soviet Union is always aggressive, or that the United States always knows what is best for the Western alliance – while it impedes the expression of contrary ideas.

Tropes of gender and pathology operate with particular power because they tap deep emotions having to do with the body, with personal ties, and with basic, often unexamined beliefs about "natural" relationships that are in fact socially constructed.[4] If we return to the interview at NATO, we can see the message inscribed in the "shorthand" of gendered metaphors. A description of the alliance as a conventional "marriage" with the United States as husband, or as a relationship between a "macho stud" and a partner eager to be "ravish[ed]" makes it seem necessary, and natural, that the United States exercise predominance in the alliance rather than seeking a more balanced sharing of power.

In terms of the question of "cooperation or control?", this chapter addresses the issue of why most U.S. officials probably would have answered, "cooperation," while they were exercising something more like sophisticated control. U.S. officials often responded to an ally's resistance to American policy with emotive language that depoliticized and trivialized the difference of opinion. Such emotion-laden language read political disagreements as evidence that the ally was unreasonable or incapable. A former U.S. diplomat with experience in Europe observed that his compatriots tended to regard "the political fears and ambitions of our allies . . . as passing irrationalities."[5] With varying degrees of intentionality, U.S. officials used language that depicted difficult allies as beings that were in some way diminished from the norm of a healthy male: sick patients, hysterical women, naive children, and emasculated men. Such images of the needy inspired altruistic language, and so helped transform American control into American caring.

Such images of the needy were also a key aspect of an enormously influential document of the early Cold War, George Kennan's long telegram of February 1946. Kennan, whose language was metaphorically rich and whose emotions ran close to the surface, constructed verbal images of the Soviet Union as a rapist exerting "insistent, unceasing pressure for penetration and command."[6] Repeating the word "penetration" five times in reference to the Soviets' insistent intrusion, Kennan juxtaposed against this hyper-masculine monster an image of effete European nations.[7] He wrote that the Europeans "are tired and frightened by experiences of the past, and are less interested in abstract freedom than in security. They are seeking guidance rather than responsibilities. We should be better able than [the] Russians to give them this."[8] In Kennan's depiction, Europeans are diminished clients: tired, frightened, and wanting only security and guidance. Although categories of gender are only implied here, the Europeans suffer a general enervation. They are certainly not like robust Americans – or the too-robust Soviets.

Although Kennan, at the time of NATO's founding, was less convinced of the necessity for the alliance than were other officials such as Dean Acheson, he was in the mainstream of American policy-makers in believing that the primary purpose of NATO was not to fight against a Soviet invasion, which they did not expect,[9] but rather to deal with what they perceived as Western Europe's lack of confidence and other psychological frailties. In appraising Europeans' apparent fear of the Soviets, Kennan in January 1949 assumed for himself the insightful gaze of the diagnostician, while assigning to Europeans the lesser position of those who could not see their own emotions clearly. In his draft notes for a lecture, he wrote: "all signs that this is a sublimated fear – fear of own inadequacy." In a formulation that suggested an image of the never-satisfied wife, he commented that the United States had already "satisfied them on economic score; if we would satisfy them on military [score], there would be something else." Kennan judged NATO to be "pure psychological warfare," in which the target was the Western Europeans as well as the Soviets. In a recommendation that indicated the utility of the alliance for guiding the psychological outlook of Europeans, he suggested that "we must exhibit more confidence in them than we may actually feel – string them along a little."[10] Kennan's comment also expressed the sureness of American officials that they could manage the psychology of their needy allies.

Even after the onset of the Korean War, Kennan described NATO's value for the European allies as "psychological-political" rather than military – and then commented that this emphasis on the psychological was appropriate because "the peoples in question are irrational." NATO "will cause them to *feel* better, which is after all what we want."[11] Kennan's discussion of allied relations in terms of supposed psychological problems helped justify the tendency on Washington's part to manipulate its associates – "cause them to *feel* better," as Kennan put it – rather than deal with them forthrightly as fully capable actors. We get some sense of how emotive language is often self-censored or censored by others when we note that, according to the original document in Kennan's papers at Princeton, the passage just quoted was part of Kennan's statement to a meeting of U.S. diplomats. Yet the "summary minutes" of that meeting, published in the Foreign Relations of the United States series, does not include Kennan's reference to the allies' alleged irrationality.[12] Either Kennan edited the emotive language from his oral presentation even though it expressed his stated feelings about the allies, or the official who drafted the minutes edited it from the written record, after the striking language had made an oral impact.

Kennan was only one of many U.S. officials who depicted the allies as partially incapacitated and needing direction, not just because the Europeans' military and economic power could not match America's, but also because their rationality, health, or masculinity seemed in some way impaired. In many episodes of the Cold War, American officials juxtaposed images of the allies as effeminate, effete, or otherwise lacking in robust masculinity, with depictions of the Soviets as aggressively hyper-masculine. Representing the danger as one of seduction and/or rape, U.S. officials expressed and reinforced gendered conceptions that naturalized America's predominance in the alliance.

For example, at the 1954 Berlin conference, Soviet foreign minister Vyacheslav Molotov made an appeal to French foreign minister Georges Bidault. Molotov argued that on the basis of Russia's and France's common trauma from German militarism in the world wars, the two nations should oppose the rebirth of the German military under the guise of the proposed European Defence Community (EDC). Paris and Moscow had much to cooperate about, Molotov stressed, and their "difference in social systems need not serve as [a] barrier between them."[13] Recording this appeal, C. D. Jackson, a special assistant to President Dwight Eisenhower, wrote that Molotov "practically wooed Bidault in public." Jackson "slipped [assistant secretary of state for European affairs Livingston] Merchant a note saying `I didn't think he would get his hand above Bidault's knee so soon.'" Jackson went on that "Merchant laughed and left the note in front of him where it was solemnly read by JFD[ulles] a while later. He turned around and winked."[14]

We get an insight into the power dynamics encoded in Jackson's language when we consider the effect of hypothetically switching the positions assigned to Bidault and to Dulles. If the Soviet minister had been appealing to U.S. interests, it would have seemed strange – and highly transgressive – for Jackson to represent that move as Molotov placing his hand above Dulles's knee. Yet Jackson's discourse assumed that taking liberties with the French was to be expected: the mock surprise was that Molotov would "get" to an intimate part of Bidault's body "so soon." A key point here is that Jackson's sexualizing of this political episode both drew on pre-existing gendered stereotypes about French susceptibility and actually reinforced those stereotypes. Jackson's cheerful obscenity made the vulnerability and subordination of France seem natural and inevitable, grounded in the body and in emotion. Although it is unclear from the text, and perhaps was unclear to Jackson, whether Molotov's advance was to be coded as heterosexual or homosexual, in either case the French leader was positioned by Jackson's discourse as passive and open to penetration. Merchant's laugh and Dulles's wink signalled that they got the point of Jackson's analogy. Moreover, the laugh and the wink marked a brief abatement in the formality and tension of the confer-ence, a moment when the boys, including the usually strait-laced Dulles, bonded together on the basis of reinscribing the familiar story of the partly raping, partly seducing Soviets and the vulnerable French.

While the juxtaposition of Soviet power and French weakness suggested the metaphor of sexual overmastering, a combination of rape and seduc-tion, it should be noted that another part of this document coded Bidault very differently. In praising a speech in which Bidault had endorsed American policy on Germany and on the EDC, Jackson depicted him as "a hero" with "guts." As Jackson's language demonstrated, the governing logic or pattern of gendered metaphors is not that a person, nation, or policy is always masculine or feminine. Rather, writers or speakers generally code as masculine that which they understand to be positive, and they generally code as feminine that which they understand to be negative. In the context of the Atlantic alliance, "positive" policies, actions, or statements are generally those with which the observer agrees. An action by Bidault in accordance with U.S. purposes, as Jackson perceived them, was a masculine action, requiring "guts" and even heroism. On the other hand, an action suggesting that the French were inclining toward Soviet policy – or acting independently – was somewhat paradoxically coded as an effeminate non-action, a position of passive, sexualized vulnerability. Molotov had his hand above Bidault's knee. Through this conflation of elements of rape and seduction in an overarching metaphor, Bidault is denied both agency and knowledge. He is both overpowered and duped.

This gendered interpretation of Bidault's interaction with Molotov forms part of a pattern in which U.S. officials represented French resistance to American policy as evidence that France of the Fourth Republic suffered from mental sickness, from an insufficiency of masculinity, and from a moral corruption in its politics and society. These categories of deficiency merged into and reinforced one another, in part through the operation of binary oppositions in the language of foreign policy-makers and analysts.

It is common Western usage of language to construct meaning by conceptualizing things in terms of pairs that require one item to be not just dissimilar, but the negation of the other. In other words, we tend to organize and define things according to what they are *not* or to what they are opposed to. The most basic binary opposition is between the self and the rest of the world: there is me and not-me and, by an easy extension, the us and not-us. In the case of the very different or alien, there is the same and the other. When the French resisted American aims for the Atlantic alliance, U.S. officials often reacted with emotive language that drew much of its force from such binary oppositions as self/other, we/them, healthy/sick, sane/crazy, masculine/feminine, rational/emotional, logical/illogical, moral/corrupt, disciplined/uncontrolled, sound/foolish, civic/selfish, trustworthy/unreliable, good/wicked, active/passive, objective/subjective.[15]

These binary oppositions help shape meaning. The first term in each set is more highly valued by society, usually by both women and men. Because the terms in each of the pairs are mutually exclusive, binaries help accentuate differences, thus underplaying the possibility of a position intermediate between the opposites. For example, if descriptive language codes French policy as a manifestation of sickness and codes American policy as a manifestation of health, such language undermines the notion that each policy is the expression of legitimate, though different, national interests. The organization of these binaries encourages people to assume linkages and spillovers within the set of positive terms – such as self, healthy, sane, sound, rational, logical, objective, and masculine from the above list – and comparable links within the set of negative terms, such as other, sick, crazy, foolish, emotional, illogical, subjective, and feminine.[16]

Because people conventionally assume that the differences between masculine and feminine are so basic and so natural, spoken or written language often maps these perceived differences onto other oppositions, such as rational/emotional and objective/subjective. Since at least the time of Aristotle, both women and men have commonly – though not universally – assumed that men by nature were more rational and objective, and that women by nature were more susceptible to illness and folly.[17] It is important to note that when I use the words "masculine" or "feminine" I am not talking about the behavior of specific or all men and women, but rather the hegemonic, conventional view of masculinity and femininity that tells us how men and women should, and supposedly do, behave. Although powerful, discourses about the masculine and the feminine do not necessarily correspond to the behavior of actual people. Furthermore, a woman may act or talk "like a man" and a man may act or talk "like a woman."

We should keep these dynamics of gender and binary opposition in mind as we examine how Americans explained to themselves and represented French resistance to U.S. policies in the Cold War. There is a tradition in the United States and also in Britain to refer to France and to the French with an abundance of metaphor and personification. These tropes often gender France as feminine, as in the French self-image of Marianne, who can be a quite positive figure. But the feminization of France is also a vehicle for the expression of ridicule and invective. To refer to "those French" is often to bring on a knowing laugh or snicker. Although France has not posed a military threat to either the United States or Britain since the defeat of Napoleon, France has frequently tried to thwart American and British aims in the interests of its own agenda. During the Cold War era, France often appeared to Americans as recalcitrant, but not seriously dangerous. U.S. officials tended to trivialize the French for their efforts at a more independent policy. From 1940 to 1958, Americans often represented France or the French government as one or more of a series of stock characters, who were wayward but ultimately unthreatening and who were usually maligned women: the whimsical airhead, the flirt, the hysteric, the seductress, the female who was willful and wrong-headed, and the woman who was out of place in the public sphere.[18]

In 1953, *Life* magazine, whose publisher Henry Luce had close ties with the Eisenhower administration and whose photographs did much to shape the perceptions of the American public when television was still in its infancy, editorialized against France's "impossible political habits" in terms that suggested that the French were too feminized to govern themselves properly. Observing the French government's divisions, its reluctance to adopt the EDC, its harrowing war in Indo China, and its yearning for some amelioration of the Cold War, *Life* trivialized and depoliticized French concerns by representing them as evidence of out-of-control femininity. Although *Life* was a private magazine, its influence was so public that the French government formally protested over the editorial.[19]

A strictly unintellectual U.S. citizens' concept of government in France, the *Life* essay maintained, might be something like this:

> The building where the National Assembly convenes is really a theater . . . . The show on the stage is produced and played in by the current premier and cabinet ministers; the members of the Assembly make up the audience. The show always opens with a rollicking bedroom farce involving Marianne – the beautiful girl who symbolizes the Republic – and the prime minister and cabinet members, who rush around and hide behind and under things whenever there's another knock on the door. From time to time a big can-can chorus comes running on stage and starts kicking away to loud Offenbach music. Then the stage darkens: Edith Piaf in a spotlight begins to sing a sob ballad about how tough things were during the war for French politicians. She is interrupted by a hubbub between a man and a woman sitting in a nearby box: They turn out to be Marianne – this time played by Zsa Zsa Gabor – and the U.S. State Department, played by W.C. Fields. Zsa Zsa is sore because, while he's told her repeatedly that she's the loveliest woman in the world, he hasn't once told her she's also the most formidable. He does so and slips a billion dollar bill in her stocking. Every now and then members of the audience grow bored and start wandering out to the buffet . . . We don't envy anybody who is trying to make sense of French politics. It would be pleasanter to concentrate on the things Frenchmen have given civilization to make life more worth living: great painting, prose, architecture, the best food and drink, the best ways to make women look and smell lovelier. Unfortunately, the whole world – of which France is a part – is in a political crisis which demands everybody's first attention.[20]

The *Life* essay invited its American readers to appropriate the authoritative gaze, that is, to assume the privileged perspective of the observer who could accurately perceive and understand the whole picture. As the magazine put it, from the viewpoint of "strictly unintellectual U.S. citizens" – a description that to most Americans meant commonsensical, clear-eyed people like themselves – and from the viewpoint of many U.S. congressmen, who had authority because they controlled the purse strings of foreign aid, the French government was "really" a raucus stage show. Despite the seriousness of the Cold War, which "demands everybody's first attention," the French government dissipated its energy in "a rollicking bedroom farce," a form of theatre in which each player had her own, self-serving agenda. I use the feminine form of the pronoun because, according to *Life*, the officials in the French government were nearly all women or emasculated men. In addition to Marianne, there was Edith

Piaf, Zsa Zsa Gabor, and "a big can-can chorus." Instead of acting like courageous men in a time of world crisis, the ungendered "premier and cabinet ministers rush around and hide behind and under things whenever there's another knock on the door."

The essay suggested that the United States did not have to try "to make sense of French politics" because French politics made little sense. Instead of meaningful process, there was rote performance and chaos: "the show always opens" with a farce; "from time to time" the chorus runs on stage; Zsa Zsa interrupts Edith Piaf; "every now and then" the legislators "grow bored" and "wander" out to eat. Although this emasculated France appeared incapable of serious achievement, it still insisted on being told that it was, as Zsa Zsa put it, "formidable" – having, in this context of *double entendre*, not only sexual allure, but also national grandeur. While its W.C. Fields characterization mocked the State Department for being too indulgent of useless allies, the editorial still coded the United States as masculine. Appearing a few days after Eisenhower's inauguration, the editorial contrasted the orderly United States, with its single, inevitably masculine chief executive, and unstable France, with its fragmented government and feminized officials. An accompanying editorial lauded the "muscular feats" of American industry and government.

According to *Life*, France's basic problem stemmed from its focus on beauty, consumption, and refinement – aspects of life usually associated with the feminine and the private sphere – at a time when the "political crisis" of the Cold War demanded the masculine, public endeavors of stable politics, economic production, and military armament. Prescribing a solution, *Life* stressed the dichotomy between "individual Frenchmen," who were differentiated and unambiguously gendered, and the feminized collectivity of "France." Repeating the formulation "individual French-men" three times in a short paragraph, the editorial stressed that these men had to use "work" and "logic" to retake the public sphere, and then dedicate a reformed, re-masculinized France to building and defending Europe. Just as *Life* criticized the French for allowing a rampant intrusion of femininized frivolity into the public sphere of their government, so too did the U.S. government criticize the French for intruding themselves into the public sphere of international politics by thwarting the decision to establish a European Defence Community.

In the early 1950s, much of the American frustration with France stemmed from French resistance to ratifying the EDC. In October 1950, France, led by René Pleven and Robert Schuman and influenced by Jean Monnet, proposed the Pleven plan for a European army that would include German soldiers integrated in the lowest units. The French initiated this idea in response to American determination to begin rearming West Germany and to their own fears that the Soviet Union might follow up the Korean invasion with a direct or an instigated attack on Western Europe. After long negotiations and much revision of the Pleven plan, the EDC proposal emerged in May 1952. This proposal, which still required ratification by the participating governments of France, West Germany, Italy, and the Benelux, provided for a European army that would reduce French military independence and provide for a greater degree of German military organization than the Pleven plan had envisaged.[21]

The Truman and Eisenhower administrations embraced the EDC because it addressed the delicate problem of how to maintain U.S. predominance in an alliance of largely independent nations. As Secretary of State Dean Acheson explained, the EDC – for the member governments – meant "giving up a lot of what is called sovereignty." Much of that power would flow to the American commander of NATO, who "could take any unit in the European Army and put it wherever he wants."[22] To its advocates in America and Europe, the EDC appeared particularly useful because it would integrate the Germans into a European army, thereby reducing the danger of revived German militarism while heading off the Germans' resentment at being contained. The EDC would not discriminate against Germany because the military independence of all its members, including France, would be similarly limited. The EDC "would mean the disappearance of the French national army. This was unthinkable," protested a close associate of General de Gaulle.[23] De Gaulle commented that if the United States found military integration such a good idea, "why does she not merge with Mexico and Canada and South American countries?"[24] In 1953–54, the French government repeatedly postponed a vote on the EDC, and parliamentary hostility to the plan grew. The Eisenhower administration responded with what a French foreign ministry official described as the "strongest and most indiscreet pressure that I have ever seen brought to bear on a French government."[25]

The point of this narration is that the French government had strong, rational reasons of national interest to oppose the EDC, which would sharply curtail French independence even as it rearmed Germany. The postponement and final rejection of the EDC was France's way of considering a complex, divisive issue and then saying no to its powerful ally. Yet when the National Assembly, in August 1954, finally turned down the scheme on a procedural vote, outraged U.S. officials trivialized French concerns by representing them as evidence of irrationality by "wayward, unreflecting, illogical France."[26]

When the National Assembly rejected the EDC, U.S. ambassador to France C. Douglas Dillon cabled Washington. Dillon, whose banking family had long operated in Europe and still owned a famous French vineyard, was himself a major figure in postwar diplomacy. An experienced diplomat, he would become undersecretary of state in the Eisenhower administration, secretary of the treasury under Kennedy and Johnson, and one of the so-called "wise men" who would help Johnson de-escalate the Vietnam War. Despite his sophistication and his affinity for France, Dillon described the rejection in loaded language that assumed the universality of U.S. aims while denigrating French concerns. While Americans aspired to the "EDC and the European ideal," their French opponents were motivated by "selfish, nationalistic, or stubborn contrariness and pride."[27] Grouped with these negative markers, French nationalism seemed petty and unjustified, especially when juxtaposed against the "European ideal," whose coincidence with American interests remained unmentioned.

Dillon's cable set up another opposition between, on the one hand, the "great native intelligence and vitality" of "the vast majority of Frenchmen . . . deeply attached to the Western alliance" and, on the other hand, "a heavy layer of selfishness, defeatism, neutralism, negativism and cynicism." On one side stood average French people with their "native intelligence" and "vitality," a silent but "vast majority" that supported America's universalist policies. On the other side was a near-alien "heavy layer" of outspoken, destructive negativists: the strata of French intellectuals who opposed the Cold War, the rearmament of Germany, and their nation's dependence on the United States. Although "common sense" rationality was conventionally associated with the masculine, the "impractical" rationalization of too sophisticated French intellectuals appeared to American observers as emasculated and decadent. Dillon portrayed the French as living in the past, indulging in "delusions of grandeur" and becoming a "museum" as the United States planned for the future.

As the cable proceeded, Dillon's language changed progressively from matter-of-fact, nearly colorless phraseology to more emotive, personifying language that constructed "the French character" as a singularity and "France" as a mentally ill patient. A major shift in tone occurred when Dillon represented France as a person in pieces, who needed to "pull herself together." The feminine pronoun here did not necessarily signify anything more than the convention of representing certain nations as "she." But in this case, Dillon went on to describe France as the pathologized "weak sister" of the Western alliance: "France is undoubtedly ill and the chart presently indicates high fever. Shock treatment is indicated, merited and sound therapy. But the voltage must be carefully controlled so as not to kill off the patient."[28] It is significant that during the decade when Dillon described France as a mental patient, women made up more than two-thirds of the population in U.S. mental hospitals; most of the doctors in those hospitals were men; and the doctors relied heavily on massive electric shock therapy. The treatment destroyed memories of the past and made patients more tractable.[29] In this metaphor, Dillon figured the United States as the understanding yet controlling doctor or husband, who should "exercise almost superhuman patience and forbearance" – while regulating the voltage of the electricity.[30]

Both the operation of linguistic binary oppositions and the gendered biases in mental treatment encouraged Americans to represent French opposition to the EDC as evidence of an illness often linked to the feminine. Marshal Shulman, a former adviser to Dean Acheson, reported from France that "neither logic, French national interest, nor calm reason were factors in the [EDC] discussion."[31] Acheson himself suggested that "France is like a member of our own family who is mentally ill."[32] If the French were not logical or reasonable and perhaps were even crazy, why take their ideas seriously? By pathologizing their political differences with the allies, Americans were reassuring themselves that they knew what was best for the French and for other nations. In terms of diplomats in the field trying to influence decision-makers back in Washington, a message such as Dillon's cable about the sickness of France was also an argument for not getting too tough with the "weak sister." At the same time, however, the language of pathology and of gender also enabled U.S. officials to justify their political pressure on the ally with the discourse of care and treatment.

In the aftermath of Washington's opposition to the Suez invasion, U.S. officials again represented French resentment as evidence of a client's psychological problem. Such language expressed two assumptions: that state department officials had the diagnostic abilities of a psychologist, and that one could analyze "the French" as if they were a unitary actor. Yet these officials had only pop notions of psychology, and a nation or a nation of people is more far diverse and complex than any individual. Nevertheless, American officials bandied about the language of pathological psychology because it fitted their conception of the alliance: an association of nations with differences in their mental stability as well as their military power.

In November 1956, Charles Yost, minister of the embassy in Paris, referred to the ubiquity of such psychological discourse when he cabled:

"As Department is fully aware, French state of mind has been abnormal since 1940."[33] Yost reported that the Egyptian nationalization of the Suez canal had "produced extreme psychological tension throughout France," which had required "some violent release." Rather than saying that the French decision to invade Egypt was faulty, Yost denied that reason and wisdom were relevant categories when appraising French decision making: "whether it was reasonable or wise had little pertinence." Asserting that the French people and leaders were "not at present in [a] logical frame of mind," he diagnosed the condition as "bordering on traumatic shock." Sent out under Dillon's signature, Yost's message warned Washington to be more careful of French feelings: "If [the French are] exposed to . . . further 'humiliations' over coming months, they are capable of quitting UN and NATO and retiring into neutralistic isolation from which they would hope to make separate deals with Soviets." Putting *humiliations* in quotations marks signaled both Yost's understanding that the French did feel humiliated by U.S. actions and the diplomat's acceptance of Washington's position that such feelings were largely "without foundation."[34] Yost's linkage of psychological disturbance with Soviet deals pointed to the basic assumption of U.S. officials that the healthy, normal behavior for Western Europe was maintaining the alliance with America and the hostility toward the Soviets. In this construction, neutralism and dealing with the Soviets appeared as the abnormal behavior of a nation suffering "traumatic shock."

While slipping comfortably into Yost's discourse, embassy official Ridgway Knight pushed the pathology metaphor still further. Yost had found the French "bordering on traumatic shock"; Knight, however, dropped the qualifier "bordering on" and referred to "the French case of 'traumatic shock' (as Charlie Yost puts it)." Knight's term "psychopathic" was another intensification. Although Yost used the psychology metaphor in part to justify greater forbearance toward France, Knight employed the trope to argue that dealing directly with France would not work because the French "don't really wish to be satisfied." Knight made plain how common it was for U.S. officials to use language that diminished the French when he commented to State Department counselor Douglas MacArthur II that "I have been speaking about this increasing-nationalist-isolationist French jag for some time."[35] The word "jag" likened French actions that were independent of the United States and the Western alliance to a binge of drunkenness or other dissolute behavior. "Jag" also connoted a spree, that is, actions so abnormal that they could not continue for long without serious mishap. "Nationalist-isolationist" referred back to Yost's formulation of "neutralistic isolation" and reinforced the tenet that for the allies to deal directly with the Soviets was pathological behavior.

American representations of France as feminine dropped off sharply after de Gaulle, who affected a consciously patriarchal air, assumed leadership in June 1958. As de Gaulle replaced the divided, parliamentary government that Americans had criticized as lacking in masculine resolve, U.S. policy documents and the popular press used masculine-coded language to describe him as "towering," "lionhearted," "magnificently strong," as the "Providential Man" with "iron composure."[36] In 1960, France exploded its first atomic weapon, and however much U.S. policy-makers disliked the independence of the *force de frappe*, they interpreted this achievement to mean that France had become a more serious power. In 1962, France ended its draining colonial war in Algeria, again rein-forcing the sense in America and elsewhere that France under de Gaulle was regaining mastery of itself. Indeed, the 6-foot-6-inches tall president seemed to American leaders not simply to be looking them in the eye but to be looking down at them. Washington officials found overbearing de Gaulle's insistence on an equal voice for France in managing NATO and his push for a more autonomous French policy. They often coded the general's stubbornly nationalistic policy as pathological self-aggrandizement and the crotchets of a too-old leader.

Although the feminization of France became less explicit after 1958, gendered discourses remained significant as markers of the anxiety felt by U.S. officials at France's upsetting of the political order built on NATO and on the Cold War. In 1966, when de Gaulle pulled France out of NATO, Lyndon Johnson responded that the French president was trying to "divorce France" from its normal "commitments and activities," even as the United States was attempting to "keep the [remaining] family of fourteen together."[37] When de Gaulle improved relations with Moscow, indignant American officials saw France as engaging in a "rather indecent flirtation" and then climbing "in bed with the Soviet Union."[38] Given the intimacy of the Western alliance and America's assumption of the patriarchal role in that grouping, it is not surprising that Americans coded a more independent French policy as sexual betrayal.

The U.S.–French rift of 1966 also brought into prominence the distinc-tion between the unavoidably masculine figure of de Gaulle and the more easily feminized representation of the French nation. In March, de Gaulle sent President Johnson a letter announcing that France would formally leave the NATO integrated command and asking that the United States pull its troops out of France. Although not surprised, Johnson and his top advisers believed this was a serious threat to NATO and to America's hegemonic position in Europe. In his carefully worded letter in reply to de Gaulle, Johnson concluded with a strangely ungrammatical sentence: "As our old friend and ally, her place will await France whenever she decides to resume her leading role [in NATO]." As Johnson's chief aide on Europe explained, the letter emphasized the "distinction between de Gaulle (and *his* policies), and France (and our relations with *her*)." But the syntax of the letter to de Gaulle, with its dangling modifier, created a further distinction. In the context of the sentence, "our old friend and ally" referred not to France but to the *place* of France, a place currently empty because of that country's evacuation from the Alliance. According to the logic of this construction, France could only be a "friend and ally" when she was in her "place." Although references to a nation as "she" and "her" was rhetorical convention, this juxtaposition of gender-coded words did more. It feminized France as a nation led astray by de Gaulle's seductive promises of grandeur. The legitimate and genuine interests of France lay in a different "place," the letter implied, namely with the dependable man at home, who loyally waited for her to take up her "leading role" in NATO – which he dominated.[39]

Because metaphors of gender and of pathology are so handy for signifying, and for naturalizing, relations of unequal power, we find them spread across diplomatic discourses. Such language is certainly not restricted to American depictions of France.

In their postwar relations with the Federal Republic of Germany, U.S. officials believed it necessary to appear in favor of policies over which they felt deep ambivalence. A fundamental assumption of American policy was that the deepest yearning of Germans was reunification. Although U.S. officials ritually endorsed the cause of reunification so as to retain the allegiance of West Germany, they believed that actual reunification could involve a nightmare deal in which Moscow gave up East Germany in return for Bonn's leaving NATO. In the 1960s, U.S. officials also feared that the building of national nuclear forces by France and Britain would eventually produce demands within the Federal Republic for a German nuclear force. Such a force could wreck NATO because most West Europeans agreed with the Soviets' vehement opposition to it. The Johnson administration hoped to escape this problem by "tranquiliz[ing] German nuclear ambitions" with a placebo, the Multi-lateral Force (MLF).[40] Not daring to allow the Germans actual equality with the French or British, Americans focused, as Undersecretary of State George Ball put it, on using the MLF to give the Germans the "*feeling* that they are respected, first class members of the Atlantic Alliance" and the "*sense* that they are in on an equal basis."[41] Germany's sensitivity about its non-nuclear status stemmed in large part from the weakening of America's nuclear credibility. Particularly with Robert McNamara's doctrine of flexible response, growing numbers of Germans, French, and other Europeans feared that the United States was raising the nuclear threshold so high as to make unlikely a nuclear response to a limited Soviet invasion of Western Europe. McNamara himself increasingly believed that the consequences of such nuclear retaliation were too cataclysmic. Although U.S. officials wanted to calm German anxieties, they did not want to share final control over using their nuclear forces nor did they want to sacrifice the American homeland in an all-out nuclear exchange. In sum, Washington officials were deeply concerned and deeply torn about basic elements in the U.S.–German relationship. Perceiving this ambivalence, West German leaders often voiced insecurity about the genuine ambiguities and uncertainties in their relationship with Washington.

Failing to see their own role in aggravating German insecurity, U.S. officials often used language that pathologized and trivialized the Germans' concerns. Some of the metaphors linked pathology and gender, particularly when they imputed mental problems to the Germans. After all, to call a man deficiently rational was not quite to insinuate that he was hysterical, but in the Cold War context, he was also not altogether manly. Adviser Henry Kissinger hinted at this kind of emasculation when he told John F. Kennedy that West Germany was "a candidate for a nervous breakdown."[42] Another Kennedy adviser referred to "the neurotic majority of German politicians," while National Security Adviser McGeorge Bundy, providing an alternative pathology, "thought the present West German Government was schizophrenic."[43]

U.S. officials referred to West Germany with language that connoted other kinds of diminution. Dean Acheson, an important adviser to the Kennedy and Johnson administrations, wrote after a trip to Germany that

[U.S. officials,] in being exasperated and irritated by the neurotic and irrational conduct of German officials – and often the German public – are making the mistake of a busy parent annoyed by the pressing of a high strung, insecure, but affectionate – almost too affectionate – child. It is a mistake to take what it says literally; and the worst thing to do is to shout at it or to slap it.[44]

Like Dillon and Yost, Acheson urged forbearance by appealing to – and so reinforcing – preexisting stereotypes of the ally as a diminished nation. Acheson's reference to a "child" naturalized the Federal Republic's juridical status as an incomplete, less than fully sovereign state. It is normal for a parent to tell a child what to do. While a parent should make allowances for a child's "high-strung, insecure" behavior, the adult need not take seriously childish fears and fantasies. The analogy fits the inclination of U.S. policy-makers to soothe the Germans rather than deal forthrightly with German political concerns.

Acheson's characterization reinforced the assumption that it was the Americans, and not their allies, who had the authoritative or correct gaze on political and military issues. Although the Americans as parents might become "exasperated and irritated" – emotions that did not detract from one's clear vision of reality – the Germans exhibited "neurotic and irrational conduct," that is, behavior that accorded with neither reality nor reason. Acheson underscored the supposed difference in gaze when he wrote that "it was a mistake to take what [the child] says literally." Although Acheson's language – "neurotic," "irrational," "high-strung," "insecure," "almost too affectionate" – depicted a child, these descriptives also fit conventional imagery of the feminine. Whether as the feminine or as the child, West Germany did not measure up to the masculine, adult norm personified by the United States.

Other U.S. officials offered variations on the theme of diminution. A State Department analysis pointed out the "unspoken" assumption in U.S. policy "that the Germans may once again become the sick children of Europe, and that their care and feeding is a matter of nervous concern to us."[45] George Ball thought it important to "keep" the West Germans "from getting off the reservation."[46] He agreed with President Johnson that the Federal Republic had to remain "on a leash."[47] Francis Bator believed that for Bonn, "the truth is dangerous medicine. We will have to feed it to the Germans in very small doses and very gradually."[48] The metaphors used here suggested problem children, discontented Indians, straying dogs, and frail patients. Despite the diversity of the images, they all suggested troublesome beings that were the objects of action by more rational superiors.

Throughout the Cold War, metaphors of gender and of pathology remained available to those officials or analysts who sought to emphasize the "Soviet threat." Just as Kennan at the onset of the Cold War employed emotive language to signify the Soviets as a hyper-masculine, monstrous force, two decades later other officials used similar representation to de-legitimate what they feared as uncontrolled *détente* along the German–German border. As foreign minister Willy Brandt reached out to the German Democratic Republic, a U.S. State Department analysis in October 1968 characterized his nascent *Ostpolitik* as "the near-pathetic speeches and statements of the Bonn leaders overflowing with 'good will' and asking friend and foe for sympathy and at least 'understanding.'" The

State Department document concluded from this behavior that West Germans "are not only jittery and frightened, but that they feel helpless." The language here – "near-pathetic," "jittery," "frightened," and "helpless" – coded the West Germans as emasculated. The discourse suggested that West Germans had lost their self-discipline and their ability to uphold necessary boundaries. The position of the word "overflowing" next to "leaders" suggested that not only the statements and speeches of Bonn officials, but also those officials themselves were spilling over with feminized concerns of sympathy, "good will," and "understanding" – not the stuff of *realpolitik*. Furthermore, the document argued, the West as a whole had demonstrated "marked passivity" in the face of the invasion of Czechoslovakia in August 1968 and appeared "rather soft" on the issue of access to Berlin.

In language that recalled Kennan's long telegram, the State Department document contrasted the insufficient masculinity of the West with the invasive hyper-masculinity of the East. "Coldly systematic and inexorable," the East Germans were becoming "harder and harsher" and appeared ready to "demonstrate to Bonn its utter impotence and helplessness." East Germany would accomplish this final rape and emasculation "by sudden rapid thrusts" of "specialized forces" into West Berlin.[49] This characterization of détente as making the West vulnerable to emasculation did not mean that the U.S. government opposed détente as such. Rather, détente was a contested policy; this document represented thinking that remained locked in the Cold War paradigm; and even proponents of détente such as Henry Kissinger wanted the United States to control the process and to prevent a race to Moscow.

In the early 1980s, when many Europeans opposed the Reagan administration's bombing of Libya and campaign against Nicaragua, some U.S. officials tried to de-legitimate the political content of such criticism by attributing it to the inadequate masculinity of those "Euro-fags." Similarly, when massive numbers of West Germans protested against the deployment on their territory of Pershing II missiles, a defense intellectual explained that "those Krauts are a bunch of limp-dicked wimps."[50]

Although this chapter focuses on the emotive language used by U.S. officials to naturalize their superiority and to depoliticize the allies' contrary points of view, such language was not, of course, a monopoly of Americans. Rather, tropes of gender, pathology, and other figures of speech – which draw their emotional power from deeply felt notions about the body, the psyche, and the supposed immutable order of the most private aspects of life – are available to any people who believe themselves superior to, and able to judge, others.

It is not surprising, therefore, to find that British Treasury and Foreign Office officials used such discourse, notably in 1945–46, when they still hoped to regain their prewar prominence and to guide their less sophisticated transatlantic cousins. British analysts clung to a structure of meaning based on the perceived opposition between their masculine rationality – "ripe and calm wisdom," as John Maynard Keynes put it – and the Americans' less than masculine emotionalism.[51] The British ambassador in Washington depicted American leaders as suffering from "uneasy bewilderment," "fear of the unknown," "baffled dismay," and "a constant disposition to prefer the emotional to the rational approach." Furthermore, the Americans were "nervous," "lack[ed] stable purpose," and put their "faith in the magic of large words."[52] To counter U.S. bragging about the atomic bomb – that "hubbub of emotional talk" – the United Kingdom would marshal its own super weapon, namely "lucid . . . appeals to reason and the logic of hard fact."[53]

British officials similarly felt superior to the French, particularly when the latter resisted EDC, giving up the Saar, and rearming Germany. In 1952, when R.H. Scott in the foreign office wrote that policy differences with Paris stemmed from "French impotence" and from France's "place as the sick man of Europe," Foreign Secretary Anthony Eden minuted "Very good" next to the comment.[54]

In 1950–51, the British worried that the United States would explode the Korean conflict into a war involving China and possibly the Soviet Union. They complained about the Americans' "highly excited state," "absence of realism," "impulsiveness and tendency to plunge ahead, sometimes in anger."[55] Recording these judgments, ambassador to London Walter Gifford de-legitimated and thereby dismissed the criticism by positioning the British on the debased side of the rationality/irrationality dichotomy. He dismissed British fears of escalation, and charges that the United States was "confusing fundamental social upheavals in Asia with Soviet machinations," as British "instinctive and emotional reactions," reflecting "contradictions, illogicalities and even blind spots." Gifford concluded that the British disagreed with America's hard-line stance against China because they were "unable to grasp [the] facts."[56]

By 1963, Britain's power relative to the United States had declined further, and in the soul-searching following the French veto of London's bid to join the Common Market, top Foreign Office analysts examined the basic assumptions of British foreign policy. In dealing with the central fact of "dependence upon the United States," Roland Butler cited the assessment of Patrick Dean, ambassador to the United Nations. Dean defended British policy by noting that "we tend to underrate the extent to which we already oblige the Americans to 'appease' us." Butler then commented:

> This suggestion of a rather *feminine* role for Great Britain in relation to the United States illustrates the fact that while diplomacy is necessarily based upon power, power can . . . be exploited diplomatically upon three main levels: first . . . as naked force, as in the policy of Hitler . . . [the Cuban missile crisis] . . . or General de Gaulle's prohibition of British entry into the Common Market. Second, power, if genuine, can be kept discreetly latent, breeding power merely by its existence rather as capital accrues interest . . . It is latent power which can impart an underlying drive to diplomacy of a rather traditionally British kind, *suaviter in modo, fortiter in re*. Latent power can, however, be allowed to slip down to the third, bottom, level, where it becomes so submerged as to suggest weakness.[57]

In this sophisticated analysis, Butler discerned the position of British policy within the gendered discourses that operated – sometimes openly, at other times implicitly – in the power relations of the Western alliance. He understood that British policy at its smartest could play a "feminine role" to "oblige the Americans to 'appease' us," as Dean had put it. Although Butler was bold in acknowledging Britain's "feminine" position, he remained anxious that "latent power" could "slip down" to "weakness," that is, to abject emasculation. To succeed in its overall foreign policy, Britain had to maintain its "genuine" power, by which Butler meant nuclear weapons. "Their abandonment," he warned meant "impotence." As long as the United Kingdom held on to this marker of great nation, masculine status, British power could remain in a feminine position, "discreetly latent, breeding power merely by its existence." The massive destructiveness of nuclear weaponry, a power that scientists and government officials had associated with the masculine since 1945,[58] would keep Britain safely masculine even as it assumed a shrewdly "feminine role." Butler further legitimated the "feminine" strategy by linking it with the masculine realm of finance, where "capital accrues interest."

Even as Butler perceived the advantage to Britain in pursuing a skillful policy of suasion and conservation of power, he emphasized that this more passive tactic had to be based on the masculine-coded power of nuclear weaponry and dedicated to the "underlying drive" and "resolute deeds" of a masculine-coded foreign policy. In common with their American counterparts, British officials generally valorized the masculine over the feminine. And, like most women and men, they assumed that the socially constructed differences between feminine and masculine were in fact "natural," immutable differences based on biology. Although few women actually participated in foreign affairs, gender norms acted as organizers in the discursive differentiation between what was strong and weak, right and wrong, healthy and sick, legitimate and illegitimate, and rational and irrational in foreign policy.

For American officials to refer to France's rejection of the EDC as indicating a feminized mental illness or to label German discontent with the Cold War as emasculation did not mean that the French people were really mentally ill or that the German people were really emasculated. Nevertheless, the use of such language made it easier for U.S. officials, who generally predominated in alliance decision-making, to depoliticize and trivialize allies' disagreements. Emotive language of gender and of pathology disparaged and so helped exclude viewpoints that differed sharply from those of U.S. officials. Such exclusion may have narrowed the range of acceptable options in pursuing, for example, a relaxation of tensions with the Soviets. Such exclusion of different viewpoints certainly limited the degree of democratic decision-making within the alliance.

The persistence of emotive language in diplomatic documents, despite the self-censorship of officials trying to write as objectively as possible and the censorship of discreet scribes, who in their memoranda of conversations edit out the juicier material, should prompt us to reflect on our prevailing model: rational policy-makers arriving at rational decisions that are later analyzed by rational diplomatic historians. Although there is of course a large measure of rationality in these processes, there is also present deep emotion and even irrationality. It would be unfair to expect policy-makers to commit themselves to certain policies and ideas and not become emotionally engaged. Tropes of gender and of pathology are a rhetorical device by which policy-makers can express emotional judgments, but do so in language that envelops, and legitimates, their emotion in the powerful logic and "natural" order of the body and morality.

In reading the documents, we diplomatic historians have generally not focused on emotive language. Assuming that language is transparent, we tend in our own writing to reinscribe, with little comment, the discourses of policy-makers. We generally travel away from the metaphor, focusing on denotation rather than connotation. In part this focus is because attention to elaborated, "flowery" prose itself carries a connotation of the feminine, and our field remains a domain of masculine discourse, regardless of the women who are now prominent in it. Inasmuch as we all try to read documents closely, we should try to read them for their emotive as well as their rational meanings and to discern how emotive meanings can actively restrict rational analysis.

Notes

1. Interview with American official on the NATO international staff, 16 Feb. 1995, Brussels.
2. *Ibid.*
3. George Lakoff and Mark Johnson, *Metaphors We Live By* (Chicago: University of Chicago Press, 1980); Murray Edelman, *The Symbolic Uses of Politics* (Urbana, Ill.: University of Illinois Press, 1964), pp. 65–66.
4. For discussion of the strong tendency to represent the political situation with bodily symbolism, and vice versa, see Mary Douglas, *Purity and Danger: An Analysis of Concepts of Pollution and Taboo* (London: Routledge, 1966), pp. 115–22; Mary Douglas, *Natural Symbols: Explorations in Cosmology* (London: The Cresset Press, 1970), pp. vii–ix, 63–71.
5. Harold van B. Cleveland in Ninth Steering Committee Meeting, "Atlantic Policy Studies," 18 Feb. 1964, p. 9, Record Group (RG) vol. 111, Council on Foreign Relations Archives, New York City.
6. *FRUS*, 1946, 6, p. 706.
7. *Ibid.*, pp. 702, 704, 706.
8. *Ibid.*, p. 709.
9. This is a major theme in Melvyn P. Leffler, *A Preponderance of Power: National Security, the Truman Administration, and the Cold War* (Stanford: Stanford University Press, 1992).
10. Quoted in Frank Costigliola, 'The Nuclear Family: Tropes of Gender and Pathology in the Western Alliance', *Diplomatic History*, vol. 21 (Spring 1997), p. 166.
11. Quoted in *ibid.* (emphasis in the original).
12. *FRUS*, 1952–1954, 6, pp. 643–65.
13. *Ibid*, 1952–1954, 7, pp. 913–16.
14. *Ibid.*, p. 921.
15. Helen Haste, *The Sexual Metaphor* (New York: Harvester Wheatsheaf, 1993), p. 85; Carol Cohn, "Wars, Wimps, and Women: Talking Gender and Thinking War," in Miriam Cooke and Angela Woollacott, eds., *Gendering War Talk* (Princeton: Princeton University Press, 1993), pp. 229–30.
16. Cohn, "Wars, Wimps, and Women," 228–29.
17. Nancy Tuana, *Women and the History of Philosophy* (New York: Paragon Press, 1992), pp. 4–9, 34–44, 67–70, 114–17; Haste, *Sexual Metaphor*, pp. 32–34; Genevieve Lloyd, *The Man of Reason: "Male" and "Female" in Western Philosophy* (London: Methuen, 1984),

pp. 2–16, 103–108; Evelyn Fox Keller, *Reflections on Gender and Science* (New Haven: Yale University Press, 1985), pp. 7–9, 87–89.

18. During the Second World War, U.S. officials including President Franklin D. Roosevelt commonly demeaned France as an impossible or sick woman. See Frank Costigliola, *France and the United States: The Cold Alliance since World War II* (New York: Twayne, 1992), pp. 22, 40.

19. See Pierre Mélandri, *Les Etats-Unis face à l'unification de l'Europe* (Paris: Université de Paris I, 1980).

20. *Life*, 26 Jan. 1953, 34.

21. Charles C. Cogan, *Oldest Allies, Guarded Friends: The United States and France Since 1940* (Westport, Conn.: Praeger, 1994), pp. 75–95; Costigliola, *France and the United States*, pp. 90–101.

22. See Costigliola, *France and the United States*, pp. 92–93.

23. *FRUS*, 1952–54, 6, p. 1198.

24. *New York Times*, 11 Nov. 1953.

25. Jean Lacouture, *Pierre Mendès France* (Paris: Seuil, 1981), p. 275. See also *FRUS*, 1952–54, 5, pp. 1033–85; Pierre Mélandri, "Les difficiles relations franco-américaines," in François Bédarida and Jean-Pierre Rioux, eds., *Pierre Mendès France et le mendèsisme* (Paris, 1985), pp. 251–59.

26. *FRUS*, 1952–1954, 5, p. 949.

27. *Ibid.*, 6, p. 1444

28. *Ibid.*, p. 1445.

29. U.S. policy-makers repeatedly characterized troublesome allies as neurotic or hysterical, conditions that have been linked with the feminine even when experienced by men. Medical literature in the nineteenth and in most of the twentieth centuries described the female hysteric as an "unusually intractable and self-assertive" woman, who was often locked in a power struggle with her husband and/or doctor, and who exhibited, as a 1968 psychiatric manual put it, a personality that was excitable, unstable, over-reactive, immature, and vain. Doctors distinguished between women, who had a natural predisposition toward hysteria and who could suffer the condition without having had any external traumas, and men, who if traumatized sufficiently by warfare or other stress, could become hysterics. Wartime psychiatrists tended to believe that the hysterical man suffered a process of feminization. He had lost control of his emotions, and he was acting like a woman by giving in to his sensitivity or cowardice instead of acting and dying like a man. These beliefs about hysteria demonstrate that even as gendered discourse assigns gender to human conditions

and afflictions, men and women can take different positions within that gendered discourse. See Carroll Smith-Rosenberg, *Disorderly Conduct: Visions of Gender in Victorian America* (New York: Oxford University Press, 1985), pp. 210, 212; Ursula Link-Heer, "'Male Hysteria': A Discourse Analysis," *Cultural Critique*, 15 (Spring 1990), 191–220; Elaine Showalter, *The Female Malady: Women, Madness, and English Culture, 1830–1980* (New York: Pantheon, 1985), pp. 3–4; Susan Sontag, *Illness as a Metaphor; and, Aids and its Metaphors* (London: Penguin, 1991), p. 74.

30. *FRUS*, 1952–54, 6, p. 1445.
31. Marshal Shulman to Dean Acheson, 5 Oct. 1954, box 28, Dean Acheson papers, Yale University, New Haven, Connecticut.
32. Dean Acheson speech at Johns Hopkins University, 19 Mar. 1959, copy in 611.41/3-1959, RG 59, National Archives.
33. *FRUS*, 1955–57, 27, p. 89.
34. *Ibid.*, pp. 90–91.
35. Ridgway B. Knight to Douglas MacArthur II, 30 Nov. 1956, 740.5/11-3056, RG 59, National Archives.
36. National Security Council, "Operations Coordinating Board Report on U.S. Policy on France," 9 Nov. 1960, NSC files, National Archives; David L. Schalk, "American Opinion of General de Gaulle's Algerian Policy, 1958–1962," paper presented at the conference celebrating the centennial of Charles de Gaulle, New York University, 7–8 Apr. 1990.
37. Press briefing, n.d. [June 1966], box 8, Rostow's Memoranda to the President, National Security File (NSF), Lyndon B. Johnson Presidential Library, Austin, Texas (hereafter LBJL); Johnson to Secretary Rusk, 4 June 1966, *ibid.*; Rostow to the President, 9 June 1966, *ibid.*
38. Ambassador Charles Bohlen to Secretary of State, 31 Mar. 1965, box 171, NSF, LBJL; David Klein to McGeorge Bundy, 29 Apr. 1965, *ibid.* On the conflation of sexual and political threats, see Neal Hertz, "Medusa's Head: Male Hysteria under Political Pressure," in Hertz, *The End of the Line: Essays in Psychoanalysis and the Sublime* (New York: Columbia University Press, 1985), pp. 161-93 and Lynn Hunt, *The Family Romance of the French Revolution* (Berkeley and Los Angeles: University of California Press, 1992), pp. 89–123.
39. Francis Bator to the President, 18 Mar. 1966, (emphasis added); Johnson to de Gaulle, 22 Mar. 1966, IT34, White House Central Files, LBJL.
40. "The Case Against Offering the Germans Ownership in Nuclear Hardware," 9 Dec. 1965, box 186–187, NSF, LBJL.
41. Ball to the President, 5 Dec. 1964, no. 1978/431A, Declassified

Documents Reference Service (hereafter DDRS) (emphasis added).

42. Kissinger to the President, 6 Apr. 1961, box 117, President's Office Files (hereafter POF), John F. Kennedy Presidential Library, Boston, Massachusetts.

43. Unsigned memorandum to the President, "The U.S. and de Gaulle – The Past and the Future," 30 Jan. 1963, box 116A, POF, JFKL; Memorandum of telephone conversation between McGeorge Bundy and George Ball, 12 Mar. 1965, 11:40 a.m., box 4, George Ball papers, LBJL.

44. Acheson to Frida Seabury, 29 Oct. 1963, box 28, Dean Acheson papers.

45. Walt Rostow to Bundy, "A Re-examination of Premises on the German Problem," 10 Dec. 1965, NSF Country File, Germany, box 186–187, LBJL.

46. Ball telephone conversation with J. William Fulbright, 23 Aug. 1965, box 6, George Ball papers.

47. "Memorandum of Discussion of the MLF at the White House, at 5:30 P.M., April 10, 1964," NSF Subject File, box 23, LBJL.

48. Bator to Bill Moyers, 15 Mar. 1966, box 3, Francis Bator papers, LBJL.

49. "Impending Berlin Crisis," [Oct. 1968], box 189, NSF Germany, LBJL.

50. Quoted in Cohn, "Wars, Wimps, and Women,' p. 236.

51. *Documents on British Policy Overseas* (hereafter *DOBPO*), ser. I, vol. 4, p. 14.

52. *DOBPO*, ser. I, vol. 4, p. 9; *ibid.*, ser. I, vol. 3, pp. 13–15.

53. *DOBPO*, ser. I, vol. 3, pp. 18–21.

54. R.H. Scott minute, 25 Nov. 1952 on O. Harvey to William Strang, 10 Nov. 1952, F.O. 371/101741, Public Record Office (hereafter PRO), London.

55. *FRUS*, 1951, 4, pp. 895–96.

56. *Ibid.*, pp. 895–98.

57. Roland Butler, "A New Perspective for British Diplomacy," 24 May 1963, F.O. 371/173334, PRO (emphasis added).

58. Carol Cohn, "Sex and Death in the Rational World of Defense Intellectuals," *Signs*, 12 (1987), 694–701; Brian Easlea, *Fathering the Unthinkable: Masculinity, Scientists, and the Nuclear Arms Race* (London: Pluto Press, 1983), pp. 5–12, 146–72.

Ambivalent about America: Giorgio La Pira and the Catholic Left in Italy from NATO Ratification to the Vietnam War

James Edward Miller

We are aware in America of your noble and inspiring work . . . especially the tireless way you have fought to bring the healing spirit of Christ into the red battlefield.

Clare Boothe Luce to La Pira, 1953

[La Pira] has followed me with telegrams since I met him . . . in Florence in 1962 . . . I have stopped answering them, as our Rome embassy advised me he was a publicity seeker.

Averell Harriman to Dean Rusk, 1965

Anti-Americanism comes in many forms and degrees. Over the last five decades, Americans have become accustomed to images of raging mobs from Tripoli to Tehran burning the symbols of the United States, attacking both its citizens and its buildings. Equally frequent are displays of shrill cultural anti-Americanism, most recently associated with Jack Lang. Soviet bloc propagandists incessantly attacked all facets of the "American Way of Life" for forty-five years. Allied governments have occasionally engaged in anti-American rhetoric as part of their electoral strategy. Various currents of the European right, from Le Pen's unreconstructed French version of fascism to Italy's reformed former fascists, display strong resentment on cultural and political levels against the nation that played a major role in liberating Europe from right-wing totalitarianism and then in shaping the postwar international order. Less attention has been paid to the critique of the United States that thoughtful and usually restrained European Catholics have expressed throughout the twentieth century. Yet, the very persistence of Catholic ambivalence, together with its rooting in philosophical and religious values, poses a potentially important ideological challenge to the U.S. model of democratic development while simultaneously placing serious demands on U.S. diplomatic dexterity.

The end of the Cold War has changed the relationship between the Roman Catholic Church and the U.S. government, ushering in an era of growing public criticism by the Vatican of the operating principles of the American economy and society. Recent papal encyclicals, above all *Centesimus annus* and *Res Sociales Solicitudines*, have underlined the Vatican's profound differences with many of the basic premises that guide U.S. activities in areas such as foreign assistance, international economics, and the role of the state. Pope John Paul II has used his trips to the United States to criticize pointedly elements of American social policy, especially the handling of reproductive rights. Even at the height of its Cold War cooperation with the United States, the Catholic Church nurtured strong doubts about the philosophical underpinnings of the great transatlantic democracy and about the longer term effects of certain U.S. attitudes and policies on the faithful. The United States, after all, was an important product of an Enlightenment culture whose values the Vatican has never ceased to dispute. Moreover, the United States was a land whose dominant form of Christianity was Protestant. It had a long, and occasionally violent, tradition of anti-Catholic prejudice. The rapid penetration of "Americanism" – the social, political, and cultural values that American literature, music, and, above all, film have diffused in Europe since the beginning of this century -thoroughly alarmed a wide spectrum of opinion, including Catholic intellectuals and prelates. Americanism was equally disturbing to many Marxist and Catholic left political activists. Ignoring their differences on social and political issues, Italy's political right and left agreed that American mass culture was a threat to Europe.[1]

Nevertheless, the Vatican, and with it Catholics of all political viewpoints, found themselves drawn into an increasingly close collaboration with the United States as mid-century approached. Concern about the onward march of totalitarianism, particularly its communist variant; fear that the Church's principal base of operations, Italy, would fall into the hands of forces unalterably opposed to religion; and persistent courting by President Franklin D. Roosevelt promoted a rapprochement between the United States and the Vatican. Roosevelt and his successor, Harry S. Truman, actively expanded the areas of common interest through the work of their special representative to the Vatican, Myron Taylor. U.S. economic reconstruction aid to war-torn Europe won the Church's backing. The two presidents carried on a unique personal correspondence with Pope Pius XII that stressed philosophical convergence on a series of larger issues. At the same time, the Vatican slowly revised its judgment about democracy, overcoming concerns about the effects of pluralism, and came to understand that, in many circumstances, this form of government was a useful and probably indispensable tool for protecting and forwarding Catholic interests.[2]

Underlying this edifice of cooperation was a common anti-communism. The parallel but independent efforts of the United States and the Vatican during the Italian electoral campaign of 1948 powerfully reinforced the triumphant Christian Democratic (DC) party. In the years that followed, Pope Pius XII and a series of U.S. ambassadors in Rome strongly supported those elements of the DC that favored a policy of uncompromising confrontation with the Italian Communist Party (PCI).[3]

This mutual effort to marginalize the PCI became bogged down in the early 1950s because changes in international relations, domestic political considerations, and the persistent efforts of the DC's own left wing pushed successive Italian governments to find a *modus vivendi* with the Communists. Even as staunch an anti-communist as Prime Minister Alcide De Gasperi repeatedly accepted compromises that favored the gradual inclusion of the Communists inside the structures of Italian democracy. After De Gasperi's defeat in the highly polarized elections of June 1953, Christian Democratic leaders slowly accepted the PCI's claim to a fuller role in the democratic process, albeit as the perpetual party of opposition. Practical considerations – above all, lowering the tensions that threatened to erupt into civil conflict – motivated the Christian Democrats. Mario Scelba, the DC's iron-fisted former interior minister (and future prime minister), told U.S. ambassador Clare Boothe Luce that "the U.S. was too concerned about communism" and that with continuing American "trust and aid . . . Italian democracy would handle communism in its own way."[4]

The DC's left wing provided a strong push in the direction of a careful and gradual rapprochement with the Italian left, beginning with its Socialist component. Convinced that to establish democracy firmly in Italy required the inauguration of a strong welfare state, the Catholic left searched out contacts with those forces most favorable both to a large state role in economic planning and to a primary policy focus on treating the vast inequalities created by Italy's industrial transformation. They found them, of course, on the Marxist left. While never abandoning its philosophical opposition to totalitarianism, the DC left believed their party should seek the collaboration of the Marxist mass parties on a large number of specific programs. Moreover, the Catholic left could point to the cooperation between the DC and the Marxist left in the wartime national resistance as proof that collaboration was not only possible but desirable. During the writing of Italy's constitution, the luminaries of the DC left – Giuseppe Dossetti, Amintore Fanfani, Giorgio La Pira, and Aldo Moro – played a major role extending that collaboration. The resulting document reflected the agreement of Marxists and Catholics that the state had a primary role in organizing society and in protecting Italy's working population from exploitation by modern capitalism. By the mid-1950s, a project for Socialist–Christian Democratic cooperation in power, the "Opening to the Left," moved to the center of the Italian political debate, to the horror of conservative Italians, the Vatican's leadership, and the U.S. government.[5]

Florence's mayor, Giorgio La Pira, was in the forefront of the effort to create a center–left coalition at both the local and national level. A slight, jovial, bespectacled mystic with a genial smile, La Pira had a propensity for lacing his public statements with biblical imagery, a sure touch for symbolic gesture, and an enormous talent for practical politics. He enjoyed a considerable following within both Italian society and the Catholic Church and easy access to the centers of power in both. La Pira mirrored all of the contradictions in the relationship of Catholicism with the United States.[6]

Sicilian-born, Florentine by adoption, an orthodox Catholic in all matters of faith and morals, a democrat, anti-fascist, and internationalist, La Pira combined to an unusual degree qualities that attracted the admiration of both Americans and Italians. Ambassador Luce courted the mayor, while Communist leader Palmiro Togliatti and Socialist chief Pietro Nenni publicly praised him. The saintly archbishop of Florence, Elio Cardinal Dalla Costa, was his warmest supporter throughout the postwar years. In 1994, the Catholic bishops of Italy endorsed La Pira, who is currently undergoing the process of canonization, as a model for the comportment of a Christian in public life.

La Pira earned this stature by his courageous personal opposition to Fascism during the dictatorship, through his central work in the drafting of Italy's postwar constitution, from his conduct as Vice Minister of Labor in De Gasperi's fifth government, in his role as a spokesman for the poor, and, above all, for his performance as mayor of Florence during the turbulent 1950s. La Pira's exceptionally ambitious view of his own role and that of his city led him to take positions that increasingly put him in a frontal confrontation with U.S. policy.[7]

The conflict between the Catholic left and the United States was rooted in divergent views of the objectives of society. Whilst most Americans stressed individualism, Catholics of all political hues were brought up on ideals of social solidarity that stressed the potential for greed implicit in untrammeled individual power. Pope Leo XIII's 1891 encyclical letter, *Rerum Novarum*, had endorsed an active role for Catholics in ameliorating the sharp social cleavages created by nineteenth-century capitalism and pointed to the important role of government in mediating between the powerful few and the masses of underprivileged in order to create a just society.

La Pira took this papal teaching to heart. In a series of controversial articles published in the DC left's journal, *Cronache sociali*, in the late 1940s, he employed a mix of scriptural citations, Keynesian economics, Thomistic philosophy, and appeals to conscience, to demand that the Italian government and Italy's industrialists subordinate the profit motive to meeting the basic requirements of the poor. A strong, ethically directed, and interventionist state was critical to La Pira's political vision.[8]

La Pira had experienced first hand the dangers of a movement that aimed at creating an all-powerful state. He rejected all forms of racism, totalitarianism, and aggressive warfare. This opposition to totalitarianism was balanced by a willingness to seek contact with its adherents. Dialogue with individuals who embraced views opposed to his was part of La Pira's Christian dialectic. Acting as a missionary in politics, La Pira sought common ground with the men of the Marxist left in order to advance projects that favored the poor, and in the belief that good will and Christian example would eventually win them from error. His friendships with a variety of Marxists, including the brilliant but morally compromised Togliatti, scandalized conservatives and subsequently left him open to charges of being a "dupe."[9]

La Pira's attitude toward the United States paralleled his approach to the left. He was, at best, ambivalent about the United States' assumption of the role of leader of the Christian West. He rejected both the consumerism and secularism that were central to the "American Way of Life." When Don Luigi Sturzo, the founder of Italian Christian Democracy, returned from wartime exile in the United States espousing free market capitalism, La Pira commented that he had suffered a "cretinization" during his years in America. On the U.S. litmus test of support for the North Atlantic Treaty (1949), La Pira failed. However, at the same time, he was eager to encounter Americans and engage in a dialogue with them. He appreciated the democratic values of the United States while retaining profound suspicions about its public philosophy. He visited the United States as Florence's mayor in 1964 to promote the tourist trade and in search of high-level political interlocutors. In the tensest years of the Cold War, American leaders failed to appreciate La Pira's subtle anti-communism. Ultimately, they decided that his ambivalence about the

United States and readiness to seek allies on the left was an outright embrace of communism.[10]

La Pira and U.S. leaders suffered from an extremely deep cultural "disconnect." Neither his Catholic education nor his practical experience in Italian politics prepared La Pira to deal effectively with the United States. He bombarded U.S. officials with lengthy, scripture-laden, insistent correspondence during and after his years as mayor of Florence. It generally struck Americans as either irrelevant or mildly irritating. His baroque style of communication, while useful in successfully navigating the patronage politics of Italy, was incomprehensible to most American officials. Operating in a highly pressurized environment, American policymakers expected a high degree of synthesis, brevity, and directness in correspondence and discussion.[11]

During the 1940s, La Pira was one of the leaders and spokesmen of the *Cronache sociali* group of left-wing intellectuals ("the Professors") who prodded the De Gasperi government to place strict limits on its association with Italy's economic elites and commit the state to a greater role in the management of the economy. Their goal was a national economic policy based on a policy of full employment, carried out through forceful state intervention. In promoting these Catholic corporatist ideas, the Professors borrowed heavily from the economic theories of John Maynard Keynes. They supported the efforts of the U.S. Economic Cooperation mission in Italy to use Marshall Plan money (counterpart funding) as a tool for expanding employment because it provided a model of the type of state intervention the Professors desired. They praised the New Deal for its success in moderating the worst excesses of capitalism, meeting the immediate needs of the unemployed, and carving out an expanded social role for government.[12]

While Roosevelt was something of a hero to the Catholic left, the Professors, like many Italians on the center and center–left, were distinctly less attracted to the foreign and domestic policies of the Truman administration. They feared the U.S. anti-communist policies would profoundly polarize Europe, playing into the hands of reactionaries. The Dossetti group disliked the loss of autonomy inherent in American leadership of the war-weakened states of West Europe. While agreeing with the United States on the need for European unification, they wanted a more autonomous role for the European states. Above all, they feared the creation of a United States-dominated military bloc that they believed would cement the existing social and political order into position. The DC left, for which *Cronache sociali* was the leading spokesman, promoted Europe's role as a "Third Force," operating independently of the two major contenders in the Cold War in order to moderate their behavior. During the debates over NATO ratification in 1949, the DC left was a vocal critic of the proposed new defense structure.[13]

Evident in the Professors' critique of the North Atlantic Treaty was a deep ambivalence about the United States. One of their spokesmen disapprovingly lumped U.S. materialism together with Soviet totalitarianism as threats to the West, insisting that the Americans did not represent the Christian values that stood at the root of European civilization. Some years earlier, Dossetti had contrasted Soviet "vitality" with the "moral bankruptcy" of the United States. He urged Italy and the Vatican to avoid an already evident drift into the U.S. sphere of influence.[14]

Defeated on the issue of Italian membership in NATO, the Professors continued to hammer the government on a wide range of social issues. Foreign policy passed to the back-burner and questions of housing, economic planning, and redistribution of wealth dominated the DC's internal political debate for most of the 1950s. La Pira's decision to abandon the national stage and return to Florence was a practical response to the need to confront the nation's pressing internal problems at a grassroots level.

Withdrawal to local politics and administration saved La Pira from direct involvement in a series of débâcles that broke the power of the DC left on the national level. Participation in the 1950 election campaign drastically changed his public image. The invitation to run as the DC's candidate was the product of the recognition by all factions of the DC and the allied parties of the center and right that only a "social" Catholic could oust the administration of the city's popular Communist mayor, Mario Fabiani. In 1950, La Pira mounted a successful campaign against the city's Communist-dominated administration by polarizing voters along a Christian–Communist ideological divide. In the eyes of most observers, the mayor of Florence represented a bulwark against the red menace. He polished this image during the first years of his administration aided by an obstructionist Florentine PCI. La Pira's social activism, with its concentration on finding homes, jobs, and food for the poor, and his deep concern for children won national and international applause in great part because it appeared to blunt the appeal of the Marxist left. Social Catholicism seemed the best tool available to Italians seeking to defeat the PCI.[15] La Pira further burnished his anti-communist credentials by publicly endorsing a proposal to place a NATO headquarters in Florence. Dismissing Communist protests as a political ploy, the mayor told the city council that Italy had a legitimate right to defend itself.[16]

By 1953, the United States' new ambassador, Clare Boothe Luce, whose twin passions were her Catholic faith and anti-communism, regarded La Pira as a solid ally of basic American objectives. Over the next three years, the two corresponded, exchanged visits, and established a warm personal rapport. Mrs. Luce appeared at one of the mayor's international peace conferences and even contributed an essay to a subsequent publication. She expressed moral support for La Pira during the critical conflict over the closing of the Pignone factory.[17]

La Pira, however, was already moving along lines that would profoundly disturb Italian conservatives, and ultimately changed his public image in both Italy and the United States from that of an anti-communist stalwart to that of a woolly-headed dupe of the PCI. In 1950, for example, while wooing U.S. investment, the mayor quietly cooperated with left-wing forces trying to block Italian involvement with the war in Korea.[18]

The Pignone crisis of 1953–54 brought La Pira's social and political views fully into focus, caused profound distress for large numbers of Italian anti-communists, revealed the solid support he enjoyed at all levels of the Catholic Church, and laid the basis for future alliance with the Marxist left. Nenni, who had staked his political future on the center–left, summarized La Pira's new role when he referred to Florence's mayor as the "point man of the Catholic left."[19]

Pignone, a machine tools and industrial equipment company, was one of the major employers in Florence and a leading element in Italy's advanced industrial sector. It was also a money-loser that badly needed a large infusion of cash to bring it into technological parity with international competitors. In October 1953, Pignone's owner, Franco Marinotti, decided to concentrate his investments in other parts of his Snia Viscosi business empire, and ordered Pignone shut down. The city faced the loss of over 1,700 jobs, many high-paying and high-skilled. La Pira's plans for a balanced local economy and continued growth faced extinction. The loss of Pignone's skills, salaries, and tax base would undercut his carefully nurtured programs for expanding housing, employment, and public services. It also struck directly at his ethical view. La Pira insisted that private profit had to take a back seat to the community good. The mayor initially tried to talk Marinotti out of his decision through a combination of blandishments, moral exhortation, and political pressure. When this approach failed, La Pira launched a *jihad*. He backed a workers' occupation of the factory, excoriated Marinotti in a series of open letters, enlisted every available source of pressure, including the Communists, under his banner, and ultimately convinced the head of Italy's state oil monopoly, Enrico Mattei, to purchase the factory.[20]

La Pira's ultimate victory owed much to solid support from the Catholic

Church. The Vatican endorsed his economic reasoning. Cardinal Dalla Costa rallied the local Church behind the strikers. However, united Catholic backing of La Pira's full employment economics could not protect him from a strong reaction from the political right. Economic conservatives were aghast at the mayor's assault on the rights of private property. Refusing to recognize the degree to which La Pira had outflanked the PCI on the Pignone issue, conservatives of all stripes were outraged at his willingness to accept Communist cooperation, even in a subordinate role. The mayor's governing coalition began to unravel. Recognizing that he could not forward his ambitious plans for public infrastructural investment in Florence with his existing partners, and correctly calculating that a change in electoral laws would put an end to the DC's majority on the city council in the elections of 1956, La Pira began to look to the left, in the form of the Socialist Party, as a future partner in government. His response to the Pignone crisis delighted the reformist left. He built up further credit by unveiling an increasingly left-wing socio-political agenda. A small but highly publicized example of the mayor's reaching to the left was the first limited but distinctly anti-American move undertaken by his administration. In 1956, La Pira, to a chorus of approval on the left, cancelled plans for an exhibit of Florentine artistic masterpieces in the United States.[21]

La Pira's decision to seek allies on the left came just as a glacial movement toward cooperation between DC and PSI got underway on the national level. The mayor moved too quickly for national events. The new Christian Democratic party secretary, Amintore Fanfani, was determined to create such a partnership, but was held in check by the party's right. Fanfani could not permit local party leaders to get out too far ahead of him. The DC secretary used longstanding ties of friendship and political alliance to restrain the Florentine mayor. Although the elections of 1956 created the numerical basis for a center–left coalition at Florence, La Pira, faithful to instructions from Fanfani and concerns expressed by the Church, ultimately renounced the mayoralty and withdrew from local politics, in the name of party unity and Catholic solidarity.[22]

In a 1964 letter to Nenni, La Pira claimed that during the 1950s, "Italy had a vast and significant international `political space': the Mediterranean, the Third World, the bridge between Russia and America, [and] Latin America." This expanded Italian role was, in good part, a result of his efforts, La Pira continued, and he lamented its decline as a result of the Atlanticist obsession of Italy's governing parties. La Pira's claims were greatly exaggerated, but they provide a mirror to his objectives.[23]

During the six years of his first term of office, the mayor created an institution that severely discomforted conservatives, caused a serious break with the Vatican, and ultimately raised doubts about his reliability among U.S. officials. La Pira's "*convegni*" (congresses) brought together representatives of the communist and neutralist worlds with those of Western governmental and non-governmental organizations for discussions that, during the 1950s, increasingly focused on peaceful resolution of the ideological and political conflict of East and West. La Pira's inspiration was Florence's role as host for the 1439 ecumenical council that briefly achieved a reconciliation of Eastern and Western Christianity. The mayor envisioned Florence (and himself) mediating world peace. He invited men of "good will" to meet in a Christian Florence that was prosperous, modern, and productive, and at the same time, as the greatest museum of the Renaissance, a defender of cultural tradition. A model society, inspired by Catholic values, and actively seeking to serve others, La Pira's Florence would launch initiatives designed to ameliorate or cure mankind's major woes. The mayor's ambitious list of objectives for the congresses included the settling of the Arab–Israeli conflict, ending the Cold War, reduction of nuclear armaments, decolonization, achieving the full entry of communist China into the international community, and ending world hunger.[24]

Man's crises, the mayor explained, ultimately were religious and metaphysical in nature and required religious and metaphysical responses. The *convegni* gave men of all cultures and political backgrounds a venue for discussions, while displaying Florence as both a great cultural center and a contender for investment in the fields of science and technology. La Pira's grandiose sense of the "mission" of Florence found little resonance among the West's leaders, but he still pressed forward.[25]

The first two congresses, held in 1952 and 1953, stressed theological themes that increased the mayor's reputation for otherworldliness and aroused little concern among international observers, as Ambassador Luce's involvement testified. The communist states, although invited, declined to send representatives. Beginning in 1955 with the meeting in which a representative sample of world mayors participated, the peace congresses, and those of the late 1950s dealing with the Mediterranean, attracted more attention, alarmed many observers in the West, but also won admiration on the left. The Mediterranean project illustrated La Pira's ability to view Italy's problems in a larger, long-term perspective. It foreshadowed current European Union efforts to establish meaningful dialogue with the other states of the region. In the context of the Cold War of the 1950s, the peace and Mediterranean congresses' efforts to promote international understanding were less significant to critics than the legitimization they offered to both the Soviet bloc and Italy's Communist Party. In 1955, for example, La Pira took advantage of the participation of the mayors of Beijing and Moscow, to announce that the "Republic of Florence" recognized the People's Republic of China. In 1956, he supported Egypt against Britain, France, and Israel during the Suez crisis. La Pira's pronouncements frequently surprised and embarrassed fellow Christian Democrats, especially those in the ministry of foreign affairs. They irritated the right and center of the Italian political spectrum, many churchmen, and, at times, the allies of Italy.[26]

In the mid-1950s, La Pira's formerly solid backing from the Church began to crumble. The Jesuit review, *Civiltà Cattolica*, frequently an unofficial mirror for Vatican views, attacked the 1955 congress. At about the same time, the Vatican sent a strong anti-communist and strict disciplinarian, Ermenegildo Cardinal Florit, to serve as coadjutor archbishop to the aging Dalla Costa. As La Pira's friend and patron gradually removed himself from daily administration of the archdiocese, relations between the local Church and Florence's leading Catholic layman became increasingly tense. Dalla Costa died in 1961. La Pira's approach to the Socialists lacked critical Church support and cover.[27]

Exploiting the Church's changed attitude, lay opponents, led by Florence's most influential daily, *La Nazione*, exploited the *convegni* to create a new image of the mayor. No longer the steadfast opponent of godless red hordes, La Pira was recycled as a holy simpleton. In truth, the mayor invited such a characterization. His speech and his writings were heavy larded with biblical imagery that had ever less appeal to the public imagination as Italy's secularization proceeded. He was given to grandiose rhetoric that lent itself to ridicule. Frequently, his projects were so far out of his reach that they seemed ridiculous.[28]

The right found La Pira's relationship with both Italian and Soviet communists yet more appalling. The rapprochement that began during the battle over Pignone grew as the mayor took more radical positions on foreign policy. La Pira's readiness to permit the PCI to use the Cascina park for its annual mass rally, the *Festa dell'Unità*, offered the already aroused right an opportunity for a direct confrontation. The national press, taking up themes developed by *La Nazione*, charged that the holy simpleton was opening the way for the Communists to achieve full political legitimization. La Pira became "the red fish in the holy water font": a threat to democracy in Italy.[29]

After handing over power to a prefectural administration in 1957, La Pira disappointed his critics by failing to fade away. Returning to parliament in 1958, Florence's ex-mayor continued quietly to lay the basis for a center–left government on both the local and national levels and launched himself into a new public career as a missionary of international peace. He began to correspond with a number of Soviet bloc leaders, including Khrushchev. These actions were simply an extension of the mission he had carved out with the *convegni*. The meetings had confirmed La Pira's view that the North Atlantic alliance was a hindrance to the pursuit of many of Catholicism's and Italy's real interests. In particular, he felt that the pro-NATO outlook of many Italian leaders blinded them to Italy's real interests in the Mediterranean and to the universal need for peace. His critical views of NATO were widely known, applauded on the left, and aggressively stated over the years. They built an image of La Pira as anti-American.[30]

In December 1957, La Pira visited the Holy Land and criticized U.S. policy in the region. His views on the need for more Italian involvement in the Middle East found an important listener in Fanfani, whose brief prime ministership (June 1958 to January 1959) coincided with the Lebanese crisis. Fanfani's activism in the region was designed to offer Italy as an interlocutor between the United States and radical Arab regimes. The pro-Arab tone of Italy's foreign policy aroused the ire of C. L. Sulzberger of the *New York Times*, who fulminated against the prime minister and his advisors.[31]

Involvement in the Middle East was the preliminary for La Pira's next major sally on the international plane. In August 1959, he visited Moscow. During this trip, he enjoyed an audience with Khrushchev, made favorable comments about the Soviet system, and incautiously suggested that the communist state was expanding religious freedom. La Pira returned home to face an avalanche of bad publicity on the right and an impressively good press from the left. Most importantly, he whetted the ambitions of Fanfani and Italy's president Giovanni Gronchi for a Kremlin visit that would combine international publicity with the opportunity for Italy (and themselves) to play a major role on the world stage. La Pira's enthusiasm for East–West dialogue remained at fever pitch. Writing about a September 1961 dinner for participants in one East–West meeting, Nenni dryly commented: "Naturally La Pira was there."[32]

By the late 1950s, La Pira was a spokesman for an international opening to the left that would replace United States–Soviet Union confrontation with the type of intense and continuing dialogue that was the key to Italian political stability. He also campaigned for profound changes in the relationship between the West and Arab states. Neither of these projects was welcome in Washington where any kind of an opening to the left, whether through greater legitimization of the Soviet system or of its radical Arab nationalist allies, was regarded as dangerous to the stability of the international order.

In February 1961, La Pira led the Florentine DC into political partnership with the Socialist Party, creating one of the first center–left governments in Italy. The experiment provoked a violent three-day takeover of the city's streets by neo-fascist thugs. Exploiting the images created by his political opponents, the neo-fascists justified their act by claiming the mayor was turning the city over to the Communists. In spite of the mayor's pleas for police assistance, the DC-led national government failed to intervene effectively, a sure sign of trouble for La Pira and the center–left. Once again La Pira was too far ahead of his party. Support within the DC for the center–left was strictly limited. (Fanfani, for example, would lose enthusiasm for the project when it no longer offered him a path to power.) On issues of international relations, La Pira was light years away from the national DC leadership. Prime Minister Aldo Moro, the first man to guide a national center–left government, as well as an alumnus of the *Cronache sociali* group, was representative of that leadership. While not opposed to an improvement in Italian–Soviet and general East–West relations, he had no desire to isolate the party or the Italian state from its powerful ally, the United States. Nor would he permit the opening to the left to divide the DC's conservative and reform wings. As a result, on both the local and national level, the DC–PSI partnership proved rocky. The Christian Democrats fought to limit reform while the Socialists discovered that a desire to retain power at any cost limited their leverage to promote change.[33]

The Florence version of the center–left endured for four years. The cooperation between the Socialist and Christian Democratic components of the La Pira junta was excellent. They were hamstrung on many issues by opposition from the smaller Social Democratic Party. In addition, La Pira faced opposition from within his own party and from an emerging younger generation of Socialists. These forces combined with business interests to block many of the coalition's major objectives. The great achievement of La Pira's center–left administration (1961–65), passage of an innovative city plan, was obstructed and then watered down by the Christian Democratic-led national government which responded to businessmen's complaints that its extremely detailed zoning regulations and social engineering implications threatened their profit margins.[34]

Faced with continuing difficulties while governing, La Pira again reached leftward. Informal cooperation with the Florentine PCI increased, further outraging conservatives. Following a setback in the 1964 local elections, the mayor's determination to find a governing formula that would encompass the Communists provoked direct intervention by the leadership of the Social Democratic and Christian Democratic parties. For the Socialists, a DC–PCI government was a nightmare. Younger Socialists insisted that "La Pira was a problem." They demanded his removal. The two parties' national leaders agreed to push the mayor aside. The Florentine church, in the person of Cardinal Florit, stood on the sidelines while the Vatican, in an essay in its official mouthpiece, *Osservatore Romano*, attacked La Pira for seeking alliances with the PCI. Ironically, in the ensuing political confusion, Florence ended up with precisely the type of political solution the DC had been trying hard to avoid. The Socialists and Communists formed a short-lived city administration.[35]

Driven again into the political wilderness, La Pira turned to foreign policy as the platform for his Christian activism and as a vehicle to reknit his ties to the Vatican. The war in Vietnam was the logical issue upon which La Pira might relaunch his political career. He sincerely believed that the conflict threatened to explode into an East–West confrontation that would trigger nuclear war. Moreover, the existence of significant Catholic minorities in the two Vietnamese states heightened the Vatican's interest. The Church's concern about the direction of U.S. policy became intense after the bloody 1963 overthrow of the South's Catholic strong-man, Ngo Dinh Diem. Vatican efforts to secure a peaceful settlement of the conflict accelerated. In October 1965, Pope Paul VI visited the United States to address the United Nations and for private talks with President Johnson which the Vatican hoped would encourage a settlement. The Pope's meeting with Johnson came to nothing. The two men exchanged polite compliments. The Americans were not interested in Vatican media-tion. A parallel papal overture to the new South Vietnam government met a negative response. An informal approach to North Vietnam was the last available path and La Pira was an attractive intermediary. His passionate concern about nuclear war and determination that Italy do more to avoid a clash of the great powers, his good relations with communist leaders, his Third World ties, his well-honed political skills, his close but independent relationship with the Vatican, and his proven record as a disciplined Catholic, all suggested his suitability for the mission. More-over, the mayor had an outstanding invitation from Ho Chi Minh, the North's president, to visit Hanoi. For La Pira, an additional incentive was the effect a triumph on the scale of aiding in the settlement of the Vietnam War would have on his two critical constituencies: the left and the Catholic Church. With the backing of these two forces and international prestige won from brokering a settlement, he could reclaim leadership of the reform movement in Florence and Italy. In November 1965, the mayor and an aide, mathematics professor Mario Primicerio, set off for Hanoi with the informal backing of the Church.[36]

In Hanoi, La Pira met with Ho Chi Minh and returned to Italy with what he believed to be a peace offer from the North Vietnamese. The mayor passed along the details of the "offer" to Italy's foreign minister, Fanfani, who was also serving as president of the U.N. General Assembly. Fanfani, in turn, brought La Pira's report to the attention of the U.S. ambassador to the United Nations, Arthur Goldberg, and through him, to President Johnson. According to La Pira, Ho was ready to proclaim an immediate cease-fire and to meet the President anywhere, without any preconditions, including North Vietnam's long-established precondition for the withdrawal of U.S. troops, to discuss a peaceful settlement.[37]

The Americans were skeptical. The purported peace offer in fact reiterated Hanoi's "four points," including the demand for the creation of a coalition government in Saigon prior to talks. Moreover, the La Pira initiative came just as the Johnson administration was recovering from a public relations buffeting caused by the publication of comments highly critical of its Vietnam policy attributed to Adlai Stevenson, the U.S. ambassador to the United Nations until his sudden death that spring. Simultaneously, the United States faced intense internal and foreign pressure to declare a bombing pause over North Vietnam. Under these circumstances, the U.S. government was very cautious about information coming from informal diplomatic soundings, especially when carried out by a well-known critic. Adding to the sense of incredulity in Washington was La Pira's contradictory statement that the North was willing to drop its preconditions to talks accompanied by an offer restating Hanoi's major demands.[38]

La Pira's credibility was a major stumbling block to further exploration by the United States. In 1964, La Pira had publicly attacked Italy's President Giuseppe Saragat for taking pro-NATO and pro-American positions. In the spring of 1965, shortly after his ouster as mayor, La Pira helped to coordinate a city council motion that condemned U.S. bombing raids on North Vietnam. His subsequent lambasting of U.S. actions attracted the attention and praise of China's prime minister, Chou En Lai. While La Pira naively believed that he could serve as an honest broker, Washington viewed him as a fellow-traveller.[39]

American officials suspected that La Pira was party to a North Vietnamese-designed set up: bringing a phony peace offer whose rejection would further embarrass the United States before world public opinion.

They asked Fanfani, in his dual official roles, to go back to the Vietnamese for confirmation. Fanfani's inquiries met with a two-week silence from Hanoi. Concluding that the Communists were about to spring a propaganda trap, the United States went public about the La Pira initiative, publishing its exchange of correspondence with Fanfani. La Pira was outraged. The correspondence exposed the Italian foreign minister to public embarrassment. Coming just weeks after Rome's decision to recognize the People's Republic of China was leaked to the press, Fanfani's involvement with La Pira and Hanoi plunged Italy's credit to new lows with Washington. La Pira's initiative suffered a final blow when Hanoi denied that Ho had made the offer the former mayor had reported.[40]

La Pira's amateurism was evident. He heard what he want to hear during his talks with Ho. He then used Fanfani to raise the level of his access to Washington. Despite his past record as a vocal critic of both NATO and the United States, La Pira apparently discounted the possibility that the Johnson administration would have little faith in a man who was publicly identified with anti-war and anti-American politics. It is hard to imagine a scenario better calculated to arouse a negative reaction in Washington or to injure the reputation of Italian diplomacy.[41]

Within weeks, La Pira compounded these errors, reinforcing his image of credulity, and fatally undercutting his chances for personal political resurrection. Two days after Christmas, the neo-fascist weekly, *Il Borghese*, published an interview that La Pira had given to one of its best-known and most aggressive journalists, Gianna Preda. Nenni drily commented: "There was something in it for everyone." La Pira eulogized Mussolini, Fanfani, and de Gaulle, attacked Prime Minister Moro's pro-American positions, blasted the Socialists, allowed that "the communist danger doesn't exist," and poured out his bile at the United States, particularly Secretary of State Dean Rusk ("Rusk doesn't know anything"). The former mayor then worsened this situation by attempting to deny his comments. The astute Ms. Preda returned fire by revealing that the meeting had taken place in Fanfani's home on the initiative of the foreign minister's wife. Fanfani, who had remained in New York, resigned immediately.[42]

In a letter written during the last days of 1965, Nenni admonished a penitent La Pira: "The sad *Borghese* affair is easy to pardon. Unfortunately, its consequences are very serious."[43] Nenni proved accurate in ways he probably could not have imagined. Ironically, La Pira's bungled diplomatic effort marked a turning point in U.S.–Vatican relations. The rebuffs the Johnson administration delivered to the Vatican over Vietnam appear to have determined a fundamental revaluation of the Catholic

Church's relations with the United States. In the 1967 encyclical letter *Populorum Progressorum*, the Pope launched into a vigorous criticism of U.S.-style economic and political liberalism and free trade. The Vatican also promoted rapprochement with America's arch-nemesis communist China, while drawing closer to North Vietnam by a consistent advocacy of an end to U.S. air raids on the North. The Christian Democratic politicians who ran Italy moved more cautiously in the same direction. The domestic threat of insurrectionary action by the PCI had long since dimmed. Europe's Cold War effectively had ended. The development of the European Community offered an alternate pillar of support to Italy. While rarely confronting the United States, Italy quietly pursued a more independent policy, disassociating itself from the United States on Vietnam, backing a softer line toward the Soviet Union, expanding its trade into East Europe and among the radical states of the Middle East, while taking a hostile stance toward the United States' major ally in the region, Israel. The change in Vatican policy and the subtler Christian Democratic moves were noted by the PCI, and helped lay the groundwork for a more open shift in Communist foreign policy and ultimately for an Italian Communist Party offer to create a new version of the opening to the left, "the Historic Compromise." This initiative, partially realized in the mid-1970s, caused acute discomfort in Washington. Its architect was Aldo Moro, the hyper-cautious, pro-American prime minister who had been a target of La Pira's ire a decade earlier.[44]

La Pira, an isolated, if much honored, DC elder statesman, could take comfort from the changes in party and Church positions. He spent the decade that followed his peace mission débâcle immersed in charitable works in Florence and in the pursuit of peace in Vietnam. La Pira's sense of impending nuclear disaster grew with the years as did his diffidence toward the United States. Convinced that the "generals" were in control at Washington, he pleaded with Nenni to promote another Italian diplomatic intervention to secure a cease-fire. The Socialist leader politely declined to get involved, as did others. La Pira's increasingly desperate pleas to Washington fell on deaf ears. In an April 1968 memorandum to presidential advisor Walt Rostow, State Department Executive Secretary Benjamin Read commented: "[La Pira's] telegram is another in a voluminous series of peace messages. In view of La Pira's well-known position on Vietnam and other issues, it is recommended no reply be made."[45]

Nevertheless, La Pira's views continue to animate Italian Catholic debate on domestic and foreign policy. In 1995, his disciple Primicerio won election as mayor of Florence at the head of a coalition of Catholics and former Communists. Italy's ambivalence about U.S. foreign policy objectives, particularly its anti-communist biases, grew in the 1970s to the point that Moro began to believe that Washington was actively plotting against him. Whilst the United States could still count on Italy on such critical questions as the emplacement of Euromissiles, it had to contend with occasional *contretemps* such as that provoked by its decision to force the hijackers of the cruise ship *Achille Lauro* to land on Italian territory and the philo-Arab policies associated with another Catholic politician, albeit one of markedly different background, Giulio Andreotti. In 1991, the United States found itself faced with a pacifist coalition of former Communists and Catholics of various backgrounds whose opposition to its Kuwait policy (Desert Shield/Desert Storm) enjoyed the blessing of Pope John Paul II. Taken together, these policy divergences provided further evidence that the ambivalence toward America displayed by La Pira and the Catholic left in the early Cold War years was an attitude grounded in the main currents of Catholic thought. The challenge for American policy-makers remains to stress convincingly those elements of world view that unite rather than divide two important carriers of the Western tradition.[46]

Notes

In preparing this chapter, I have been able to utilize two unpublished pieces by Roy Domenico, "Community and Internationalism: Giorgio La Pira and Italy's Catholic Left in the Cold War," a paper presented at the 1990 annual meeting of the American Historical Association, together with an untitled revision. I would like to thank Professor Domenico for the use of these essays.

Although I am associated with the Department of State as an editor of the series *Foreign Relations of the United States* and as the chairman of the Italian Area Studies seminar of the Foreign Service Institute, this chapter was prepared without access to any material not available in the public domain. The chapter itself does not reflect the opinions of the Department of State or the United States government.

1. On the diversity of anti-American feeling among Italian elites of differing political persuasions, see the essays of Stephen Gundle, "Il PCI e la compagna contra Hollywood," and Bruno F. P. Vanrooji, 'Decenza e dollari. I cattolici italiani e Hollywood," in D. Ellwood

and G. P. Brunetta, eds., *Hollywood e Europa* (Florence: Usher, 1991), pp. 113–48 and Michela Nacci, "Le barbarie del conforto" and Angelo Ventrone, "L'avventura americana della classe dirigente cattolica," in P. P. D'Attore, ed., *Nemici per la pelle* (Milan: Angeli, 1991), pp. 81–108, 141–60.

2. One of the fruits of this "cultural" rapprochement was the publication by Myron Taylor of certain of the more high-minded exchanges between Pius XII and the two American presidents. (*Wartime Correspondence Between President Roosevelt and Pope Pius XII* (New York: Macmillan, 1947) and *Correspondence Between President Truman and Pope Pius XII* (New York: Macmillan, 1952)). Ennio Di Nolfo has published a much wider range of U.S. documentation on policy toward the Vatican together with an insightful analysis in *Vaticano e stati uniti, 1939–1952* (Milan: Angeli, 1978).

3. On the parallel efforts of the Vatican and United States, see James E. Miller, "Taking Off the Gloves: the United States and the Italian Elections of 1948," *Diplomatic History*, 7 (Winter 1983), 35–56. On the pope's confrontation with the PCI, see Sandro Magister, *La politica vaticana e l'Italia, 1943–1978* (Rome: Riuniti, 1979). See also, *Foreign Relations of the United States* [henceforth *FRUS*], 1955–57, vol. 27 (Washington: GPO, 1992), pp. 273–75; and *FRUS*, 1958–60, vol. 7 (Washington: GPO, 1993), pp. 453–54, 567–70.

4. *FRUS*, 1952–54, vol. 6 (Washington: GPO, 1986), pp. 1640–45, 1672–75. Luce, whose plan for the PCI was repression, called this meeting "most baffling, futile, and disconcerting."

5. Giorgio La Pira, "Il comunismo," (1947) in M. Glisenti and L. Elia, eds., *Cronache sociali* (S. Giovanni Valdarno, 1962), pp. 755–62; "Schema di una linea politica," in L. Merli [Giovanni Di Capua], ed., *Antologia della base* (Rome: EBE, 1971), pp. 81–85. On U.S. responses to the "Opening" proposal, see William Colby and Peter Forbath, *Honorable Men* (New York: Simon and Schuster, 1978), pp. 110–30; N. Pistelli, "Interclassismo," in L. Merli, ed., *Antologia di S. Marco* (Rome: EBE, 1972), pp. 80–83; F. Malgeri, *Storia della DC* (Rome: Cinque Lune, 1987–89), 4 vols., vol. 1., pp. 125–27.

6. On the centrality of La Pira to postwar Italian politics, see the comments of G. Baget Bozzo, *Il partito cristiano al potere* (Florence: Valecchi, 1974), vol. 2, p. 310n.; Giorgio Galli and P. Fracci, *La sinistra democristiano* (Milan: Feltinelli, 1962), p. 295; Pier Luigi Ballini, "La democrazia cristiana," in E. Rotelli, ed., *Ricostruzione in Toscana* (Bologna: Il Mulino, 1981), vol. 2, pp. 114–15; P. Pombeni, *Il gruppo Dossettiano e la fondazione della democrazia italiana* (Bologna:

Il Mulino, 1979), p. 157; Franco Zeffirelli, *Zeffirelli* (New York: Weidenfeld and Nicolson, 1986), p. 17.

7. La Pira's followers, who continue to play an active role in Florentine cultural life, provide a good picture of his views in the publications of the Cultura editrice house. See, for example, S. Biagio Di Mondavi, *La Pira e la politica* (Florence, 1987); Antonello Antonelli, *Giorgio La Pira* (Florence, 1987); Salvatore Carlino, *Storia e testimonianza* (Florence, 1990); Salvatore Carolino, *Il senso della storia negli scritti di Giorgio La Pira* (Florence, 1990).

8. For the texts of La Pira's essays on the social question, see Giorgio La Pira, *L'attesa dei poveri gente* (Florence: Libreria editrice fiorentina, 1977). See, also, Sandro Leoni, *La formazione del pensiero politico di Giorgio La Pira* (Florence: Cultura, 1991) and Domenico, "Community and Internationalism."

9. Pombeni, *Gruppo Dossettiano*, pp. 68–69, 230–32; L. Fiorello, "I fondamenti teorici del impegno politico di Giorgio La Pira," in G. Roggerone and L. La Puna, eds., *Novecento minore* (Lecce: Massapica, 1977), pp. 198–99; Richard Webster, *Cross and Fasces* (Stanford, Ca.: Stanford, 1960), p. 146; E. E. Agnoletti, "Attraverso il centrosinistra," *Testimonianza*, 21 (April 1978), 371–80; Fioretta Mazzei, *La Pira* (Florence: Libreria editrice fiorentina, 1980), p. 84.

10. Telegram 40 from the Department of State to the Consulate in Florence, 1 Oct. 1964, Lyndon B. Johnson Presidential Library, National Security File, Italy, vol. 2. (Hereafter this will be abbreviated LBJL, NSF with indication of series and folder title.) La Pira's harsh comments on Sturzo are cited in Dino Messina, "Cattolici ricomminciare da Sturzo," *Corriere della Sera* (7 Feb. 1966).

11. See the comments of Read to Bundy, 25 Feb. 1965, LBJL, NSF, Italy, vol. 3. For an example of La Pira's style, see his statement to the Florence city council, 18 June 1964, in U. De Siervo, Gianni Giovannoni, and Giorgio Giovannoni, eds., *La Pira sindaco* (Florence: Cultura nuova, 1989), vol. 3, pp. 339–77. One of the few U.S. officials with whom La Pira communicated effectively, Clare Boothe Luce, shared not only his Catholicism but also an affection for the rotund phrase. My comments are also influenced by a long-term familiarity both with La Pira's works acquired in the course of writing a history of postwar Florentine politics and long observation of the operations of the U.S. foreign policy bureaucracy.

12. Piero Roggi, *I Cattolici e la piena occupazione* (Milan: Giuffre, 1983), pp. 52–53, 56; S. Linaro, *Storia dell'Italia repubblicana* (Venice: Marsilio, 1992), pp. 108–109.

13. On the positions of the DC left, see the 1948 and 1949 essays in Glisenti and Elia, eds., *Cronache sociali*, pp. 130–44, 211–12, 310; Malvestiti to De Gasperi, 26 Apr. 1951, in C. Bello, ed., *Lettere al presidente* (Milan: Bonetti, 1964), pp. 179–87; C. Pizzinelli, *Scelba* (Milan: Longanesi, 1982), pp. 113-14. Interview with Paolo Emilio Taviani in G. Rossini, ed., *De Gasperi e l'età del centrismo* (Rome: Cinque Lune, 1990), p. 193.

14. Glisenti and Elia, eds., *Cronache sociali*, pp. 130, 144; Richard Drake, *The Aldo Moro Murder Case* (Harvard: Harvard University Press, 1995), p. 12.

15. "The Christian Conqueror of a Red City," *Saturday Evening Post*, 15 Nov. 1952; "The Mayor of Florence," *Commonweal*, 1 May 1953; "The Incredible Mayor of Florence," *The Reporter*, 6 Oct. 1955.

16. The mayor's statement came during a 10 Oct. discussion. See, Florence, *Atti del consiglio comunale*, 1951, pp. 516–19.

17. Among the exchanges between the two, see La Pira to Luce, 8 Feb. 1953, Luce to La Pira, 25 Feb. 1953; La Pira to Luce, 13 July 1953; La Pira to Luce, 12 Oct. 1953 with attachments; La Pira to Luce, 19 Nov. 1953; all in Library of Congress, Manuscript Division, Clare Boothe Luce Papers, Ambassadorial File, 1953 Lap-Laz.

18. Domenico, untitled redraft of "Community and Internationalism." La Pira's courtship of Luce had little to do with foreign policy issues. The mayor was eager to maintain U.S. investment in two interrelated parts of the Florentine economy: tourism and the handicrafts industry. The U.S. was very aware of the power it could bring to bear on Florence's economy and well-informed about the level of Communist penetration in city unions. Reed to Department of State, 23 Oct. 1951, National Archives, Record Group 84 (Records of Department of State Diplomatic Posts), Records of the Florence Consulate, Accession 61 A 473, 510.23 Trade Complaints; the U.S. Embassy in Italy to the Department of State, 19 May 1952, *ibid.*, 510.21.

19. P. Nenni, *Tempo di guerra fredda. Diari*, ed. G Nenni and D. Zucaro (Milan: Sugar: 1981), p. 622.

20. On the Pignone crisis, see *Libro Bianco sulle officine Galileo* (Florence, 1959), pp. 111–13 and Francesca Taddei, *Il Pignone di Firenze* (Florence: Nuova Italia, 1980). The letters exchanged between La Pira and Marinotti are in LC, Luce Papers, Ambassadorial File, Press: Marinotti–La Pira.

21. On the motivations for and reaction to La Pira's decision to oppose the U.S. exhibit, see Archivio della città di Firenze, Gabinetto del sindaco, Atti 1956, fasc. 1201–1400, Opere di arte. On La Pira's

swing left, see P[iero] C[alamandrei], "Il comunista bianco," *Il Ponte*, Dec. 1953, pp. 1613–14.

22. Interview with the Giovannoni brothers, Florence, 25 May 1993; Malgeri, *Storia della DC*, vol. 3, pp. 371-92; Galli and Fracci, *Sinistra democristiana*, pp. 212–14.

23. La Pira to Nenni, 8 July 1964, Fondazione Nenni, Archivio, serie C, Carteggio Nenni–La Pira.

24. Mazzei, *La Pira*, pp. 74, 91–92; La Pira to Fanfani in Amintore Fanfani, *Giorgio La Pira* (Milan: Rusconi, 1978), p. 114.

25. La Pira, "Discorso su Mattei," 27 Nov. 1962 in De Siervo and Giovannoni, eds., *La Pira sindaco*, vol. 3, p. 155; La Pira, *Lettere a claustrali* (Milan: 1978), pp. 235–38; La Pira, *Le citte sono vive* (Brescia: La Scoula, 1957), p. 70. On the declining influence of La Pira in the West, see Alfonso Prandi, "Conclusione su La Pira," *Il Mulino*, 5, Apr. 1956, pp. 267–75.

26. Mazzei, *La Pira*, p. 93; Bozzo, *Il partito cristiano*, pp. 55–56, notes that Fanfani had to provide backing to La Pira to head off criticism within the DC. Interviews with Giorgio and Gianni Giovannoni, Florence, 26 Sept. 1991 and 25 May 1993.

27. Piero Di Loreto, *La difficile transizione* (Bologna: Il Mulino, 1993), p. 138; Linaro, *Storia*, p. 399. The relationship between La Pira and Florit, made difficult by the Communist issue, was further poisoned by a clash between the authoritarian cardinal and parishioners in La Pira's beloved satellite city of Isolotto. See Giampaolo Taurini, "La Pira e il dissenso cattolico fiorentino," *Testimonianza*, 21 (April 1978), pp. 326–77.

28. *Il Mondo*, 30 Sept. 1958.

29. See the careful analysis of the intertwined Pignone/Cascina issues in Nicola Pistelli, *Scritti politici*, ed. E. De Mita (Florence, 1967), pp. 760–64.

30. La Pira to Nenni, 17 July 1964, Fondazione Nenni, archivio, serie C, Carteggio Nenni–La Pira; Giovanni Di Capua, *Nicola Pistelli* (Florence: EBE, 1969), p. 194; De Siervo and Giovannoni, eds., *La Pira sindaco*, vol. 2, pp. 31–32; Alberto Cecchi, "La Pira e il PCI," *Testimonianza*, 21 (April 1978), p. 354.

31. *FRUS*, 1958–60, vol. 7, pp. 466–73, 477–79; C. L. Sulzberger, *Last of the Giants* (New York: Macmillan, 1970) pp. 516–17; Bozzo, *Il partito cristiano*, pp. 100–101; Piero Ottone, *Fanfani* (Milan: Longanesi, 1966), p. 134; G. Baget Bozzo and G. Tassani, *Moro* (Florence: Sansoni, 1983), p. 175.

32. A. Lugli, *Giorgio La Pira* (Padua, 1978), p. 53; Di Loreto, *Difficile*

transizione, pp. 316–18; Pietro Nenni, *Anni di centro sinistra. Diari*, ed. G Nenni and D. Zucaro (Milan: Sugar, 1982), p. 189; *FRUS*, 1958–60, vol. 7, pp. 581–82. On the mayor's relationship with the Soviets, see Vittorio Citterich, *Un santo al Cremlino* (Torino: Paolino, 1986).

33. De Siervo and Giovannoni, eds., *La Pira sindaco*, vol. 3, pp 35–36; La Pira to Scelba, 14 Mar. 1961, Archivio centrale dello stato, Ministero del interno, gabinetto, partiti politici, busta 61, fasc. 195/P/31/MSI-Firenze; Spencer Di Scala, *Renewing Italian Socialism* (Oxford: Oxford University Press, 1988), pp. 121-22; Nenni, *Anni di centro sinistra*, p. 445.

34. Mariella Zoppi, *Firenze e l'urbanistica* (Rome: Autonomie, 1982), pp. 113–14; Giorgio Morales, "Centro sinistra vecchio e nuovo a Firenze," *Il Ponte* (Feb. 1964), 170–96.

35. Interview with Lelio Lagorio, Florence, 4 Oct. 1995; Agnoletti, "Attraverso il centro sinistra"; Remo Gumelli, "Il grillo della Cascina," *Politico*, 15 May 1966; Nenni, *Anni di centro sinistra*, p. 457.

36. Roy Palmer Domenico, "America, the Holy See, and the War in Vietnam," in Peter Kent and John Pollard, eds., *Papal Diplomacy in the Modern Age* (Westport, Conn.: Praeger, 1988), pp. 203–19. On La Pira's concerns about the Vietnam War, see La Pira to Nenni, 31 Aug. 1964 and 27 Dec. 1965, both Fondazione Nenni, archivio, series C, Carteggio, Nenni–La Pira; Mazzei, *La Pira*, p. 120.

37. *Anni di centro sinistra*, pp. 568–69. The exchange of notes between Fanfani and the President, together with the State Department's official comments, are in Department of State, *Bulletin* (Jan. 1966), 10–13.

38. Nenni, *Anni di centro sinistra*, pp. 568–69; Rusk to Fanfani, in Department of State, *Bulletin* (3 Jan. 1966), pp. 12–13.

39. E. E. Agnoletti, "Giorgio La Pira," *Il Ponte* (31 Oct. 1977), 1086–91; Read to Bundy, 2 Apr. 1965 with attached telegram La Pira to Lyndon Johnson, 27 Mar. 1965, LBJL, NSF, Italy, vol. 3.

40. Nenni, *Anni di centro sinistra*, pp. 565, 569–70; Memorandum of Telephone conversation between Bundy and Ball, 22 Nov. 1965, 6 p.m., LBJL, George Ball Papers, Italy.

41. Harriman to Rusk, 27 Dec. 1965, Library of Congress, Harriman Papers, Special Files, Subject Files, Lap-Laz; Nenni, *Anni di centro sinistra*, pp. 571–72; Memorandum of telephone conversation between Bundy and Ball, 22 Nov. 1965, 6:10 p.m., LBJL, Ball Papers, Italy.

42. Nenni, *Anni di centro sinistra*, pp. 571, 573; Malgeri, *Storia della DC*, vol 4, p. 35; Baget Bozzo and Tanassi, *Moro*, pp. 212-17; Ottone, *Fanfani*, pp. 186-87; Memorandum of telephone conversation between

Ball and Italian Ambassador Fenoaltea, 19 Dec. 1965, noon, LBJL, Ball Papers, Italy; Telegram 1644 from the Embassy in Italy to the Department of State, 28 Dec. 1965, LBJL, NSF, Italy, vol. 4.

43. Nenni to La Pira, 29 Dec. 1965, Fondazione Nenni, archivio, serie C, Carteggio Nenni–La Pira.

44. See also the essays in Austin Ramey and Giovanni Sartori, eds., *Eurocommunism: The Italian Case* (Washington: American Enterprise Institute, 1978), esp. pp. 183–97; Palmiro Togliatti, *Togliatti e il centro sinistra* (Florence: Cooperativa editrice universitaria, 1975), vol. 2, pp. 1249–63, 1287–91; Baget Bozzo and Tanassi, *Moro*, pp. 287–88.

45. La Pira to Nenni, 23 Feb., 27 Mar., 26 Sept., and 30 Nov. 1967, Fondazione Nenni, Series C, Carteggio Nenni–La Pira; La Pira to Bargellini, 29 Nov. 1966, and La Pira to Moro, 19 and 21 Nov. 1966, both in Fondazione La Pira, archivio, busta 76, alluvione, carteggio; Read to Rostow, Library of Congress, Harriman Papers, Special Files, Subject Files, Lap-Laz.

46. Drake, *Moro Murder Case*, pp. 30, 214. See also, La Pira to Nenni, 7 Aug. 1964, Fondazione Nenni, archivio, serie C, Carteggio Nenni–La Pira.

Part III
The Defense Relationship

– 6 –

What Price Solidarity?
European–American Nuclear
Interdependence in NATO

Beatrice Heuser

In the Cold War, solidarity within NATO was derived from the recognition of an interdependence of the security interests of West Europeans and North Americans. But NATO's structure was asymmetric: dominated by the United States' nuclear might on the one hand, but weakened by the greater likelihood of nuclear use against West European territory on the other. In the first half of the Cold War, Canada, Britain, France, West Germany (and indeed other NATO allies) all discovered the problems as well as the benefits of U.S. nuclear deployment on their soil, and particularly the loss of sovereignty over their own territory which it entailed.

Britain and France, by acquiring nuclear weapons on their own, managed to redress this imbalance in their relations with the United States to some extent, but in different ways: Britain, by becoming the closest partner of the United States in joint planning; France, by detaching itself from NATO's integrated military structure. Canada, like Britain, chose integration with the United States, but unlike Britain without an independent national fallback option. West Germany found a solution only in urging joint consultation within NATO about the principles of nuclear use and in arguing for joint planning arrangements. These were created, once France had left the integrated military structure, in the Nuclear Planning Group, which paved the way for better relations between the United States and its dependent allies in the second half of the Cold War.

The North Atlantic Treaty of April 1949 was founded on the recognition of an interdependence of the security of West Europeans and North Americans. It was seen as in the interest of all members of NATO (the organization based on the Treaty) on the European, Asian, and North American continents that the Soviet Union should not be allowed to increase the sway of its power further. Bound together by this treaty, the member states sought to deter the Soviet Union from such a course of action.

NATO harnessed the military and economic might of the United States, but particularly its nuclear arsenal, to the defense of Canada, Britain, France, the Benelux countries, Portugal, Italy, Denmark, and Norway, and later also to the defense of Greece, Turkey, West Germany, and Spain. Until Britain acquired nuclear weapons in the 1950s and France in the early to mid-1960s, the United States had a monopoly among Western nations, which was to endure in terms of quantity even after the two European powers had joined the nuclear "club." Yet the United States also enjoyed the singular advantage compared with all other NATO members of being protected from any Soviet conventional attack by the Atlantic to the East, the Pacific to the West, and by the considerable land mass of Canada to the North. The United States was thus less vulnerable, and yet also more essential, than its allies in NATO as a deterrent counter-weight to the threatening strength of the Soviet Union and its satellites. This unequal distribution of vulnerability and responsibility engendered structural strains within the alliance itself.

Initially, technological limitations which affected the range of U.S. nuclear delivery vehicles made it necessary for America to seek forward bases (in Europe, the Middle East, and Asia) where it could station its bombers, and later also its short-range and medium-range nuclear missiles. But, in time, the belief grew among some NATO members that their own security was only safeguarded if nuclear weapons were deployed on their territory, and if they had some influence on the way in which they would be used. This belief, which during the Cold War came to be a firmly held tenet of NATO, was never shared universally among all NATO member governments, nor among all the citizens of the member states. For the obvious corollary of such deployment was that, from a Soviet point of view, these bases were prime targets for Soviet preventive strikes. This was acknowledged as early as 1950 by the U.S. government.[1] Indeed, preventive strikes, or at least launch-on-warning (what in Warsaw Pact terminology was termed "meeting strikes"), remained one of the key features of Soviet nuclear strategy until the end of the 1980s.[2] From the very beginning of NATO, this created concern throughout Western Europe over the potential consequences of offering one's territory to the United States for bases.

This chapter will focus on the reactions of Canada, Britain, France, and West Germany to the issue of the stationing of U.S. nuclear forces on their soil. While the situation of the Federal Republic of Germany was always noticeably different from that of France and Britain, let alone

Canada, there was concern in all four countries about U.S. bases and about the American reluctance to inform (let alone consult) allies about the ways in which Americans might use their nuclear weapons. As we shall see, the respective governments of the four countries drew different conclusions from the dilemma with which they were faced. On the one hand, there was the belief in the deterrent effect of a show of solidarity within the alliance, and of a tightly centralized nuclear release system in American hands that could be brought into action quickly without being delayed or even obstructed by a lack of consensus among the allies. On the other hand, there was the fear of becoming the victims of Soviet preventive or punitive strikes in a crisis over which one had no influence. The choice was thus between alliance solidarity and the assertion of independence.

In 1943, while American scientists were pursuing research which was to lead to the development of the first two atom bombs in history, scientists from many other nations were in fact involved in this project. This international effort, code-named "Tube Alloys," received the support not only of the United States, but also of the British and Canadian governments. In recognition of this support, an agreement was concluded among the three governments in Quebec in 1943, in which Britain and the United States pledged themselves never to "use this agency against each other." Furthermore, they agreed that they "will not use it against third parties without each other's consent."[3]

Three years later, however, after the Second World War had ended, the U.S. Congress passed the McMahon Act, aimed at restricting both the development and the control and use of nuclear weapons to U.S. authority alone, and aimed at shielding the secrets of nuclear technology as much as possible from foreign powers, be they friend or foe. Congressmen like McMahon and Vandenberg found the Quebec agreement objectionable, and Congress coupled the surrender of the British veto to economic aid to the United Kingdom (UK). A *modus vivendi* agreement was negotiated as a compromise in 1948, allowing Britain access to limited nuclear aid in return for British and Canadian supplies of uranium to the United States. But the *modus vivendi* agreement summarily annulled the Quebec agreement.[4]

Canada and the United States negotiated a separate agreement in 1947 over the use by the United States of military bases in Canada,[5] but this did not include any provisions about U.S. use of Canadian bases for nuclear operations.[6] In December 1949, the NATO Defense Committee approved the first NATO strategy paper, the "Strategic Concept for the Defence of the North Atlantic Area" (D.C.6/1), which later was interpreted by the United States as committing its allies to lending the United States all necessary support (including the provision of air bases) for the implementation of the strategy.[7] The relevant passage read: "Basic undertakings: . . . a. Insure the ability to carry out strategic bombing promptly by all means possible with all types of weapons, without exception. This is primarily a U.S. responsibility assisted as practicable by other nations."[8]

While legal details of the Canada–United States base agreement were still being negotiated, the Korean War erupted, creating a greater sense of urgency. Goose Bay, Labrador – from where, according to U.S. estimates, 75–100 percent of Soviet strategic targets in the Urals, the Moscow–Leningrad area, and the Don basin could be reached – had been identified by the United States as the best location for "the principal [U.S.] S[trategic] A[ir] C[ommand] advance assault base" even before the outbreak of war in the Far East. Now Washington felt the need for making more extensive use of this base. On 18 August 1950, the U.S. Joint Chiefs of Staff requested immediate permission from the Canadians to move the 43rd Medium Bomber Group of the USAF's Strategic Air Command (SAC) to Goose Bay for a six-week period, "against a general emergency."[9] With the permission of the Canadian government, the bombers carried nuclear weapons.[10]

The bombers were removed again in November, at the end of the six-week period of their original deployment, not least because it became impossible for the crews to stay on in their tents as winter drew near: there were no suitable buildings in Goose Bay to house them. At the beginning of October, the U.S. representatives on the Permanent Joint [US–Canadian] Board on Defense requested the permission to construct buildings at the base and to move the bomber group back.[11]

The Canadian Department of External Affairs was aware of the implications. Its response, toward the end of October 1950, was to seek agreement from the U.S. State Department "that there will be no storage of special weapons [the euphemism for nuclear weapons] at Goose without the express approval of the Canadian Government."[12]

While the 43rd Medium Bomber Group was being redeployed from Goose Bay to Tucson, Arizona, in mid-November 1950, an embarrassing incident occurred. One aircraft developed engine trouble and had to jettison its payload (nuclear weapons or their components) near the St. Lawrence river, causing a heavy explosion or explosions near the villages of St. André de Kamouraska, St. Simeon, and Pointe au Persil, fortunately without causing more than public excitement there.[13] It seems that the operational components were not fitted to the bomb or bombs that were lost in this way, and the explosion, although of considerable force, was merely of a conventional nature. Nevertheless, this created in the Canadian government the strong desire to be informed in advance of any movement of U.S. nuclear weapons to, from, and through Goose Bay.

Furthermore, Ottawa wanted to retain the right to approve or veto any use of Goose Bay (or other bases in Canada, such as Harmon) for SAC's air attacks. Indeed, it was suggested in Canada's Department of External Affairs that "No U.S. conventional or atomic bombs may be dropped on any enemy targets in Canada without the express advance approval of the Canadian Prime Minister."[14]

Secretary of State Lester Pearson, Chairman of the Chiefs of Staff Committee General Charles Foulkes, and a number of other high-ranking officials and military men agreed at a meeting held the following spring that Canada's geographical location was about its only asset in negotiations with the United States, and that Canada would be ill-advised to give the Americans a free hand in advance to use Canadian bases. Yet they did not want to adopt the uncompromising language proposed by the Department of External Affairs. Instead, they noted that Canada wished to retain sovereign control of these bases in peacetime, including the insistence on advance notification of any use for nuclear purposes.[15] In May 1951, the Canadian Ambassador was instructed to tell the U.S. Secretary of State that his government expected to be consulted (and not merely notified) before any use was made by the United States of Canadian bases for nuclear purposes, even just for storage purposes, and indeed before any overflight of Canada with aircraft carrying nuclear weapons. Yet "in the event of a major outright Soviet attack against continental North America . . . we would not object to immediate retaliation by the US Strategic Air Command with all available means and from all available bases. . . . In these circumstances, we would not insist on prior consultation, but would, of course, wish to have as much prior notification as possible."[16]

Five years later, Canada granted the United States use, without any restrictions, of Canadian bases for refuelling tanker aircraft.[17] Canada thus tried to strike a bargain for itself in which it would retain sovereign control over its territory and bases in peacetime, at least where nuclear weapons were directly involved. It also tried to retain a veto over U.S. use of nuclear weapons from Canadian territory, unless North America itself had been attacked first by the Soviet Union. The North American space was seen as indivisible by both Canada and the United States, and Canada agreed to be integrated into a North American air defense system, including nuclear ground-to-air missiles, to be launched from Canadian soil against any invading bombers.[18] The command remained ultimately with the United States – this concession was the price Canada was prepared to pay for the security it derived from solidarity with the United States.

Turning to America's other privileged partner, Britain, we find that, as early as 1945, British military planners and their scientific advisers expressed the fear that the Soviet Union might one day bomb Britain with nuclear weapons. In their view, this could only be forestalled through deterrence: Britain itself had to own nuclear weapons with which it could threaten to retaliate, in the hope of frightening the Soviet Union away from such a course.[19]

Britain itself only tested its first atomic bombs after the Soviet Union, and the situation was thus reversed: the Soviet Union could threaten Britain before Britain was able to deter it. But, even prior to the first Soviet atomic test, American bombers had been moved to British bases during the Berlin Blockade of 1948, in the hope that this would deter the Soviet Union from drawing on its conventional military might in order to secure its goals. Moreover, even as early as 1946, the Spaatz–Tedder agreement had provided for the use of British air bases by U.S. military aircraft in peacetime.[20] Since 1948, U.S. nuclear-capable bombers have been stationed continuously in Britain, augmented as time passed by medium-range nuclear missiles (first Thor at the end of the 1950s, and then Cruise missiles in the early 1980s). British bases were used many times for operations both related and unrelated to NATO missions, and are still being used in this way at the time of writing.

It seems that until the U.S. air raid on Libya in 1986, there was relatively little concern about the American use of British bases for non-nuclear missions. But from the very beginning of nuclear research cooperation during the Second World War, successive British governments had felt a strong desire to be consulted as equals by the United States on any nuclear use, and particularly nuclear use from bases in Britain.

As we have seen, the Quebec agreement gave Britain the right of veto against any nuclear use by the United States. By annulling the Quebec agreement, the *modus vivendi* agreement of 1948 also cancelled the British right to a veto of U.S. nuclear use.[21] The poignancy of this only became completely clear to the British government in December 1950, after the outbreak of the Korean War. In an ambiguous statement, President Truman had not ruled out the use of nuclear weapons in this context. Moreover, as we now know, Truman had authorized, in August 1950, that nuclear weapons be deployed both to Goose Bay in Canada and to the U.S. strategic bomber group in the United Kingdom.[22] Both the British and the Canadian governments were thus aware that if strategic nuclear forces were to be used by the United States in these circumstances, they would be used from Canadian and British territory respectively – and both London and Ottawa were consequently directly affected by Truman's statement.[23] The British Prime Minister, Clement Attlee, felt called upon to travel to Washington in person to stake his own claim to consultation, notwithstanding the contents of the *modus vivendi* agreement. Truman was generous in his own private assurances to Attlee that he would be consulted before the United States decided to use the bomb. But his Secretary of State, Dean Acheson, and other members of Truman's administration persuaded him not to make any such concession in writing. The final communiqué merely stated: "The President states that it was his hope that world conditions would never call for the use of the atomic bomb. The President told the Prime Minister that it was also his desire to keep the Prime Minister at all times informed of developments which might bring about a change in the situation."[24]

While, in the light of their private conversations, Attlee took this to be a commitment to consultation on the part of Truman, there was no agreed record of the meeting, and thus nothing that Attlee had to prove that Truman had agreed to more than was contained in the communiqué.[25] (On 13 April 1951, the Canadian ambassador in Washington was told that with regard to consultation, his country was offered "the same arrangement that had been offered to the United Kingdom." Lester Pearson in Ottawa thought that this did not amount to very much.[26])

It soon dawned on the British government that the communiqué alone was not enough even to give Britain a veto over the use of British bases by the United States for nuclear missions. The United Kingdom government requested further talks and the Americans were persuaded to concede that there had to be explicit British agreement "before the United States used atomic weapons from Britain," as such "use of British bases involved British sovereignty." In January 1952, Winston Churchill, once again in office as Prime Minister, persuaded President Truman to issue the following joint communiqué: "Under arrangements made for the common defense, the United States has the use of certain bases in the United Kingdom. We reaffirm the understanding that the use of these bases in an emergency would be a matter for joint decision by His Majesty's Government and the United States Government in the light of the circumstances prevailing at the time."[27] This communiqué lent itself to different interpretations on opposite sides of the Atlantic. First of all, it was a communiqué, not a treaty ratified by parliaments. And as such, it was, second, not necessarily binding on later Presidents of the United

States. John Foster Dulles, President Eisenhower's Secretary of State, believed that this commitment was valid only if time and circumstances permitted such consultation, and Eisenhower himself explicitly excluded any commitment to consultation with Britain that amounted to a global veto on U.S. nuclear use.[28] As Paul Warnke, head of the U.S. Arms Control and Disarmament Agency under President Carter, commented three decades later to a British journalist,

> If you mean that at a time of crisis you could be quite confident that American nuclear weapons could not be launched from your territory without your agreement, then I think you'd be deluding yourselves . . . no piece of paper, no matter how well intentioned, is going to make any real difference at a time of crisis – the country that physically controls the weapon is going to make the decisions.[29]

And the country physically controlling the air bases with its own military forces, with special rights enshrined in the successive Emergency Powers Bills passed by United Kingdom governments, was the United States.[30]

British officials and governments alike, however, always interpreted the Churchill–Truman communiqué as binding all subsequent governments on both sides of the Atlantic. Indeed, their faith was so great that they sought no additional assurances from the United States on a British veto on the use of Cruise missiles when the decision was made to deploy them in Britain during the early 1980s.

This faith in the United States was not shared by important sectors of the public, i.e. the anti-nuclear movement in Britain, whose members voiced their concern over the loss of British sovereignty to the United Staters in this context.[31] Even individuals who approved of the Thatcher government's nuclear policies showed some discomfort in view of the fact that no explicit agreement on a British veto over U.S. use, such as a "dual key arrangement," had been negotiated.[32]

Also, Britons never ceased to worry about being targets for preventive nuclear strikes from the Soviet Union. Even high-ranking members of the British military establishment continued to see Britain as "very much in the forefront as a strategic target for the USSR from the outset of war."[33] Such fears were revived by the stationing of American Cruise missiles in Britain in 1983–84. Many Britons believed that in this way, Britain once again became an area threatened by preventive strikes.[34]

Admittedly, however, from the early 1950s onwards, Britain was informed in much greater detail than any other European power would ever be of U.S. nuclear strategy. On his visit to Washington in January

1952, Churchill requested to be shown SAC plans, and his request was met. Gradually, throughout the 1950s, the British built up with the Americans a far-reaching cooperation on nuclear targeting and planning.[35] This was in good part due to the fact that Britain had some valuable commodities to offer in this bargain: not only its British, but also its overseas bases in the Middle East and in South-East Asia. From 1952 onwards, and particularly after Britain had tested its first nuclear device in 1953, Britain and the United States jointly planned strategic nuclear operations against the Soviet Union from the British mainland, from bases in the Middle East (mainly Cyprus),[36] and against China from bases in the Far East.[37]

Far Eastern contingency planning for joint nuclear operations with the United States, for example if the North Koreans and Chinese should resume military action after the 1953 armistice in the Korean War, or in the event of an attack on Britain's and America's allies in the South East Asian Treaty Organization (SEATO), had definitely started by 1954.[38] The role of Britain in the context of the French request for nuclear help to relieve Dien Bien Phu in Indo-China that year shows how close the Anglo-American nuclear relationship had become. At the last moment, the British refused to join in trilateral talks concerning the use of nuclear weapons in this context, thus effectively signaling their opposition to such a course of action (something which then became publicly known).[39] Eisenhower may have been swayed by the British opposition, which went against the advice of his own Chairman of the Joint Chiefs of Staff, Admiral Radford.[40]

The British–American special nuclear planning relationship was underpinned by the Nassau Agreement of December 1962 (see chapter 7). By assigning its V-bomber force and, later, its submarine-based nuclear force to NATO, Britain engaged in further joint planning with the United States in which targets were assigned to both forces in the General (nuclear) Strike Plan (GSP) of NATO. This was an area where other European allies were at best allowed to contribute to the formation of guidelines through the Nuclear Planning Group (NPG).[41]

Being so closely involved with U.S. planning from the 1950s, and remaining so with regard to the European theater even after the British withdrawal from east of Suez, Britain thus had available a form of cooperation that – as we shall see – was denied to the other European nations. Whatever the actual text of any secret British–United States agreement on the use of British bases may have said, the British derived their confidence in the Americans from their joint planning for targeting and, indeed, from the British flag officer who permanently represents Britain in the SAC command centre in Omaha, Nebraska. It has been on this level that the British have known that they can exert influence, and not only at the level of agreeing on the general guidelines to govern such targeting. Solidarity of this sort was so valuable for them that it is not surprising that the price of being the "US air strip No. 1" (as George Orwell called it in his novel *1984*) was worth paying.

This American closeness with Britain was denied to other members of the alliance. Nevertheless, as Marc Trachtenberg has persuasively argued, Eisenhower tried to circumvent, to as great a degree as possible, the restrictions placed on his Administration by the McMahon Act, aiming to place a large proportion of the American nuclear forces at the disposal of the European members of NATO. While, for the purposes of satisfying the stipulations of the McMahon Act, all nuclear warheads and bombs, even those stockpiled in Europe, had to be kept under American control in peacetime, Eisenhower's aim seems to have been to make this control a nominal one, and to enable at least a good number of the European allies to be able to use nuclear weapons in their own defense if attacked by the Soviet Union or the Warsaw Pact.[42] Similarly, Eisenhower pre-delegated to the Supreme Commander of the Allied Forces in Europe (SACEUR) the right to release nuclear weapons in certain prescribed circumstances.[43] Moreover, American commanders anywhere had the right to release tactical nuclear weapons when their own forces were under direct attack.[44]

Initially, these arrangements satisfied the European allies, including the French, who approved along with all other NATO members the "massive retaliation" (and immediate nuclear use) doctrine contained in the NATO strategy document MC48, adopted by NATO's Military Committee on 22 November 1954. This document described it as essential, in order to create a "major deterrent to aggression" and a "successful forward defense in Europe against Soviet military aggression," that the Soviets be convinced that in "the event of aggression they will be subjected immediately to devastating counter-attack employing atomic weapons."[45]

The French Fourth Republic had proved very ready to host U.S. bases on its territory after the Second World War. France, indeed, became the most important bridgehead for U.S. forces. While the United Kingdom was of greater importance as a launch pad for the U.S. Air Force, France's ports were of greater importance in supplying forces deployed on the central front. The pipeline system established to move fuel from the French ports into the central front area was also vital. It was France, not Britain or Germany, where the allies chose to establish the NATO headquarters (Supreme Headquarters of the Allied Powers in Europe, SHAPE), and the United States opted to put the headquarters of the Unites States

Forces in Europe (HQ EUCOM). This was a logical choice flowing from the location of SHAPE, as both were headed in personal union by the same general as supreme NATO commander in Europe (SACEUR) and highest-ranking American commander in Europe. For easier co-ordination, the Headquarters of the Allied Forces Central Europe (AFCENT), the Headquarters Allied Land Forces Central Europe (LANDCENT), and the Headquarters Allied Air Forces Central Europe (AIRCENT) were also all established in France.

While France was deeply involved, of course, in all planning for land operations in Central Europe (the Commander-in-Chief, Central Europe – CINCENT – was French), the French leadership were aware that they were excluded from U.S. nuclear planning (while Britain, as we have seen, was involved in such planning from 1952). French officers at the Pentagon-based Standing Group of the NATO Military Committee (the Standing Group consisted of U.S., British, and French representatives) were aware that this was going on between the British and the United States, while the French, despite being members with the United States and Britain of what was effectively NATO's tripartite emergency executive, were kept at arm's length like all other European allies.[46] This was, of course, extremely vexing for the French. Furthermore, the influence of the British leaders on Eisenhower when the question of nuclear use at Dien Bien Phu arose added both to France's resentment of the special Anglo-American relationship and to its determination to become a nuclear power itself.[47]

As we have seen, exclusion from planning also vexed the Canadians. In 1954, when he was prodded by Lester Pearson about the need for nuclear consultation within the alliance, John Foster Dulles explained that he was ready to agree to some very secret discussions among some chosen members of the alliance – all fifteen members would be too much. Dulles thought that besides the United States and Britain, Canada should be in this exclusive club, and also France.[48]

But this reform of proceedings was not carried out. France remained excluded from the strategic nuclear planning process. Indeed, France was so far excluded that in an oral history session held by the French branch of the Nuclear History Program in Paris in 1990, military officers who had been in positions with access to important planning information in the 1950s and early 1960s disagreed as to whether the United States had ever stored nuclear weapons in France during that period, and whether U.S. tactical aircraft were allowed to use French bases when they carried nuclear bombs. It seems that the U.S. ambassador in Paris first requested permission to bring nuclear warheads or bombs onto French soil in

October 1952. The French minister of foreign affairs, Robert Schuman, refused the request. In April 1954, Schuman's successor, Georges Bidault, also refused a second American request. In March 1957, the United States returned to the charge, and the ensuing negotiations became intertwined with SACEUR General Lauris Norstad's proposal that the European NATO allies should be given American Medium-Range Ballistic Missiles (MRBMs), with the warheads remaining in U.S. custody. To this, the French government, headed by Gaillard, appears to have replied that France would only accept these weapons if France were to be given full national control over the missiles and warheads. When de Gaulle came to power in mid-1958, he confirmed this view.[49]

Despite Eisenhower's and SACEUR General Norstad's intentions to give the Europeans access to nuclear weapons in this way and, in consequence, the means of their own nuclear defense, there seem to have been grave problems with communication between them and the Europeans. In September 1958, de Gaulle visited Norstad at his headquarters in France and asked him to explain to him NATO's defense planning. In the presence of his international staff, Norstad gave a résumé to de Gaulle. Upon this, de Gaulle supposedly asked to be told where in France U.S. nuclear missiles were deployed, and which targets were assigned to them. General Norstad is said to have replied: "General, I can only reply if we are both alone." When the other officers had left the room, Norstad reportedly said: "Well, General, I cannot reply to your questions, to my very great regret." Upon which de Gaulle replied: "General, this is the last time, please repeat that [to the United States] that a French decision-maker hears such a reply."[50] This account thus implies that nuclear weapons (warheads or bombs or even complete missiles with warheads installed) were deployed by American forces in France, despite the previous French governments' refusals, and that Norstad would not tell the President of France where these were deployed.

The timing of this incident is crucial. It was immediately after this humiliation that de Gaulle – well aware of joint British–United States planning through the briefing he had received from General Gallois, one of the French representatives in Washington[51] – sent his famous memorandum to the U.S. President and the British Prime Minister, proposing a reform of NATO. He wanted the creation of a concertation mechanism between the United States, Britain, and France which went beyond that of the Standing Group, which also considered developments in other parts of the world (the Quemoy-Matsu crisis had just occurred), but which crucially would also concert strategic nuclear planning. He added that if his proposal were not implemented, France would demand a revision of the North Atlantic Treaty, in accordance with its Article 12.[52] It is worth recalling that similar proposals had led to the creation of the NATO Standing Group in 1950 and that Prime Minister Pierre Mendès-France had proposed a similar tripartite concertation between Britain, France, and the United States on nuclear matters even in 1954.[53] De Gaulle's request for a *directoire à trois* was therefore nothing new.

President Eisenhower, already with a bad conscience *vis-à-vis* Congress and other alliance partners in respect of the exceptional relationship with Britain which he had allowed to develop in the nuclear field, was not prepared to see it grow into the three-power directorate desired by France. Neither he nor, of course, the British were prepared to see the creation of a formal tripartite structure that went beyond the limited brief of the (military) Standing Group, and that would have made all other NATO members feel excluded. The most that Eisenhower (and the British) thought they could concede was *ad hoc* meetings among the three powers.[54] *Ad hoc* meetings of three, however, offered France no guarantee that no other informal meetings between the British and the Americans would take place without the French. Nor did they give France the right to know about the nuclear planning of its allies. From 1959, de Gaulle took decisions true to his threat of September 1957. He began to withdraw parts of the French armed forces from the integrated military structure of NATO, or refused to assign them to it when they returned from the Algerian War.[55]

Meanwhile, France was itself – and despite U.S. opposition (humiliating in view of the help that was now being given to Britain) – turning into a nuclear power. Indeed, one could almost say that France's determination to become a nuclear power against the odds of economic constraints and U.S. opposition was strengthened by the United States' ignoring French wishes in the context of both Dien Bien Phu in 1954 and the Suez operation of 1956. France's first nuclear test took place in 1960.[56]

As France moved from the test to the construction of its first bomber force, the United States made a last bid to gain a veto, not only over the French, but also over the British nuclear force. In December 1962, the Nassau offer of Polaris missiles based on nuclear submarines was made to both France and Britain. While the British Prime Minister Macmillan cleverly managed to build in an escape clause that allowed for British national control, de Gaulle suspected a trap, and refused to participate in the scheme. In the same press conference in which he announced his decision on Polaris, de Gaulle declared his opposition to British membership of the Common Market – in part, as a punishment for the privileged relationship Britain enjoyed with the United States.[57]

Instead of choosing continued dependence on the United States for its security, France chose independence. From 1964, Mirage IV aircraft – the first French delivery system for nuclear weapons – were entering service. By the end of 1965, the Mirage IV strategic nuclear force was fully operational. France had an independent nuclear deterrent and thus an ultimate guarantor of French security. No longer was de Gaulle prepared to pay the price of humiliation and dependence to show solidarity with the United States. On 7 March 1966, he sent the second of his famous memoranda: France requested the withdrawal of all foreign forces and also all NATO organizations from French soil.[58]

This affected SHAPE and the American HQ EUCOM, the HQ of AFCENT, the HQ of LANDCENT, and the HQ of AIRCENT. It meant that LIVE OAK, the planning centre for Berlin contingencies limited to the United States, France, and Britain as occupying powers, had to be moved out of France. It further affected logistic installations, the NATO Central Europe pipeline system, the NATO Maintenance Supply Services System, the NATO Hawk Production Organization, airfields, naval base installations, and, finally, the NATO Air Defense Ground Environment (NADGE) system, even though France decided to continue its membership in NADGE. Apart from HQ EUCOM, the United States had to move stocks and depots out of France and abandon the airfields it had used. Canada, and even the FRG, had also used facilities in France which they were now asked to leave.[59]

France thus put its own sovereignty above alliance solidarity. Considering the different treatment which the United States gave to the United Kingdom on the one hand and to its other allies on the other, particularly where nuclear planning was concerned, this decision is intelligible. It is not without irony, however, that France until the mid-1980s refused to tell the West Germans, in turn, what French short-range nuclear targets would be. This meant that the French would not tell the Germans where on their territory French short-range nuclear weapons would explode. French governments thus gleefully visited the injustices they themselves had received upon their neighbors.

West Germany's starting point was totally different from that of America's Second World War allies, Canada, Britain, and France. As the successor of the conquered, occupied enemy of these allied powers, the newly formed Federal Republic of Germany (FRG) was hardly in a position to impose its own rules at the beginning of the nuclear age. U.S. forces on the soil of West Germany were equipped with short-range nuclear weapons even before the FRG was admitted into NATO. Until then (in 1955), Bonn was told next to nothing about NATO, let alone

U.S. nuclear strategy, and West German leaders were consistently wrong-footed by Washington on the subsequent evolution of U.S. and NATO thinking in the second half of the 1950s.

When the FRG finally began to set up armed forces, Chancellor Adenauer and his military advisers were still under the impression that the Bundeswehr was needed to create the ability for NATO to repel a large-scale Soviet and/or satellite aggression in Western Europe using conventional means.[60] But, in the meantime, unbeknownst to Bonn, NATO strategy had moved on from the original one emphasizing large conventional and nuclear forces to "Massive Retaliation," a strategy putting emphasis only on nuclear deterrence. While the Bundeswehr was being built up, the Americans were beginning to scale their conventional forces down, building up their tactical nuclear weapons capacity instead. U.S. and U.S.-dominated NATO strategy now planned for the use of nuclear weapons on German soil, as NATO's Carte Blanche exercise of June 1955 revealed. The high assumed casualty figures of the exercise leaked to the press.[61] A further newspaper leak, this time in Washington in July 1956, announced further cuts in conventional forces, as favored by U.S. Admiral Arthur Radford (Chairman of the Joint Chiefs of Staff).[62] This seemed to make nonsense of Adenauer's claims to the West German parliament that Germany's manpower was irreplaceable and urgently needed by NATO. Radford was also happier than Eisenhower about the existing legislation in the United States which barred America's allies in Europe from access to U.S. nuclear weapons (or, more accurately, nuclear warheads).[63]

In the spring of 1957, another NATO exercise (Lion Noir) assumed the complete destruction of Frankfurt on the Main in the process of defending NATO territory from a Warsaw Pact attack.[64] Shortly after this exercise, Eisenhower's Secretary of State, John Foster Dulles, visited Bonn. He asked the Germans (and other allied forces on the central front) to integrate (tactical) atomic delivery vehicles into their conventional fighting forces – artillery, air force, and missiles.[65] Before 1957, there were no operational arrangements for giving non-American forces access to U.S. battlefield nuclear weapons even after hostilities had begun. If the Soviets attacked, only the American forces in Europe could have responded with short-range nuclear weapons. With any intelligence about this, Soviet commanders would have acted logically if they had directed their forces towards the non-nuclear (i.e. non-American) forces deployed in West Germany.[66] But Eisenhower, as we have seen, was keen to give the Europeans a greater degree of involvement in their own nuclear defense: this was confirmed as U.S. policy with National Security Council paper NSC 5707/8 of June 1957.[67]

Into this context fell the negotiations with European NATO members about the deployment of MRBMs, which we have referred to earlier. Britain proved willing to accept Thor missiles; Italy and Turkey were keen to station Jupiter missiles.[68] While this was being negotiated, the U.S. government went so far as to negotiate the sale of Matador cruise missiles to West Germany.[69] But this decision ran into hot domestic opposition in the United States and, ultimately, fewer systems were deployed with the West German armed forces than had originally been approved.[70] This was, in part, an expression of the opposition to "nuclear sharing" with allied forces (with the exception of those of Britain), which came to the fore particularly during the Kennedy administration. Although Kennedy shared Eisenhower's wish to forestall further nuclear proliferation within NATO,[71] he did not agree on the means adopted by Eisenhower to pursue this policy, the nuclear stockpiling programme. While Kennedy's administration (as that of Johnson after him) was constrained by promises made by Eisenhower, the preferences underlying U.S. nuclear policy from 1961 were different, and this contributed to the confusion in the signals that Washington gave to the European allies about its own aims and intentions.[72] The West German government was never properly consulted over any of these moves in American thinking, which seemed to change fundamentally about once every year from 1955 onward.[73] In view of these continual fluctuations in American policy, the German government was unable to make any sense of what NATO strategy was supposed to be.[74]

Eventually, a range of different nuclear missiles were given or sold by the United States to European NATO allies, including West Germany, on whose territory the concentration of nuclear forces was higher than on that of any other NATO state.[75] The nuclear warheads, however, remained in U.S. custody, which means that it would have required the approval both of the American President and of the German government to release missiles with nuclear charges. But, at least, the Germans exercised militarily with these systems and knew roughly how they would be used.

This was not the case for a long time with regard to Atomic Demolition Munitions (ADM). Initially, there was ignorance about the particularly large fall-out of the ADM ground-bursts. This made ADM much less suitable for the defense of densely inhabited areas such as West Germany than, for example, for Italian Alpine or remote Turkish mountain passes. In addition, unless one was prepared to pre-position ADM in advance of hostilities (which would have made it difficult to guard them), it would have been difficult to obtain release orders in time for them to be used in forward-based locations, before these were overrun by Warsaw Pact forces. If, on the other hand, they were kept in closely U.S.-controlled storage sites until release orders were given well after the outbreak of hostilities, one could hardly hope to deploy them in time along the intra-German border.

ADM were assigned to SACEUR's control at the latest during the Cuban missile crisis in 1962, but were initially only given to U.S. forces. The German Federal Government wanted them also for areas where there were no U.S. forces.[76] The problem of command and control arose from this. At the beginning of 1962, the Germans – like the French in 1958 – did not even know how many U.S. nuclear weapons were deployed on German soil.[77] The German government was very keen to be told, and also to obtain at least a negative say (that is, a veto) with regard to nuclear use on German territory, including that of East Germany (the GDR).[78]

The commitment made by the United States to consult with allies before nuclear release was limited, however. Under Eisenhower, the U.S. National Security Council agreed in February 1956 that, if time permitted, the United States should consult appropriate allies, including NATO, before the final decision to use nuclear and chemical, bacteriological, and radiological weapons was made by the President.[79]

This formulation foreshadowed the Athens Guide-Lines, agreed at the NAC meeting in May 1962.[80] It meant that consultation would only take place if U.S. decision-makers thought there was the time to do so, something that was more worrying for the FRG, a country in the front line of a potential conflict with the Warsaw Pact, particularly if – as was likely – many of the targets for American weapons would be found on German (including West German!) territory. Moreover, SACEUR's Emergency Defense Plan (EDP) was approved by NATO's Standing Committee (the United States, Britain, and France), while West Germany had no influence on its formulation.[81]

The full implications of U.S. planning with regard to ADM became known only to a small group of West German military planners as late as 1964/65, when the West Germans and the Americans jointly conducted a study on "principles and guidelines for the use of ADM." The West Germans, on whose territory these weapons would have been used, wanted only very small ADM to be used, to limit collateral damage to a minimum. In addition, they wanted them to be used early, and as closely as possible to the inner German border.[82] The American planners, however, had plans to use ADM with considerable yields (up to two or three times that of Hiroshima) throughout most of West Germany, including in West German towns![83] It is thus not unintelligible, and not merely a matter of prestige, that the German government henceforth wished to have a say in the timing, yield, and choice of location of ADM.[84]

Otherwise, German planners considered – in studies conducted in the early 1960s – that it was in West Germany's interest if SACEUR's deterrent stance (embodied in his ability to release nuclear weapons swiftly, as soon as the Americans authorized it) were not undermined by lengthy consultation with allies.[85] Even after the ADM exercise, Bonn strategists thought there would be more disadvantages than advantages resulting from a veto for all allies. It was in West Germany's interest, it was concluded, to surrender some degree of sovereignty.[86] What Bonn wanted, however, was a veto over the release of nuclear weapons from West German territory, and also against targets in East Germany.[87] The FRG did not seek any arrangement whereby it could release nuclear weapons independently, but, instead, sought to have a finger on the safety-catch in relation to the use of the nuclear weapons belonging to allies on German territory.[88]

Either way, the FRG had a strong interest in sharing responsibility in the planning for nuclear use, the selection of targets, and – short of actually controlling release – the decision to use nuclear weapons. As early as 1959, Franz Josef Strauss, as Defense Minister, formulated the need for a planning group where the FRG could have its voice heard (as it was not a member of the NATO Standing Group).[89]

While West Germany continued to be denied a formal veto over nuclear use from its own territory, many of its aims were attained after the NATO reforms of 1966–69 following France's withdrawal from the integrated military structure. The FRG was included in the Nuclear Planning Group – foreshadowed by various German proposals since 1959 – which was established in 1967 to determine the general principles which should guide nuclear use. The NATO WINTEX exercises practiced the use of consultation mechanisms which it was hoped would make it possible (time and circumstances permitting, according to the Athens formula) to consult even non-nuclear members of the alliance before nuclear release. The second half of the Cold War thus introduced more consultation and concertation. This was crucial to the sense of solidarity within NATO. For West Germany and Italy, which had no acceptable alternative to nuclear dependency, and for smaller states like the Netherlands, which could not afford a domestic nuclear weapons programme, security could only be found through alliance solidarity. But the conditions to make alliance solidarity (and dependence on the nuclear protectors) acceptable took decades to work out.

Initially, U.S. attitudes were very difficult for its allies to accept (notwithstanding Eisenhower's and Norstad's "nuclear sharing" policies). Canada, Britain, France, West Germany, and other countries had problems with the deployment of U.S. weapons on their territory (even if this was supposed to enhance their own security) since they did not even have the basic knowledge about where the weapons were positioned or how many there were.

As early as 1949, Denmark had protested against the first strategy paper of NATO, which had spelled out the obligation to assist the United States in carrying out its strategic bombardment. The Danish representative thought the Soviets might take such cooperation with the US as "a pretext for dropping an A-bomb on Copenhagen" at the outbreak of war.[90] Denmark was persuaded to drop its objections, but henceforth was determined not to accept U.S. nuclear weapons on its soil.

By 1961, the Ministry of Defense in Bonn believed that the Norwegian government had obtained a special agreement from SACEUR and the NATO Standing Group (United States, Britain, and France) that it would be consulted in advance on any use of nuclear weapons on Norwegian territory.[91] Spain, not a member of NATO until much later, retained its special control of U.S. air bases on its soil which had been negotiated bilaterally even under Franco and Truman.[92]

All members of NATO wanted protection and security, and none had any trouble with recognizing that the prime source of protection and security was the United States. Solidarity with the United States was thus worth paying for in terms of a certain loss of independence. But the U.S. refusal even to tell allies how many nuclear weapons were stationed on their soil, or where they were, or how they were to be used, including against targets on allied territory, made it very difficult for allies to accept their dependence.

In this context, the decision of France to withdraw from the integrated military structure in 1966 is easier to understand. The decision went along with the constitution of a separate French nuclear force (despite consistent U.S. opposition). This option was not, however, open to many other NATO allies, either for political or economic reasons or both. They had to try to make their voices heard in other ways, through nuclear consultation.

When we look back on NATO's history, it is fair to say that during the first two decades of its existence, the senior partner in NATO expected its junior partners on both sides of the Atlantic to pay high prices for the solidarity of the alliance. But the shock of French withdrawal worked wonders: the second half of NATO's history shows a considerably better record of solidarity and mutual consultation.[93] As Brigadier Kenneth Hunt said at the time, the service done to NATO by France in 1966 may unwittingly have been a very positive one[94] – one, indeed, from which France herself now stands to benefit.[95]

Notes

1. Gregory Donaghy for the Department of Foreign Affairs and International Trade, ed., *Documents on Canadian External Relations* [henceforth *DCER*], vol. 16, 1950 (Ottawa: Canada Communications Group, 1966), Doc. 828, p. 1468.
2. See Beatrice Heuser, "Warsaw Pact Military Doctrine in the 1970s and 80s: New Findings in the East German Archives," *Comparative Strategy*, 12 (1993), 437–57.
3. Simon Duke, *US Defence Bases in the United Kingdom: A Matter for Joint Decisions?* (London: Macmillan for St. Antony's, 1987), p. 39.
4. Duke, *US Defence Bases*, pp. 41–43.
5. I would like to acknowledge with gratitude the help given by Dr. Christopher Cook with regard to the Canadian source material.
6. *DCER*, vol. 13, Doc. 868.
7. For this interpretation, see *DCER*, vol. 16, p. 1469.
8. *Foreign Relations of the United States* [henceforth *FRUS*], 1949, vol. 4 (Washington: United States Government Printing Office, 1975), p. 355.
9. *DCER*, vol. 16, pp. 1468f.
10. *DCER*, vol. 16, p. 1488, Note of 2 Dec. 1950.
11. *DCER*, vol. 16, pp. 1468f.
12. *DCER*, vol. 16, Doc. 831, p. 1478.
13. "Explosion Shakes Villages," *Montreal Gazette*, 11 Nov. 1950.
14. *DCER*, vol. 16, Doc. 838., pp. 1491–97.
15. James Eayrs, *In Defence of Canada: Growing Up Allied* (Toronto: University of Toronto Press, 1980), p. 245.
16. *Ibid.*, pp. 246f.
17. *Ibid.*
18. *FRUS*, 1955–57, vol. 19, pp. 474, 498, U.S. National Security Council discussions of this point, May 1957.
19. Julian Lewis, *Changing Direction: British Military Planning for Post-War Strategic Defence, 1942–1947* (London: The Sherwood Press, 1988), pp. 187, 201. See also Alan Macmillan, "British Atomic Strategy 1945–52," in John Baylis and Alan Macmillan, eds., "The Foundation of British Nuclear Strategy, 1945–1960," *International Politics Research Papers* No. 12 (Dept. of International Politics, University College of Wales, 1992), 41.
20. Duke, *US Defence Bases*, pp. 195–96.
21. *Ibid.*, pp. 42–43.
22. *DCER*, vol. 16, p. 1488, Note of 2 Dec. 1950. It seems that the

bombers deployed to Britain in 1948 during the Berlin crisis, although in principle nuclear-capable, were not fitted with nuclear weapons. See Sheila Kerr, "Hotline to Moscow: Donald Maclean and the First Berlin Crisis," in Beatrice Heuser and Robert O'Neill, eds., *Securing Peace in Europe, 1945–1963: Thoughts for the Post-Cold War Era* (London: Macmillan, 1992).
23. Eayrs, *In Defence of Canada*, pp. 247–49.
24. Duke, *US Defence Bases*, p. 66.
25. Alan Bullock, *Ernest Bevin: Foreign Secretary* (Oxford: Oxford University Press, 1985), pp. 821–25.
26. Eayrs, *In Defence of Canada*, pp. 250f.
27. Duke, *US Defence Bases*, pp. 69–72, 77–80.
28. Jan Melissen, *The Struggle for Nuclear Partnership: Britain, the United States and the Making of an Ambiguous Alliance, 1952–1959* (Groningen: Styx, 1993), pp. 11–13.
29. David Fairhall, "Nuclear Safety-Catch," *Guardian*, 7 June 1983.
30. Duncan Campbell, "Secret Laws for Wartime Britain," *New Statesman*, 5 Sept. 1985; Duncan Campbell, "If War Came Close We Would Have New Masters," *New Statesman*, 13 Sept. 1985.
31. Campbell, "Secret Laws for Wartime Britain"; Campbell, "If War Came Close We Would Have New Masters."
32. Ian Aitken, "I would press Polaris button, says Thatcher," *Guardian*, 1 June 1983; John Pardoe, "Faith in Defence the Nato Way," *The Times*, 3 June 1983; David Fairhall, "Nuclear Safety-Catch," *Guardian*, 7 June 1983.
33. Sir John Barraclough, "Britain's Strategic Nuclear Deterrent," *NATO's Fifteen Nations*, vol. 27, no. 1 (Feb.–Mar. 1982), 35.
34. Duncan Campbell, *The Unsinkable Aircraft Carrier: American Military Power in Britain* (London: Michael Joseph, 1984), pp. 316–38; Jeannette Buirski, "How I Learnt to Start Worrying and Hate the Bomb," and Ann Pettitt, "Letter to My Neighbour," both in Dorothy Thompson, ed., *Over Our Dead Bodies* (London: Virago Press, 1983), pp. 15–28 and 89–107.
35. Ian Clark and Nicholas J. Wheeler, *The British Origins of Nuclear Strategy, 1945–1955* (Oxford: Clarendon Press, 1989), pp. 150f.
36. Public Records Office, Kew, Richmond, Surrey [henceforth PRO] AIR8/2271, "Military Strategy for Circumstances Short of Global War 1960–1970," mid-March 1961.
37. E.g. PRO, DEFE 5/99, COS(60)14 of 25 Jan. 1960; DEFE 4/132, Appendix "B" to JP(60)16(Final) of 21 June 1960, pp. 5, 10.
38. PRO, AIR 8/2271, CAB 2416/AUS(A)/7125, note by R.C. Kent,

Assistant Under Secretary (Air), 29 Sept. 1960; and *ibid.*, summary of JP(60)16(Final), "Military Strategy for Circumstances Short of Global War," discussed in mid-March 1961.

39. "Le Foreign Office fait une mise au point modérée à la suite de l'article de «Life»," *Le Monde*, 15 Jan. 1956 and the famous interview with John Foster Dulles, "On the Brink of War," *Life*, Jan. 1956.

40. Greg Herring and Robert Immerman, "Le jour où nous ne sommes pas entrés en guerre: la politique américaine au moment de Diên Biên Phu," in Denise Artaud and Lawrence Kaplan, eds., *Diên Biên Phu: L'Alliance atlantique et la défense du Sud-Est asiatique* (Lyon: La manufacture, 1989), pp. 116–27.

41. Paul Buteux, *The Politics of Nuclear Consultation in NATO, 1965–1980* (Cambridge: Cambridge University Press, 1983), pp. 202–206.

42. Marc Trachtenberg, "La formation du système de défense occidentale: les Etats-Unis, la France et MC48," in Maurice Vaïsse and Frédéric Bozo, eds., *La France et l'OTAN, 1949–1996* (Brussels: Complexe, 1996), pp. 121–23.

43. *Ibid.*

44. *FRUS*, 1955–57, vol. 19, pp. 203f, 493, 506.

45. NATO, M.C. 48 (Final) of 22 Nov. 1954, "COSMIC TOP SECRET," copy no. 267, p. 2, paragraphs 2 and 3. Document declassified by NATO at the author's request.

46. (Admiral) Marcel Duval and Yves Le Baut, *L'Arme nucléaire française: Pourquoi et comment?* (Paris: Kronos, 1991), p. 24; interview with General Pierre-M. Gallois, Paris, May 1991.

47. Duval and Le Baut, *L'arme nucléaire française*, pp. 6–38.

48. Eayrs, *In Defence of Canada*, p. 266.

49. Patrick Facon, "Les bases américaines en France, 1945–1958: un enjeu politique," in Vaïsse, Mélandri, and Bozo, eds., *La France et l'OTAN*, pp. 140–43.

50. Jean Lacouture, *De Gaulle: Le souverain, 1959–1970*, vol. 3 (Paris: Seuil, 1986), p. 466.

51. *Ibid.*

52. "Mémorandum du général de Gaulle au Président des États-Unis d'Amérique, et au Premier Ministre du Royaume-Uni, 17 septembre 1958," in Dominique David, ed., *La Politique de défense de la France: Textes et documents* (Paris: Fondation pour les Études de défense nationale, 1989), pp. 130–31.

53. Trachtenberg, "La formation du système," p. 120.

54. PRO, FO371/159668, 10 mars 1961: "The problem of France and the emergence of further nuclear powers."

55. Frédéric Bozo, *La France et l'OTAN: De la guerre froide au nouvel ordre européen* (Paris: Masson, 1991), pp. 93–101; Frédéric Bozo, "Chronique d'une décision annoncée: le retraint de l'organisation militaire (1965–1967)," in Vaïsse, Mélandri, and Bozo, eds., *La France et l'OTAN*, pp. 331–58.

56. Maurice Vaïsse, "Un dialogue de sourds: les relations nucléaires franco-américaines de 1957 à 1960," *Relations internationales*, 68 (Winter 1991), 407–23.

57. Press Conference of President de Gaulle of 14 Jan. 1963, *Charles de Gaulle – Discours et Messages 1963* (Paris: Plon, 1974), pp. 61–79.

58. "Lettre du Général de Gaulle au Président Johnson, 7 mars 1966," in David, ed., *La Politique de défense de la France*, pp. 132–33.

59. Brigadier Kenneth Hunt, *NATO without France: The Military Implications*, Adelphi Paper 32 (London: IISS, Dec. 1966).

60. Christian Tuschhoff, "Die MC 70 und die Einführung nuklearer Trägersysteme in die Bundeswehr, 1956–1959," *Nuclear History Program Arbeitspapier* (Ebenhausen: Stiftung Wissenschaft und Politik, n.d.), pp. 30, 55.

61. "Atom Alarm in Bonn," [Frankfurt/Main] *Abendpost*, 14 July 1955; "Debatte über die Atomkriegführung am Samstag," *Frankfurter Allgemeine Zeitung* [henceforth *FAZ*], 15 July 1955; "Über 1,7 Millionen Deutsche wären getötet worden [1.7 million dead and 3.5 million wounded]," [Dortmund] *Westdeutsches Tageblatt*, 18 July 1955.

62. Hans Meyer, "Die neue Strategie der USA," *Bremer Nachrichten*, 26 July 1959; "Rückzugsstrategie," *Kasseler Post*, 26 July 1959; "Der Hintergrund der Generalsreisen," [Koblenz] *Rhein-Zeitung*, 26 July 1959; Immanuel Birnbaum, "Amerika denkt um," *Süddeutsche Zeitung* [henceforth *SZ*], 26 July 1959.

63. Meeting of the National Security Council, 11 Apr. 1957, *FRUS*, 1956–58, vol. 19, p. 474.

64. Hans Henrich, "Sozialer Faktor Atombombe," *Frankfurter Rundschau*, 24 Apr. 1957; "Frankfurt gegen Atomwaffenversuche," *Stuttgarter Zeitung*, 27 Apr. 1957.

65. Transcripts of interviews with Strauss of 1988, pp. 93f. (a much edited rendering of this is to be found in *Erinnerungen*, p. 357).

66. Transcripts of interviews with F.J. Strauss of 1988, p. 96.

67. Cf. *FRUS*, 1956–58, vol. 19, pp. 473, 496, 506, and NSC5707/8 of 3 June 1957, pp. 512f.

68. See Leopoldo Nuti, "The F-I-G Story Revisited," in *Storia delle Relazioni Internazionali*, vol. 13, no. 1 (1998), pp. 69–100.

69. "Taktische Atomwaffen führen zum grossen Krieg," *Hamburger Echo* (SPD), 7 June 1958; [Dortmund] "Fragwürdige Verteidigung," *Westfälische Rundschau* (SPD), 7 June 1958; "Mit der grossen Bombe gekoppelt," *Die Welt*, 7 June 1958; "Ist der Atomkrieg unteilbar?," *FAZ*, 9 June 1958; "Widerspruch zur NATO-Strategie: die `Ketzerei' des Generals Panitzki," [Stuttgart] *Christ und Welt*, 12 June 1958.

70. Christian Tuschhoff, "Causes and Consequences of Germany's Deployment of Nuclear Capable Delivery Systems, 1957–1963," Occasional Paper No. 9 of the Nuclear History Program (College Park, Md.: CISSM, University of Maryland, 1994), 12.

71. *FRUS*, 1956–58, vol. 19, p. 474.

72. Christian Hoppe, *Zwischen Teilhabe und Mitsprache: Die Nuklearfrage in der Allianzpolitik Deutschlands, 1959–1966* (Baden-Baden: Nomos, 1993), pp. 41–70.

73. "Die USA prüfen ihre Rüstungspolitik," *SZ*, 8 Feb. 1960; Herbert von Borch: "Die letzte Schranke," *Die Welt*, 9 Feb. 1960; "Amerikas Luftwaffe stützt die Kritik General Powers," *FAZ*, 9 Feb. 1960; "Verwirrung in Amerika über die Verteidigung," *FA*, 11 Feb. 1960; "Abschreckungstheorie unzureichend," *SZ*, 10 Aug. 1960; "Streit um die US-Luftstrategie," *Industriekurier*, 1 Dec. 1960.

74. Catherine M. Kelleher, *Germany and the Politics of Nuclear Weapons* (New York: Columbia University Press, 1975), p. 52.

75. Gerd Scharnhorst, "Die modernste Waffe der Bundeswehr," *Welt am Sonntag*, 6 Sept. 1964. The article gives the later range of Pershing I missiles (1100 km).

76. Letter from FüB to the Minster of Defence (Dec. 1962), Nuclear History Program collection in Bonn [henceforth NHP Bonn] Doc. 114, pp. 1f.

77. "Sprechzettel für den Besuch des Herrn Ministers bei General Norstad" (5 Mar. 1962), NHP Bonn, Doc. 88, p. 5.

78. "Mitspracherecht bei Kernwaffen nötig," *Stuttgarter Nachrichten*, 7 Apr. 1962; "Atomfriede," *Sonntagsblatt*, 15 Apr. 1962.

79. *FRUS*, 1956–58, vol. 19, p. 205.

80. "Strategische und nukleare Planung der NATO" (8 Feb. 1962), NHP Bonn, Doc. 86, p. 3.

81. PRO, DEFE 13/254, British Defence Staff Washington to the MoD in London, 23 Apr. 1962.

82. "Wesentliche Ergebnisse der deutsch-amerikanischen Studie: 'Grundsätze und Richtlinien für den Einsatz der ADM'" (May 1965), NHP Bonn, Doc. 155, pp. 1–5; see also Christoph Bluth, *Britain, Germany and Western Nuclear Strategy* (Oxford: Clarendon Press, 1995), pp.

87–93. I am very grateful to Professor Bluth for having made these documents available to me.

83. "Wesentliche Ergebnisse der deutsch–amerikanischen Studie."

84. This study is probably at the origin of the great "Atomic Mines" or "Trettner Proposal" debate of December 1964 and early 1965. See Kelleher, *Germany and the Politics of Nuclear Weapons*, pp. 214f.

85. "MRB-Problematik: hier: Kommentar zum Fragebogen" (20 Oct. 1962), NHP Bonn, Doc. 110, p. 2; "Grundsätze der Verteidigungs-politik" (23 Jan. 1963), NHP Bonn, Doc. 119, pp. 19f.; "Vorschlag für Einleitungsvortrag Minister" (for von Hassel talks in Pentagon, Feb. 1963), NHP Bonn, Doc. 128, pp. 36f.; "Untersuchung über Inter-allied Nuclear Force" (9 Apr. 1963), NHP Bonn, Doc. 132, p. 115.

86. "Kurzstudie über Zweischlüsselsystem" (15 Dec. 1965), NHP Bonn, Doc. 162, p. 5.

87. "Deutsches Veto Recht" (14 Apr. 1966), NHP Bonn, Doc. 164, p. 6.

88. "Die nukleare Frage" (23 Aug. 1965), NHP Bonn, Doc. 160, pp. 2f. This formulation was used a year later by the new Chancellor Kurt Georg Kiesinger: "Kiesinger wiederholt Verzicht auf Atomwaffen," *Die Welt*, 20 Dec. 1966.

89. "Atomare Mitbestimmung für Kontinentaleuropa," [Düsseldorf] *Der Mittag*, 26 Aug. 1959.

90. *FRUS*, 1949, vol. 4, p. 355.

91. FüB III 1 to Leiter III (30 June 1961), NHP Bonn, Doc. 69, p. 3. Unbeknownst to them, the Canadians had sought, and it seems obtained, even more far-reaching concessions in the early 1950s.

92. Cf. Jill Edwards, "Relations between the US and Franco's Spain," in Heuser and O'Neill, eds., *Securing Peace in Europe, 1945–1963*.

93. See Ivo Daalder, *The Nature and Practice of Flexible Response: NATO Strategy and Theater Nuclear Forces since 1967* (New York: Columbia University Press, 1991), and Bluth, *Britain, Germany and Western Nuclear Strategy*.

94. Hunt, *NATO without France*, p. 2.

95. France decided in December 1995 to return to the planning fora of NATO.

7

Interdependence and Independence:
Nassau and the British Nuclear Deterrent

Lawrence Freedman and *John Gearson*

Graham Allison used his study of the Cuban Missile Crisis to develop his ideas on the "bureaucratic politics model" as an alternative explanation for policy outcomes to the established concepts of the "rational actor model."[1] The bureaucratic politics model has been criticized on a number of grounds, not least of which is that it is by no means clearly supported by the Cuban case study. It very much reflects the American experience, and arguably a 1960s experience, prior to the active involvement of Congress in foreign affairs. It seems to be particularly appropriate for national security policy rather than other areas of foreign policy, largely because of the critical roles played by the separate armed services. They can be seen to have an "organizational essence" which transcends the demands of particular Administrations and which encourages a tendency towards policy advocacy, in which the service and national interests naturally merge into one another.

Not long after Nikita Khrushchev's attempt to introduce missiles into Cuba had obliged the Kennedy Administration to confront its most important adversary, its own decision to cancel the Skybolt air-to-surface missile led to a crisis with America's most important ally. Britain had come to depend on Skybolt to prolong the life-span of its nuclear deterrent. Now it appeared that the United States was seeking to push the United Kingdom out of the nuclear business by removing this important prop. In an already scheduled summit at Nassau between the President and Prime Minister Harold Macmillan in December 1962, an alternative prop was found in the form of the Polaris submarine-launched ballistic missile.

Given the British government's commitment to some form of nuclear strike force, the shift to Polaris was undoubtedly the correct decision. The implementation of the policy was relatively unproblematic and by the end of the decade Britain had built four submarines, each able to carry sixteen American A-3 Polaris missiles carrying British warheads.[2]

This force is only now coming out of service as the new Trident fleet becomes operational. Trident itself represents confirmation of the validity of the concept adopted hurriedly in 1962, and indeed was negotiated under the terms of the Polaris Sales Agreement of 1963.[3] The main advantage of the Polaris force was that it was relatively invulnerable to surprise attack, so that Britain could assure retaliation. While an air-based deterrent was always prone to obsolescence, a submarine-based force could only be undermined by substantial breakthroughs in anti-submarine and anti-missile technologies.

The question to ask, therefore, is not why Polaris was adopted in 1962 but why it had *not* been adopted in 1960 when the decision had been made to purchase Skybolt? This question is relevant to the study of bureaucratic politics as the answer does point to the policy as a product of the balance of bureaucratic interests. It also appears to strengthen even more the case for the study of bureaucratic interests in policy-making by focusing on the collusion between the air forces, and the navies, of the United Kingdom and the United States.

This chapter consequently considers the issue of "why Polaris?" in terms of what it reveals about the bureaucratic politics in both countries, and the interaction between the two governments. The case study is helped not only by the release of official records, but also by the recent publication of two books dealing with this issue.[4] In addition, we have the advantage of the proceedings of an oral history conference in 1992 in Washington. The purpose of this meeting was to examine the Nassau conference, and a number of key players at the 1962 conference participated. We have also been fortunate in having access to the interview notes of Professor Richard Neustadt, who was commissioned by President Kennedy to report on why these two close allies had experienced such a monumental misunderstanding.[5]

This chapter does not deny the importance of bureaucratic politics in setting the agenda for policy-making and shaping decisions. It does, however, point to the conditional aspects of this. There is a direct relationship between the influence of the armed services and the ability and readiness of the center to assert itself. In the end, and despite bureaucratic pressures, the key decision-makers remain political leaders and decisions with a compelling bureaucratic logic still require some sort of functional logic.

The period covering the late 1950s and early 1960s was one not only of great turbulence in international politics, but also of transition in the management of defense. The management problem in both the United States and the United Kingdom stemmed from the dominance of the policy-making arena by the three armed services, organized independently of each other, often working with mutually contradictory doctrines, and led by career officers loyal to their own service above all else. Fortified by the conviction that their service was critical to national survival, the individual chiefs were often tenacious in the promotion of their service view.

This had important consequences. The chiefs often could only agree on the basis of asking the government to meet all their collective manpower and equipment demands.[6] They had no basis for agreement when it came to hard choices on priorities. This meant that the civilian staffs in the American Department of Defense and the British Ministry of Defence were required to take on this task. The line of least resistance was to divide the spoils on an historical basis, so that each service had equal reasons for grievance. It took a determined government to shift the balance.

The severity of this problem varied according to personalities and circumstances. In the period we are considering it was unusually severe. This was for two reasons. First, during the early part of the 1950s, the Conservative government in Britain and then the Republican administration in the United States had taken fright at the fiscal implications of the rearmament programs set in motion under the combined impact of the deterioration of East–West relations in Europe and then the onset of the Korean War in 1950. It proved impossible to sustain a broadly based expansion of the armed forces. The context was, therefore, one of continuing pressure on the defence budgets of the two countries, which undermined the potential for cooperation between the three services.

Second, both governments determined that the answer to this problem lay in nuclear deterrence. Fighting a war had become an extraordinarily expensive business. If, as likely as not, nuclear weapons were going to be used, then it would also end in mass destruction all round. The threat of this prospect, both governments decided, should be used to deter – thus allowing for savings in conventional capabilities which were now only needed for situations in which there was no risk of total war. At the time, this approach privileged the two air forces. It represented a logical continuation of the doctrines of strategic bombardment which both had used to justify the need for independence from the other two services, but which had been undermined by the uncertain achievements of the strategic bombing campaigns of the Second World War. Nuclear weapons appeared to have rescued the doctrine, for now the threat from the air appeared irresistible in a way that had not been the case from 1939 to 1945.

Thus, in Britain, the 1957 Defence White Paper signalled a whole-hearted commitment to nuclear deterrence. This was used as a means to cut spending on conventional weapons and, in particular, to cut back on air defenses and forces based in Germany, and also to abolish conscription.[7] In the face of official backing for nuclear deterrence, the army and the navy in both countries felt obliged to warn of the dangers of excessive reliance on this doctrine. There were many types of conflict, they pointed out, for which nuclear weapons would be quite inappropriate and, even with an East–West confrontation, if deterrence should fail there would still be a need for substantial conventional forces. The scenarios in which nuclear weapons might be used were hard to envisage. This led the navies and the armies to argue that the reductions in conventional forces meant a shrinkage in military potential, especially in the apparently non-vital areas which had a habit of leading to significant military commitments.[8]

By the end of the 1950s, the dangers of over-dependence on nuclear deterrence represented the basic thrust of most academic writing on security policy, and were also coming to be recognized in official circles. This might have simply led to a re-balancing of defence provision among the three services were it not for a major and coincidental technological change.

This was the start of the missile age. To the air forces, the arrival of nuclear-tipped missiles represented a major threat to the dominance of the manned strategic bomber. The threat took two forms. First, missiles seemed a much more straightforward way of delivering munitions to a target. While initially they might lack the accuracy of the manned bomber, this could be expected to improve. Second, they were probably accurate enough to threaten bomber bases. A country relying on manned aircraft for its deterrent risked their loss in a surprise first strike. The first test of a Soviet Inter-Continental Ballistic Missile (ICBM) and the launch of the world's first Earth satellite, Sputnik I, in 1957 underlined this danger. Reluctantly, the air force might shift from manned bombers to ICBMs, but then there was a further risk. As the accuracy of ICBMs improved, they could threaten the other side's ICBM bases as well, thus raising the spectre of "the reciprocal fear of surprise attack" as each side might be tempted to get its missile strike in first.[9] This prospect encouraged the search for systems that could survive disarming strikes. The obvious methods were mobility and concealment, and this argued for putting missiles in submarines.

Ideas of this kind represented a major challenge to the "organizational essence" of the two air forces. Instead of the USAF's Strategic Air Command and the RAF's Bomber Command together taking responsibility for the credibility of deterrence, they could see this role slipping away to the U.S. Navy (USN) and the Royal Navy (RN). This might leave them only with the so-called "tactical" roles, acting in support of ground and maritime operations. Not that the USN and RN were desperately enthusiastic about this new responsibility. The admirals had become rather attached to carrier battle groups. They were not anxious to see funds diverted from the surface fleet to the nuclear role. Against this, of course, there were many in both navies who saw the acquisition of the nuclear role as an excellent opportunity. Naval reluctance when it came to acquiring the nuclear role was never as great as air force opposition to relinquishing it.

The USAF fought hard to get a successor to the B-52, introduced in the mid-1950s, only to be thwarted by successive administrations until they eventually achieved some success with Ronald Reagan. They consistently proclaimed the virtues of the manned bomber. They did, at least, have the consolation of a substantial ICBM force.[10] Even here, when it came to designing a successor to the Minuteman force, introduced during the 1960s, progress was slow. The successor – the M-X – was obliged to demonstrate high survivability. The schemes to achieve this consistently appeared extraordinarily complex and far too expensive, so that in the end only a small force was introduced. By contrast, submarine-launched missiles moved effortlessly from one new generation to the next – Polaris, Poseidon, Tridents 1 and 2.

The choices were even starker in Britain. The V-bomber force entered service just as the implications of the missile age were becoming inescapable. The country found it impossible to keep up with the most advanced technology. Its effort to build a land-based missile – Blue Streak – faltered in the face of a combination of high cost and imminent obsolescence. The pressure on the budget was such that Britain lacked the option of a "triad" – the American rationalization for maintaining a combined force of bombers, ICBMs, and Submarine-Launched Ballistic Missiles (SLBMs). It had to choose, and it soon became apparent that the choice was conditional on a transfer of the relevant technology from the United States. The implications for the inter-service balance were, thus, much more stark in Britain than they were in the United States.

In both countries, the army, navy, and air force often probably felt closer to their sisters across the Atlantic than they did to each other. In the late 1950s (after the two governments had agreed in 1958 that nuclear information could now be shared), Bomber Command and SAC had begun to work together to plan the nuclear campaign against the Warsaw Pact. The USN and the RN had always worked closely together. In both cases, lines of communication were good. Indeed, when Skybolt was conceived, the USAF sought the support of the RAF *before* the Defense Department had even begun to consider the project.[11]

This was, in fact, the high point of Anglo-American interdependence in the nuclear field. Having successfully demonstrated a capacity to operate independently, with a successful H-bomb test and the coming into operation of the V-bomber force, Britain could achieve true interdependence. During the 1960s, it became progressively harder to demonstrate that British capabilities made much difference to the overall quality of the Western deterrent. This was not the case in the late 1950s. The nuclear relationship between the two countries, which had been restored through the Agreement on Atomic Cooperation in July 1958, amending the McMahon Act,[12] was genuinely two-way as the United Kingdom had an independent technological base upon which American nuclear scientists could now draw, as well as stocks of Plutonium and other special materials which were then in short supply. Indeed, the Americans had been impressed with the breadth of British knowledge in atomic matters – "surpassing ours in at least one case" one U.S. official noted.[13] The atmosphere was truly one of cooperation, at least from the British perspective.[14] Furthermore, from the start of this cooperation, the furnishing of missile technology to the British tended to be linked (at the very least tacitly) to basing rights for American-manned missile forces – a link that was to prove crucial at Nassau.[15]

The sense of interdependence also permeated the working relationships between the Foreign Office and the State Department, and the two political leaderships, although again the need was felt more strongly in the United Kingdom than in the United States. For Prime Minister Harold Macmillan, a top priority had been to revive the special relationship after the débâcle of Suez.[16] Britain was a declining but still great power which had been "present at the creation" of the atomic bomb. As such, she sat at the nuclear high table by right, not sufferance. However, to stay in the game, American help had to be sought to share the costs of maintaining this nuclear status. Eisenhower appeared to accept this and, despite some internal opposition, noted that the exchange of nuclear information should be "full and generous."[17]

However, while Britain's position as a nuclear power was being undermined by the pace of technological advance, its position as a "European power" was being undermined by the steady revival of France and Germany, and by the fact that, contrary to all precedent, they were working closely together rather than in opposition. The vision of a united Western Europe, which provided the foundations of increased prosperity as it banished the prospect of another great war, was seen as increasingly compelling. Macmillan himself had been obliged to succumb to it, as the UK government's initial aloofness and scepticism when the Treaty of Rome was first signed was shown to have been more than mistaken. In the United States, there was an increasing conviction that it would be best all round if European integration accelerated and, if this was the case, could the United States continue to allow Britain a privileged position, especially in the nuclear sphere? One idea, gestating during the late 1950s, was for all the European nuclear assets to be pooled in a joint medium-range ballistic missile (MRBM) force.[18]

As Britain struggled to adjust to the new realities of military technology and political change in Europe, there were few attempts to overhaul decision-making. The two big decisions under consideration in this chapter – the decision to opt for Skybolt in 1960 and Polaris in 1962 – were taken with a decision-making process which still put the government in a position of arbitrating among service demands. It lacked the capacity to set the defence agenda for itself, other than by setting budgetary guidelines. In the United States over this period there was a revolution in defense decision-making. Robert McNamara, President Kennedy's Secretary of Defense, further developing a centralizing process begun by his predecessor, Thomas Gates, took firm control of the Pentagon. American decision-making was shaped by inter-service rivalry but, with the budget allowed to increase, McNamara was able to deploy formidable analytical capabilities to shape the programme.

The problem for the United Kingdom in 1960 was to find a delivery system to take the deterrent through the 1960s and beyond. The British had suffered a succession of humiliating set-backs as the technologies involved outstripped their capabilities. Efforts focused initially on how to extend the life of the V-bombers through the development of the Blue Steel stand-off missile, which would reduce the need for the increasingly vulnerable V-bombers to penetrate the clearly effective Soviet air defenses.[119] It was then decided to develop an Intermediate-Range Ballistic Missile (IRBM) called Blue Streak, to keep Britain in the race while missiles emerged as the future. British technological vulnerability was revealed by the fact that Blue Streak was substantially based on American designs. It eventually became apparent that it would be obsolete by the time it became operational. Stuck in fixed sites, liquid-fuelled, and slow to prepare for launch, Blue Streak would be vulnerable to surprise attack by new, faster, Soviet missiles. In 1960, it was cancelled.

This left an embarrassing hole in the British nuclear programme, with no obvious alternative. The British deterrent would lack a delivery vehicle once the V-bombers went out of service and a missile programme was bound to be expensive. The USAF appeared to have an ideal solution – Skybolt. Skybolt was an air-launched stand-off missile which could be attached to the V-bombers, allowing them to remain in service longer than had hitherto been thought possible. The size of the V-bomber force had been progressively reduced as debates took place as to how much was enough for minimum deterrence. However, the force *was* operational, and offered the flexibility of a recallable strike force. Although the RAF was concerned about the potential loss of independence that purchase of Skybolt would entail, the fiscal realities of the Skybolt option were too telling – and it would provide additional range over the British Blue Steel, which was suffering development problems.

Yet there were problems with Skybolt which could be appreciated even at that time. It was no more certain to perform as expected than Blue Steel and doubts about its viability were regularly voiced.[20] Most importantly, it was dependent upon a continuing commitment to a manned bomber force by the American government. At best, it was just one of many American nuclear delivery systems under consideration or development and was by no means of central importance to the American nuclear arsenal.[21] Furthermore, for the Americans, extending the operational mission of the manned bomber in the defence suppression mission (for which longer-range missiles were ill-suited) using Skybolt offered marginal benefits. Such a mission involved a relatively small warhead – which was not ideal for the much more substantial British mission. Macmillan was well aware of this and was keen to order enough missiles for Britain to have a say in the design of the weapon.[22] The British were even warned that if the Americans dropped the Skybolt project themselves, it was unlikely to be kept going for the United Kingdom alone, apparently to no avail.[23] Above all these factors was another – Skybolt was a highly speculative project. This point was never fully appreciated by British ministers, who lacked suitable civilian experts to assess the project properly.[24]

Profound doubts also existed about Skybolt as a mobile deterrent invulnerable to attack. The V-bomber force had been reduced so much as to call in question the RAF's ability to maintain standing patrols in an era when alert times had fallen to only four minutes, as the Minister for Aviation, Duncan Sandys, pointed out.[25] The bomber lobby discounted this – the Secretary of State for Air, George Ward, tried to reassure Macmillan that such a warning time was not bad if the Skybolt-equipped

V-bombers were left in dispersal positions at the end of runways and claimed that, for deterrence purposes, it was not even important. The criticism, however, was telling.[26]

By contrast, Polaris was mobile, invulnerable to surprise attack, and could be maintained at a high state of readiness. Its invulnerability reduced the pressure for an instant decision to launch, which had been one of the major drawbacks of the Blue Streak missile. What, therefore, might have been the reasons against choosing the system?

One problem with Polaris was target coverage. Now that Britain coordinated strategic planning with the United States, there was a concern to target those Soviet forces which directly threatened Britain but which might be lower down on the American list of priorities for initial attack, as well as to help clear a path for the main thrust of any nuclear strike through the suppression of Soviet defenses.[27] Increasingly, though, as American target coverage grew and the expected size of the V-bomber force declined, it was counter-city targeting which came to prevail in British thinking about an independent but minimal deterrent. The acquisition of a Polaris-based missile force would tend to emphasize the counter-city mission because, while being safe from surprise attack, the submarine-based missiles would be fewer in number and relatively inaccurate compared with a V-bomber force. It would be suitable for defined military targets.

As early as 1959, and before Polaris was seriously considered, the basic criterion for "minimum deterrence" was put at 50 percent destruction of forty Soviet cities and industrial centres by the British Nuclear Deterrent Study Group.[28] This fitted in well with the fact that targeting Soviet forces was becoming more and more difficult for the small British force. It was already apparent to Whitehall that the purely military requirements relating to a particular targeting strategy would not be permitted to determine the overall size of the British deterrent force.[29] Nonetheless, in 1960, as the Royal Navy had only recently started to coordinate targeting plans with Bomber Command, it might have seemed too early to shift publicly to a system which was so clearly restricted in the roles which it could play.

Whatever the targeting issues, the precise type of system was not absolutely crucial to meeting the core objectives of British policy. The strategic rationale derived essentially from the doubts over the American guarantee to Europe continuing in the era of ICBMs. Macmillan saw the British deterrent's strategic purpose as primarily a trigger for the American nuclear arsenal.[30] This was not a rationale that was easy to expound in public. The Americans were understandably wary of such arguments, but they had their own reasons for continuing to help Britain. In particular, they were anxious to avert further conventional force cuts by Britain, and also hoped to draw Britain into schemes for a multilateral nuclear force.

Another problem with Polaris was that the technology was not yet certain although, of course, this was also the case with Skybolt.[31] It also seemed to have strings attached. There was a link in the American eyes with the NATO MRBM force, and this would have further undermined the independent nature of the British deterrent. A further disincentive to the pursuit of Polaris was the evidence that existed that the United States was less ready to provide Polaris than Skybolt. Despite the fact that the Americans were pushing to establish a Polaris submarine base in Scotland and that this became, in effect, the *quid pro quo* for the supply of American missiles, the British attempt to use Holy Loch to get Polaris out of the Eisenhower administration encountered resistance.

Macmillan wanted to make sure that something was agreed as soon as possible to avoid the appearance of the United Kingdom's defense policy being "aimless."[32] As he noted to the Defense Secretary, Harold Watkinson, "We must not be straddled between Polaris and Skybolt and getting neither one of them."[33] In 1957, he had tended towards reliance on a missile force, but Eisenhower had encouraged him to keep up the development of manned bombers.[34] By 1960, the choice facing Britain was more acute and, significantly, an election was due in America in the autumn. In the short term, at least, there seemed to be powerful arguments in favor of Skybolt: it was cheaper, appeared to make possible the extended deployment of an existing asset, the V-bombers, and offered operational flexibility. It offered first and foremost a financial saving over most alternatives which recommended it to the Prime Minister, who did not look forward more than seven or eight years in financial terms according to one official.[35]

Furthermore, there was no logical reason why the two forces should have been seen as being in opposition to each other. Opting for Skybolt could be presented as a useful stopgap measure in the expectation that Polaris would later be available (or could be obtained). On this point, it should be noted that the RAF, unsurprisingly, did not accept the technical arguments for the medium-to-long-term obsolescence of the manned bomber at all – they were hoping and planning for Skybolt 1 to be followed by Skybolt 2 and 3, probably on future aircraft such as the TSR2.[36] To the Aviation Minister, Julian Amery, Skybolt appeared a modern sophisticated weapon system which, despite the differing missions envisaged for it, was still an improvement on Blue Steel.[37]

Yet while the RAF, abetted by the USAF, argued strongly in favour of retaining its role as the carrier of the strategic deterrent, the Royal Navy appeared strangely agnostic, preoccupied with surface ships and defending its budget against attempts to unload upon it the cost of the nuclear deterrent. This does not mean to say that the RN was ignoring Polaris: there had been a team since 1958 in the United States monitoring the programme and a liaison officer was based in America.[38] Even so, Solly Zuckerman recalled seeing no sketch costings for a Polaris system until December 1962.[39]

It was not so much that the RN was uninterested in Polaris, but that it understood the bureaucratic realities of 1960. The RAF was committed to its deterrent role and would fight to retain it, so long as there were serious options. If the RN made a play for Polaris, and was successful, then it could expect to be told to find resources from its own budget. Better to wait to be asked to take on the role, which would help it hold on to its established ships and missions. To others, who believed that Polaris was the right choice for the country, this strategy was inappropriate. When serious advocacy was required, it was not provided.[40] But this was not only the RN's fault. There was a serious lack of analytical capability in the Ministry of Defense to provide the government with a disinterested study on the best long-term option. For example, when it was reported that the B-70 bomber had been cancelled, the MOD argued that this merely made the case for Skybolt stronger in the United States, since it would be useful in extending the operational life of the existing B-52 bomber.[41] This analysis reflected a British standpoint where extending the life of a bomber was essentially on grounds of cost, and underestimated the range of nuclear choice facing the Department of Defense and the American tendency to purchase the best system, not the cheapest. Nor did the British government even consider a joint study with the United States to assess the alternative options.

There is evidence that Thomas Gates would have been quite sympathetic to a British request for Polaris.[42] The American readiness to help was not really tested until after the Skybolt deal had been agreed. A visit by Macmillan in June 1960 was proposed, but only if it was thought he could secure Polaris as a result. The visit did not occur.[43] All his government did was attempt to preserve the option for the future. This was very much Watkinson's approach during the negotiations – secure the cheapest option of Skybolt and continue discussions regarding Polaris.[44]

When the deal to purchase Skybolt had been outlined in March 1960 by Macmillan and Eisenhower, it was for the supply of Skybolt "or to acquire in addition or substitution a mobile MRBM system." The British took this to mean a Polaris force independent but assigned to Supreme Allied Commanders, Atlantic (SACLANT), the Americans possibly to mean British acceptance in principle of a European MRBM force. A memorandum from the Americans stated it was not "appropriate to consider a bilateral understanding on Polaris until the problem of Supreme Allied Commanders, Europe (SACEUR)'s MRBM requirements has been satisfactorily disposed of in NATO." The following line welcomed "the assurance that, in the same spirit of cooperation, the UK would be agreeable in principle to making the necessary arrangements for US Polaris tenders in Scottish ports."[45] Macmillan decided that this ambiguity was worth the political difficulty of accepting an American nuclear submarine base not far from the major population centre of Glasgow and declared himself "fully satisfied that we shall get what we need."[46]

Macmillan's confidence was not altogether unreasonable given that United Kingdom–United States memoranda tended to refer to "Skybolt and Polaris."[47] As soon as the Skybolt deal was settled, the British concurrently discussed obtaining Polaris – to be assigned to SACLANT as part of the Holy Loch arrangement – as a means of averting the tricky question of the NATO MRBM force. Macmillan's calculation may well have been that by agreeing to Skybolt, the principle of the independent deterrent was assured and, through the Polaris NATO MRBM force, its future as well could be assured – if he was nimble enough. Watkinson returned from America to report that a swap of Polaris for Holy Loch was not acceptable to the Americans, who regarded the deal as having been Skybolt for Holy Loch, but that the sale of an American submarine was possible.[48]

Unlike de Gaulle in France, Macmillan was not bothered by reliance on America for advanced high technology. This was essentially a symbolic difficulty not a conceptual one for him, as long as the government maintained control of the fateful decision-making. There had been some pressure to keep up research for a British-designed cruise missile, the X12, eventually to replace Skybolt and preserve Britain's independence, but this in the end was axed.

However, senior voices were raised questioning the method of decision adopted in the Skybolt case – essentially a deal worked out on the hoof by the Prime Minister in America and then implemented as quickly as possible by the Ministry of Defence. Just how bizarre the whole process had been is illuminated by Zuckerman. When he first received a briefing in Washington on Skybolt, he claims the Defense Secretary Thomas Gates barely knew about the project (which according to John Rubel was then little more than a "thin pile of papers"). Two weeks later, Macmillan and Eisenhower had agreed in principle on the Skybolt deal.[49] The Chancellor, Heathcoat Amory, complained to the Minister of Defence about "making such a commitment on the spur of the moment, with no examination of the merits of the various alternative courses" and acutely noted that the government appeared to be "plunging wildly from one weapon to another."[50] Amory continued to argue against Skybolt in cabinet and even questioned continuing with the deterrent at all but, faced with Macmillan's opposition, eventually accepted the cabinet decision to procure Skybolt.[51]

Unknown to the British, two months *before* the deal was finally signed with the Americans, the Missile Panel of the U.S. President's Science Advisory Committee recommended cancelling Skybolt, noting that if it was not cancelled it should be developed as quickly as possible to "capitalize on what may turn out to be a relatively short useful life."[52]

Meanwhile, the RAF was reporting that Skybolt was completely on schedule, was "being given, and would continue to be given, top development priority."[53] To be fair to the RAF, Macmillan was also told directly by Eisenhower substantially the same thing. The American interest in supplying a Polaris force outside of the NATO MRBM force had waned by then and Macmillan was careful not to mention Polaris directly when expressing concern about the future of Skybolt to the President.[54]

Having decided to purchase Skybolt, the British government was put in a difficult position when the programme ran into difficulties and the spectre of cancellation arose. Much of the debate over events in 1962 has centred on why the British failed to pick up the signals from the United States that Skybolt was in trouble.[55] Robert McNamara had identified Skybolt as a candidate for the axe long before the decision was actually made.[56] He was aware of the problems that this might cause for the British but, given that his responsibility was not foreign policy, he did not fully appreciate just how serious those problems might be. A Joint Chiefs of Staff (JCS) paper of February 1961 on principal problems in the political area made no mention of Skybolt as an issue for the British.[57]

Perhaps part of the problem was Britain's difficulty in coming to terms with McNamara, who was something of a phenomenon. The managerial techniques he brought to the Pentagon from the Ford Motor Company, where he had briefly been president, were far beyond anything seen before in the American government. The sophisticated methodologies of programme budgeting and systems analysis, leading to decisions being made on the basis of detailed quantitative comparisons provided by very bright, but also very young, recruits from the "think-tanks" was all very alien to the British who were more ready to trust the reasoning powers developed through a classical education, tempered by intuition and a keen sense of tradition. They called the new American approach "Hitchcraft" after Charles Hitch, McNamara's budget director. On Skybolt, as with all his own programmatic questions, McNamara just presumed that the British would conduct their own studies and reach their own conclusions on need.

The limited studies which had been undertaken in the United Kingdom supported Polaris. Interest in the system had continued following the Skybolt deal. Concurrently, the target coverage of British nuclear planning had been reduced under financial pressures and also, possibly, because of doctrinal pressures from America.[58] The end result of this was that, at the close of 1962, there were fewer strategic objections to the adoption of the Polaris system because the coverage envisaged in the plans could be met by a SLBM force, negating the need to retain the bomber. Polaris now fitted Britain's strategic doctrine, could take the country into the future with a survivable system, and ensured that the policy of nuclear interdependence with the United States would continue.

However, despite this work, the most striking thing about the run-up to the Nassau summit was not so much how insensitive the Americans had been to the dilemma they were handing to the British, but how little the British had begun to think it through for themselves. As early as January 1962, when Aviation Minister Julian Amery had met with President Kennedy and been told that Skybolt was a rotten weapon system, he almost "fell off his chair" with surprise. Kennedy had added, "Why don't you take Polaris?"[59] This hardly suggests an attempt to force Britain out of the nuclear game, and indicates that Kennedy himself was wholly sold by then on the virtues of a sea-based as opposed to an air-based deterrent. Why then had Polaris neither been offered nor requested prior to the meeting at Nassau in December?

It had been obvious for some time that there were some sharp discontinuities between the Eisenhower and Kennedy administrations. The most blatant of these was the anti-nuclear tilt, as Robert McNamara pushed for "flexible response" to reduce dependence on nuclear deterrence. The British had already recognized the need to move in this direction, but were still taken aback at the remorselessness of McNamara's logic, especially when it developed into hostility toward allies holding an independent nuclear capability. It says something for the attention being paid to these trends that the British appear to have missed the significance of McNamara's remarks to the Athens NATO summit (May 1962) that small nuclear forces were dangerous, costly, and prone to obsolescence.

They only took notice when he made the same point publicly the next month at Ann Arbor.[60] It was assumed to be an assault on the legitimacy of the British force (although the main target was undoubtedly France).[61] The Ann Arbor speech was seized upon by the British right-wing press as a crippling blow to the United Kingdom's independent deterrent.[62] The Labour Party, too, exploited the government's embarrassment and McNamara was forced to issue a statement denying that RAF Bomber Command was the target of his speech. This was then followed by an awkward stage in Anglo-American relations following the Cuban Missile Crisis and Dean Acheson's tactless remarks about Britain having lost an empire and not having found a role.[63] There were grounds for suspicion that the Americans were out to push the British out of the nuclear game completely. It was not unreasonable to suppose that Britain was being priced out of its role as a nuclear power.

While the defense professionals preoccupied themselves with the technology of the competing systems, foreign policy professionals had distinctly different preoccupations.[64] As one State Department official put it, "This is basically not a technical military issue, and we are on the wrong wicket – both in the UK and here – if it is being handled through military channels." Other channels produced more opposition to a move to Polaris on both sides of the Atlantic. In both countries, the bureaucracy split between the foreign offices and the military establishments.

Those Americans who criticized the necessity to continue with an independent British nuclear deterrent were not without sympathizers within the British government itself, although this was not of course true of the Prime Minister. Within the Cabinet, there was some scepticism as to whether the whole effort was worthwhile. Edward Heath, the Lord Privy Seal and chief European negotiator, put a higher priority on joining the Common Market; Reginald Maudling, the Chancellor of the Exchequer, was concerned about the additional expenditure involved in preserving a modern deterrent; while Ian Macleod, the Leader of the House of Commons and Rab Butler, the Home Secretary and later Deputy Prime Minister, were apparently not sold at all on the political gains afforded by an independent deterrent.[65] For the anti-nuclear elements within the bureaucracy, the nuclear deterrent was an expensive and wasteful military asset giving limited diplomatic advantage at high political cost. Powerful voices such as the cabinet secretary had questioned for some time whether it would not be better to "reinvest" the nuclear asset before it became worthless, to gain political objectives.[66] The Foreign Office and the State Department were preoccupied with the political fall-out from any British–American nuclear deal. British diplomats at times appeared to support the State Department's arguments against the utility of the independent deterrent because of the threatened cost in other areas of foreign policy.

According to a number of British civil servants interviewed by Neustadt, this was an opportunity to get out of the nuclear business. (Such officials, therefore, were later frustrated with Kennedy for not being tough enough with Macmillan at Nassau.)[67] They seemed to have concluded that the sooner the British were forced out of the nuclear game the better, and that Britain's long-term interests were damaged by sustaining ministerial delusions regarding the "independent" deterrent for longer than was necessary. In this they were, of course, very close to the views of the State Department Europeanists who were pushing to keep the British deterrent linked to manned bombers and thus impose a finite duration on that deterrent.

This meant that the issue in 1962 was not necessarily Skybolt versus Polaris but, in reality, some nuclear strike force or none at all. For Macmillan, the issue with regard to the choice of missile, and the whole method of choosing, had to be judged by reference to the preservation of Britain's nuclear status. In this context, the American decision to axe Skybolt was not necessarily decisive if some way could be found for Britain to take over the development costs.

Macmillan was aware of the political balance inside the three services, which was still geared to manned aircraft as the source of Britain's nuclear deterrent. He was also aware of the dangers of opening up the nuclear issue again. Macmillan's attachment to Skybolt was sincere inasmuch as he had negotiated the deal and defended it on a number of occasions in the House of Commons. This was the current policy and he had come to be identified with it. Scrapping Skybolt would suggest that he had made the wrong decision in 1960. It also risked giving the question undue prominence at a time of sensitive negotiations with the French over the Common Market, as well as opening up the larger question of whether Britain could afford to stay in the nuclear business at a time when financial pressures were, as ever, severe.

For all these reasons, Macmillan was not, at first, inclined to seize this opportunity to get Polaris. His initial reaction was to defend Skybolt and this was his public position until he reached Nassau. If the plan could be rescued, it would avoid a row with the right wing of the Tory Party, deny the Opposition an issue, not annoy the RAF and the aviation industry, and avoid the introduction of potentially awkward issues with the Treasury or the need to place the matter on the cabinet agenda.[68]

Minister of Defence Peter Thorneycroft's attachment to Skybolt was rooted in his cabinet position and role as a leading light of the Tory right wing. This was a time of considerable speculation about the succession to Macmillan. The right wing of the Conservative Party was in an anti-American frame of mind and it was consequently in his interest to avoid the appearance of supplication in the face of American bullying. It is a matter of speculation whether he did all he could to avoid the fall-out over Skybolt in advance of Nassau.[69] His initial response to the troubles faced by Skybolt was to assume that the United States dare not drop it if this would mean a crisis for the British. As a former aviation industry minister, he had defended Skybolt forcefully in the Commons in support of his Prime Minister. Although he claimed, after the event, that, when warned about the possible cancellation of Skybolt, he instantly knew that Polaris was the system to go for, he made no serious attempt at the time to make such a case to the Americans. When he met with Robert McNamara, no progress was made on an alternative to Skybolt. McNamara was not going to offer something before a request was made; Thorneycroft was reluctant to ask for something that had not been offered.

In effect, McNamara had almost inadvertently decided the issue when he arrived in London to meet Thorneycroft. He made public American doubts about the quality of the system and announced to the press that "all five flight tests attempted thus far have failed."[70] As Macmillan later observed, the lady had been "violated." The easy option of a quiet deal to get the programme back on track was therefore stymied by the fact of Skybolt's cancellation becoming public knowledge. It is not unreasonable to suppose that if the violation had not occurred, Skybolt might still have been sustained as an option. Despite a miserable parliamentary session for Thorneycroft, it was not jettisoned prior to Nassau.

Nonetheless, despite the violation, Macmillan still did not want to discuss alternative options with the cabinet prior to meeting Kennedy. By keeping the Skybolt issue alive until he got to Nassau, he would be free to deal on his own terms with the Americans. It also suited him to let the crisis atmosphere grow. Furthermore, while the adverse publicity attracted by Skybolt left the Prime Minister with little choice but Polaris, he could not be certain that a negotiation between the two bureaucracies would produce the desired result. Most seriously, a formal request for Polaris would have required a cabinet debate and allowed the "no deterrent" option time to gain adherents. Tim Bligh (principal private secretary to Macmillan) and Michael Carey (deputy cabinet secretary) both confided to Neustadt that the cabinet opposition to continuing with the deterrent could have made itself felt if only it had been given time to crystallize.

Hence it was in Macmillan's interest to avoid any detailed discussion of the Skybolt problem in advance of his meeting with Kennedy. Once face to face with the President, he would thrash out a deal and face the cabinet with a *fait accompli*, and bounce them (rather than the President) into a Polaris deal. Neither the Chairman of the U.S. Joint Chiefs of Staff (Maxwell Taylor) nor the Chief of the Defence Staff (Lord Mountbatten) were invited to Nassau. Mountbatten was furious, although he was personally content with Polaris. However, while Kennedy was also without his Secretary of State, Macmillan had three heavyweights – Thorneycroft, Lord Home (Foreign Office), and Duncan Sandys (Commonwealth) – who would present powerful backing to any agreement and leave less scope for dissenters in London.[71] In the event, the cabinet was given four hours to give its views on the Polaris offer rather than four days or four weeks. Bligh believed that if they had had more time, the cabinet would have urged a longer study. Macmillan himself believed he had one chance to get Polaris and that this was it.[72]

For the same reason, if there was any resistance to the sale of Polaris on the American side, then he did not want it to gather pace by having his hand revealed too early or lose the opportunity of bringing pressure to bear on Kennedy by making him feel guilty (for denying the British something that was still viable and was only being cancelled for American domestic financial, rather than technical, reasons). The President would be aware of how unfortunate it would be to land a friendly Prime Minister in desperate political trouble in such an insensitive manner.[73]

Macmillan argued at Nassau that there was a moral commitment for the United States to supply the British with a viable nuclear force. Although none of the key players on the American side had any knowledge of what Eisenhower and Macmillan had agreed in 1960 (thereby illuminating the lack of institutional memory which is one of the problems with the American system), McNamara, Rusk, and the President agreed that such a commitment must have been made, whatever the documents said.[74]

The President was well aware in advance of Nassau how important Skybolt's cancellation was for Macmillan: his very "political survival" was involved.[75] In fact, a sale of Polaris to Britain was essentially agreed on by Kennedy in advance before the Nassau meeting.[76] Thus, in some ways it was not the American President who was bounced into giving Britain something he did not want to, it was the British cabinet which was bounced into accepting something it was not sure it wanted. The day after the deal to supply Polaris to Britain, a Skybolt test firing was carried out successfully (Macmillan noted this was "rather provoking").[77]

In the end, despite the absence of Skybolt, the V-bomber force's operational life was much longer than expected: it remained in service until the 1980s when it was used to bomb the Falkland Islands – using missiles mounted with electrical components and fittings made for Skybolt twenty years earlier.[78]

Though the claim was later made that Nassau did set back Britain's European policy and preserved the illusion of a special relationship, the truth of this is debatable. The goal that was apparently lost at Nassau was hardly realizable in any case. De Gaulle's veto of Britain's membership of the Common Market was unlikely to have been averted even if Britain had been left out in the nuclear cold by the United States. Nor would it have made much difference to France's own nuclear programme – although domestic opposition to Britain's privileged nuclear relationship was often couched in terms of its effect on proliferation, notably on France and, potentially, on Germany.

Pushing the British away would merely have encouraged an uncoupled nuclear relationship across the Atlantic, making American command and control of nuclear policy all the more difficult. Furthermore, the European policy of the State Department depended on the Tory moderates who were clustered around the Prime Minister supporting his move into Europe. Bringing down Macmillan might have brought into power the nationalistic right wing of the party or a deeply ambiguous Labour Party. This was the contradiction at the heart of the State Department's opposition to the Nassau deal.

Contradiction or not, it was a reality of which Macmillan was aware. Hence, the advantage of summit diplomacy as a means of ensuring that bureaucratic politics on either side of the Atlantic did not determine Britain's nuclear future. In the end, the politicians weighed up their arguments and took a purely political decision which, rather coincidentally, proved to be the correct strategic choice as far as the weapon system was concerned.

The outcome of Nassau consequently demonstrated that few of the vital decisions of foreign policy can really be attributed to the pulling and hauling of bureaucratic agencies. If the 1960 decision had taken this form, it was because central government allowed the balance of power and interest between the services to shape the outcome. The key absence then was not only the lack of an analytical capability which could have provided a serious technical evaluation of the two alternatives, but the lack of ministerial clout sufficient to force through the logic of such an evaluation against the wishes of the most affected service and in face of the relative indifference of the apparent beneficiary.

By the time of Nassau, this deficiency was already coming to be recognized, as a result of a succession of poor procurement decisions and under the influence of the "McNamara revolution" in the United States. Soon, under Denis Healey, the Ministry of Defence was under tighter control. Macmillan chose Polaris in the end because, in practice, the only alternative was no system at all and the end of any pretence to an independent nuclear deterrent. Macmillan's skill at Nassau was less in convincing Kennedy to let him have Polaris without strings, than in ensuring that there was no serious national or transatlantic debate on the much more drastic option. The paradox was that a government used to a rapid turnover in strategic systems, and taking yet another momentous decision for reasons of short-term expedience at "one of the worst prepared summit meetings in modern times,"[79] stumbled on a solution which lasted for almost three decades.

Notes

1. Graham T. Allison, *Essence of Decision: Explaining the Cuban Missile Crisis* (Boston: Little Brown, 1971). See also Morton Halperin, *Bureaucratic Politics and Foreign Policy* (Washington, D.C.: Brookings Institution, 1974).
2. Peter Nailor, *The Nassau Connection: The Organisation and Management of the British Polaris Project* (London: HMSO, 1988).
3. Ministry of Defence, *The Future United Kingdom Deterrent Force* (Defence Open Government Document 80/23: July 1980).
4. Ian Clark, *Nuclear Diplomacy and the Special Relationship: Britain's Deterrent and America 1957–1962* (Oxford: Clarendon Press, 1994) and John Baylis, *Ambiguity and Deterrence: British Nuclear Strategy 1945–1964* (Oxford: Clarendon Press, 1995). See also Jan Melissen, *Summit Diplomacy and Alliance Politics: The Road to Nassau, December 1962* (University of Leicester: Discussion Papers in Diplomacy, 1995).
5. The Neustadt Report was delivered on 15 November 1963 to the President, who read it at Palm Beach on 17 November before leaving for Texas, where he was assassinated. It was declassified in April 1992 as a case program of the Kennedy School of Government (C16-92-320.0), although a version of it was published in 1970 as Richard Neustadt, *Alliance Politics* (New York: Columbia University Press, 1970). This remains a standard account of the affair. See also Andrew

Pierre, *Nuclear Politics: The British Experience with an Independent Strategic Force 1939–1970* (London: Oxford University Press, 1972).

6. Lawrence Korb, *The Joint Chiefs of Staff: The First Twenty Five Years* (Bloomington: Indiana University Press, 1976).

7. See Martin Navias, *Nuclear Weapons and British Strategic Planning 1955–1958* (Oxford: Clarendon Press, 1991).

8. On the criticisms of Sir Gerald Templer, the Chief of the Imperial General Staff (CIGS), and the First Sea Lord, later the first Chief of Defense Staff (CDS) Mountbatten, see Clark, *Nuclear Diplomacy*, p. 116. The case in the United States was made most forcefully by General Maxwell Taylor. See his book, *The Uncertain Trumpet* (New York: Harper & Row, 1960).

9. These ideas are discussed in Lawrence Freedman, *The Evolution of Nuclear Strategy* (London: Macmillan, 1989).

10. Strategic Air Command was manned by the Air Force.

11. Solly Zuckerman, *Monkeys, Men and Missiles: An Autobiography 1946–1988* (London: Collins, 1988) p. 235, quoting John Rubel of the Department of Defense.

12. Wartime British–American co-operation on nuclear research had been terminated by the McMahon Atomic Energy Act of 1946, which prohibited the passing of nuclear information to foreign nationals. See Timothy J. Botti, *The Long Wait: The Forging of the Anglo-American Nuclear Alliance 1945–1958* (New York: Greenwood Press, 1987).

13. Joseph Wolf (Dir. Office of Political Affairs, U.S. Mission to NATO) to BEL Timmons (State Dept.) 15 Sept. 1958, RG59 Records of the Office of European Regional Affairs, Box 1, Lot 61D252, Folder: RA Correspondence 1958, US NARS.

14. John Thomson, First Secretary, U.K. embassy, Washington 1960, Oral History Conference, Wilson Centre 1992.

15. Eisenhower had agreed in principle to supply Britain with IRBMs (Thor or Jupiter) in a meeting with Macmillan in March 1957. One "concept of deployment" envisaged four squadrons of missiles being transferred to the United Kingdom, two in British hands and two under American control. Eisenhower favoured using the term "lend-lease." Memo of Conversation, Eisenhower and Macmillan, Bermuda 22 Mar. 1957, Whitman Files Int Series Box 3 Folder: Bermuda Conf (3) DDEL.

16. The most useful account of Harold Macmillan's career remains the official two-volume biography by Alistair Horne *Macmillan 1891–1956* (London: Macmillan, 1988) and *Macmillan 1957–1986*

(London: Macmillan, 1989). See also "The Skybolt Crisis 1962," Colloquium by Alistair Horne, 3 Mar. 1983, Woodrow Wilson Centre, Washington, D.C.

17. Memcon, Eisenhower and Dr Libby, 23 Aug. 1958, DDEL.

18. David Schwartz, *NATO's Nuclear Dilemmas* (Washington, D.C.: Brookings Institution, 1983), especially chap. 5.

19. Just how effective was brought home to the British by the shooting down of the U-2 spy plane over Russia in May 1960. Macmillan noted, "It could of course now be said that the bomber is of no use." Macmillan to Lloyd, 7 May 1960, PREM11/2983.

20. Notably by Solly Zuckerman, the chief scientific adviser to the Ministry of Defence. However, Zuckerman was discounted by the RAF as in the RN lobby and too closely linked to Mountbatten. Clark, *Nuclear Diplomacy*, pp. 7–8.

21. Eisenhower was told that Minuteman could do anything Skybolt could and more, Memcon, Eisenhower and Kistiakowsky, 7 May 1960, DDE Diary Series Box 50, Folder: Staff Notes, May 1960 (2), DDEL.

22. The Prime Minister proposed one hundred as a figure likely to make the Americans take the British seriously (one hundred was the eventual order). Macmillan to Watkinson, 10 May 1960, PREM11/3261.

23. Record of meeting, Watkinson and John Rubel (Dep. Dir. of research & engineering, DOD), 25 May 1960, DEFE13/195, PRO.

24. Zuckerman, *Monkeys, Men and Missiles*, pp. 237–53.

25. Sandys to PM, 25 Feb. 1960, DEFE13/195.

26. Ward to PM, 1 Mar. 1960, DEFE13/195.

27. Lawrence Freedman, "British Nuclear Targeting," *Defence Analysis*, vol. 1, No. 2 (1985).

28. Clark, *Nuclear Diplomacy*, pp. 133–34.

29. *Ibid.*, p. 128.

30. Henry Brandon, *Special Relationships: A Foreign Correspondent's Memoirs from Roosevelt to Reagan* (London: Macmillan, 1988), p. 138.

31. In 1958, Polaris (which then had an estimated range of no more than 1500nm) had even been mooted as a possible mobile land-based MRBM system likely to be more acceptable to European allies than the fixed site Thor and Jupiter rockets. Memo, Ballistic Missile Panel to J.R. Killian, 18 July 1958, White House, Office of Special Assistant for Science and Technology, Box 12, Folder: missiles Apr.–Dec. 1958 (3), DDEL.

32. Record of meeting, Macmillan and Watkinson, 20 May 1960, PREM11/3261, PRO.

33. Macmillan to Watkinson, 10 May 1960, PREM11/3261.

34. Memo of Conversation, Eisenhower and Macmillan, Bermuda 22 Mar. 1957, Whitman Files Int. Series Box 3 Folder: Bermuda Conf. (3) DDEL.

35. Alan Pritchard, Oral History Conference, Wilson Centre 1992.

36. *Ibid.*

37. Julian Amery, Oral History Conference, Wilson Centre 1992.

38. Alan Pritchard, Oral History Conference, Wilson Centre 1992.

39. Zuckerman, *Monkeys, Men and Missiles*, p. 266.

40. John Thomson, Oral History Conference, Wilson Centre 1992.

41. Note, A. Earle (DCDS) to Watkinson, 15 Jun. 1960, DEFE13/195 PRO. (Shortly afterwards, the B-70 was reinstated.)

42. A proposal emerged (apparently from Gates) for the United States to supply the British with two or three submarines on a lend-lease basis while the United Kingdom built its own. Polaris missiles would be bought by Britain to put in them, to be assigned to SACLANT, which would count as the U.K. contribution to the NATO MRBM force, relieving Britain of any further NATO MRBM obligations. Note to the PM, Bishop, 2 June 1960, PREM11/3261.

43. Note to the PM, P. de Zulueta, 23 May 1960, PREM11/3261, PRO.

44. Watkinson to Macmillan, 12 May 1960, PREM11/3261, PRO.

45. PM's Visit to Washington, 26–30 Mar. 1960, CAB133/243, PRO.

46. Macmillan to Watkinson, 29 Mar. 1960, DEFE13/195, PRO.

47. Caccia to London, 10 May 1960, PREM11/3261.

48. Watkinson to Macmillan, 7 June 1960, PREM11/3261.

49. Zuckerman, *Monkeys, Men and Missiles*, p. 236.

50. Amory to Watkinson, 22 Apr. 1960, PREM11/3261, PRO.

51. Cabinet Defence Committee meeting, 25 May 1960, PREM11/3261 PRO.

52. Report by the missile panel, 20 July 1960, White House Office of Special Assistant for Science and Technology, Box 12, Folder: Missiles Jul.–Sept. 1960 (6), DDEL. Zuckerman warned Watkinson in September that Skybolt was by no means certain to be developed, Zuckerman to Watkinson, 22 Sept. 1960, DEFE13/195.

53. DRS to MOD, 21 Sept. 1960, DEFE13/195.

54. Macmillan to Eisenhower, 26 Oct. 1960, PREM11/3261.

55. Indeed, warnings had been passed directly to Watkinson by James Douglas (Deputy Secretary of Defence) on 21 Oct. 1960, PREM11/3261.

56. President-elect Kennedy's National Security Policy Committee had identified Skybolt as ripe for ditching even before he took office.

Pre-presidential papers Box 1074, JFKL. A DOD report to McNamara on Skybolt in May 1961 had noted that while there were no serious doubts as to the technical feasibility of Skybolt, justification for the Skybolt "solely as a weapon to be carried by the B-52 appears to be very marginal." Memo re Skybolt, Harold Brown to McNamara, 11 May 1961, NSA.

57. Principal Problems in the Political Area, JCS Paper, 13 Feb. 1961, NARS.

58. See Clark, *Nuclear Diplomacy*, chap. 11 for discussion of this issue.

59. Julian Amery, Oral History Conference, Wilson Centre 1992.

60. Remarks by McNamara, Ann Arbor, 16 June 1961, NSA.

61. Bundy to Kennedy, 1 June 1961, NSA. American opposition to the French nuclear programme was rooted in the fear of subsequent proliferation, especially to the Germans.

62. *Daily Mail*, 18 June 1961.

63. Acheson went on to say, "Britain, attempting to work alone and to be a broker between the US and Russia, has seemed to conduct a policy as weak as its military power." Address by Dean Acheson at West Point, 5 Dec. 1962, Neustadt Papers Box 19, Folder 12/62, Skybolt Folder 2, JFKL.

64. Henry Owen to George Ball, 13 Dec. 1962, NSF Box 238–46, Folder: Trips and Conf: Nassau, Briefing book 12/62, JFKL.

65. Tim Bligh interview with Neustadt, 31 July 1963.

66. In January 1961, Norman Brook had concluded "on purely military grounds, and assuming continued cohesion between the US and UK, there is no great need for an independent British contribution to the strategic nuclear deterrent of the West. And over the years ahead its military value to the West will decline." Memo by the Secretary of the Cabinet, 18 Jan. 1961, CAB133/244.

67. One Foreign Office planner told the Americans that he could not understand why the Prime Minister was pleased with Nassau, adding that a truly multilateral role for Britain in nuclear matters was more attractive for the country. Memcon, Rostow and John Barnes, 2 Mar. 1963, NSF Box 171–173, JFKL.

68. De Zulueta interview with Neustadt, 16 Aug. 1963.

69. Zuckerman commented at the time that Thorneycroft's judgements were all "political" and went so far as to suggest that no British politicians based their decisions on nuclear weapons procurement on strategic grounds, or indeed even understood the realities of such weapons. Zuckerman interview with Neustadt, 12 July 1963.

70. *The Times*, 12 Dec. 1962; Clark, *Nuclear Diplomacy*, p. 372.

71. Melissen, *Summit Diplomacy*. pp. 18–20.
72. The study idea was Bundy's favored solution too.
73. This was Macmillan's sixth encounter with Kennedy and the two had already established a comfortable rapport.
74. Neustadt interview with Dean Rusk, 8 May 1963.
75. Current political scene in U.K., 13 Dec. 1962, NSF Box 238–246, Folder: Trips and Conf: Nassau, Briefing book 12/62, JFKL.
76. See Baylis, *Ambiguity and Deterrence*, p. 324 and Clark, *Nuclear Diplomacy*, pp. 411–12.
77. Macmillan to Kennedy, 24 Dec. 1962, NSA.
78. Zuckerman, *Monkeys, Men and Missiles*, p. 254.
79. George Ball, *The Past Has Another Pattern: Memoirs* (New York: Norton, 1982), p. 265.

Part IV
Towards a United States of Europe: Do Personalities Make a Difference?

8

European Insiders Working Inside Washington: Monnet's Network, Euratom, and the Eisenhower Administration

Pascaline Winand

During the Cold War, key American policy-makers considered European unity as a potential element of stability and prosperity for the West and as a factor of strength for the Atlantic Alliance. They were part of a network of American and European friends and colleagues who seemed to "co-conspire" – a word coined by Walter Hallstein – to further the cause of European integration. The association of these Americans with officials who later occupied high-level positions within the European Communities or in European national governments, or with atypical personalities such as Jean Monnet, who did not necessarily operate from an official power base, dated back to the Second World War or earlier, as in the case of the Dulles–Monnet connection. While there were, of course, other European "insiders" in the United States, this chapter focuses on Jean Monnet (whom Robert Schaetzel, one of Kennedy's foremost advisers in European affairs, once singled out as the "closest friend" of the United States), Max Kohnstamm,[1] one of Monnet's trusted advisers, and their American connections. As we shall see, informal contacts among Monnet's network of Europeanists played a central role in shaping American policy towards European integration in specific cases, while Monnet's American contacts also helped to strengthen his own hand in Europe. Although Monnet's position was not always powerful in Europe, especially during de Gaulle's presidency, his Action Committee for the United States of Europe was not his sole power base. The American connection was an essential element in his lobbying strategy for key European projects. A few examples drawn mostly from the Eisenhower administration will serve to illustrate this point. First, however, it is advisable to introduce some of Monnet's American contacts.

As François Duchêne has pointed out in his excellent biography of Monnet, "Donald Swatland, the Cravath lawyer who would have been a secretary of state had he not refused, said that Monnet had an even better address book in the US than Churchill."[2] Eric Roussel's equally impressive biography of Monnet is a further testimony to the vastness of the latter's network in the United States.

Monnet's American connections were many, both at higher and lower levels of the U.S. government and outside of government. Some predated the Second World War. For example, Monnet had met John Foster Dulles at the Versailles Peace Conference of 1919, where Dulles was acting as legal counsel to Bernard Baruch, the U.S. representative on the Reparations Commission.[3] Dulles and Monnet were of the same vintage year of 1888 and soon became friends.[4] Following the Peace Conference, after a short stint as Deputy Secretary to the League of Nations in Geneva, and after devoting time to reorganizing the Cognac family business, Monnet became the Vice-President of the Société française Blair and Co. Foreign Corp. in Paris.[5] From then on, he was in touch with many of the movers and shakers of Wall Street, as well as leading journalists such as Walter Lippmann, with whom he shared a Eurocentric view of the world and a commitment to multilateralism. McCloy and Dulles were soon numbered among his friends.[6] During those years, Monnet frequently visited Dulles's New York home.[7] During the Second World War,[8] Monnet worked for five years in the British Supply Council in Washington, which Dulles advised as legal counsel. This facilitated frequent contact between the two men, who often exchanged ideas on European unity, while Monnet further strengthened his knowledge of Washington's ins and outs. At that time the Monnet galaxy included top-level officials such as Secretary of War Henry L. Stimson, "Jack" McCloy, by then Stimson's Assistant Secretary, Philip Graham of the *Washington Post*, and Assistant Secretary of State for Economic Affairs Dean Acheson.

As U.S. high commissioner to the new Federal Republic of Germany, McCloy was instrumental in convincing Secretary of State Acheson to support the Schuman Plan, which Acheson first viewed as the biggest cartel ever. Another member of Monnet's network, Professor Robert Bowie, the founder of Harvard's Center for International Affairs, served as general counsel to McCloy and advised him on how to implement Law 27, a ruling from the Allied High Commission which aimed at deconcentrating the German coal and steel industry. Encouraged by McCloy to coordinate work on Law 27 with the Schuman Plan negotiations, Bowie frequently collaborated with Monnet in Paris, and became a friend. Bowie worked closely with U.S. Ambassador David Bruce's staff in Paris and, particularly, with William Tomlinson, a brilliant treasury official, whose dedication to Monnet and European integration knew no bounds. Tomlinson, Bruce (who greatly admired Monnet for "his fertile inventive mind"),[9] and McCloy were instrumental in convincing Washington to endorse Monnet's proposal for a European Defense Community, albeit in a modified form.

Monnet's circle also included George Ball, who later, providentially, became one of Kennedy's top advisers in European affairs. Ball first met Monnet during the Roosevelt administration, in the context of administering Lend-Lease. An excellent lawyer, Ball benefited from high level contacts in political Washington. He helped Monnet word various proposals which allowed him to bypass Washington's hurdles. Among many cooperative ventures with Monnet, Ball became involved in the preparation of the European Coal and Steel Community (ECSC) Treaty after the announcement of the Schuman Plan in May 1950,[10] and thus had the peculiar privilege of being "a private American actively working for a participating government."[11]

During the Eisenhower and Kennedy administrations, Monnet used his American contacts in a way which enabled him to exert considerable influence, although he did not hold any official position during much of the period. This was so even during the Eisenhower administration, which many have described as a military administration. By then, Monnet's contacts included no less than Secretary of State Dulles and President Eisenhower himself. Dulles proved an important asset to Monnet's lobbying efforts in favor of European integration. Contacts at lower echelons in the U.S. government were also useful. There were privileged communication channels through Tomlinson and Bruce in Europe. Other friends and sympathizers of Monnet included Stanley Cleveland, the Consul at the U.S. Embassy in France; Bowie, who headed the State Department's Policy Planning staff; and Undersecretary of State Walter Bedell Smith. In private circles, McCloy (now chairman of the Chase National Bank in New York), Ball, and others were frequently helpful to Monnet. Fruitful associations continued under the Kennedy administration.[12]

While Kennedy's more open administrative style facilitated access to Washington's otherwise heavy organizational machinery, the configuration of American Europeanists in his administration gave Monnet relatively easy access to Washington's decision centers, this despite Kennedy's not initially being a Monnet convert. First as Undersecretary of State for Economic Affairs, then as Undersecretary of State, Ball was an invaluable asset to Monnet. In the area of European affairs, he became the number one man, above all on issues of economics and European integration. Averell Harriman, another of Monnet's friends, was a former member of the Truman administration and one of the instigators of the Marshall Plan who gradually gained influence under Kennedy, rising from roving ambassador to Assistant Secretary of State for Far Eastern Affairs and to Undersecretary of State for Political Affairs. Meanwhile McCloy served as Kennedy's principal disarmament adviser, Bowie came in as a consultant, and Acheson advised Kennedy on foreign policy.[13]

Robert Schaetzel, who worked in the Bureau of European Affairs in the State Department, also belonged to Monnet's circle. He became Ball's senior assistant when the latter was Undersecretary of State for Economic Affairs. As the result of a year's research at the National War College in 1954–55, Schaetzel had become an expert on the peaceful uses of atomic energy. He later proved useful to Monnet in gathering U.S. support for Euratom, and particularly during the negotiations for the U.S.–Euratom agreement.[14] He was also a close friend of Kohnstamm, who became Vice-President of the Action Committee for the United States of Europe.[15]

As chairman of the Policy Planning Council, Walt Rostow, and his assistant, Henry Owen, also played key roles in European affairs. An early supporter of European unity, Rostow had known Monnet since the Second World War while Owen met Monnet for the first time at the beginning of the Kennedy administration. During Monnet's frequent visits to Washington, Owen came to appreciate his intelligence and his knack for obtaining advice on how to lobby most effectively for his views in the United States. Yet Owen's own interest in European integration was first aroused by Kohnstamm.[16]

On the ambassadorial side, Bruce now became ambassador to London, a key position for the negotiations surrounding British entry to the Common Market, a policy strongly advocated by the Kennedy administration and Monnet. Meanwhile, McGeorge Bundy established his quarters in the White House as special assistant to the President for national security affairs. Bundy's "European" credentials included working in Washington for the agency responsible for implementing the Marshall Plan in 1948. During the Kennedy administration Monnet became a friend.[17]

Having thus caught a small glimpse of Monnet's U.S. network, we shall now give examples of how it functioned in practice, mostly under the Eisenhower administration and with an emphasis on Euratom. As we shall see, while some of Monnet's lobbying efforts were crowned with success, some of the policies he and his American friends pursued met with defeat. Did Monnet use the Americans to lobby for his views in Europe, or did

Americans use Monnet, the "inspirateur" as de Gaulle called him, as a tool of American policy in Europe? The question is probably irrelevant as persuasion went both ways and frequently operated in informal ways in a sort of cross-fertilization process.

After North Korea's invasion of South Korea, when Monnet inspired and Pleven presented a proposal for the creation of a European army, the U.S. government opposed the plan, which it suspected to be a device to delay German rearmament and to insure that Germany's second-rate status remained. It also found the plan badly conceived militarily. Although a proponent of European unification, General Eisenhower remarked that the proposal seemed "almost inherently to include every kind of obstacle, difficulty, and fantastic notions that misguided humans could put together in one package."[18] President Truman, Acheson, and George Marshall also initially shirked association with the project. Thanks to the adroit efforts of McCloy and Ambassador to France David Bruce, who urged Eisenhower to talk with Monnet, the Frenchman (who was then known as "Mr. Europe" in the United States) was instrumental in convincing Eisenhower to support the plan by focusing on its political aspects.[19] Eisenhower's change of heart in favor of the European army proposal was eventually a decisive factor in overcoming Truman's and Acheson's initial doubts on the matter.

Both as Supreme Allied Commander, Europe, and as President from 1953, Eisenhower strongly backed European integration, hoping that the European Defense Community (EDC) would lead to a European federation. To him, the political and economic unification of Europe became a *sine qua non* for the permanent security of the West. Without it, there could be no long-term economic health to the region and without economic strength, adequate military force could not be maintained. Eisenhower's recurring nightmare was that the Russians would spend the United States into bankruptcy. A united Europe would prevent this from happening as it would strengthen the alliance, not only by providing desirable markets for American goods but also by contributing more to common defense. The EDC offered the prospect of cutting down the number of American troops on the continent, which would further reduce costs.

From the very beginning of the Eisenhower administration, Monnet, convinced that the ECSC and the EDC would not succeed without American backing, lobbied his American contacts to send clear signals of American support for European integration. Along with Adenauer and Alfred Gruenther, Eisenhower's former chief-of-staff at SHAPE, Monnet first succeeded in convincing Dulles and Eisenhower to appoint David

Bruce (although he was a prominent Democrat) not only as U.S. Observer to the EDC Interim Committee but also as American Representative to the ECSC, and observer of progress made towards the creation of a European political community. For Monnet, this appointment symbolized the U.S. commitment to European integration efforts as a whole, not just in the field of defense. In case the EDC should fall by the wayside, Monnet tried to convince Americans that the ratification of the EDC was not the only decisive factor for the advancement of European unification.[20] As part of this strategy, he and his collaborators at the High Authority launched a full-blown lobbying effort in Washington to obtain the official reaffirmation of American support for the fledgling ECSC, in part through an American loan to it. Monnet hoped that such a loan would not only strengthen the ECSC, but would also indirectly enhance the chances of the EDC by stressing U.S. support for European integration. Monnet insisted that the loan must be of an amount sufficient to "capture European imagination" and give a sufficient push to get the EDC Treaty ratified. An agreement was eventually signed on 23 April 1954. Unfortunately this was too late to rescue the EDC.[21]

When the EDC foundered in the French Assembly on 30 August 1954, American supporters of European integration were disappointed. Their reaction to the Messina Conference in early June 1955 was lukewarm, all the more so since one of its only tangible results seemed to have been to divest Monnet of his post as President of the High Authority of the ECSC. The disenchantment with European integration was best evidenced by Bruce's resignation in January 1955 from his post as U.S. Representative to the ECSC (his appointment had symbolized, in the words of Dulles, "the great importance which the President and the US Government attach to the movements in Europe to develop a unified six nations Community"[22]). In addition, Dulles was noncommittal toward Monnet's plea for a U.S. Mission to the ECSC, which Monnet asked to be kept separate from European intergovernmental organizations, such as the Organization for European Economic Cooperation (OEEC) or NATO, as a confirmation of the American commitment to supranationality. Bruce was not replaced until 1956. By then, however, what was popularly known as the "Relaunching of Europe" was well on its way, and Monnet proved resilient.

Shortly after leaving the High Authority, Monnet decided to launch his Action Committee for the United States of Europe, whose creation he proudly announced on 13 October 1955. He then set out to convince Dillon, Dulles, and Eisenhower of the importance of his Committee.[23]

Dulles, who, when talking to Adenauer in the United States shortly after Messina, had expressed regret that his friend Monnet was no longer in a position to help in the area of European integration, now decided to resume collaborating with him, despite the fact that the Frenchman no longer occupied an official position.

On 10 October 1955 – three days before Monnet launched his Committee – the State Department announced Eisenhower's decision to establish a separate American Mission to the ECSC as a token of the importance the United States attached to the Community. Walton Butterworth was later appointed to the position, with the special rank of ambassador. He subsequently also became representative to the EEC and Euratom, an appointment which was intended as a further demonstration of U.S. support for European supranational integration.[24] Monnet's efforts, therefore, were eventually crowned with success.

Why did it take so long for the Eisenhower administration to reaffirm U.S. support for European integration after Messina? First of all, there was a lack of agreement within the State Department and among U.S. representatives abroad on what was meant by "European integration."[25] By the end of 1955, the Eisenhower administration, in part through Monnet's coaching and that of other "good Europeans," had finally opted for the supranational six-nation approach as opposed to "cooperative arrangements" such as the OEEC which did not involve transfers of sovereignty in favor of a supranational authority such as the High Authority of the ECSC. The lukewarm attitude of the United States towards the Free Trade Area negotiations initiated by the British and, subsequently, towards the European Free Trade Association, can be traced back to this tendency to favor "genuine integration" *à la Monnet*, not only because of the "expected economic and technical advantages,"[26] but also because this kind of integration was thought to lead to European political union. Only such a union could capture the imagination of European nations and especially of West Germany. By channeling German energies towards European integration, one would increase economic efficiency in Western Europe, while creating a new link between Germany and the West, thereby strengthening the Atlantic alliance.

Another reason for maintaining a relatively reserved attitude towards European integration after the EDC saga was that the defeat of the EDC had shown that it was best for the United States to speak with a soft voice. Therefore, as a matter of strategy, the U.S. administration tried to refrain from making too many public comments on European integration, except when asked to do so by Europeans. Spaak and Monnet encouraged such discreet tactics until well after Messina.

Yet the Americans, acting from the sidelines, exerted considerable influence on the EEC and Euratom negotiations. Top policy-makers frequently listened to Monnet, something which partially explains why American support for Euratom and the Common Market initially had a lopsided appearance. Although some of his closest advisers, including Kohnstamm and Pierre Uri, thought that the Committee must take the Common Market more seriously, Monnet had a strong tendency to place Euratom first on his list of priorities and the EEC second. Whereas Euratom could "identify the Community with the power of the future and capture public imagination," Monnet and his emissaries told American officials in April 1955 that the Common Market seemed to be "a pretty nebulous project"[27] for the Six, and especially for the French, with a slim chance of being ratified. For a while, priorities in the Eisenhower administration closely paralleled those of Monnet. Both the lack of in-depth discussions of the potential effects of a European Common Market on the United States, prior to the signing of the Rome Treaties, and frequent statements by Dulles, who insisted that the approval of Euratom should not be delayed by Common Market negotiations, substantiated the priority of Euratom in high-echelon American policy making.[28]

Besides being an asset for European integration, Euratom had other qualities to commend itself. Dulles and Eisenhower hoped to use it to discourage the production of atomic weapons in Europe and prevent nuclear proliferation,[29] in part by dissuading Europeans from building an isotopic separation plant for the enrichment of uranium.[30] But while the State Department and the White House mostly lent a sympathetic ear to Monnet and Euratom, the project encountered substantial opposition from parts of the American administration. This included the American Atomic Energy Commission (AEC) and its chairman, Lewis Strauss.

The State Department and the AEC were mostly at odds on the bilateral agreements with future Euratom members. Strauss, doubting that Euratom would soon come into existence and anxious to show Congress progress in the peaceful uses of atomic power abroad, was reluctant to delay bilateral negotiations. By contrast the State Department insisted that bilateral agreements be postponed in order to convince the Six that they would be better off dealing with the United States on a multilateral rather than a bilateral basis, thereby strengthening the Euratom concept. Dulles, urged on by Monnet and others, made a special effort to delay a bilateral agreement with Germany since the French might resent it greatly, and since giving substantial bilateral aid to Germany before the Euratom Treaty was signed up might weaken their interest in the supranational approach. Wanting to move toward a more equal relationship with the

United States, Monnet wrote to the members of his Committee that separate bilateral agreements between each European government and the United States would lead to a situation where Europe would become the "atomic satellite" of the United States.[31]

Meanwhile, Dulles also defended Euratom to the British. By early 1956, two plans for European nuclear development competed with each other: an OEEC plan conceived as a cooperative enterprise, and the Spaak Committee's study for a European atomic organization with supranational characteristics. No longer participating in the Spaak discussions, the British became determined promoters of the OEEC plans, to the detriment of the Spaak proposals.[32] The United States was not supportive of such tactics, and Dulles made it clear to Macmillan that the Americans favored creating an atomic agency in Europe that would appeal to the Germans while also reconciling French and German interests.[33] In addition, while the United States could conceivably provide classified information to a group of countries acting as a single state, such as a supranational Euratom, for security reasons it could not do so for a loose association of countries such as the OEEC.[34]

Dulles further came to Euratom's rescue by pointing out to its U.S. opponents that Euratom's high degree of supranationality guaranteed an integrated and more efficient control than would be possible were atomic energy programmes to be administered by several national authorities.[35] The alternative was far from attractive: uncontrolled national atomic programmes leading to atomic weapons programmes – in other words, nuclear proliferation. Monnet's thinking on the matter did not differ much from that of Dulles: he was hopeful that France and other European countries might one day renounce atomic weapons. This of course made him *persona non grata* with the French Commissariat général à l'énergie atomique.

Meanwhile, the advocates of the six-nations approach within the American administration further insisted that a Euratom safeguards system would not necessarily compete with the universal control system of the International Atomic Energy Agency (IAEA). Despite the merits of the IAEA, the agency could not be expected to have access to classified material and, since it included the Russians, it would "undoubtedly be in for a good deal of rough sailing." As progress toward the IAEA would be relatively slow, why not rely on a regional control system such as Euratom to serve as a stepping stone to the IAEA? Once the IAEA was completely operative, Euratom might then be treated as one nation by the International Agency.[36] To be sure, the issue of control loomed large in the negotiation of the Euratom Treaty and in debates on Euratom within the Monnet Committee. Control by Euratom, as Monnet well knew, was one of the preconditions for support of Euratom by the German socialists, who were key members of his Committee.

If the control of the United Nations or, for that matter, that of the United States was not replaced by European control, Monnet told Kohnstamm in mid-July 1956 that "there would be no Euratom and no Europe. The US must choose."[37] On the French side, Robert Marjolin, who also had many friends in the United States, put it bluntly: "if the American control were not suppressed, Euratom would never hold the ground against French nationalism."[38] But while Monnet got satisfaction on that point, Guy Mollet's announcement in July that Euratom would not prove an obstacle to a potential French decision to build nuclear weapons flew right in the face of the demands of the German socialists, who insisted on an exclusively pacific Euratom. Monnet and his team now set out to find other ways to breathe life into Euratom. Here again, U.S. support ranked high among Monnet's lobbying arsenal.

Suez helped magnify the need for energy sources that would reduce Europe's excessive dependence on Middle Eastern oil. But something else was still needed to seize upon that momentum. Soon, the Monnet Committee recommended appointing a committee of "Wise Men" to draw up an emergency programme for the production of atomic energy in Europe, with concrete indications of financial and research needs. The committee would start operating even before Euratom was set up. The idea emerged on 2 September in conversations between Monnet, his assistants Kohnstamm and Van Helmont, and the Canadian Secord, who acted as Monnet's technical adviser.[39] The French Prime Minister, Guy Mollet, soon gave the full approval of his government for the proposal of the Three Wise Men. By 6 November, Adenauer and Mollet wrote to Paul-Henri Spaak asking him to "undertake the necessary démarches" to nominate the Three Wise Men.[40]

The Wise Men committee, consisting of Louis Armand, Franz Etzel, and Francesco Giordani, was effectively established during a meeting of the foreign ministers of the Six at Brussels on 16 November 1956. Their mandate was "to report within two months on what quantities of atomic energy can be produced in [the] six countries in the foreseeable future, and on the means whereby this can be achieved."[41] The next day, Monnet told American Ambassador Dillon that "a broad scale and generous program of US support for Euratom, both in the supply of materials and in technical cooperation," might do much to repair Atlantic solidarity. Monnet recommended showing strong American support for Euratom as soon as the treaty had been signed.[42] Here again, as he had done with the U.S. loan to the ECSC, Monnet hoped to use the United States as the midwife of another European venture.

When the Three Wise Men handed in their report to the Six in May 1957, "A Target for Euratom" already contained the seeds of the U.S.–Euratom agreement, which Kohnstamm envisioned as a kind of atomic Marshall Plan.[43] Pointing out that the average cost of electricity in the United States amounted to about two-thirds of what it was in Europe, "Target" spoke of the benefits to be derived by the United States from "the large-scale industrial application of atomic power" in Europe. Europeans, on the other hand, would gain from American technical expertise in atomic energy, while the United States would also provide fissile materials to get the power plants going. U.S. and European industries, as well as the American and the European Atomic Energy Commissions, would undertake joint projects to develop new reactors or adapt old ones. "Target" spoke of a "two-way traffic, a close partnership as equals" which could be built "between the US and Euratom and their respective industries."[44] The report insisted that a joint U.S.–European programme would be a key asset in fending off the growing economic menace of excessive dependence on Middle Eastern oil. In order to reduce fuel imports, the report (thereby well deserving its name) aimed at a target of 15-million-kilowatt nuclear-power capacity within ten years. Well in the Monnet tradition, this ambitious figure was posted much more as a political necessity to emphasize the urgency of the situation, than as a technically realistic target.[45] Technical realism and political necessity were frequently at odds when the Three Wise Men, the so-called "technicians," and those whom Kohnstamm called the half-Wise, who tended to emphasize the political stakes, set about to produce the final report. Kohnstamm, the German Dr. Regul, and Secord, belonged to that group, and wrote most of the report, after consulting with European and American experts.[46]

All told, bringing about the final report was an exhausting experience, especially for Kohnstamm, the Wise Men's Secretary. As Adenauer's favorite and as Vice-President of the High Authority, Etzel was a very busy man, although he was useful for providing infrastructure and money for writing the report.[47] Yet he did not want to go too far, especially since "the Germans were not all over-enthusiastic" about the initiative, and this included Strauss, who "accumulated problems as the minister of atomic affairs." A well-known and well-connected Italian scientist, Giordani was cautious about not damaging his professional reputation, while Armand was brilliant but also rather chaotic. On the whole, the Wise Men were rather reluctant to follow Monnet – who communicated with

Luxembourg through "enormous telexes"[48] – and give political clout to the report. During the Three Wise Men's visit to the United States, Kohnstamm was in the uncomfortable position of having to steer the wheel from the back seat.

The Three Wise Men planned to come to the United States in early 1957. Just a few days before Christmas 1956, Strauss and Dulles issued a press release inviting them to America for conversations with government officials and the private sector.[49] Meanwhile, Monnet came to the United States in mid-January 1957 to prepare the ground for a speedy ratification of the Euratom Treaty. Upon returning to Europe, he emphasized to the members of his Committee the importance of establishing an association between Euratom and the United States through Euratom that would then lead to a partnership between equals in mutual interest.[50] Monnet insisted that such a mutually profitable agreement would be a first for the old Europe that since the Second World War had been receiving all too many "aids and grants." The Wise Men would help define the contents of the agreement.[51] Further tilling the ground for a profitable visit of the Wise Men and their ally, Kohnstamm, Monnet then sent numerous letters to his American friends, making sure that they understood the true significance of the visit.[52] He took special care to introduce Kohnstamm, who was officially to accompany the Three Wise Men and whom he presented as his very intimate friend. In mid-January, Monnet's friend, Swatland, had arranged for a private meeting between Monnet and Lewis Strauss. Monnet now asked him to organize a similar meeting with Kohnstamm, the Wise Men, and Lewis Strauss. Writing to Dulles's secretary, Monnet asked that Kohnstamm's phone calls be treated as his own had been in the past, and go directly through to Dulles. Monnet then wrote to Dulles that he should fully trust Kohnstamm and asked for a favor. Could Dulles please arrange for his two "very good friends," the Wise Men Louis Armand and Franz Etzel, to be received by the President?[53] Monnet further prepared the ground for the visit of the Three Wise Men by sending Kohnstamm ahead as their emissary. Ambassador Butterworth, the U.S. representative to the ECSC, accompanied the Wise Men to the United States, which gave an added aura of officialness to the visit. Butterworth was invaluable in suggesting useful tactics for dealing with Washington pundits: before leaving for the United States he told Kohnstamm not to ask for money, but preferably for other kinds of help.

"The Wise Men are not coming to Washington with hat in hand and palm extended," Kohnstamm told journalists in Washington. They were coming to see how Europe could use atomic energy to be less dependent on Middle East oil supplies for its own survival. Thus introduced, the Wise Men and their entourage[54] arrived in the United States on 3 February. The next day, Dulles met with them and arranged for the group to see the president.[55] During the meeting with Dulles and other officials, including Bowie, Butterworth, Smith, Schaetzel, and Cleveland, all of them belonging to Monnet's network, Armand made a striking presentation on the need for Euratom. Atomic energy, he emphasized, was necessary both to meet the energy gap and to shield European countries from economic underdevelopment, which could lead to political unrest.

Two days later, Eisenhower concluded an interview with Etzel by giving assurances that Euratom would have the full backing of his administration and himself. On 8 February, a joint communiqué welcomed "a fruitful two-way exchange of experience and technical development, opening a new area of mutually beneficial action on both the governmental and the industrial level and reinforcing solidarity within Europe and across the Atlantic." In order to help the Wise Men with technical problems in meeting their objective, the communiqué recommended appointing a joint group of American and European experts. The State Department and the AEC having thus publicly given their blessing to Euratom, the Wise Men proceeded to obtain the support of American industry.

The trip proved successful. But even though Monnet had paved the way for a successful venture and Eisenhower backed the whole enterprise (he reportedly told Dulles that: "if these fellows tell the experts to go to Timbuctoo, they must go to Timbuctoo"[56]), there were still many loose ends left undone. Much background work had also been necessary. For example, Kohnstamm, not fully trusting the Wise Men's political sense, arranged to have a private conversation with AEC Chairman Lewis Strauss before the Wise Men met him and without them knowing about it. For Kohnstamm, the Wise Men had not "the faintest idea . . . how to deal with the Americans . . . in these informal ways in which you can do so much in the US."[57] Monnet and Kohnstamm were, indeed, well versed in these ways. Negotiations with the AEC and the State Department, Kohnstamm remembered vividly, "were carried out partly in the bathroom of Gerry Smith's house, where we had dinner together. Because you couldn't do it with Etzel and company present. There weren't that many rooms, so I remember being in a real bathroom talking with Gerry Smith and I don't know who from the Atomic Energy Commission."[58]

In March 1956, Washington confirmed that American experts, as had been decided[59] during the Wise Men's visit to the United States, would be available to go to Luxemburg by the middle of the month. It was the result of the common initiative of Bowie, Smith, and Kohnstamm.[60] On

22 March,[61] an AEC delegation composed of four top technicians from the AEC[62] arrived in Luxemburg. They came several times and soon turned into a single team with the Europeans, working together at Kohnstamm's *Maison Rouge* in Luxemburg with pleasant interludes. The atmosphere was one of friendship:

> Our house was their home, we had dinners and meals . . . We had endless meetings. Vanderweyden who had been a professional trumpetist in a jazz band, played the trumpet . . . Here were open-minded technicians, nice fellows, who began to see they were in a major political adventure, backed by their own President, so they went all out, no holds barred . . . We were really one group trying to solve the problem . . . no one in the newspapers noted we were working together.[63]

On this last count, Armand could, provisionally, utter a sigh of relief, for the CEA did of course not look with any sympathy on collaboration with U.S. experts.

"Target" was completed on 4 May. It was a convincing plea for diminishing European overdependence on Middle East oil. It also ran counter to many of the CEA's ambitions. Arguing that American light-water reactors were technologically superior to the French natural uranium ones, the report directly challenged French hopes for a preferential market in the Community.[64] By 7 May, Strauss issued a communiqué acknowledging the Wise Men's report and pledging American technical and material help. That same day, Monnet's Committee distilled the political heart of the report in a short statement:

> Our September resolution, proposing the nomination of the "Three Wise Men," emphasized that "the power supplies of Western Europe determine the progress or decadence of our countries." The work of the "Three Wise Men" confirms, if confirmation were necessary, the gravity of our situation and the urgency of rapid action. The results of their mission show that it is necessary and possible to achieve, with the help of the US, Canada, and Great Britain, an atomic electricity production programme whose target is the installation in our countries by 1967 of nuclear centres of power of 15 million kW, giving an electricity production greater than those of all the conventional power stations and dams which exist today in France or Germany.[65]

On the whole the press was favorable.

Once the Euratom and EEC treaties were signed, the road was open to an American joint programme with Euratom. The Soviet Union's launching of Sputnik in October 1957 facilitated the efforts of Euratom supporters. Not only did it directly challenge the credibility of the American nuclear guarantee to Western Europe, but it was also a patent demonstration that the Soviet Union had surpassed the United States in rocket technology. How could the United States meet the challenge? One option was to try to catch up with the Soviet Union by emphasizing research in rocket development. Another was to concentrate on developing civilian atomic power, an area in which the Soviet Union seemed to lag behind. Seen in this light, Euratom offered the opportunity to test American nuclear power plants on a large scale.

Two Europeanists from the State Department, Schaetzel and Cleveland, made a special trip to Luxemburg to discuss the odds of a joint U.S.–Euratom programme with Kohnstamm prior to his departure for the United States in October 1957.[66] Kohnstamm hoped that an agreement with the United States would make all the difference between a research Euratom, which to him was not very exciting, and a power-producing Euratom. The Action Committee and the same team which had drafted Target would lay the ground for the agreement.

On 1 January 1958, the Euratom and EEC treaties went into effect. Yet Euratom did not get off to a flying start. Armand, its new president, fell sick at the very beginning of his mandate. The railwayman, missing Paris and ill-at-ease as an administrator, suffered a serious breakdown. For internal political reasons in the Netherlands, Kohnstamm was denied a seat on the Euratom Commission. In addition, the Six failed to decide on a location for the new institutions. In fact, Euratom was largely inoperative during the first year of its checkered existence; there was a cruel lack of leadership. While nominations for the Euratom Commission lagged behind, and the Commission subsequently failed to meet or to achieve any results, Kohnstamm was Euratom for the Americans.[67] Not surprisingly, in the light of these unpromising beginnings, the American connection and a proposed agreement with Euratom acquired added importance as possible galvanizers. Armand felt that without the programme with the Americans, Euratom would not amount to much.[68]

In the United States, interest in the development of a civilian atomic energy programme showed in the organization of numerous meetings and conferences shortly after the Sputnik shock. In mid-October, Columbia University, where Eisenhower had once been president, hosted a conference on American atomic power at Arden House while the Atomic Industrial Forum held its fourth annual conference about one week later. Kohnstamm, whom Monnet trusted to negotiate the U.S.–Euratom joint agreement, attended both meetings. He also took part in a Council on

Foreign Relations (COFR) study group on Western European integration which Ball chaired and which mainly investigated ways Euratom could cooperate with the United States in building power stations in Europe. While in the United States, Kohnstamm also touched base with the State Department and the AEC. Gerard Smith, who had just been appointed as Assistant Secretary of State for Policy Planning, assured him of his support while suggesting that the initiative in the United States should come from Admiral Strauss. Subsequent conversations confirmed that the way to obtain the joint agreement was not by exerting political pressure via the Joint Committee on Atomic Energy (JCAE) on Congress, but by going through the AEC and the President.[69] The problem with the AEC was that it leaned towards favoring a programme of subsidies to prop up the American atomic industry by making it more competitive in foreign markets. The alternative, a joint demonstration programme with Euratom and the concomitant development of U.S.-type reactors in Europe on a large scale, had not yet won favor. In an effort to court the top man at the AEC, Kohnstamm met with Strauss twice during his stay.[70]

Kohnstamm then set out to lobby the Export-Import Bank. Monnet's friend Samuel Waugh, who was now the president and the chairman of the board of directors of the bank, was the ideal contact. With him, Kohnstamm discussed the feasibility of a loan to Euratom, thereby setting the stage for a new "political" loan such as the previous American loan to the ECSC. After Kohnstamm had left the United States, Schaetzel, who had worked for Waugh in the past, further pressed his former boss to bring in the Export-Import Bank to support Euratom. Monnet himself, he anticipated, would do the rest of the work during Waugh's imminent visit to the ECSC in Luxemburg. At the end of October, Kohnstamm, who had in practice not had time to discuss his plans with Monnet beforehand, now had the opportunity for a good chat. He found Monnet "entirely in favour" of the agreement.[71] During the following months, Kohnstamm and his American friends lobbied continuously for the agreement.

Meanwhile, toward the end of November, Kohnstamm called a meeting in Luxemburg with the Americans to evaluate the feasibility of a joint U.S.–Euratom programme. Kohnstamm insisted that Euratom needed an outside stimulus from the United States right from the moment of its official birth in January 1958. Without American backing, he said, there would be few U.S.-type reactors constructed in Europe, and Europe would be left mostly with voluminous graphite-gas reactors (with which the French and the British had the most experience). In order not to stake Europe's atomic future on just one type of reactor, he suggested, the

United States and Euratom might share the cost of experimenting with at least four demonstration power reactors of different types in the European market. The graphite-gas reactor, much favored by the French military because its by-product of plutonium could be used in bombs, would thus be only one of the demonstration reactors. One must also experiment with a heavy-water natural-uranium reactor, with which Canada had the most expertise, and of course, with those reactors preferred by the United States: General Electric's Boiling Water Reactor (BWR) and Westinghouse's Pressurized Water Reactor (PWR). By the end of the meeting, participants agreed that Euratom's proposal for a joint programme with the United States should only speak of the "extensive development of U.S.-type reactors in Europe."[72] This had far-reaching implications for Euratom's future.[73]

In the meantime, Schaetzel wrote to Kohnstamm emphasizing the need to foster high-level U.S. backing for the joint programme in order to silence voices in the United States that criticized it for building reactors in Europe rather than at home. Monnet could do the necessary lobbying in America and persuade Eisenhower and the "other big bosses" to support the project. But it was equally crucial to "insure a sympathetic and effective staff follow-through" of the project in the United States, to compensate for Euratom's lack of experienced staff during its first months of operation. Lastly, Schaetzel suggested that the Monnet Committee hire experts to draft a detailed plan addressing the technical and organizational aspects of the proposal and counseled putting pressure on Douglas Dillon, the newly appointed Deputy Undersecretary of State for Economic Affairs, who was responsible for supervising the entire American foreign aid programme and would most likely be charged with defending the project in Congress. In the end, Dillon's role indeed proved decisive. His testimony in favor of a Euratom-controlled safeguard system helped assuage the reservations of the "redoubtable" JCAE in Congress.[74]

Philip Farley of AEC and Kohnstamm met twice in mid-December to devise a strategy for using Monnet most effectively. Monnet was scheduled to come to Washington in January. By that time, Armand would have taken up his functions as president of Euratom and could "get agreement in principle from the Euratom Commission that Euratom ought to undertake a power demonstration programme for the construction of a million kW by a given date, *mainly in enriched uranium power reactors.*"[75] Once in Washington, Monnet could then easily point out that a detailed "prospectus" was necessary to work out the terms of the agreement and ask the United States to agree to provide technical, political, and economic experts in order to help Euratom draft a preliminary prospectus. Kohnstamm was hesitant to ask the advice of experts from the national atomic energy programmes of the Six, who might have lacked enthusiasm for the project in view of their own national interests. He thus once again turned to American experts.[76]

Monnet arrived in the United States at the end of January 1958. After lengthy discussions with him, Schaetzel and his staff secretly prepared memoranda outlining points to be raised with Strauss in a forthcoming meeting: Euratom must truly be a joint programme and support for it should come soon since Congressional hearings were imminent and Euratom member countries were inclined to develop their programmes along national lines. Monnet and the Americans agreed that although the United States must take the initiative to speed up the process this must not be done openly. Confidential discussions with Armand and other Euratom Commission members to prepare for a visit by Armand to the United States and the release of a statement showing a U.S.–Euratom agreement in principle to a joint programme would do the job. American experts would fly to Europe to assist the Euratom Commission in drafting the details of the programme. Soon Strauss and Acting Secretary of State Christian Herter recommended to Eisenhower that he approve in principle a cooperative U.S.–Euratom agreement, the contents of which mostly followed Monnet's, Kohnstamm's, and Schaetzel's advice. Eisenhower obliged, and Monnet then met with him. The proposed agreement planned to encourage the construction of several U.S.-type reactors. Europeans would bear most of the cost, while the United States would provide about half the financing for the reactors with a loan. It would also foster U.S.-European research cooperation in developing U.S.-type reactors to be constructed by Euratom, as well as advanced reactor types. Upon Monnet's and Schaetzel's recommendation, the programme was to be made public only after talks were held with the Euratom Commission in order to preserve its political impact and to demonstrate that the initiative had come from the Europeans.[77]

During the next few months, the strategy worked out by Schaetzel, Monnet, and Kohnstamm unfolded. But Kohnstamm had his own Scylla and Charybdis: "Scylla: asking too much of the Euratom Commission. Charybdis: disappointing the Americans."[78] Talks began in mid-February 1958 in Luxemburg. Schaetzel, Van der Weyden, and some of their colleagues joined Butterworth and members of the Euratom Commission to signify American interest in the programme. A working party with European and American experts was set up to study the possibility of initiating a U.S.–Euratom programme for the development of full-scale prototype reactors and to prepare for Armand's visit. In late February,

Butterworth transmitted to Armand an invitation from Dulles and Strauss to come to Washington in April to discuss the U.S.–Euratom programme. This invitation now gave an aura of officialdom to the proposed agreement. Unfortunately, illness prevented Armand from going, and Kohnstamm had to go in his stead. In early March 1958, he flew to the United States. He wanted to develop a schedule and a procedure that the working party should follow in order best to achieve congressional ratification of the joint programme before Congress adjourned in the summer.[79] The study group then met in Luxemburg from 20 March to 3 April. American experts reported to Butterworth, while representatives of Euratom reported to Kohnstamm.[80] The result was a detailed first draft of a "Memorandum of Understanding" signed by Kohnstamm, Butterworth, and Cook, which contained the essence of a future joint agreement.[81] Despite this auspicious beginning, talks soon bogged down.

The reason for this delay was again the protracted debate on the control by Euratom of its own safeguard arrangements, in other words "Euratom's control in opposition to Vienna control" or U.S. control.[82] The debate, which Monnet and Kohnstamm had thought concluded, was now reopened. As we have seen, Monnet felt very strongly that a European organization controlled by the United States would fail to be a first step towards a more equal relationship with America. He and Kohnstamm also rightly feared that De Gaulle, who had just returned to power, would never accept a joint U.S.–Euratom programme under American control. While the State Department mostly sided with Euratom, the AEC insisted on unilateral inspection rights by the United States to prevent Euratom from using American nuclear materials for military purposes. Was it wise to encourage Euratom to develop its own regional controls? While the International Agency in Vienna was busy developing global controls, would not Comecon then be tempted also to establish its own regional controls?[83] This point remained a bone of contention even though the chairman of the AEC had previously given his approval to the preliminary draft of the Euratom Treaty back in March 1957. Failing to achieve a common position on this issue, the State Department and the AEC were ill-equipped to face Congress and request a joint agreement with Euratom. In the meantime, by the beginning of May, the joint working group, which had met in Washington to put the last touches to the memorandum of understanding, had completed its work. Hoping to speed up negotiations, Monnet met with Dulles on 10 May. By the end of the month, the Euratom Council of Ministers signed the Memorandum of Understanding and initialed an Agreement of Cooperation. Yet the AEC continued to object to signing these documents, leading the *New York Times* to pinpoint "a disturbing lack of coordination among different government agencies" and to criticize the AEC for objecting "to an agreement already negotiated."[84]

In a last-minute effort, Kohnstamm asked for an appointment in New York with André Meyer, an old friend of Monnet and a very respected merchant banker with a top position at Lazard Frères. Meyer promised he would call Dulles and try to put some pressure on the White House. Acheson said he also would intervene in favor of the agreement. In addition, Kohnstamm, with the help of Monnet's journalist friends and George Ball, mounted a huge press campaign in the United States in favor of the agreement. In the end, Eisenhower ended the debate by siding with his Secretary of State. By 17 June, the president had approved the Memorandum of Understanding, which was then signed by Strauss, Dulles, and Eisenhower himself. On 23 June, Eisenhower sent an agreement to Congress for approval. The memorandum set forth two objectives:

A. To bring into operation by 1963, within the European Atomic Energy Community, large-scale power plants using nuclear reactors of proven types, on which research and development has been carried to an advanced stage in the US, having a total installed capacity of approximately one million kilowatts of electricity and under conditions which approach the conventional energy costs in Europe. B. To initiate immediately a joint research and development program centered on these types of reactors.[85]

This was by no means the end of the checkered career of the U.S.–Euratom agreement. The JCAE seemed in no hurry to initiate hearings on the subject. Monnet, Armand, Kohnstamm, and their American contacts then persistently lobbied the JCAE and the administration for its rapid approval. Somewhat unwisely, however, they also came to identify the success of Euratom with the success of the joint programme. In early July, Kohnstamm suggested that Monnet should write to Dulles and McCloy. The latter could prove useful to Monnet once more because he was a good friend of McCone, who had just been appointed the new chairman of the AEC. On 13 July, Monnet wrote to Dulles asking him to use his "influence and energy to make sure that the agreement pass[ed] Congress before the holidays." As a postscript, he added: "I understand that Sen[ator] Clinton Anderson is the difficulty and might be extremely susceptible to some attention!"[86] Senator Anderson, a Democrat from New Mexico and the influential vice-chairman of the JCAE, was indeed the main roadblock. An undiplomatic move on the part of President Eisenhower further complicated matters.

Hearings on the U.S.–Euratom programme were scheduled to start before the JCAE on 16 July, but the committee decided to delay them for another week. A few days earlier, Eisenhower had written a letter to the ranking Republican member of the Appropriations Committee on Public Works: the President disapproved of the additions the JCAE had appended to the programme of domestic reactor construction that the administration had just sent to Congress. Having consistently resisted building domestic reactors with government money in the hope that the private sector would shoulder the responsibility of atomic power production, Admiral Strauss was seen as the main culprit. Many believed that he must surely have advised the president to write the letter since he had recently become Eisenhower's adviser for nuclear affairs. At any rate Eisenhower's letter angered the Joint Committee, and especially Anderson, whose personal dislike for Strauss was well known in Washington. The senator convinced his colleagues on the JCAE to cancel the 16 July hearing on the Euratom agreements. When the hearings eventually did open on 22 July, Congress, and most of all Anderson, repeatedly pointed to the advantages granted to Euratom that were denied to the domestic programme.[87]

In late July, Kohnstamm returned to Washington for a last round of lobbying. Despite Anderson's antagonism, things started looking up for the agreement. Most of the other members of the JCAE were generally favorable to a joint programme, all the more so since American industry favored it as a way of gaining export markets in Europe and of experimenting with American reactors on a large scale. The Middle East crisis in Jordan and Iraq further helped Euratom supporters, by demonstrating once again Europe's need for alternative energy sources. Finally, Dillon adroitly pointed out during the hearings that, if the United States refused to go along with the agreement, Europe might be perfectly justified in looking elsewhere for its supply of fissionable materials. In the end, the constant lobbying efforts of Monnet's friends helped bring the JCAE along. It was a rather strange lobbying operation since Kohnstamm lobbied alongside the State Department, and to a large extent the AEC, to bring the JCAE around. Meanwhile, Ball, who continued to advise Monnet from his law firm, made efforts to approach Anderson privately. General Julius Klein, appointed by Euratom Commissioner Krekeler, also contributed to the lobbying campaign. Klein, whose headquarters were in Chicago, had other offices in New York and Washington as well London and Frankfurt. A great actor, continuously smoking a huge cigar, he typified the lobbyist.[88] Acheson's intercession on behalf of the programme also proved helpful. Walter Reuther, president of the United Automobile Workers of America, "probably the most influential man in the sphere of

American trade unions," and one "of the rare people who seemed to have a great influence on Senator Anderson," similarly put pressure on the senator, while Kohnstamm himself met with Anderson.[89] Finally, Samuel Waugh's support for Monnet aided in obtaining a long-term loan of $135 million from the Export-Import Bank to Euratom.[90]

By the end of August, Congress had granted its full approval to an International Agreement with Euratom pursuant to Section 124 of the Atomic Energy Act of 1954.[91] After the summer recess, Congress approved an Agreement for Cooperation between Euratom and the United States, which was nothing less than a legislative version of the "Memorandum of Understanding." On this occasion, Monnet sent Kohnstamm a telegram congratulating him.[92] The official signing of the U.S.-Euratom agreement took place in Brussels on 8 November 1958. "The signature on Saturday was a solemn occasion," wrote Kohnstamm,

> There were hundreds and hundreds of people, all terribly important no doubt, but it was a strange feeling not to see, with the exception of Am Bishop and Walt Butterworth, any of the Washington friends, who did it! At luncheon afterwards Walt Butterworth made a very nice speech and told a story about two boys driving around Washington past the Archives Building and reading the inscription "The past is the preface." One boy asked the other "what does it mean?" Thereupon the other answers: "All it means is `you ain't seen anything yet.' It was very nice, and I think we should take these words as our motto.[93]

It now remained to execute the joint agreement. But organizational changes within the AEC made it difficult to develop clearly defined guidelines for implementing it.[94] On the European side, Armand suffered from a nervous breakdown. He could not take part in the official signing of the U.S.–Euratom agreement in November and eventually resigned in February 1959. De Gaulle's coming to power did not, of course, help the cause of Euratom. The U.S.–Euratom agreement gave him and the French Commissariat à l'energie atomique ready-made arguments for criticizing Euratom as an extension of American technology. In 1961, Etienne Hirsch, who had replaced Armand as the head of Euratom, and whom de Gaulle disliked as too "European," was not reappointed to his position. By contrast, Hirsch's successor faithfully followed the directives of the French government, and Euratom's supranational character became less and less credible. The decline in oil and gas prices further doomed Euratom. Only in 1973 did they rise sufficiently to make nuclear power competitive. In addition, results of the joint U.S.–Euratom agreement were disappointing. Only three light water reactors were built under the programme. Their total capacity did not exceed 750 MWe, which looked insignificant when compared with the 15,000 MWe the Wise Men had predicted in their report. Additional agreements were negotiated with the United States in 1960 and later with the Kennedy administration, but the Kennedy team soon denounced cooperation with Euratom as a draining-off of American technology, while Euratom did not have much to offer.[95]

Yet the hopes of Monnet and Kohnstamm for an equal partnership had run high, as evidenced by a letter Monnet wrote to a member of his Committee in early June 1958:

> The US would supply 30 tons of enriched uranium, this goes by far beyond Eisenhower's offer to supply 20 tons of fissionable materials to the entire world . . . One must emphasize the importance of this agreement, which establishes organic links on an equal basis, at the nuclear level, between the US of America and the US of Europe. In particular, this agreement fully recognizes the right for Euratom to own and exclusively control materials . . . This political recognition of equality of US-Euratom relations is accompanied by a true reciprocity at the technical level.

The Kennedy administration continued to support European integration for many of the same reasons as the Eisenhower administration had done. They also had additional reasons of their own. Continuity between the two administrations was insured in part by Europeanists in both administrations who had close ties to Monnet. In August 1960, Kennedy asked Adlai Stevenson to help him develop a programme of action for the first few months of the new administration "somewhat reminiscent of the celebrated Hundred Days of the first term of Franklin Roosevelt." Stevenson then commissioned Ball to write the report for him. He, in turn, asked Monnet to contribute to the project by helping him define American policy toward Europe. The final product heeded the suggestions of Monnet and his colleagues, and included a twenty-page paper outlining a plan for a "Policy for Partnership Between a United Europe and America within a Strong Atlantic Community."[96] Despite Monnet's lobbying efforts and those of his American friends, however, the idea of a partnership of equals between Europe and the United States, as well as British entry into the European Community, mostly fell victim to de Gaulle's roadblocks, and his fear of a Europe dominated by the United States. For de Gaulle, Monnet's association with the United States was always decidedly too close.[97]

Notes

1. Born in 1914, the Dutchman Max Kohnstamm, who later became one of Monnet's assistants for the Action Committee for the United States of Europe, shared with Monnet an early acquired first-hand experience of the United States and an admiration for the New Deal. In 1938, Kohnstamm accepted a scholarship from the American University in Washington, D.C. From October 1938 to August 1939, he studied in Washington and was then allowed to travel extensively in the United States to see in the field what New Deal agencies were doing.
2. François Duchêne, *Jean Monnet, the First Statesman of Interdependence* (New York: W.W. Norton, 1994).
3. Townsend Hoopes, *The Devil and John Foster Dulles* (Boston: Little, Brown and Company, 1973).
4. Alfred Grosser, *Les Occidentaux* (Paris: Fayard, 1978), p. 138. On Dulles's friendship with Monnet, see: Eleanor Dulles, recorded interview by Douglas Brinkley, May 1987, and Eleanor Dulles, interview with Pascaline Winand, Apr. 1990.
5. Jean Monnet, *Memoirs* (New York, Doubleday, 1978), pp. 102–106.
6. In early 1927, Monnet left for Warsaw, where he and his young collaborator, René Pleven, endeavored to save the zloty. In this instance, as in many others, Monnet enlisted the services of Dulles, *ibid.* Later on, Dulles, then head of Sullivan and Cromwell, convinced William Nelson Cromwell, his titular superior, to support a partnership between George Murnane, one of his old friends and associates, and Monnet. R.W. Pruessen, *John Foster Dulles: The Road to Power* (New York: Free Press, 1982), pp. 118–19.
7. Many years later, when Dulles lay on his hospital bed, dying of cancer, Monnet wrote to him fondly remembering the years before he joined the U.S. government, their friendship, and Dulles's "kindness to [him] in New York," Jean Monnet to John Foster Dulles, 14 May 1959, Fondation Jean Monnet pour l'Europe (hereafter FJM).
8. One of Monnet's contributions to the war effort was to convince Roosevelt to stimulate war production to such an extent that America would become "the great arsenal of democracy," Roosevelt's famous phrase, for which he was indebted to Monnet.
9. Eric Roussel, *Jean Monnet* (Paris: Fayard, 1996), p. 636.
10. For more details see: Pascaline Winand, *Eisenhower, Kennedy and the United States of Europe* (London and New York: Macmillan/St. Martin's, 1993, 1996 paperback ed.).

11. George Ball, *The Past Has Another Pattern, Memoirs* (New York: W.W. Norton, 1982), p. 89.

12. For a detailed discussion of American policy towards European integration during the Kennedy administration, see, Winand, *Eisenhower*.

13. Although he did not formally belong to the administration, Acheson became a foreign policy adviser to Kennedy. His report on NATO, a study commissioned by the President, unequivocally stressed the importance of European integration for the United States and the Western world, emphasizing the crucial variable of Franco-German solidarity.

14. In 1959, Schaetzel, as a recipient of a Rockefeller Public Service Award, had also spent a year in Europe on sabbatical leave from the State Department. His task was to study the origins of the European Communities.

15. When Monnet came to Washington during the Kennedy years, he frequently used Schaetzel's office. See: Fondation Jean Monnet pour l'Europe, *Témoignages à la mémoire de Jean Monnet* (Lausanne: Centre de recherches européennes, 9 Nov. 1989), p. 487.

16. Henry Owen, recorded interview by Pascaline Winand, Washington D.C., 17 Oct. 1990.

17. In the 1950s, he also taught at Harvard a course in modern foreign policy, which dealt mainly with European foreign policy. Many of Bundy's friends had also been friends of Monnet during the war. McGeorge Bundy, recorded interview by Pascaline Winand, 1 March 1989.

18. Louis Galambos, ed., *The Papers of Dwight David Eisenhower: NATO and the Campaign of 1952*, vol. XII (Baltimore and London: Johns Hopkins University Press, 1989), no. 304.

19. Monnet reportedly pointed out that the key part of the plan was not its military, but its political and human aspects: by making the Germans and the French serve under the same uniform, one would also unite people and create a common European outlook, a solidarity of destiny.

20. By contrast, some of his American friends, and particularly Dulles, initially focused the bulk of their energy on getting the EDC through, and recommended getting tough with the French to do so.

21. For a more detailed discussion of the negotiations for the loan, see: Pascaline Winand, "Eisenhower, Dulles, Monnet and the Uniting of Europe," in Clifford P. Hackett, ed., *Monnet and the Americans* (Washington D.C.: Jean Monnet Council, 1995).

22. Dulles to Jean Monnet, 19 Feb. 1953, AMF/46/6/1, FJM.

23. After the defeat of the EDC, Monnet indeed reached the conclusion that one would have to work with key representatives from democratic political parties and non-communist trade unions of the Europe of the Six to obtain a parliamentary majority on other European projects in the future and to put pressure on governments to progress on the road to European unity. The Committee later played a key role in helping to obtain parliamentary majorities for the ratification of Euratom and the EEC.

24. *Department of State Bulletin*, XXXIII, 24 Oct. 1955 and Pierre Mélandri, *Les Etats-Unis et le "défi" européen 1955–1958* (Paris: Presses universitaires de France, 1975), p. 63.

25. Meanwhile Jean Monnet made this amply clear in his letter to the leading figures who agreed to join his Action Committee in October 1955. The letter served as a sort of constituting charter for the Committee: "Mere cooperation between governments will not suffice. It is indispensable for States to delegate certain of their powers to European federal institutions responsible to all of the participating countries as a whole." Press Release, Creation of Action Committee for a United States of Europe, 13 Oct. 1955, FJM.

26. *FRUS*, 1955–57, vol. 4, Circular Telegram from the Secretary of State to Certain Diplomatic Missions, 6 Mar. 1957, pp. 534–36.

27. *FRUS*, 1955–57, vol. 4, Memorandum of Conversation, Department of State, 20 Apr. 1955. Words from Mr. Albert Coppé, p. 288; Monnet, *Memoirs*, pp. 417–30.

28. See, for example, *FRUS*, 1955–57, vol. 4, Memorandum of Conversation, Department of State, 14 May 1956, p. 441.

29. *FRUS*, 1955–57, vol. 4, Memorandum of Conversation, Washington, 25 Jan. 1956, p. 397, and Telegram from the Secretary of State to the Embassy in Belgium, Washington, 24 May 1956, p. 443.

30. Both the Secretary of State and the President intended to thwart French hopes for using such a plant within the framework of Euratom. A Euratom enrichment plant would, indeed, have allowed the French to defray the costs they would incur by constructing a plant themselves, thereby helping them fulfill their ambitions for nuclear independence. The carrot to be put in front of the mouths of the six European donkeys was nothing less than the promise to provide substantial quantities of Uranium 235 at a very advantageous price. With the new low price for American enriched uranium, the price of European-produced Uranium 235 would be double or triple that offered by the United States. American tactics worked: during the

early months of 1957, the Six gradually abandoned the idea of building their own enrichment plant. On 12 December 1956, the United States also declassified data from the first American enriched-uranium power plant in Shippingport, Pennsylvania, which was to go into operation only nine months later. This was done to insure that the European pool would prefer American technology to British technology, thereby preserving an important export market for American industry. For the best account of United States interests in controlling the development of Euratom, and preventing the construction of an enrichment plant, see Mélandri, *Défi*. On the fear that the United Kingdom might be preferred to the United States as a source of material and assistance, see, for example: *FRUS*, 1955–57, vol. 4, p. 395.

31. Monnet to Pleven, 24 Jan. 1957, FJM. The matter was settled by January 1957 upon consultation with the Six, who agreed to transfer their benefits or obligations under bilateral agreements with the United States to Euratom. By so doing, any German, Italian, French or other bilateral atomic energy agreement with the United States lost its potentially adverse effect on the Euratom negotiations.

32. "OEEC Plan Favoured by Britain," *The Times*, 14 Feb. 1956 and "Atomic Plans for Europe: Britain Supports OEEC Scheme," *The Times*, 29 Feb. 1956, reference in Darry A. Howlett, *Euratom and Nuclear Safeguards* (London: Macmillan, 1990).

33. *FRUS*, 1955–57, vol. 4, note 4, p. 370.

34. *Ibid.*, Memorandum from the Deputy Under Secretary of State (Murphy) to the Director of the International Cooperation Administration (Hollister), Washington, 16 Feb. 1956.

35. See, for example *FRUS*, 1955–57, vol. 4, Memorandum of Conversation, Washington, 25 Jan. 1956.

36. Howlett, *Euratom and Nuclear Safeguards*, pp. 71, 74.

37. Max Kohnstamm's diary (hereafter MKD), p. 158.

38. *Ibid.*, p. 157.

39. *Ibid.*, p. 265.

40. Copie. Lettre de MM. Mollet, et Adenauer à P.H. Spaak, 6 Nov. 1956, Secrétariat, Conférence intergouvernementale pour le Marché Commun et l'Euratom, Bruxelles, le 9 Nov. 1956, Max Kohnstamm's dossiers (hereafter MKS), D4.

41. European Coal and Steel Community High Authority, Information Service, 21 Nov. 1956, Press Release.

42. *FRUS*, 1955–57, vol. 4, Dillon to the Department of State, 19 Nov. 1956, pp. 487–89.

43. Duchêne, Interview with Max Kohnstamm (hereafter Duch int), p. 122.

44. Note sur la conversation avec M. Schaetzel, 12 Nov. 1956, MKS; *A Target for Euratom*, Report submitted by Louis Armand, Franz Etzel, and Francesco Giordani at the requests of the governments of Belgium, France, German Federal Republic, Italy, Luxemburg, and the Netherlands, May 1957, MKS.

45. As François Duchêne has pointed out, 15 million was larger than the combined electrical output of France and Germany in 1957, yet the figure was not that excessive since "Britain's programme, already under way, aimed at 6-million-kilowatt capacity by 1965 for a population a third as large." Duchêne, *Monnet*, p. 301.

46. For a list of experts who were consulted, see MKS, D4. According to Kohnstamm, Regul worked on the statistics, and he, Kohnstamm, wrote the introduction of "Target." U.S. experts joined the half-wise in Luxemburg to give them part of the technical back-up for their arguments.

47. Pascaline Winand, interview with Max Kohnstamm, 1991.

48. Duch int, p. 141.

49. *FRUS*, 1955–57, vol. 4, Memorandum from the Assistant Secretary of State for European Affairs (Elbrick) and the Special Assistant to the Secretary of State for Atomic Energy Affairs (Smith) to the Secretary of State, Washington, 3 Dec. 1956, pp. 491–95; Invitation of Mr. John Foster Dulles and President Lewis Strauss for the Wise Men's visit to the United States, released to the press on 21 Dec. 1956, MKS.

50. "une association sur un pied d'égalité dans un intérêt mutuel."

51. Monnet to René Pleven, Paris, 24 Jan. 1957, MKS.

52. The letters were addressed to André Meyer of Lazard Frères in Wall Street; John McCloy of the Chase Manhattan Bank; Donald Swatland of Cravath, Swaine, and Moore; Gerard Smith; Robert Bowie; and John Foster Dulles.

53. Monnet to Meyer, Paris, 30 Jan. 1957; Monnet to Smith, Paris, 30 Jan. 1957; Monnet to McCloy, Paris, 30 Jan. 1957; Monnet to Swatland, Paris, 30 Jan. 1957; Monnet to Bowie, Paris, 30 Jan. 1957; Monnet to Dulles, Paris, 30 Jan. 1957; Monnet to Miss Barnaw, Paris, 30 Jan. 1957, MKS.

54. The personal assistants of the Three Wise Men were: Mr. Albonetti (personal assistant of Giordani); Mr. Ernst, assisting Etzel; Mr. Ravelli, assisting Armand; Kohnstamm. The list of participants for the U.S. trip also included Regul, Secord, as experts; Mr. Mande and Mr.

Quoiani, as assisting experts; as well as two secretaries and three interpreters, and a representative of the Secretariat of the Intergovernmental Conference at Brussels.

55. Warren Unna, "Atoms for Europe," *Washington Post*, 2 Feb. 1957; Dulles to Monnet, 4 Feb. 1957, John Foster Dulles papers, Box 120, Princeton Library.

56. Duch, int, p. 300.

57. Pascaline Winand, interview with Max Kohnstamm, 1991.

58. Duch, int, p. 142.

59. The four American experts were Mr. Cook, Mr. Andrew Vander Weyden (Deputy Director of the Division of International Affairs of the AEC), Mr. Fine, and Mr. Roddis.

60. Atomic Industrial Forum, Inc., Euratom Committee Meeting with U.S. Representatives, 13 Feb. 1957, MKS; Kohnstamm to Monnet, 10 Feb. 1957, MKS.

61. The first trip of American experts to Luxemburg had to be postponed for a few days. The reason was lack of preparation on the part of the Wise Men and their team and the prospect of an event of some magnitude, the signing of the Euratom and EEC treaties in Rome.

62. This included Richard Cook, the AEC's deputy general manager; A. Vander Weyden, Deputy Director of International Affairs; Fine, Director, Division of Operations Analysis; and Louis Roddis, Jr., Deputy Director, Division of Reactor Development.

63. Duch int, pp. 140–45.

64. Duchêne, *Monnet*, p. 305.

65. *Action Committee for the United States of Europe, Statements and Declarations 1955–67* (London: Chatham House, 1969), p. 23.

66. Schaetzel to Kohnstamm, 1 Oct. 1957, K5, MKS.

67. Duch, int, p. 229.

68. *Ibid.*, p. 296.

69. Bob Schaetzel of the State Department, Smith warned Kohnstamm, was unpopular in the AEC: MKD, pp. 4121–22.

70. For more details, see Winand, *Eisenhower, Kennedy and the United States of Europe*.

71. Kohnstamm to Schaetzel, 6 Nov. 1957, MKS, D5.

72. Allen Vander Weyden of AEC and Louis Boochever of the Office of European Regional Affairs in the State Department also attended the meeting. See *FRUS*, 1955–57, vol. 4, Memorandum by the Scientific Representative of the Atomic Energy Commission at the Embassy in France (Bishop), Paris, 27 Nov. 1957, pp. 565–69.

73. While the graphite-gaz and heavy-water natural-uranium reactors

both used natural uranium, American reactors required enriched uranium. Developing American reactors in Europe had the disadvantage of making European power plants dependent on a steady flow of enriched uranium from the United States, since Euratom ultimately decided not to build its own enrichment plant. Neither Kohnstamm nor Armand seemed to entertain grave doubts on the matter. Armand believed that natural-uranium plants were too large and could probably not be economically developed on a large industrial scale. On the other hand, enriched uranium power plants utilized light (natural) water and took up relatively little space and were consequently those of the future. Associating Euratom with the nuclear power plants of the future, where the United States was far ahead of Europeans, and gaining access to American technology by constructing and developing light-water reactors jointly with the United States, held precedence over guaranteeing Europe's independence from the United States for enriched uranium. Europe would be free to plan ahead. In the long run, France and Great Britain would then be able to compete with the United States in the construction of breeder reactors, which utilized very enriched uranium. Armand's gamble proved him right on one count: the PWR and the BWR light-water reactor types currently provide more than 90 percent of all the electricity generated by nuclear power plants. Yet light-water reactors also turned out to be far more costly to develop than experts had originally projected. Armand's vision of the development of a world market for nuclear fuels and easy European access to uranium turned out to be wrong, in part because of American nonproliferation policy. Kohnstamm and Armand did not anticipate this development at the time, hoping that U.S.–Euratom cooperation would make Europe more of an equal partner to the United States.

74. Proposed Euratom Agreements, Hearings before the JCAE, Congress of the United States, 85th Congress, second session on the proposed Euratom agreements and legislation to carry out the proposed cooperative agreement, pp. 84–85; Schaetzel to Kohnstamm, 26 Nov. 1957, Kohnstamm to Schaetzel, 5 Dec. 1957, Schaetzel to Kohnstamm, 6 Dec. 1957, K5, MKS.

75. Italics added.

76. Schaetzel to Kohnstamm, 17 Dec. 1957 and Philipp Farley, Memorandum for the File, 23 Dec. 1957, MKS.

77. Memorandum for the Record, 1/7/58, White House Central File, Alpha File B 2137, O.F. 181, Dwight D. Eisenhower Library; Memorandum, " Meeting with Admiral Strauss," 27 Jan. 1958, MKS;

Memorandum, "Various Aspects of U.S.–Euratom Relationships," 27 Jan. 1958, MKS; Schaetzel to Kohnstamm, 28 Jan. 1958, MKS; Memorandum for the President, 28 Jan. 1958, Whitman File, Dulles–Herter, Box 7, DDEL.

78. MKD, p. 4139.

79. Kohnstamm met with Schaetzel, Vander Weyden, Cleveland, Mr. Cook (Deputy General Manager of AEC), Dillon, Shepard Stone, and Senator Pastore. See "Schedule for Max Kohnstamm," MKS.

80. Among the American delegates were such top-level officials of AEC as Richard W. Cook, Deputy General Manager of AEC, and Vander Weyden, while Stanley Cleveland (Office of European Regional Affairs) and Robert Schaetzel (Office of the Special Assistant to the Secretary) represented the State Department.

81. Doc. EUR./W.P. 11/58 E, United States Delegation, Joint U.S.– Euratom Working Party, MKS; Report of the Joint Euratom–United States Working Party, 3 Apr. 1958, MKS.

82. Duch int, p. 294.

83. Duchêne, *Monnet*, p. 314.

84. "Brief Outline of Proposed Joint US–Euratom Program," 5/19/58, M6, MKS; Phyllis D. Bernau to Jean Monnet, 9 May 1958, JFD, Box 132, Princeton Library (hereafter PL); Groupe de travail États-Unis Europe, Brussels, 30 May 1958, K6, MKS; *New York Times*, 9 June 1958.

85. The "total capital cost of the power plants, exclusive of fuel inventory, was not to exceed $350,000,000. Of this amount $215,000,000 was to be provided by participating European facilities and other capital sources and up to $135,000,000 was to be provided by the U.S. as a long term credit to Euratom." The research and development programme was to last for ten years, with each party contributing $50,000,000 for the first five years and a similar amount for the remaining five years. "History of the Joint US–Euratom Program," 23 Apr. 1959, MKS D7. On the loan, see, Samuel Waugh to Kohnstamm, 15 Aug. 1958, MKS D6.

86. Kohnstamm to Armand, 7 July 1958, MKS; Kohnstamm to Monnet, 1 July 1958, K6, MKS; Monnet to Dulles, 13 July 1958, JFD, Box 137, PL.

87. Ball to Kohnstamm, 18 July 1958, K6, MKS; J.C.A.E., Euratom Hearings. For a detailed discussion of the hearings see Mélandri, *Défi*, pp. 174–79.

88. Kohnstamm to his wife, 2 Aug. 1958.

89. *Ibid.*; note pour Monsieur le Président Hirsch, 17 Nov. 1959.

90. Kohnstamm to Pastore, 7 July 1958, MKS; Ball to Kohnstamm, 18 July 1958, MKS; Schaetzel to Acheson, 29 Aug. 1958, Acheson Papers, Manuscript and Archives, Yale University Library; Samuel Waugh to Kohnstamm, 15 Aug. 1958, MKS.

91. This special International Agreement was needed to establish the legal basis for allowing the United States to enter into an agreement with a group of countries such as Euratom, as opposed to a single country.

92. Duch int, p. 241.

93. *Department of State Bulletin*, XL, 12 Jan. 1959, pp. 69–74; Kohnstamm to A. J. Vander Weyden, 14 Nov. 1958, D2, MKS.

94. Ball to Kohnstamm, 20 Nov. 1958, MKS.

95. Henri Tessier du Cros, *Louis Armand: Visionnaire de la Modernité* (Paris: Editions Odile Jacob, 1987), pp. 256–66 and Charles-Lavauzelle, *op. cit.*, pp. 119–25.

96. Schaetzel to Kohnstamm, 4 Oct. 1960, Department of State, Washington, MKS; "Report to the Honorable John F. Kennedy from Adlai E. Stevenson, November, 1960," Personal Papers of Robert Schaetzel, Bethesda, Maryland, pp. PA 1–20.

97. For an in-depth discussion of the Kennedy period, see Winand, *Eisenhower, Kennedy and the United States of Europe*, pp. 140–350.

9

Do Personalities Make a Difference?
Washington Working with Europeans

Klaus Schwabe

The issue raised in this chapter must be viewed in the general context of how international relations can be interpreted in terms of social history. Basically, there are two approaches to this problem: the primarily economic approach, which analyzes diplomacy as the result of economic interests sustained by specific pressure groups. The classic of this type of interpretation remains William A. Williams' *The Tragedy of American Diplomacy*. One of his disciples in Germany has been Hans Ulrich Wehler.[1]

The other approach is based on social history in a narrower and more precise sense. It tries to see diplomacy as influenced or, perhaps, even determined by certain groups, mostly elites, within a given society. For example, this approach might focus on the diplomatic corps of a given country, on its social standing, on the values shared by its members, their collective world view, their definition of the national interest of the country they are serving, and, above all, their collective or individual contribution to the conception and the implementation of their country's foreign policy.[2]

This chapter belongs to the latter category of inquiry. It will raise and attempt to answer these questions:

1 Is it possible, in the context of post-Second World War American society, to identify an elite that had a specific impact on the execution of U.S. foreign policy?
2 If this is the case, what was the contribution of this elite or individual members of it to America's European policies in the decade from 1947 until 1957 – that is, the period between the launching of the Marshall Plan and the signing of the Treaty of Rome establishing the Common Market in Europe?
3 At what point is it possible to identify contributions leading to

achievements in implementing that policy; where, on the other hand, is it necessary to fix responsibility for the failures?

4 If this can be done, what were the reasons for success or failure in specific cases?

5 Finally, and most importantly, could such reasons in any way be traced back to the social structure and societal position of this elite?

This chapter will be subdivided into three major sections: first, I propose to tackle the general problem of elites and their role in American post-Second World War foreign policy; second, five case studies will be presented which should give an idea of how an American diplomatic "elite" contributed to various turning points in America's European policy from 1947 until 1957. This part of the chapter, in turn, will be divided into three chronologically defined subsections dealing with the Truman administration, the beginnings of the Eisenhower administration until the demise of the EDC, and the period from late 1954 until the Treaty of Rome. Third, some general conclusions will be drawn from these case studies in the light of the questions raised at the beginning of this chapter.

The impact of elites on America's foreign relations is a problem that many studies have touched, but only a few have really focused their attention upon. There is the more or less Marxist-inspired denunciation of the "Power Elite" by C. W. Mills and the debunking treatment of "The Best and the Brightest" by David Halberstam – both syntheses that seem to have become methodically more or less obsolete.[3] Significantly, the most recent studies starting out from something like a social-elitist approach and at the same time related to the period under discussion in this chapter were (like Halberstam's book) presented not by professional historians, but by journalists: in 1986, Walter Isaacson and Evan Thomas published a widely read and, in many ways, brilliant – even provocative – collective biography of some members of what they call the foreign policy establishment of post-Second World War Washington.[4] A few years later, it was succeeded by Kai Bird's massive biography of John J. McCloy with the characteristic subtitle, "The Making of the American Establishment."[5] Associative intuition rather then analytic abstraction is the strength of these two publications. Still, due to the richness of the material they present, I will use them as the point of departure and frame of reference. In addition, Pascaline Winand, in her recent book on United States European policies during the Eisenhower and Kennedy adminstrations,[6] has added significant information on the networks through which America's foreign policy in the postwar years was conducted. There are two more recent publications which offer further information: the volume of collected essays edited by Clifford P. Hacket, dealing with Jean Monnet's Washington connections,[7] and the study by John Lamberton Harper analyzing Franklin D. Roosevelt's, George F. Kennan's, and Dean Acheson's attitudes towards Europe.[8] Most recently, two authors, François Duchêne and Eric Roussel, produced biographies of Jean Monnet, both of them rich in new evidence and, each in its own way, penetrating and perceptive, shedding further light on the foreign policy establishment in Washington.[9]

The relatively high number of studies devoted to a group of outstanding personalities instrumental in carrying out America's post-war European policies is all the more significant as similar studies for earlier periods of American diplomacy, for example for the Paris Peace Conference of 1919, seem to be lacking. The just-mentioned authors do not really provide any more general explanation of why elitist groups grew up and happened to influence America's foreign policy precisely during those post-war years, and not in other phases of American foreign relations. They do succeed, however, in uncovering the intimate network of outstanding personalities which surrounded the American Secretaries of State George Marshall, Dean Acheson, and, to some extent also, John Foster Dulles, in those crucial early years of the Cold War – a network which Hacket simply calls a "club" and which Isaacson/Thomas define as a "cross section of the postwar policy Establishment" and a network based on a "collective identity."[10]

It is true, as Isaacson/Thomas demonstrate by analysing origins – that is, region and ancestry – that this American "network" did not share a common background, and thus differed from similar networks in Europe. Some of its members, like Averell Harriman, Robert Lovett, Charles Bohlen, David Bruce or Dean Acheson, as well as John Foster Dulles, descended from well established "houses," while others, like John McCloy, Louis Douglas, Robert Murphy, or George Kennan, were typical upstarts. Regardless of this difference, the careers of these men converged. All of them attended prestigious private schools (most of them Grotton) and Ivy League universities (most of them Harvard); most of them entered either corporate law or business and, as a rule, were connected with Wall Street banking. Career officers in the diplomatic service like Kennan and Bohlen were a minority. It was characteristic that many of them – like Harriman, Lovett, or McCloy – easily switched from business to the foreign service and back, thus establishing lasting links between "Wall Street" and "Foggy Bottom."[11] In all cases, their professional careers brought them into close touch with representatives of Western European countries, the most prominent being Jean Monnet, and thus helped develop a distinctly Atlanticist world view. The formative experience they shared was the collapse of the international order established at the Paris Peace Conference in 1919 and the ensuing Second World War. In one capacity or another, most of them, as Isaacson/Thomas point out, served in the Roosevelt administration. In many ways, their nucleus was the all-important Department of War, with Henry Stimson at its helm. It was here that, in carrying out the Lend-Lease programme, techniques of assuring and coordinating a flow of supplies across the Atlantic were tried out and that plans for the post-war reconstruction of Europe were hatched. Stimson's successor, James Forrestal, inherited this role from him. John McCloy, serving as Under Secretary of War, occupied a position at the core of this network and developed close ties with people such as Dean Acheson, George Ball, Averell Harriman (with whom he had already had business relations during the 1920s), George Marshall, Paul Nitze, and Robert Lovett, and thus founded his reputation as the proverbial "Mr. Establishment."[12] On the basis of the experience which he gained in this position – not least because of his friendship with Dean Acheson – he was later considered (in May 1949) to be qualified for the all-important assignment of the first U.S. high commissioner for the newly founded Federal Republic of Germany.[13]

Henry Stimson, Roosevelt's Secretary of War, not only established a network which survived well into the post-war era, he also carried on the tradition of impartial public service in America that went back to the beginning of this century. His membership of the Republican Party notwithstanding, he set the example of a disinterested, independent, and competent public servant – thus introducing a "meritocracy" into public life, an elite sharing basic values such as personal integrity and independent judgment.[14] As Henry Kissinger put it in retrospect, after 1945 American "foreign policy had been enobled by a group of distinguished men, who, having established their eminence in other fields, devoted themselves to public service . . . an aristocracy dedicated to the service of this nation on behalf of principles beyond partisanship."[15] It is true that only a few of them – such as Lovett or Kennan – consistently shunned even nominal partisan allegiance, that most of them were aligned with the Democratic, some with Republican party, and that a few of them (such as Harriman) actually were prominent financial contributors to their respective party (in Harriman's case, the Democrats). Isaacson/Thomas, however, make the point, and the other above-mentioned authors imply, that none of these personalities had any leanings towards the extremist wings within their respective parties, that all of them, instead, cultivated an "instinct for the center"[16] – subordinating partisan ideologies to what they considered to be the requirements of America's leading role as a world power. To various degrees, all of them had experienced the disillusion arising from the failure of Soviet–American cooperation soon after Nazi Germany's surrender, and thus became converts to a policy of containment *vis-à-vis* Soviet encroachments in Europe.[17] Partly in conjunction with the onset of the Cold War, partly (as in the case of McCloy[18]) earlier and independently of it, they recognized the necessity of rebuilding Europe and integrating Germany into this process. Most of them agreed that Franco-German reconciliation was a cornerstone of that process.[19]

Everything said so far is limited to the top rank of the foreign-policy elite. Personalities of the (then) middle rank who should also be mentioned are William Tomlinson (Treasury), Paul Nitze (State Department), and George Ball – all three legal experts – or the academician Robert Bowie.[20] Some of them, such as Tomlinson, Ball, and – to an extent – Bowie, had established particularly close working relationships with Monnet and his staff in the Commissariat du Plan responsible for modernizing French industry.[21] For the sake of clarity, a distinction should be made at this point between policy-*making*, which, as will be seen, was the domain of the top rank of this elite, and policy *implementation*, which generally was the task of the lower-ranking officials. The latter's specific contribution often cannot be traced even in the primary sources (as in the case of Tomlinson) and, therefore, will only be marginally discussed in this chapter.

As Isaacson/Thomas show, the members of the top elite had an intimate knowledge of each other and at the same time were familiar with many "representatives" of the middle rank. In some cases, this knowledge went far back to the time of common enrollment in a particular school. It was then based on professional ties and, in the case of the career officers of the State Department (such as Bohlen, Kennan, or Murphy), on shared diplomatic experiences. Such long-term bonds created a background of mutual trust and patronage, and facilitated cooperation and a basic consensus that transcended occasional differences of opinion as they arose (for example, between Bohlen and Kennan). What helped overcome such controversies was the consensus on the basic tenets of America's postwar foreign policy: the belief that the future of Europe continued to be the primary challenge to U.S. diplomacy; that the control by one predominant non-democratic power of the Old World had to be prevented by all methods; that the Western-oriented part of Europe had to be transformed into a closely knit unit strong enough to withstand Soviet pressures; and that West Germany at least, if not the whole of Germany, had to contribute to the reconstruction of Europe as an integral part of it.[22]

As noted above, this foreign policy elite had been created by the war. In most cases, it shared the memory of service in the Roosevelt administration. As Isaacson/Thomas suggest, the decision of the U.S. government in 1947 to embark upon a policy of actively promoting European reconstruction and some measure of European integration reactivated what after the war's end had become a "latent elite" once the Truman administration decided to rely on it to carry out the new programme. It is the first case of prominent action on the part of the Washington network and their cooperation with Europeans to be analysed in this chapter. In fact, as Isaacson/Thomas point out, prominent members of the elite such as Acheson, Stimson, McCloy, Harriman, Bohlen, and Kennan share the paternity for the Marshall Plan, which became their "purest achievement."[23] They agreed on the major condition on which American assistance to Europe depended, a prerequisite first made known in George Marshall's famous Harvard commencement speech of 5 June 1947: that the European recipients of the proposed American aid programme should cooperate in a common effort to rebuild Europe.

In placing members of the Washington foreign policy elite in key positions for implementing the Marshall Plan, the Truman administration made sure that this condition was actually met. In Washington, this was the task of the newly appointed Under Secretary of State, Robert Lovett, a former business partner of Averell Harriman, who in turn was to represent the newly created Economic Cooperation Administration (ECA) in Europe after having served in the Administration's Committee on Foreign Aid.[24] In August 1947, before the ECA was set up, George Kennan who, during the war, had won Harriman's respect as his adviser at the U.S. embassy in Moscow, was sent to Paris, in order to bring back onto the right track the inter-European negotiations that threatened to get bogged down in August 1947.[25] Other members of the Washington network – such as Acheson, Bohlen, and Stimson – were engaged in selling the idea of an American-sustained coordinated reconstruction effort in Europe to the American public. Later luminaries of the network such as Paul Nitze and George Ball served as liaison with Jean Monnet, the commissioner of the plan for modernizing France's industries.[26]

It is difficult in this case to single out particular representatives of the network and to define their specific contribution to the implementation of the Marshall Plan, as the day-to-day task of making it work depended on the close interaction of a number of officials responsible for doing so. The point that must be made is that this administrative cooperation, by and large, ran smoothly, and it is this fact that can be explained in part at least by the circumstance that most of the responsible Marshall Plan officials, with the significant exception of Paul Hoffman, the administrator of the whole programme, belonged to the Washington network and could count on each other.[27]

The hopefulness that underpinned the Marshall scheme, however, did not last. This brings us to the second case study in this chapter, primarily relating to interaction *within* the "network." A certain disillusionment spread when, in 1949, it turned out that the Marshall Plan had not entirely produced what it had promised. More important perhaps, European integration lagged behind American expectations. At the time the Marshall Plan was launched, the State Department, withstanding considerable pressure from Capitol Hill, was cautious not to prescribe a precise blueprint for the type of European cooperation it hoped would be adopted by the recipients of American aid. Gradually, however, and especially within the "network," the view rose to predominance that the Europeans should work out supranational structures as a starting point for long-term cooperation in the economic and, maybe, also in other fields. The prospect of a German "comeback" – the beginnings of recovery and the founding of the Federal Republic in 1949 – lent a particular urgency to this demand. It seemed to many to be high time to harness this "rising giant" economically and politically to the West.[28]

Seen from this perspective, the actual European performance was disappointing. Neither the OEEC nor the Council of Europe, in structural terms, went beyond traditional intergovernmental agreements. The principal impediment to greater integration, and on this point there was no disagreement within the "network," was Great Britain, which studiously avoided commitments that went beyond the point of no return in yielding sovereign powers to some European body.

Any supranational European integration, apparently, was not to be had as long as Britain remained a partner in the European integration effort and vetoed any progress that infringed upon its sovereign rights. This impression was confirmed in the spring of 1949, when Kennan had sounded out members of the British Foreign Office concerning their views on progress in European integration. At this point, the consensus that so far had prevailed within Washington's foreign policy elite broke down. The "network" split.[29]

A conference of U.S. diplomatic representatives held in Paris in late October 1949 discussed a proposal, submitted by Secretary of State Dean Acheson, suggesting that the "inability" of the United Kingdom "to join at this time in actions involving some merger of sovereignty should not debar some countries from such progress."[30] What Acheson suggested was a Europe of two speeds: a hard core, that is, the continental Western

European countries (including the Federal Republic), which would go ahead with integration along supranational lines, and the European "outsiders" like Great Britain, which would preserve their full sovereignty by not joining this hard core. The proposed policy was unanimously rejected by the American diplomats gathered in Paris. Charles Bohlen summarized as the "central event" of that meeting "the complete agreement that European integration without the UK was impossible."[31] Bruce added that "no effective integration of Europe would be possible without UK participation because of the belief (not without reason) held by western continental powers of potential German domination if such UK participation did not take place."[32] In spite of such daunting opposition, Acheson did not retract. "We had believed," he cabled back, "that France and other continental powers would be willing to go farther along [the] road to integration (including Germany) than would the British, and we would not wish to see this progress retarded by British reluctance." There is much evidence that Acheson did all he could to encourage the French government to take the leadership in integrating Europe, regardless of whether Great Britain would join in or not – provided, of course, that American and British backing in the field of security remained assured.[33]

Decoupling Great Britain, economically and politically, from continental European integration had been an idea that George Kennan, as the director of the State Department's Political Planning Staff, had first developed in the summer of 1949 as the result of his unsuccessful soundings in London.[34] Kennan's conception of European supranational integration confined to the continent remained controversial, and he became involved in heated debates with his close friend, Charles Bohlen, who maintained that Britain was indispensable as a participant in European integration.[35]

Acheson's insistence on this new direction of American policy on the question of European integration represented a belated triumph for the policy Kennan had recommended. It was a change of direction that can hardly be overestimated. Up to that moment, the United States had regarded Great Britain as the backbone of any development in the direction of European integration. Thoroughly disgusted and discouraged by Britain's dragging its heels over this issue, the U.S. government for the first time considered European core integration without the United Kingdom – a policy line that was going to be upheld until the early 1960s with far-reaching effects on the process of European integration itself. It was effectively the beginning of what Duchêne has called the "triple alliance" between France, the United States, and West Germany.[36] But it is important to bear in mind that it was originally a minority view within the Washington "network," sustained primarily by Kennan and Acheson.[37]

Events in Europe helped to overcome this temporary rift. Confronted with the prospect of a West Germany that the Anglo-Saxon powers would sooner rather than later relieve of the political and economic restrictions they had originally imposed on it (including international control of the Ruhr), the French government (inspired by Jean Monnet) decided to take the initiative and to propose a supranationally structured European Community for Coal and Steel – an organization that, on the one hand, would assure a continuing control of West Germany's heavy industry but, on the other, would not discriminate against the Federal Republic. Schuman and Monnet committed themselves to this proposal, clearly foreseeing that Britain would choose to stay out of the organization. Encouraged by Dean Acheson and John McCloy, who had suggested a similar idea in October 1949, they decided it was worth taking the risk. Once France itself had actually created an established fact, the Washington "network" (and this is the third case to be examined here) abandoned its disagreements and, following Harriman's example, joined Dean Acheson in wholeheartedly supporting the Monnet–Schuman proposal. Just as in the days of the Marshall Plan, key positions for influencing the negotiations for the Schuman Plan were held by members of the foreign policy establishment – above all, John McCloy in Bonn, Dean Acheson in Washington, and David Bruce, Acheson's close friend, as U.S. ambassador in Paris. George Ball, William Tomlinson, and Robert Bowie gave advice on technicalities of law and finance.[38] Ironically, Kennan, who had first conceived this change of policy, by the time the Schuman Plan was actually announced had left his position in the State Department, because he felt that his advice was no longer welcome at the top echelons of government.[39]

The functioning of the "network" became crucial during the last stage of the Schuman Plan negotiations (January–March 1950). Monnet's American friends agreed with him that the formation of a giant cartel as the result of pooling iron and coal in Western Europe had to be avoided at all costs. Not only was American interest in exports at stake, but also the firm establishment of a competitive market economy in Europe. As it turned out, the stumbling block on the road to achieving this goal was West Germany or, more specifically, the highly concentrated heavy industry in the Ruhr district. German opposition to American plans for the decartellization of the Ruhr industry had been strengthened by the progress of the Schuman Plan negotiations, which seemed to prove that Germans were again accepted as equals on the international scene and thus no longer had meekly to yield to the demands of the victorious powers of the Second World War. This new feeling of self-assurance received an additional boost with the outbreak of the Korean War and the subsequent American demand for a German contribution to the rearmament of the West. Sensing that these developments had decisively improved their negotiating position, German representatives both at the Schuman Plan negotiations and with the Western Allied High Commission took a stronger stand against American efforts to assure the deconcentration of the coal and steel industries in the Ruhr district. At stake, first, was the given structure of these industries for which an Allied ordinance (Law 27 of the Allied High Commission) had prescribed various measures of deconcentration.[40] Second, the *future* structure of the coal and steel industries in the Schuman Plan countries had to be regulated. This was the task of the Schuman Plan treaty that was being negotiated. The West German government, fearing that the Ruhr industries would have to abandon efforts at modernizing their structure and thus would be placed at a disadvantage *vis-à-vis* their competitors in the Schuman Plan pool, procrastinated both in the Paris and in the Bonn negotiations.

In December 1950, Monnet and McCloy, assisted by Bruce, Tomlinson, and Bowie, agreed on a concerted effort to break German resistance on both levels. McCloy and Bowie took charge of negotiations with German government representatives, in order to assure the full implementation of law 27, that is, the dissolution of the existing German coal and steel cartels.[41] At the same time, Monnet, assisted by Bruce, conducted negotiations in Paris aiming at provisions in the Schuman Plan Treaty that banned cartels from the future common European market for coal and steel. Weeks of hard bargaining were necessary to overcome German objections. McCloy had personally to address the affected German interest groups (industrialists, and trade unions as well) in order to alleviate the pressure these organizations were bringing to bear upon the Adenauer government. Monnet established a linkage between Germany's yielding in this issue, the signing of the Schuman Plan Treaty, and the opening of parleys preparing West German rearmament and the restoration of sovereignty to the Bonn Republic. Thus, for a time, the whole process of German integration with the West seemed to be in suspense.[42]

At the height of this struggle, the State Department offered "strongest action against Germany . . . if the Germans did not play ball on the Schuman Plan."[43] In mid-March 1950, Adenauer gave in by accepting, as a compromise, a limited degree of deconcentration. H. A. Byroade, the head of the bureau of German Affairs in the State Department, commented:

> I believe it not an over-statement to say that the Schuman Plan would not
> have succeeded but for the personal efforts of McCloy. When the going got
> rough, and particularly during the last month, it is almost a certainty that the
> French and the Germans would not have stuck together in an effort to find an
> agreed solution without some catalyst pulling them together . . . When I left
> Germany, the prospects of failure were very terrifying as the French were
> already showing signs of a complete retrenchment in their approach towards
> Germany. There can be no doubt that the failure of this Plan would have been
> a major set back to U.S. policy in Europe.[44]

Thus, McCloy does seem to have made a difference in the process of
bringing the Schuman Plan negotiations to a successful conclusion, but
so did the coordinated effort of the people of the "network" in support of
him.[45]

Only a few months later, the American High Commissioner in Germany
became instrumental in producing another "finest hour" for the "network"
by committing the United States to the project of a European Defence
Community (EDC) as the capstone of European integration. This was
closely related to the issue of a West German contribution to the military
efforts of NATO. The whole matter had been discussed unofficially
since the winter of 1949/50. It was, however, only as a result of the
outbreak of the Korean War that the question became acute. German
rearmament then became a requirement for the Truman administration.
McCloy, partly influenced by the German Chancellor, who feared an
immediate infiltration and subversion by East German agents of the
Federal Republic, was fully aware of the necessities of the situation. At
the same time, however, he was decidedly against any revival of a national
German army. Confronted by this predicament, McCloy, as early as August
1950, first conceived the idea of a European Defence Force with the same
membership as the European Community for Coal and Steel which was
under discussion at Paris at the same time. The European Defence Force
promised to kill several birds with one stone: it would help to protect
West Germany against Soviet military pressure; it assured Germany's
contribution to Western defence and, thus, a more credible deterrence
of the Soviet Union; it would control a rearmed Federal Republic; it
would silence French objections to raising any kind of German armed
force; and, last but not least, it would generally promote European
integration.[46]

A few weeks later, on 26 October 1950, Monnet, advised by David
Bruce but independently of McCloy, worked out a project for a European
Defence Organization and succeeded in persuading the French Prime

Minister, René Pleven, to launch it as a "Pleven Plan."[47] The proposed plan for a European Defence Community displayed the same organizational characteristics as the Schuman Plan. A common independent minister of defence would provide the most important supranational feature.

While not overly impressed with some details of the Pleven Plan, McCloy basically favored it and recommended making the best of it. In taking this view, he was nearly isolated within his own government. Acheson did not think very much of the suggested EDC, and the military rejected it outright as impractical.[48] The situation in Korea demanded a speedy decision in favour of raising German troops. The Pleven Plan, instead, proposed a complicated scheme, which required difficult negotiations. The Pentagon feared endless delay. In addition, it seemed unclear how the EDC would fit into NATO and how confusions in the chain of command could be avoided. By the spring of 1951, these American reservations, in combination with a continued French refusal to accept any German rearmament outside the proposed EDC, had created a perfect stalemate, even though the Pleven Plan – in the meantime – had been purged of some aspects which had clearly discriminated against the Federal Republic. This situation appeared the more ominous since, parallelling the talks on the EDC, Allied–German negotiations were being conducted, aiming at a so-called contractual agreement, which would remove Allied controls from the Federal Republic and restore a degree of sovereignty to it. More or less implicitly, Adenauer had made progress on this issue the condition of the acceptance by Bonn of German rearmament within an EDC, a step highly unpopular among West Germans. Thus, all hopes for integrating West Germany with the Free World seemed to be in jeopardy, unless the EDC came about.[49]

It was apparently one of McCloy's advisers, Robert Bowie, who suggested a way out of this impasse. Bowie proposed a meeting between Monnet and General Eisenhower, who had recently been appointed Supreme NATO Commander for the European theater, to discuss the Pleven Plan. This meeting was held on 21 June 1951. It proved to be a turning point in the early development of the EDC, for Monnet succeeded in convincing Eisenhower that the EDC, for political reasons, was the only feasible way of gaining a German defense contribution.[50] Eisenhower accepted the primacy of political over military considerations in this case and, shortly afterwards, delivered a speech endorsing the EDC as an indispensable step toward European integration. The long-term personal wishes he associated with this decision went quite far. Unless the West European countries, including West Germany, "formed *one* federated state," he noted in his diary, "the millions the United States had spent on the Economic Cooperation Administration [i.e. the Marshall Plan] would go to waste."[51]

Eisenhower's conversion to the EDC amounted to a breakthrough for this project within the American government. Acheson was finally persuaded of the necessity of the project, and on 30 July 1951, he for the State Department and Lovett for the Department of Defense officially recommended an American commitment to the EDC. Truman accepted the recommendation.[52] One of the reasons why Acheson became convinced that the EDC was the only safe method to get West Germany rearmed was the assumption that the EDC promised to survive a future American retreat from Europe and to continue to serve as a firm basis for Franco-German cooperation – a view that, later on, was adopted by the Eisenhower administration.[53]

The "network" fell into line with what looked like a promising approach toward European integration. A "cabal of friends,"[54] among them Averell Harriman, recently appointed head of the National Security Council, David Bruce, ambassador in Paris, and Lew Douglas, U.S. ambassador at St. James and brother-in-law to McCloy, was initiated, which invested all its energy in the effort to bring the negotiations for the EDC to a successful conclusion.[55] McCloy repeatedly intervened, both in Paris and in Bonn, urging the acceptance of a "permanent West European Union," in order to fend off dangers arising from a Germany not fully wedded to the West.[56]

In the final stage of the negotiations, at the end of May 1952, Acheson again assumed the role of a "catalyst" in removing the final disagreements that remained between European negotiators – obstacles that, for a time, seemed to jeopardize the previous negotiating efforts as a whole. One of these disagreements was owing to the Dutch. It arose from the difference in the dates of expiration existing between NATO and the EDC – NATO open to renegotiation after the lapse of twenty years, the EDC being in effect for fifty years. In Dutch eyes, after the course of twenty years, a situation might well develop, which, on the one hand, permitted an American withdrawal from Europe, but, on the other hand, continued to commit the Europeans to the EDC and might well result in reduced American aid to the Netherlands.[57]

As far as the French government was concerned, it demanded a binding Anglo-Saxon commitment to come to France's assistance, in case a rearmed Germany should decide to leave the EDC and thus once again became a threat to Western Europe. This seemed all the more necessary as Britain offered assistance to Western Europe only so long as it remained within NATO. But, obviously, such a commitment would involve the U.S. executive in a conflict with Congress, which would surely refuse to forego its constitutional prerogative to declare war.[58]

Finally, the Germans had problems with regard to a clause in the contractual agreements which bound a future German government after unification to abide by the existing international obligations of the Federal Republic. As some of the more nationalist-minded members of Adenauer's cabinet pointed out, this provision – in freezing Germany's post-unification status – would deprive the West of all leverage *vis-à-vis* the Soviet Union, in case the latter one day offered negotiations, and, consequently, would in fact rule out Germany's eventual unification. Acheson subordinated these difficulties to his "mature judgement that European security and thereby our own rests on France and Germany and not on France or Germany." He skillfully worked out face-saving formulas that papered over these differences, which to him, at any rate, were largely theoretical.[59] The compromises he consequently arrived at removed the final obstacles in the way of the signing of the contractual and the EDC agreements.

These events appeared to seal the final triumph of America's policy to integrate West Germany into the West by way of an EDC. First initiated by McCloy, this policy united most of the Washington "network" behind a concerted effort. As McCloy acknowledged, part of the network in Paris had been the "Bowie–Tomlinson team," which provided the legal know-how necessary to implement the policy.[60] In view of the transition from the Truman to the Eisenhower administration in 1953, it should be remembered that General Eisenhower, since June 1951, had been part of that "cabal" and, thereby, of the "network."

What followed was a lengthy process which was supposed to lead to the parliamentary ratification of the EDC Treaty and the contractual agreement. Actually, it ended with a resounding defeat for America's policy of integrating Western Europe. To what extent was the Washington "network" involved in or, possibly, responsible for this disaster? Let us first take a brief look at the chain of events that preceded the rejection by the French National Assembly of the EDC in 1954.

As François Duchêne puts it, "the EDC was rotting before the ink was dry."[61] After difficulties in other member countries such as West Germany had been overcome, the French problem remained. Opposition developed against Monnet. The strong French Socialist Party demanded that a European Political Community (EPC) be established. This was to assure political control of the EDC and the recovery of the original supranational structure of the EDC for finances, a structure that had been largely watered down during the previous negotiations for the EDC.[62] The French government, anxious to maintain Socialist parliamentary support for the EDC, passed this demand on to the other members. Negotiations to draft a treaty for the EPC, in fact, began, with Robert Bowie and the German-American political scientist, Carl J. Friedrich, acting in an advisory capacity.[63]

Progress, nevertheless, was slow, and ratification by the French parliament of the EDC was still far away. At least, this was the impression gained by American observers. In a meeting with Jean Monnet on 14 December 1952, Acheson, already representing a lame-duck administration after Eisenhower's electoral victory, bitterly complained about being left totally in the dark with regard to recent progress in European integration. Despite Monnet's assurances to the contrary, he painted a somber picture of the situation in Europe:

> It had seemed to me that the momentum had been lost, retrogression has set in, and that we might now be on the verge of disaster. I pointed out the amazing distance which the United States has gone in responding to European initiatives . . . – the OEEC, the Marshall Plan, the North Atlantic Treaty, the development of the unified command with its concomitant of the restoration of German sovereignty and German participation and the stationing of American troops in Europe. All of this . . . depended for its continuance upon Europe . . . developing here a community politically united, strong economically and militarily . . . It was not an easy thing to maintain American ground, air and naval forces in Europe . . . It was worthwhile and necessary to do what we are doing, if by so doing we were helping the Europeans themselves to build a new strong Europe. It was quite quixotic to do this if the Europeans themselves gave up the struggle. If the EDC went to pieces, I saw the gravest difficulties opening up for the new Administration.

By continuing to act the way they presently did, Acheson concluded, Germans and French risked their own defense and their future.[64] Strong words, indeed, even though not spoken in public – and words that foreshadowed the attitude the new Eisenhower administration was soon going to adopt.

The change of administrations modified, though it did not destroy, the Washington "network." Key members of it, above all Acheson himself, then McCloy (who had rejected an offer to work for the new administration), Lovett, Harriman, and Bohlen (after a brief interlude as U.S. ambassador in Moscow) "went into exile." Kennan (like Harriman) was not even asked to join the new administration. The most important change was probably the replacement of McCloy as U.S. high commissioner in

Germany by James Conant, a Harvard academic, who, as seen from the Washington perspective, was an outsider.[65]

And yet, this change of personalities did not mean a change of direction in America's policy with regard to European integration. The new administration, in practice, was even more committed (if this was possible) to this goal than had been the outgoing one. Most importantly, unlike Truman, who had largely left foreign policy generally, and European policy in particular, to his Secretary of State, Eisenhower – as we have seen – had made European integration and federation a matter of personal concern, and thus had become part of the pro-European "network." He overruled doubts his military advisers continued to have with regard to the practicability of the EDC.[66] Eisenhower's Secretary of State, John Foster Dulles, had been an American propagator of a United States of Europe as early as the Second World War, and had been one of Monnet's American friends since 1919. With exactly the same language Acheson had used, he tried to impress the fact on the Europeans that America's policy with respect to Europe did not "involve a choice between France *or* Germany," but was based "on France *and* Germany."[67] In spite of outward appearances, there was also a notable continuity of personnel in the somewhat lower levels of European policy-making. Robert Murphy, who had first met Monnet during the 1930s and had served under the Truman administration as political adviser to the Military Government in Germany, was appointed assistant Under Secretary of State. Robert Bowie, who had helped McCloy in preparing the Schuman Plan and the EDC treaties, became director of the Policy Planning Staff (succeeding Paul Nitze). At Jean Monnet's insistence, David Bruce, although a Democrat and a close friend of Acheson's, was appointed American representative at the European Iron and Steel Community with the additional responsibility of reporting about progress in the creation of a European Political Community. Last, but not least, William Tomlinson became Bruce's deputy at the seat of the High Authority of the ECSC in Luxemburg.[68] Thus, as seen from the perspective of both policy and personnel, there continued to be a strong current of bipartisanship in the administration's positive attitude toward the question of European integration.

If there was change, it was in part a tendency toward professionalization, in the sense that the new "network" was recruited from members of the State Department rather than from prominent outsiders, as had been the case under Truman. More significant, perhaps, was the change of emphasis in motivation. Even more clearly than had been the case with Acheson, Eisenhower regarded the process of European integration as a means ultimately of disengaging the United States from Europe militarily, at least as far as conventional forces were concerned. He hoped that the European Defence Community, in the end, would make Western Europe self-sufficient in the field of conventional forces so that the umbrella of American troops to help defend Europe would no longer be needed. American soldiers could then be withdrawn from Europe, and pressure on the American budget would be correspondingly eased. Ultimately, the struggle over the EDC, as viewed by the Eisenhower administration, was a question not so much of control as of "devolution" of military responsibility on the part of the United States.[69] This could mean that, once the EDC functioned, German soldiers would take the place of American ones, a disquieting perspective for the French government and not one conducive to strengthening their confidence in the EDC.[70] In fact, this motivation neutralized American threats to withdraw from Europe, in case the EDC failed to be ratified. In a similar vein, the idea of a mutual withdrawal of at least some Soviet and American forces from Europe was discussed between Dulles and his entourage as a possibility after the EDC had been set up – a step that similarly would have left France militarily alone, face to face with a rearmed Germany.[71]

Keeping this motivation to itself, the Eisenhower administration and its not-so-new European "network" used the three methods that had already been tried out by its predecessor in order to induce the recalcitrant Europeans, above all the French, to ratify the EDC: mediation, incentives, and threats – the latter both behind closed doors and in public. It appears that the matter of a European Political Community was somewhat neglected, although the Eisenhower administration knew that the Socialist vote in the French parliament depended, in part, on whether or not this objective was attained. Dulles did attempt to mediate when, in November 1953, the Dutch demanded that the powers of the EPC be extended into the economic field.[72] He also exercised the strongest pressure on Adenauer to compromise over the Saar question, where French and West German interests continued to clash.[73]

The inducements American diplomacy had to offer encompassed financial assistance, which France badly needed, in order to be able to carry on its war in Indo-China; a loan to the ECSC, which was actually negotiated; further assurances of unswerving American support to the EDC and of the continued deployment of American troops in Europe, once it had been established; and a British association with the EDC.[74] All these "carrots" were presented to France. The U.S. government also agreed to attend another Four-Power Conference on Germany, hoping to prove by this that agreement on a German settlement with the Soviet

Union was unattainable and that, for this reason, no alternative was left to France but the EDC.

From early on, Dulles also resorted to direct threats. Acheson had done the same, as we have seen. The difference was that Dulles did not hesitate to make such threats public. The best known is his prediction of an "agonizing reappraisal" of America's policy towards Europe if the EDC was not ratified.[75] This was only the culmination of a whole barrage of similar threats to which the French government and public were exposed. It was also fairly clear what Dulles implied: either a withdrawal of American troops to the periphery of Europe or, more likely, the raising of German troops for NATO without a supranational umbrella. There were two further dangers which Bruce and other American diplomats in Paris tried to impress on their French opposite numbers: first, that after the defeat of the EDC, West Germany would enter into negotiations with the Soviet Union on the unification of a neutralized Germany. Second, that a national German army would be formed and thus German militarism revived; history might then repeat itself. In the last analysis, Americans argued, the fate of the EDC would decide whether the Federal Republic would be "polarized" to the West or to the East.[76]

Ultimately, all such efforts were to no avail. In the final days of August 1954, David Bruce, trying to mobilize the French premier Pierre Mendès-France into action in favor of the EDC, felt he was speaking "to a stone."[77] In a final attempt to rescue the EDC, a conference was held in Brussels on 19 August 1954. The European participants and the United States were confronted with the French Prime Minister's proposal to strip the EDC of all its supranational features, so that it would be palatable to the French parliament. Fearing that to yield to these proposals would mean destroying the domestic base of the German Chancellor, who had staked his political future on the creation of a supranational European defence force and European integration in general, American negotiators were advised to counsel France's European partners to reject such overtures.[78] By the end of August 1954, the vote of the French National Assembly against the EDC was pretty much a foregone conclusion.

To the American pro-European "network" – be it Dulles, Acheson, Bruce, or Tomlinson – this final rejection by the French parliament of the EDC was deeply disappointing. To some, particularly Bruce and Tomlinson, it felt like a personal blow.[79] Bruce resigned from his post at the ECSC. It is true that the Western powers succeeded within weeks in solving the questions of West German rearmament and sovereignty by concluding a set of agreements that made the Federal Republic a member of NATO and placed it under special control of the newly formed Western

European Union. But no one in the American government could deny that America's policy aiming at Western European integration had suffered a grave setback.

In the context of the subject of this chapter, the question arises whether the failure of the EDC had something to do with the change of guard within the Washington "network" responsible for U.S. policies *vis-à-vis* Europe. Acheson, never an admirer of his successor, promptly blamed Dulles's ineptness for the defeat of American objectives in Europe.[80] While it cannot be denied that Dulles's public interference with the decision-making process of the French parliament was resented by a number of French politicians, it is equally true that these attempts at browbeating hesitant French members of parliament were far from unplanned. As we now know, Dulles's most sensational threat – of an "agonizing reappraisal" – was based on a well-calculated tactic and had been cleared with both the President and the responsible desks at the State Department.[81] Repeatedly, members of the pro-European "network" such as Bruce and Tomlinson pleaded for a policy of strong and public pressure on the French political establishment, and French members of parliament in particular, in order to make them aware of what was at stake.[82] At the last minute, Bruce suggested a conference of the six signatories of the EDC plus Britain and the United States with the sole purpose in mind of demonstrating France's isolation to the French public.[83] Thoroughly pro-French and warmly attached to France's culture, they firmly believed that, in demanding a speedy ratification of the EDC Treaty, they spoke in the name of France's higher national interest.[84] Their closest contact with French politics, Jean Monnet, supported them in this belief and welcomed Dulles's threat of an "agonizing reappraisal."[85] Thus, it cannot have been a lack of engagement, a lack of contact with political life in France, nor a lack of good will in understanding France, that would explain their failure to win sufficient French support for the EDC. In the concluding part of this chapter, I will attempt to assess why Washington succeeded in creating European agreement in some previous cases and why it failed to accomplish this when the EDC was at stake.

Despite the defeat of the EDC and despite the need for the United States to agree to a form of German rearmament which virtually ignored European integration, the basic orientation of the Eisenhower administration in favor of Europe's supranational integration remained unchanged. The President himself reaffirmed this policy in the National Security Council on 21 November 1955. He hoped, Eisenhower declared, that Western Europe would develop into a third great power block – "after which development," he characteristically added, "the United States would be permitted to sit back and relax somewhat."[86] Earlier, in May 1955, a consensus had been reached among U.S. envoys abroad and the State Department that the United States should continue to support integration efforts which aimed at creating supranational authority and responsibility instead of merely cooperative arrangements.[87] In pursuing this policy, the President could again rely on a group of State Department officers devoted to the ideal of European unification. Some of them, like Bowie, Murphy, and Bruce, who was appointed U.S. ambassador in Bonn, were old hands in the field. Others, such as Livingstone Merchant and Walton Butterworth, successor to Bruce as U.S. representative with the European Coal and Steel Community, were newer names to be added to the group.

Sooner than probably had been expected, the American commitment to European integration was put to the test. Trying to relaunch the integration process, Jean Monnet hit upon the project of a European Atomic Energy Commission, later to be called Euratom. This, he hoped, would unite the Europeans in another economic sector of highest importance in the immediate future. Euratom was to sponsor further research and would make fissionable material available for exclusively civilian use. As the conference at Messina in early June 1955 had generally authorized further study of the possibilities for the economic integration of Europe, Euratom became a subject of public and official debate. In pursuing his plan, Monnet encountered various obstacles. France was interested in the project, but refused to commit itself to the renunciation of building atomic weapons; in other words, it was unwilling to subscribe to the exclusively civilian character of the Euratom agreement. A statement by Prime Minister Guy Mollet, in July 1956 before the National Assembly, reaffirmed this decision publicly.[88] If France, by joining, had to renounce the production of nuclear weapons, it seemed obvious that Euratom – like the EDC – would not be accepted by the French parliament. From the German perspective, Euratom was another case of discrimination against the Federal Republic under a European disguise. Generally, it had never been popular in West Germany, as the industrial interests there preferred to obtain nuclear know-how for peaceful use directly from the United States on a bilateral basis. Later, the idea of Euratom's ownership of fissionable material came under fire as smacking of socialism. What Bonn was interested in was the economic union that the Dutch government had insisted on at Messina, and it soon established a linkage between Euratom and a common European market. The German government announced that it was willing to accept Euratom only if the negotiations would also pursue the objective of setting up a common market. Vocal politicians in

Germany, such as Franz Joseph Strauß, continued to attack the Euratom project. Adenauer himself remained non-committal until October 1956. There was one further adversary for Euratom: Britain, which had opted out of the negotiations. As London recognized, these parleys were once again trying to develop supranational structures for Europe. Instead of creating a Euratom organization, the British preferred to deal with atomic developments within the framework of the Organization for European Economic Cooperation (OEEC).[89]

Immediately after the conclusion of the Messina Conference, the State Department decided to support the Euratom project "as a way of reviving the European integration movement and . . . forging a new link between Germany and the West."[90] Attempting to implement this political objective, it met the consistent opposition of the Atomic Energy Commission, headed by Admiral Lewis Strauss, which – in the interest of exporting nuclear know-how – preferred bilateral agreements of the type approved by German industrial interests.[91] Monnet was aware of opposition of this kind and, as during the Schuman negotiations, requested American backing to overcome German resistance.[92] In Washington, the approval of President Eisenhower was needed to assure the cooperation of the Atomic Energy Commission in supporting Euratom.[93] What followed was the determined effort of "a small State Department group around Dulles and Eisenhower"[94] to navigate Monnet's project through the various rapids that threatened it, and thus to assure its adoption by the six Schuman Plan members (Britain was discouraged from interfering with this new European initiative).[95] France was given to understand that the United States would not stand in the way of its nuclear armament.[96] Against its better judgment, the U.S. government was prepared to accept the European Common Market, although it was concerned about the linkage established between it and Euratom, a link which seemed to compromise the chances of Euratom being ratified by the French parliament.[97] The American Atomic Energy Commission, finally, and potential European customers, had to be kept patient and to be dissuaded from pushing bilateral agreements on nuclear exports. Admiral Strauss continued to be opposed to this decision until December 1956.[98] Most of all, Adenauer had to be committed to silencing strong German opposition to Euratom on the grounds of its alleged socialist bias. Dulles authorized strong representations to Adenauer over this matter.[99] On 10 January 1957, a few weeks before the Treaties of Rome were signed, Monnet warned Dulles that if the United States agreed to give bilateral nuclear aid to Germany before Euratom was signed, this would probably mean the end of the project. At that point, Dulles banked on Adenauer's assuming responsibility over the issue.[100] "Without the constant involvement of Adenauer, the whole business would be lost," the Dutch negotiator Kohnstamm confided to his diary at this point. As Duchêne has noted, in many ways it was the story of the Schuman Plan negotiations over again: France needed and used the United States or, to be more precise, a pro-European American elite, as a catalyst, in order to break the resistance of German industrial interests to Euratom and to subordinate them to the higher objective of European integration.[101] It proved to be another triumph for the network of Europeanists within the State Department.

The case studies examined in this chapter should make it possible for us to arrive, at least, at preliminary answers to the questions raised at the start. There seems to be no doubt that a foreign-policy elite did exist in the United States at the outset of the postwar period. Experiences under the Roosevelt administration and the impact of the war had formed a network of foreign-policy experts partly coming from the world of high finance and corporate law, partly recruited from the personnel of the State Department. Sharing a similar educational and professional background, this elite had an Atlanticist outlook. It focused on the objective of creating conditions in Europe that would prevent another military conflict and the hegemony of a single European power over the rest of the continent, especially its Atlantic coastline. Soon, European integration along supra-national lines appeared to be the panacea for accomplishing these ends. It would also provide a means of preventing history from repeating itself. It was this outlook, in the last analysis based on a common Western heritage of values, but also on considerations of power and economic principle, that held the elite in question together – a solid ground that transcended differences as to tactics which, as we have seen, at times arose. Most members of this elite developed close ties with their opposite numbers in France, especially with Jean Monnet, and, to a more limited extent, in West Germany (Adenauer, Hallstein). The elite propagated and sustained the American commitment to European integration and made it an unquestioned basic assumption of the United States' foreign policy, to such an extent that the reshuffling of personnel which resulted from the change of administrations in 1953 did not, in reality, make any difference.

Against the background of this elite's activities, the contributions of a few individuals clearly stand out. In this context, we should mention Kennan–Acheson's 1949 option for a core-of-Europe approach. We should also refer to McCloy and his two outstanding accomplishments (both of 1951): first, having West Germany accept the Schuman Plan plus deconcentration, and then persuading the Truman administration to adopt the EDC project and, thus, to confirm America's commitment to European integration. Last but not least, we must single out John Foster Dulles and his collaborators from the State Department, and, ultimately, President Eisenhower himself, for making Euratom palatable in 1956 within the U.S. government and *vis-à-vis* Germany. In all these examples, the personalities concerned made a considerable difference by acting as sources of pressure, as catalysts, and/or as intermediaries.

There remains the disaster of the EDC. To an extent, this drama unfolded beyond the reach of any American policy-maker, and its roots have to sought in the crisis of the French Fourth Republic, a crisis – aggravated by the military defeat France suffered in Indo-China – that tended more and more to cripple the political decision-making process in Paris. Despite all this, there still remains the possibility of inadequate American responses to the situation and American ineptness in the attempt to enlist French support for the EDC. In the context of this chapter, the most relevant question is whether the change of guard, the somewhat modified Washington "network" resulting from Eisenhower's electoral victory in 1952, can be considered responsible for the failure. The answer of this writer is in the negative. It may be that Dulles lacked some of the tactical finesse needed to handle the highly delicate situation in France. But, as has been demonstrated, close ties between a rejuvenated elite in Washington and the French pro-Europeans headed by Monnet survived the change of administrations in Washington virtually intact. Dulles, in making most of his moves, listened to advisers such as Bruce, who had already counselled his predecessor Dean Acheson. After all, Acheson himself had proved as helpless as Dulles when he was confronted with the parliamentary difficulties occurring in France after 1952.

And yet, the defeat of the EDC may have had something to do with the social background and structure of the "network." Taking into a account the crisis of the French Republic and accidental events (such as, for example, Monnet's illness during the crucial weeks of the summer of 1954), it would still be possible to argue that the social make-up of the Washington pro-European elite might partly account for the setback they were exposed to when the EDC was defeated in the French National Assembly. Rising to prominence on the basis of their expertise and trained in complicated international bargaining at the highest level, this professional elite in most cases was inexperienced in parliamentary log-rolling and, more often than not, despised partisan politics. Would more familiarity with political life, in that sense, have helped them in coping with the EDC crisis in France? Would closer ties with more French representatives of parliamentary politics have helped them overcome French doubts regarding European integration? It may require further study of the individuals concerned and the times in which they lived to furnish more precise answers to these questions.

The final rejection of the EDC, at all events, suggests definite limits to the capacity of the "network" to influence the course of events abroad. If this *was* a deficiency, it was rooted in the "network"'s own most prominent quality – the ability to serve impartially what they perceived as the enlightened interest of their country and its European allies.

Notes

1. William A. Williams, *The Tragedy of American Diplomacy* (New York, 1962); Hans Ulrich Wehler, *Grundzüge der amerikanischen Außen-politik* (Frankfurt, 1984).
2. This was attempted in a conference conducted by the author: Klaus Schwabe, ed., *Das Diplomatische Korps, 1871–1945*, Büdinger Forschungen zur Sozialgeschichte: Deutsche Führungsschichten in der Neuzeit, vol. 16 (Boppard, 1985).
3. C. Wright Mills, *The Power Elite* (New York, 1956) [for example, p. 211]; David Halberstam, *The Best and the Brightest* (New York, 1972); see also the review essay by Douglas Little, "Crackpot Realists and Other Heroes: The Rise and Fall of the Postwar American Diplomatic Elite," *Diplomatic History*, vol. 13, no. 1 (Winter 1989), pp. 99–111.
4. This chapter uses the 1988 edition: Walter Isaacson and Evan Thomas, *The Wise Men: Six Friends and the World They Made* (New York, 1988) [henceforth Isaacson, *Wise Men*]. Other abbreviations used in this paper: *FRUS* (Foreign Relations of the United States: Diplomatic Papers) and NA (National Archives: Diplomatic and Fiscal Branch, Washington, unprinted sources).
5. Kai Bird, *The Chairman: John McCloy, the Making of the American Establishment* (New York, 1992).
6. Pascaline Winand, *Eisenhower, Kennedy, and the United States of Europe* (Houndmills, 1993).
7. Clifford P. Hacket, *Monnet and the Americans: The Father of a United Europe and his U.S. Supporters* (Washington, D.C., 1995).
8. John Lamberton Harper, *American Visions of Europe* (Cambridge, 1994).

9. François Duchêne, *Jean Monnet: The First Statesman of Interdependence* (New York: W. W. Norton, 1994); Eric Roussel, *Jean Monnet, 1888–1979* (Paris: Fayard, 1996).

10. Isaacson, *Wise Men*, pp. 25, 739; Hacket, *Monnet and the Americans*, p. 73. Bird defines the elite as "sharing 'the same social and political values,' thinking of themselves as 'keepers of the public trust' . . . 'persuading America to shoulder its imperial responsibilities.'" Bird, *The Chairman*, p. 18.

11. Isaacson, *Wise Men*, p. 428; Bird, *The Chairman*, p. 18.

12. Isaacson, *Wise Men*, pp. 18, 23, 29, 130f., 237, 428.

13. *Ibid.*, p. 515; Bird, *The Chairman*, p. 304f.; Hermann-Josef Rupieper, *Der besetzte Verbündete: Die amerikanische Deutschlandpolitik 1949–1955* (Opladen, 1991), p. 22.

14. Isaacson, *Wise Men*, pp. 428, 739.

15. Kissinger, quoted in Isaacson, *Wise Men*, p. 27.

16. Isaacson, *Wise Men*, p. 29.

17. *Ibid.*, pp. 30, 33, 362.

18. Melvyn P. Leffler, *A Preponderance of Power: National Security, the Truman Administration, and the Cold War* (Stanford, 1992), pp. 20, 69; Winand, *Eisenhower, Kennedy, and the United States of Europe*, p. 12; Isaacson, *Wise Men*, p. 406.

19. Bird, *The Chairman*, p. 379; Roussel, *Monnet*, pp. 482f., 518f., 636; Harper, *American Visions*, p. 282; also see Klaus Schwabe, "The United States and European integration 1947–1957," in Clemens Wurm, ed., *Western Europe and Germany: The Beginnings of European Integration, 1945–1960* (Oxford: Berg, 1995), pp. 124f.

20. Pascaline Winand, "Dulles, Eisenhower, Monnet, and the Uniting of Europe," in Hacket, *Monnet and the Americans*, pp. 121, 211, and Sherrill Brown Wells, "Monnet and the 'Insiders,': Nathan, Tomlinson, Bowie, and Schaetzel," in *ibid.*, pp. 211f.

21. See Roussel, *Monnet*, pp. 482, 601. Monnet was particularly attached to Tomlinson, whom he liked to call his "grandson." *Ibid.*, p. 483.

22. Isaacson, *Wise Men*, pp. 30, 33, 406; Winand, *Eisenhower, Kennedy, and the United States of Europe*, pp. 7, 15, 23.

23. Isaacson, *Wise Men*, pp. 406–408.

24. *Ibid.*, pp. 417f., 425.

25. *Ibid.*, p. 421.

26. *Ibid.*, pp. 429f.

27. Michael Hogan, *America, Britain, and the Reconstruction of Western Europe, 1947–1952* (Cambridge, 1987), pp. 22f., defines the consensus as a "New Deal synthesis." Also see Alan Milward, *The*

Reconstruction of Western Europe, 1945–51 (London, 1984), p. 61, although this important study does not focus on the interplay of elites in implementing the Marshall Plan.

28. Schwabe, "United States and European Integration," pp. 126f.
29. Wilson D. Miscamble, *George F. Kennan and the Making of American Foreign Policy, 1947–1950* (Princeton, 1992), pp. 288f.
30. Acheson to U.S. Embassy France, 19 Oct. 1949, *FRUS*, 1949, vol. 4, p. 470.
31. Meeting of U.S. Ambassadors at Paris, 21–22 Oct. 1949, *FRUS*, 1949, vol. 4, p. 343.
32. Bruce to Acheson, 22 Oct. 1949, *FRUS*, 1949, vol. 4, p. 435.
33. See Dean Acheson to Robert Murphy, 25 Feb. 1950, quoted in Duchêne, *Monnet*, p. 204; Harper, *American Visions*, p. 289.
34. Policy Planning Staff, "Outline: Study of U.S. Stance toward Question of European Union," 7 July 1949, in Anna K. Nelson, *The State Department Policy Planning Staff Papers 1947–1949* (New York, 1983), pp. 82–100.
35. Miscamble, *Kennan*, p. 289.
36. Duchêne, *Monnet*, p. 224.
37. Schwabe, "United States and European Integration," p. 125.
38. Roussel, *Monnet*, p. 525; Duchêne, *Monnet*, p. 212; Pierre Mélandri, *Les Etats-Unis face à l'Unification de l'Europe* (Paris, 1980), p. 245.
39. George F. Kennan, *Memoirs, 1925–1950* (New York, 1967), pp. 457f.
40. Roussel, *Monnet*, pp. 600f.
41. Duchêne, *Monnet*, pp. 217f.
42. Roussel, *Monnet*, p. 603; Mélandri, *Les Etats Unis*, pp. 313f.
43. P. Porter to J. Cullough, Present State of the Schuman Plan, 6 Mar. 1951, NA; Klaus Schwabe, "Efforts towards Cooperation and Integration in Europe, 1948–1950," in Norbert Wiggershaus, ed., *The Western Security Community* (Providence, 1993), pp. 36f.; Duchêne, *Monnet*, pp. 216f.
44. H.A. Byroad to Acheson, 20 Mar. 1951, NA. I do not share Roussel's view that McCloy's clemency action vis-à-vis Alfred von Krupp had anything to do with the Schuman Plan. Instead, it was related to the pending issue of German rearmament (Roussel, *Monnet*, pp. 603f., as compared to Bird, *The Chairman*, pp. 361f., 364f., and Thomas Schwartz, *America's Germany: John McCloy and the Federal Republic of Germany* (Cambridge, 1991), pp. 169f.).
45. Duchêne, *Monnet*, pp. 213f.; Thomas Schwartz, "Jean Monnet and Jack McCloy," in Hacket, *Monnet and the Americans*, pp. 183, 187.
46. Bird, *The Chairman*, p. 340.

47. Renata Dwan, "The European Defence Community and the Role of French–American Elite Relations, 1950–1954," manuscript article; Klaus Schwabe, "Fürsprecher Frankreichs? John McCloy und die Integration der Bundesrepublik," in Ludolf Herbst *et. al.*, eds., *Vom Marshallplan zur EWG* (Munich, 1990), pp. 525f.; Duchêne, *Monnet*, p. 227. Communications between McCloy and Monnet, apparently, were inadequate as late as the end of September 1950, because Monnet continued to believe at that date that the United States planned to raise a German national force that would be put under American command (Monnet, Note, 23 Sept. 1950, in Roussel, *Monnet*, p. 584).

48. Harper, *American Visions*, p. 301; Dean Acheson, *Present at the Creation* (New York, 1987), pp. 556f.

49. Schwartz, *America's Germany*, pp. 210f.

50. Duchêne, *Monnet*, p. 231.

51. Quoted by Winand, *Eisenhower, Kennedy, and the United States of Europe*, pp. 29f.

52. Acheson, Lovett to Truman, 30 July 1951, *FRUS*, 1951, vol. 3, pp. 849f.; Winand, *Eisenhower, Kennedy, and the United States of Europe*, pp. 28f.

53. Acheson to U.S. Embassy France, 28 June 1951, *FRUS*, 1951, vol. 3, p. 802.

54. Acheson's expression, as quoted in Isaacson, *Wise Men*, p. 518.

55. Harper, *American Visions*, p. 308.

56. Bird, *The Chairman*, pp. 377f.

57. Harper, *American Visions*, pp. 312f.; Acheson, *Present at the Creation*, pp. 643f.

58. Harper, *American Visions*, p. 288.

59. *Ibid.*, p. 322; Acheson, *Present at the Creation*, pp. 643f.

60. Tomlinson to Bowie, 6 June 1952, NA.

61. Duchêne, *Monnet*, p. 232.

62. *Ibid.*, p. 234.

63. Winand, *Eisenhower, Kennedy, and the United States of Europe*, p. 32.

64. Acheson, Memorandum of Conversation [with Monnet], 14 Dec. 1952, *FRUS*, 1952–54, vol. 6, p. 254.

65. Isaacson, *Wise Men*, pp. 559f.

66. Stephen E. Ambrose, *Eisenhower: The President*, vol. 2 (New York, 1984), p. 49.

67. Dulles to Conant, 20 Nov. 1953, *FRUS*, 1952–54, vol. 7, p. 1475.

68. Pascaline Winand, "Eisenhower, Dulles, Monnet and the Uniting of Europe," in Hacket, ed., *Monnet and the Americans*, pp. 119f.; Wells,

"Monnet and the `Insiders,'" in *ibid.*, p. 210; Winand, *Eisenhower, Kennedy, and the United States of Europe*, p. 39.

69. Winand, *Eisenhower, Kennedy, and the United States of Europe*, p. 36.

70. *Ibid.*, p. 36; Ambrose, *Eisenhower*, vol. 2, pp. 120f.; denial: Dulles, Statement to NATO Council, 14 Dec. 1953, *FRUS*, 1952–54, vol. 5, p. 463; Third Plenary Meeting, Meeting of Heads of Government, Bermuda, 6 Dec. 1953, *FRUS*, 1952–54, vol. 5, p. 1802.

71. John Gaddis, "The Unexpected John Foster Dulles: Nuclear Weapons, Communism, and the Russians," in Richard H. Immerman, ed., *John Foster Dulles and the Diplomacy of the Cold War* (Princeton, 1990), p. 69.

72. Dulles to Bruce, 21 Nov. 1953, *FRUS*, 1952–54, vol. 6, pp. 329f. Also see Renata Dwan, "The European Defence Community and the Role of French–American Elite Relations, 1950–1954," manuscript essay, pp. 6f. In spite of the valuable information we owe to the author's research on this question, it still requires further analysis.

73. Dulles to Conant, 20 Nov. 1953, *FRUS*, 1952–54, vol. 7, pp. 1474f.

74. Winand, *Eisenhower, Kennedy, and the United States of Europe*, pp. 54f.; Rolf Steininger, "John Foster Dulles, the European Defense Community, and the German Question," in Immerman, ed., *John Foster Dulles and the Diplomacy of the Cold War*, p. 87.

75. Dulles, Statement to NATO Council, 14 Dec. 1953, *FRUS*, 1952–54, vol. 5, p. 463.

76. Bruce, Diary, Memorandum, 29 Mar. 1954, Bruce Papers, Virginia Historical Society, Richmond, Virginia.

77. Bruce, Diary, 21 Aug. 1954, Bruce Papers.

78. Rolf Steininger, "John Foster Dulles, the European Defense Community," in Immerman, ed., *John Foster Dulles and the Diplomacy of the Cold War*, pp. 81f.

79. Wells, "Monnet and the 'Insiders,'" in Hacket, ed., *Monnet and the Americans*, p. 210; Douglas Brinkley, *Dean Acheson: The Cold War Years, 1953–71* (New Haven, 1992), p. 31.

80. Brinkley, *Acheson*, p. 31.

81. Winand, *Eisenhower, Kennedy, and the United States of Europe*, p. 50; Bruce, Diary, 15 Dec. 1953, Bruce Papers.

82. Bruce, Diary, 15 Dec. 1953, 29 Mar. 1954, Bruce Papers.

83. Steininger, "John Foster Dulles, the European Defense Community," in Immerman, ed., *John Foster Dulles and the Diplomacy of the Cold War*, pp. 101f.

84. Bruce to Merchant, 30 Mar. 1954, in Bruce Diary, Bruce Papers;

Wells, "Monnet and the 'Insiders,'" in Hacket, ed., *Monnet and the Americans*, p. 210.

85. Bruce, Diary, 15 Dec. 1953, Bruce Papers; Winand, "Dulles and Eisenhower," in Hacket, ed., *Monnet and the Americans*, p. 125.

86. National Security Council, Meeting, 21 Nov. 1955, *FRUS*, 1955–57, vol. 4, p. 349.

87. Winand, *Eisenhower, Kennedy, and the United States of Europe*, p. 78.

88. Duchêne, *Monnet*, p. 296.

89. *Ibid.*, pp. 290f.; Hanns Jürgen Küsters, *Fondements de la Communité économique européenne* (Luxemburg, 1990), pp. 182f.

90. Dulles to U.S. Embassy in Germany, 1 July 1955, *FRUS*, 1955–57, vol. 4, pp. 307f.; Merchant, Memorandum, 1 July 1955, *ibid.*, p. 305.

91. Memorandum of Conversation, Monnet, Dulles, Merchant, 25 Oct. 1955, *FRUS*, 1955–57, vol. 4, pp. 337f.; Memorandum of Conversation, Dulles, Strauss *et al.*, 25 Jan. 1956, *FRUS*, 1955–57, vol. 4, pp. 395f.

92. Memorandum of Conversation, Monnet, Dulles, Bowie, 17 Dec. 1955, *FRUS*, 1955–57, vol. 4, pp. 367f.; Memorandum of Conversation, Dulles, Monnet, Merchant, 25 Oct. 1955, *ibid.*, pp. 337f.

93. Dulles, Memorandum to Eisenhower, 9 Jan. 1956, *FRUS*, 1955–57, vol. 4, pp. 388f.

94. Duchêne, *Monnet*, p. 303.

95. Dulles to Macmillan, 10 Dec. 1995, *FRUS*, 1955–57, vol. 4, pp. 362–64.

96. Duchêne, *Monnet*, p. 296; Memorandum of Conversation, Dulles, Strauss, Mayer, Murville, 6 Feb. 1956, *FRUS*, 1955–57, vol. 4, pp. 406f. The U.S. ambassador in Paris had warned that Euratom would have no chance of being ratified by the French parliament if France was required to renounce the right of producing nuclear weapons (Dillon to Dulles, 3 Feb. 1956, *ibid.*, pp. 401f.).

97. Dulles to U.S. Embassy, Belgium, 24 May 1956, *FRUS*, 1955–57, vol. 4, p. 444.

98. Strauss to Hoover, 19 Dec. 1956, *FRUS*, 1955–57, vol. 4, pp. 495–97; Dulles to U.S. Embassy in Germany, 30 Mar. 1956, *ibid.*, pp. 420f.

99. Memorandum of Conversation, Dulles, Adenauer, 12 June 1956, *FRUS*, 1955–57, vol. 4, pp. 446f.

100. Memorandum of Coversation, Dulles, Monnet, 10 Jan. 1957, *FRUS*, 1955–57, vol. 4, p. 501.

101. Duchêne, *Monnet*, p. 298.

Part V
Special Relationships

–10–

Special Pleading

Alex Danchev

It is not our policy continuously to try to be one-up, as a nation, on other nations; but it is our aim to rub in the fact that we are not trying to do this, otherwise what is the point of not trying to do this?[1]

We limeys have a peculiar position to keep up, you know . . . We can't all be at the top of the tree but we are all men of responsibility. You never find an Englishman among the underdogs – except in England of course.[2]

"The Special Relationship" – the very idea of "specialness" in this sphere – a notion now over half a century old, remains radically under-thought and under-theorized. The terms themselves are commonly tricked out with inverted commas, as here. The well-read, well-respected collection edited by Roger Louis and Hedley Bull is a classic case in point. This book, entitled *The "Special Relationship"*, might be described as a treatise on inverted commas. It is prefaced as follows:

The "Special Relationship" was not the theme of the conferences [on which the book is based] . . . In discussions designed to study contemporary problems at least as much as the historical background, the label "Special Relationship" seemed to prejudice the debate . . . Yet the idea of an intimate connection, a "Special Relationship," would not go away. Indeed it haunted the discussions. Eventually it was referred to as the ghost, ever present yet elusive, derided by some but acknowledged by all. What then was the "Special Relationship"? Why was it "special"? Was it a good thing? What has become of it? Has it run its course?[3]

These little marks, the inverted commas, are evidently meant to convey something important: a certain coolness – skepticism, perhaps, or irony – a post-modern awareness that words are playthings, ideas are constructs, and nothing is as it seems. The little marks promise more: if not explication, then at least interpretation. Yet the cupboard is bare. The inverted commas are not shorthand but sham. The scholarly evasions offered above are no more illuminating than the politician's categoric imperatives. "It is special. It just is. And that's that."[4] In the literature of the special relationship, attitude trumps analysis.[5]

There has been some refinement. We have long since discarded the Evangelical mode so expertly satirized in Stephen Potter's "Hands-Across-The-Seamanship": "First lessons concentrate on the necessity of always using the same phrases, and using them again and again. No harm in the general reader memorizing one or two of them now:

> We have a lot in common.
> After all, we come from the same stock.
> We have a lot to learn from each other."[6]

The Evangelists had a sense of mission. Equally important, they also had a point of reference, the greatest Anglo-American experience of their lifetimes, the Grand Alliance of the Second World War. For them, special-ness was like the scriptures. It required not examination but exegesis, or simply revelation. The Evangelist-in-Chief was, of course, Winston Churchill. "The natural Anglo-American special relationship" (not to mention "the fraternal association of the English-speaking peoples") was his coinage and his dream. "I cannot help reflecting that if my father had been American and my mother British, instead of the other way round, I might have got here on my own," he told an enraptured Congress in December 1941. "In that case this would not have been the first time you would have heard my voice." Famously, the voice carried. For the wartime generation and its offspring, specialness was articulated in a distinctively Churchillian register – sonorous, emotional, incantatory. The same speech expressed his hope and faith, "sure and inviolate, that in the days to come the British and American peoples will for their own safety and the good of all walk together side by side in majesty, in justice, and in peace."[7] More than any other individual, it was Churchill who advertised the benefits of the relationship and dramatized its possibilities in his own life. Except as apostrophe, it did not survive him.

For some two decades, the dominant mode has been the Functional. In sharp contrast to the earlier work, this is neither militant nor inspiring. Functionalists aim to reconstruct, not convert. They take their cue from the plain-speaking Dean Acheson:

> I shall not bother you by doing what is done so often on occasions like this, of talking about all that we have in common: language, history and all of that.

> We know all that. What I do wish to stress is one thing we have in common, one desperately important thing, and that is that we have a common fate.[8]

A common fate entails common enemies, and a common interest in defeating or containing them. On this reading, the Anglo-American relationship was a combination for a purpose – first a *pax anti-Germanica* and then a *pax anti-Sovietica* – not a sentimental attachment.[9] The relationship was special (as Acheson himself privately conceded), but it was also seamy. It did not arise naturally from an existential sense of community. It had to be nurtured and, above all, negotiated.

The great exemplar of this mode of thought was the late, lamented Christopher Thorne, his *magnum opus* the dense, punning *Allies of a Kind* (1978), a brilliant disquisition on the hybridity and complexity of the wartime relationship after Pearl Harbor, perhaps best encapsulated in his own words as "remarkably close and yet particularly strained."[10] With Thorne's untimely death in 1992, the mantle passed to David Reynolds, whose strikingly assured début, *The Creation of the Anglo-American Alliance* (1981), focusing on the formative period 1937–41, was sub-titled "a study in competitive co-operation" – the epitome of Func-tionalism – and whose recent work on the years immediately following, *Rich Relations* (1995), is a masterly examination of just how special and also how foreign it was to get "somewhat mixed up together" in such a fashion.[11]

Recently, there have been unmistakable signs of a further shift, to the Terminal.[12] Here is "endism" applied to the special relationship. In keep-ing with the multiple fractures of the post-Cold War world – as witness the former Soviet Union and the former Yugoslavia – it posits a former Anglo-America. This is not reconstruction but deconstruction. Inverted commas litter the page like ticks. "Specialness" is, and always was, self-deception; "the special relationship" not so much a creation as a construct – a British construct, or, to personalize, a Churchillian one.[13] In this mode, Churchill figures more as conjurer than evangelist. For those of a Terminal persuasion, the mythicality is the reality. They are interested in Anglo-American make-believe. As at public school, games-playing reveals character. One game, in particular, has caught the imagination, largely because of its popularity with Harold Macmillan and later, *diminuendo*, with Margaret Thatcher. The name of the game is Greeks and Romans. At Allied Force Headquarters (AFHQ) in Algiers in 1943 the rules were explained to the young Richard Crossman by a worldly-wise Macmillan. "Remember," he said,

> when you go into the Hotel St George, you will regularly enter a room and see an American colonel, his cigar in his mouth and his feet on the table. When your eyes get used to the darkness, you will see in the corner an English captain, his feet down, his shoulders hunched, writing like mad, with a full in-tray and a full out-tray, and no cigar.
>
> Mr Crossman, you will never call attention to this discrepancy. When you install a similar arrangement in your own office, you will always permit your American colleague not only to have a superior rank to yourself and much higher pay, but also the feeling that he is running the show. This will enable you to run it yourself.
>
> We, my dear Crossman, are Greeks in this American empire. You will find the Americans much as the Greeks found the Romans – great big, vulgar, bustling people, more vigorous than we are and also more idle, with more unspoiled virtues but also more corrupt. We must run AFHQ as the Greek slaves ran the operations of the Emperor Claudius.

In another variant from the same period: "These Americans represent the new Roman Empire and we Britons, like the Greeks of old, must teach them how to make it go." And in the fraught circumstances of 1956–57: "We are the Greeks of the Hellenistic age: the power has passed from us to Rome's equivalent, the United States of America, and we can at most aspire to civilise and occasionally to influence them."[14]

If ever there was a Greek, it was Acheson's friend and confessor, Oliver Franks, ambassador in Washington, 1948–52.[15] If ever there was a Roman, it was George McGhee, Assistant Secretary of State for the Near East, South Asia, and Africa, 1949–51. In April 1951, these two began talks in the State Department on the ticklish issue of the Iranian oil crisis: that is to say, the Iranian threat to nationalize the Anglo-Iranian oil company, popularly known as "Anglo-Persian," the forerunner of British Petroleum (BP). Half a century earlier, Lord Curzon had written prophetically that, once British rule in India was ended, "your ports and your coaling stations, your fortresses and dockyards, your Crown Colonies and protectorates will go too. For either they will be unnecessary, as the toll-gates and barbicans of an Empire that has vanished, or they will be taken by an enemy more powerful than yourselves."[16] Anglo-Persian was a toll-gate of Empire. For the British, the oil concession was economically vital (as a source of foreign exchange as well as oil), though not indispensable. For the Americans, locked in the Cold War, Iran itself was a strategic asset. The Iranians for their part wanted the maximum benefit from their own bounty.[17] Here were all the makings of a test case, and one that the British might easily lose. Hence the Anglo-American talks.

To all outward appearances, Franks and McGhee were completely incompatible. Just thirty-nine, oil-savvy and oil-rich himself, the Assistant Secretary's invincible self-assurance and sharp tongue were enough to give British officials conniption fits. In the privacy of their correspondence, they called him "the infant prodigy."[18] A later generation might have had recourse to "Indiana Jones." Like the intrepid archaeologist, however, there was more to George McGhee, D.Phil., than met the eye. A former Rhodes Scholar, he had spent three years as a graduate student at Queen's College, Oxford, completing his doctorate in 1937. After Dallas, Texas, the Southern Methodist University, and the University of Oklahoma, immersion in Oxford had a profound effect on him, as it did on the many Rhodes Scholars propelled into government service during the Democratic cycles of the 1940s and 1960s – Philip Kaiser and Dean Rusk, to name but two. In McGhee's case, one aspect in particular left its mark. At Queen's, as at most Oxford colleges, each student had a "moral tutor" whom he would see regularly, if infrequently, and to whom he could go in case of need, moral or otherwise. McGhee was allocated to an energetic philosophy don hardly older than himself and yet, as it seemed, infinitely knowledgeable and infinitely wise. This paragon was Oliver Franks, then plying his trade as a disciple of John Locke and lecturing, appropriately enough, on God.[19]

So the stage was set for a classical confrontation. Who better to tame the new barbarian? Was this not the very essence of Greeks and Romans – the former, a philosopher, as moral tutor of the latter? Alas, it was not to be. By that time, after a long period of havering by Anglo-Persian – described as confused, hidebound, small-minded and blind by their own Labour Advisor – there was no decent way out. McGhee was genuinely sympathetic, but characteristically direct. The United States was neither willing nor able to pull Britain's chestnuts out of the fire. Anglo-Persian was duly nationalized the following month. In London, there was some reflex rattling of sabres – a tinny sound – but over Iranian oil, unlike Egyptian water, the sabres stayed sheathed. In Washington, there was only the silent calculation of future dividends.

Greeks and Romans was a British conceit.[20] It was shared (or connived at), for a while, by some Americans. As an analogy, it leaves a lot to be desired. Historically, it makes no sense. As Robin Edmonds has reminded us – one Greats man reproving another – "not only did they speak different languages. The Romans acquired their eastern provinces by defeating the Greeks in war; and they went on to pillage the immense riches of the Greek world on a vast scale."[21] Moreover, it is inescapably patronizing.

The analogy assumes that the Greeks (that is, the British) know best. The central point about the encounter between Franks and McGhee over Anglo-Persian, however, is that it was McGhee who knew better. In reality, the American matched none of the stereotypes for which he was so eagerly fitted in London. He was not anti-British, he was not a simple-minded anti-colonialist, and he was not (as the Foreign Office charged) an "appeaser" of Iran. He was simply the expert – a rare bird in Britain, as Correlli Barnett never tires of pointing out.[22] Macmillan's conception was pure fantasy. In reality, a civilizing mission was not enough. True Greeks had to get their hands dirty. Even a sub-special conception of this sort carried a further obligation – the capacity to act as well as the audacity to advise. Oliver Franks himself observed wisely that "in the Anglo-American relationship British policy has to pass the test: can the British deliver?"[23] This was an obligation acutely felt. If there is a touch-stone of British foreign policy in the post-1940 period, it is reliability *vis-à-vis* the United States. Nevertheless, there have been some embarrassing defaults. In plain truth, the British did not have the wherewithal to meet either their obligations or their aspirations. "Never forget the Greeks, Forster," the poet Constantine Cavafy once admonished E. M. Forster, as if to anticipate the analogy. "Never forget . . . that we are bankrupt . . . Pray that you – you English with your capacity for adventure – never lose your capital, otherwise you will resemble us, restless, shiftless, liars."[24]

Macmillan's persistently seductive analogy was and is a snare and a delusion. It is wonderfully revealing of a certain native *mentalité*, but as a hypothesis on the special relationship it is either irrelevant or redundant. This is not unexpected. All three modes of scholarship canvassed here – Evangelical, Functional and Terminal – tell us many interesting things about the Anglo-American relationship. None provides us with an adequate account of specialness, and certainly not one that is readily transferable. By common consent, the seminal Anglo-American experience was the Second World War, or at least (according to the former) that part of it which the latter eventually deigned to share.[25] Was the Anglo-American relationship special, therefore, in 1941? Potentially. In 1942? Emphatically. In 1943? Mostly. In 1944? Vestigially. In 1945? Hardly. That is a summary of the received wisdom. But how can we tell? On what basis can we say that the relationship was special in 1942 and not in 1945, or even that it was more special in the early 1940s than in the early 1990s? We have nothing to go on but inverted commas and the two broad categories suggested by David Reynolds – quality and importance.[26]

Can we do better? Is it possible to specify "special"? The *Oxford English Dictionary* offers, *inter alia*, "of such a kind as to exceed or excel in some way that which is usual or common; exceptional in character, quality or degree . . . Admitted to particular intimacy; held in particular esteem . . . Marked off from others of the kind by having some distinguishing qualities or features; having a distinct or individual character." Its Anglo-American examples appear under the last of these variants; disappointingly, the earliest is dated 1945. What then are the distinguishing features of a special relationship? Are there, in effect, criteria? I propose ten:

1 Transparency
2 Informality
3 Generality
4 Reciprocity
5 Exclusivity
6 Clandestinity
7 Reliability
8 Durability
9 Potentiality
10 Mythicality

Some generalizations about these criteria will be readily apparent. They are derived from the Anglo-American avatar.[27] They are highly subjective. To go further, the greatest are perhaps the first and the tenth, transparency and mythicality. They are purely qualitative. As H. C. Allen remarked, "specialness" is a term of art.[28] And they are inescapably relative. Notwithstanding the definite article – *the* special relationship – there is no absolute standard and no fixed requirement. International relationships, like any other relationships, may be more or less special. It is a matter of degree; and also a matter of comparison. "We don't go around saying, yah boo sucks, my relationship is more special than yours," said a British Foreign Secretary recently.[29] Perhaps not. But that is exactly what "we" have been thinking, or pleading, for over fifty years. Explicitly or implicitly, in other words, evaluation makes reference to others. And others are by no means disinterested. In 1993, the U.S. government accidentally released a league table of states ranked by "importance to US interests," according to a State Department study completed the previous year, shortly before the election of Bill Clinton. In order of importance, the top ten were Germany, France, Britain, China, Japan, Russia, Mexico, Israel, Canada, and Iraq.[30] Clearly one can be important – or be considered important – but not special. Clearly, also, there are a bewildering variety of cases. Some claim specialness (Japan).[31] Some disclaim specialness

(Canada).[32] Some are born special (Israel).[33] Some have specialness thrust upon them (Germany).[34] Some are special, it might be said, in spite of themselves (Russia). If the competing claims can be substantiated – and they are advanced in uncomfortably familiar terms, complete with affinities, aspersions, and the obligatory punctuation[35] – then having a special relationship is not the cultured and culture-specific pastime that the Anglo-Saxon aristos have always imagined. That notion and that type, skewered mercilessly by John le Carré in novel after novel – "Church and Spy Establishment, with uncles who sat on Tory Party committees, and a rundown estate in Norfolk . . . a strand of the finely spun web of English influence of which we had perceived ourselves the centre"; "callow Yale men in button-down shirts who believed they could outwit the worst cut-throats in Latin America and always had six unbeatable arguments for doing the wrong thing" – are now out of fashion, perhaps for ever.[36] The special relationship is "our game" no longer. It may be a game of governance, in Richard Neustadt's term, but it is a game that anyone can play – anyone with the right cards and a cool nerve – more Happy Families (or Unhappy Families) than Greeks and Romans.[37] But can *anyone* play? Are there no valid distinctions to be made between, for example, the Philippines and the United Kingdom: small islands, strategically situated; unsinkable aircraft carriers in foreign seas; handy leverage for rampageous Uncle Sam?

> Where away England, steersman answer me?
> We cannot tell. For we are all at sea.[38]

The *reductio ad absurdum* of such a proposition is that *everyone* has a special relationship with the United States, because of the overwhelming power or overweening influence of the latter;[39] or that there is no country with which the United Kingdom has not claimed a special relationship at some time in its history;[40] or, worse still, that all bilateral international relations are special:[41] insights of a kind, no doubt, but analytically barren ones.

There is no general theory. At the back of a book on the special relationship between Israel and (West) Germany – two of the more unlikely candidates – Lily Gardner Feldman has attempted "a theoretical framework for special relationships," drawing chiefly on that case history, with some brief reference to others, including the Anglo-American one.[42] Feldman is almost alone in trying to ground her argument in the existing literature on alliances and integration – a praiseworthy endeavor – but sets about it in a highly self-conscious and mechanistic fashion.[43] The result is unrevealing. Though she makes some sharp observations about terminological inexactitude and conceptual confusion, often wilful, her strongest suit is exasperation. When it comes to her own analysis, she is more therapist than evangelist. Specialness for Feldman is rather like an affective disorder. It is founded upon "mutual preoccupation," "psychological resonance," and (felt) need. The emphasis is on the emotional over the ideological, the societal over the governmental, the affiliational over the institutional. This is psychic rather than bureaucratic politics, a helpful corrective to the dominant Anglocentric assumption that the parties to a so-called special relationship are either frauds or dupes, and a salutary reminder that sentiment, properly conceived, has a role to play even in a world peopled by the likes of Henry Kissinger – who, incidentally, has more to say for the Anglo-American special relationship than his Bismarckian *alter ego* might lead one to expect.[44] As criteria, however, or simply as characteristics, preoccupation, resonance and need are at once diffuse and differentiated, for Feldman's analysis of the singular relationship between Israel and Germany is firmly embedded in one particular historical experience – the Holocaust. This is, of course, perfectly understandable, and in the nature of the case almost certainly unavoidable, but it imposes severe restrictions on the general applicability of any theoretical framework so derived.

Interestingly enough, Feldman's treatment finds an echo in another putative special relationship involving Israel. In the course of his investigation of Israeli–American relations, Abraham Ben-Zevi has constructed a "special relationship paradigm," juxtaposed with a "national interest paradigm," in an effort to capture that elusive something for which exponents of the art are always searching – the holy grail of specialness – in this case something more than cold-eyed geo-strategic (or geo-economic) calculation on the part of the United States. According to Ben-Zevi, the elements that merge into the special relationship paradigm reflect a widespread fund of goodwill toward Israel that is not restricted to the Jewish community, and an equally strong and persistent commitment to Israel's continued national existence, integrity, and security. Comprising a cluster of broadly based attitudes that underscore the affinity and similarity between the two states in terms of their pioneering nature and commitment to democracy, this paradigm emerged as a legitimate and pervasive precept as soon as Israel was established in 1948.[45]

For this author, therefore, the key criteria are durability, pervasiveness, and legitimacy. Ben-Zevi, too, holds that the affective domain is crucial. He is investigating a relationship that he takes to be special – there is a strong element of circularity here – albeit one undergoing what he calls "a continuous process of erosion and evaporation," or, in Camille Mansour's word, "trivialization" (a process both link to the exhaustion of the Manichaean struggle between the United States and the Soviet Union). The peculiar character of this relationship cannot be understood in terms of instrumentality or *realpolitik* alone. Neither the Soviet ogre nor the Jewish lobby will suffice. The contention here is Martin Wight's: "There are associations between powers that seem to be deeper than formal alliances, to be based on affinity and tradition as much as interest, to be not so much utilitarian as *natural*."[46] A new paradigm must be called in to redress the balance of the old.

These paradigms have their uses, but in Ben-Zevi's work they begin to assume a life of their own. An insidious substitution process takes place, such that it is the paradigms themselves that are said to change, rather than the phenomena they purport to describe. Thus, it is not the Israeli–American relationship (or its specialness) that is subject to erosion and evaporation in his account, but the special relationship *paradigm*. This is worrying. Paradigms are not politics. They are merely the pets and playthings of political scientists. Abraham Ben-Zevi's pets are inadequately house-trained. Furthermore, the inquiry is as unequal as the relationship. Ben-Zevi's paradigms are paradigms of *American* behavior and attitudes. Nothing comparable is offered for the other partner in the relationship, and surprisingly little analytical attention is given to the complex question of how the two interact. Ben-Zevi is interested in motives; at any rate, in American motives. He tends to ignore modalities. The effect is to suggest that the character of the relationship is determined unilaterally, not to say arbitrarily, by the United States. Specialness is like a scarce commodity (or perhaps an illegal substance), rationed and confiscated, hoarded and looted, used and abused, and traded on the black market. Washington is the dealer and the only source of supply. The habit is expensive and hard to break. Cold turkey is worse than Cold War. The peace process holds the fragile hope of eventual detox.

Much of this is extremely valuable. At the very least, there is an intuitive tension between quality and inequality, as one might say, and it is well to affirm that an international relationship can be at the same time special and unequal. Except perhaps for a certain equality of esteem – if a place can found for more sentiment – parity is not necessary for speciality. Indeed, inasmuch as the original conception of the special relationship is a twentieth-century hyphenation involving the United States (call it x-American), then parity was always more pipe-dream than premise. The closest approximation to full parity ever experienced is the Anglo-American relationship of 1941–42. American potential was infinitely greater; but the Americans themselves saw that it would take time to realize. Rarely has a great power gone to war in such a state of comprehensive unreadiness. The British, by contrast, were already organized, mobilized, and tyrannized – but benignly – by the wildcat Winston.[47] In their mutual predicament, Anglo-American needs matched. Their respective contributions, if not exactly equal, were complementary and necessary. For a long moment, London and Washington were totally interdependent, and they knew it. Here was reciprocity in action, the foundation of the *pax anti-Germanica*. "The perfect alliance would show equality of interest and commitment between the two parties, with a reciprocity of advantage." Here, too, was the moment to redeem the expectant promise of the combination from the British point of view: nothing less than a realignment of their relationship with the United States – "no longer a client receiving help from a generous patron, but two comrades fighting for life side by side," in the Prime Minister's post-Pearl Harbor invocation.[48] Churchill was always hopeful. "It is difficult to go anywhere in London without having the feeling that Britain is now Occupied Territory," wrote George Orwell in December 1943.[49] He was a good barometer. The British have been occupied in one way or another ever since, "intravenously," in Angela Carter's marvellous metaphor, or otherwise.[50] They are not alone.

The tension, therefore, remains. It is normal to be unequal; yet it seems that prolonged, gross inequality will eventually vitiate speciality. For all Tel Aviv's much-advertised intransigence, there is no denying the pronounced patron-client (or rather client–patron) flavour of Israeli–American relations. It is, in fact, a highly dependent relationship: a crippling handicap that may well be held to weaken any wider claims. When all is said and done, mendicants must mind their manners. The United States has endowed Israel with many things, including life itself. In Washington, Israel may be considered special, just as it was (and is still) considered important. But that is not enough. The character of a relationship cannot be determined unilaterally. If it could, either the relationship would not be special or the specialness would not be a relationship, but merely an imposition. Contrary to popular apperception, specialness is not a matter of grace and favor. It is not in the gift of one partner, however strong. It cannot be administered like a drug or a punishment. It is not a commodity or a crime. It is a process – a process of interaction, laced with expectation.

As in life, so in international relations: expectations are crucial. "There are great possibilities," observes John Dickey, "for strain and disappointment in a special relationship, as many can attest, but nothing is resented quite so much as the unfulfilled expectation of being consulted."[51] A willing engagement each with the other, an openness to inspection and objection, and ultimately to influence – in a word, transparency – is an exacting requirement, as the Anglo-American wartime experiment demonstrated.[52] Notwithstanding the extraordinary consonance achieved and sustained, Churchill's high expectations of "righteous comradeship" were disappointed. His characteristic reproofs to the U.S. President were all variations on the same theme. As early as February 1942: "The keynote of our relations must surely be equality." As late as July 1944: "It is, I am sure, the duty of those who bear our responsibility . . . to place themselves in a reasonable and equal relationship."[53] But these reproofs were never sent. Certainly, Churchill felt resentment, much more than we suppose. He kept it bottled up, except among his inner circle, because he had to. Squeezed uncomfortably between a great American buffalo on one side and a great Soviet bear on the other, the little British donkey might be the only one that knew the way home (so it thought); but no one was listening.[54] James Gould Cozzens's fictionalized portrait is a cruel exposure:

> Grimacing, Mr Churchill must taste . . . the gall of his situation. Fine phrases and selected words might show it almost a virtue that, far call'd our navies melt away; that on dune and headland sinks the fire; but those circumstances also kept him from the leading position. Except as a piece of politeness, he did not even sit as an equal. His real job was to palter.[55]

The circuit from conjurer to palterer runs the gamut of skepticism about the very idea of specialness. Curiously, scepticism predates specialism. It was not yet 1938 when Neville Chamberlain declared his belief that "it is always best and safest to count on *nothing* from the Americans except words."[56] The sceptics have always been uncommonly assertive. Their belief – or rather unbelief – is absolute:

> Be these juggling fiends no more believ'd,
> That palter with us in a double sense;
> That keep the word of promise to our ear,
> And break it to our hope.

As to the prospect of a special relationship, the expectations of the skeptics are best described as trivial. Their attention wanders. The process of interaction congeals. The resulting relationship is not so much ordinary as absent. With the possible exception of Edward Heath – when it mattered rather less – no British Prime Minister this century has been so conspicuously neglectful, not to say scornful, of the process of interaction with the United States as was Neville Chamberlain. The contrast with his successor could not have been more marked. Where Chamberlain was inert, Churchill had to be forcibly restrained. No sooner had the Japanese done the dirty deed at Pearl Harbor than he leapt into an ocean liner bound for Washington to confabulate with the President. Alarmingly, he lodged at the White House. The consequences were unpredictable, but it worked out well enough. Anglo-American relations were success-fully domesticated. Bath-time at the White House in December 1941 was the apogee of specialness in a hostile world:

> One morning the Prime Minister wanted to dictate while he was in his bath – not a minute could be wasted – He kept submerging in the bath and when he "surfaced" he would dictate a few more words or sentences. Eventually he got out of the bath when his devoted valet, Sawyers, draped an enormous bath-towel around him. He walked into his adjoining bedroom, followed by me, notebook in hand, and continued to dictate while pacing up and down the enormous room. Eventually the towel fell to the ground but, quite unconcerned, he continued pacing the room dictating all the time.
>
> Suddenly President Roosevelt entered the bedroom and saw the British Prime Minister completely naked walking round the room dictating to me. WSC never being lost for words said "You see, Mr President, I have nothing to conceal from you."[57]

And the moral of this tale? In the truly special relationship transparency beats mythicality every time. So they say.

Notes

Earlier versions of this chapter were presented at the Fulbright Conference at the University of Hull in 1995 and the International Theory Group at Keele. I am grateful to both audiences for their stimulation and encouragement.

1. Stephen Potter, "Hands-Across-The-Seamanship," *One-Upmanship* [1952], in *The Complete Upmanship* (London: Rupert Hart-Davis, 1970), p. 263.
2. Sir Ambrose Abercrombie in Evelyn Waugh, *The Loved One* [1948] (Harmondsworth: Penguin, 1951), pp. 12–13.

3. Wm. Roger Louis and Hedley Bull, eds., *The "Special Relationship"* (Oxford: Oxford University Press, 1989), p. vii. Cf. C. J. Bartlett, *"The Special Relationship"* (London: Longman, 1992).

4. Margaret Thatcher, speech in Washington, 21 Feb. 1985, quoted in H. C. Allen, "A Special Relationship?", *Journal of American Studies*, 19 (1985), 407.

5. There are, of course, exceptions. See David Reynolds, "A 'Special Relationship'?" and "Rethinking Anglo-American Relations," *International Affairs* 62 and 65 (1985–86 and 1988–89), 1–20 and 89–111.

6. Potter, "Hands-Across-The-Seamanship." Perhaps the most sophisticated exponent was H. C. Allen. See his *Great Britain and the United States* (London: Odhams, 1954) and *The Anglo-American Predicament* (London: Macmillan, 1960); and his own later commentary on this work, "The American Revolution and the Anglo-American Relationship in Historical Perspective," in H. C. Allen and Roger Thompson, eds., *Contrast and Connection* (London: Bell, 1976), pp. 149–77, and also "A Special Relationship?", *ibid.*, pp. 403–13.

7. The *locus classicus* of specialness is his "Sinews of Peace" speech at Fulton, Missouri, on 5 Mar. 1946, printed in Robert Rhodes James, ed., *Churchill Speaks* (London: Windward, 1981), pp. 876–84. See esp. p. 880. For his wartime thinking and speechifying, see Churchill to Roosevelt, 28 May 1943, printed in Warren F. Kimball, ed., *Churchill and Roosevelt*, vol. 2 (Princeton: Princeton University Press, 1984), pp. 225–26; Churchill to Attlee, 14 Sept. 1943, FO 954/22A, Public Records Office [hereafter PRO]; and speeches to U.S. Congress and Harvard University, 26 Dec. 1941 and 20 Sept. 1943, quoted in Martin Gilbert, *Winston S. Churchill*, vol. 7 (London: Heinemann, 1986), pp. 29–30 and 493.

8. Talk to British–American Parliamentary Group, 26 June 1952, Acheson Papers, Box 67, Truman Library.

9. *Pax anti-Sovietica* is Roger Louis's expression, derived from Richard Ullman, "America, Britain and the Soviet Threat in Historical and Present perspective," in Louis and Bull, eds., *"Special Relationship"*, pp. viii and 103–14. *Pax anti-Germanica* is mine, as far as I know.

10. Christopher Thorne, *Allies of a Kind* (London: Hamish Hamilton, 1978).

11. David Reynolds, *The Creation of the Anglo-American Alliance* (London: Europa, 1981); *Rich Relations* (London: HarperCollins, 1995). See also his "Competitive Co-operation," *Historical Journal*, 23 (1980), 233–45.

12. Christopher Hitchens, *Blood, Class and Nostalgia* (London: Chatto and Windus, 1990); John Dickie, *"Special" No More* (London: Weidenfeld and Nicolson, 1994); and, more ambiguously, Christopher Coker, "The Special Relationship in the 1990s," *International Affairs*, 68 (1992), 407–22. The latest full-length survey, however, finds life in the old dog yet. See Alan P. Dobson, *Anglo-American Relations in the Twentieth Century* (London: Routledge, 1995).

13. See John Charmley, *Churchill's Grand Alliance* (London: Hodder and Stoughton, 1995).

14. Quoted in Anthony Sampson, *Macmillan* (Harmondsworth: Penguin, 1967), pp. 65–66; Hitchens, *Blood, Class and Nostalgia*, pp. 23–24.

15. The following section borrows from Alex Danchev, *Oliver Franks* (Oxford: Oxford University Press, 1993), pp. 121 f.

16. Lord Curzon, "The True Imperialism," *Nineteenth Century*, 63 (1908), p. 157.

17. See Wm. Roger Louis, *The British Empire in the Middle East* (Oxford: Oxford University Press, 1984).

18. George McGhee, *Envoy to the Middle World* (New York: Harper and Row, 1983); Houston-Boswall to Bowker, 29 Mar. 1951, FO 371/91184, PRO.

19. Interview with Ambassador George C. McGhee, 29 Mar. 1989; McGhee, *Middle World*, pp. xvi–xvii, 334, 384. McGhee also attended some of Franks's lectures.

20. Even Ernest Bevin, that most unlikely Greek, was not immune. "The United States is a young country and the Administration was too apt to take unreflecting plunges," he told the Indian Prime Minister. "We had made it our business to try to restrain them." Strang minute, 5 Jan. 1951, FO 371/92776, PRO.

21. Robin Edmonds, *Breaking the Mould* (Oxford: Oxford University Press, 1986), p. 319.

22. Correlli Barnett, *The Lost Victory* (London: Macmillan, 1995). Cf. Alex Danchev, "Britannia in Fur Coat and no Knickers," *The Times Higher Education Supplement*, 6 Oct. 1995.

23. Oliver Franks, *Britain and the Tide of World Affairs* (Oxford: Oxford University Press, 1955), p. 35.

24. Forster to Isherwood, 16 July 1933, in Mary Lago and P. N. Furbank, eds., *Selected Letters of E. M. Forster*, vol. II (London: Collins, 1985), p. 118.

25. For recent interpretations see David Reynolds *et al.*, eds., *Allies at War* (New York: St Martin's Press, 1994).

26. In Reynolds's schema, importance relates to the partners themselves and to the world at large. With regard to the former, also see John Baylis, *Anglo-American Defence Relations* (London: Macmillan, 1984), pp. xvii–xviii.

27. Of my earlier work, they draw chiefly on *Very Special Relationship* (London: Brassey's, 1986); "In the Back Room," in Richard J. Aldrich, ed., *British Strategy, Intelligence and the Cold War* (London: Routledge, 1992), pp. 215–35; *Oliver Franks*, esp. pp. 109–135; and "To Albion's Aid with Gum and Nylons," *The Times Higher Education Supplement*, 9 June 1995.

28. Allen, "A Special Relationship?", p. 406.

29. Douglas Hurd quoted in Ian Black, "Do We Know Our Place?", *Guardian*, 25 Mar. 1995.

30. *State 2000* (Washington: GPO, 1993), p. 268, excerpted in Patrick Cockburn, "Germany Tops the US Global Pecking Order," *Independent*, 4 July 1993.

31. Roger Buckley, *US–Japanese Alliance Diplomacy* (Cambridge: Cambridge University Press, 1992); James W. Morley, "A New Partnership for a New Age," *IHJ Bulletin*, 15 (1995), 1–8. I am grateful to Masashi Nishihara for guidance on the literature of the Japanese–American relationship.

32. John W. Holmes, *Life With Uncle* (Toronto: University of Toronto Press, 1981); Lauren McKinsey and Kim Richard Nossal, eds., *America's Alliances and Canadian–American Relations* (Toronto: Summerhill Press, 1988).

33. Abraham Ben-Zevi, *The United States and Israel* (New York: Columbia University Press, 1993); Bernard Reich, *The United States and Israel* (New York: Praeger, 1984).

34. Zbigniew Brzezinski, "A Plan for Europe," *Foreign Affairs*, 74 (1995), 26–42; Martin Woollacott, "Bill and Helmut Unite around the Marshmallow Pie," *Guardian*, 13 July 1994.

35. See, e.g., Gabriel Sheffer, "Shared Values as the Basis for the US–Israeli 'Special Relationship'," in *idem*, ed., *Dynamics of Dependence* (Boulder: Westview, 1987), pp. 1–6.

36. John le Carré, *The Secret Pilgrim* and *The Night Manager* (London: Coronet, 1991 and 1994), pp. 120 and 93.

37. Richard E. Neustadt, *Alliance Politics* (New York: Columbia University Press, 1970), p. 79.

38. Joyce Cary, *To be a Pilgrim* [1942], reprinted in *Triptych* (London: Penguin, 1985), p. 498.

39. In a little-noticed passage in his "Sinews of Peace" speech, Churchill

made reference to the "special relations" enjoyed by the United States with both Canada and the South American republics. See Rhodes James, *Churchill Speaks*, p. 880.

40. Bhikhu Parekh, "Britain and America: Some Stray Thoughts," address at conference on "What Remains Special about the 'Special Relationship'?", University of Hull, 10 Apr. 1995. Jordan would be a prime example. See Richard Norton-Taylor, "Britain's 'Best King' Relationship Ends in Break with Saddam," *Guardian*, 25 Aug. 1995.

41. Holmes, *Life With Uncle*, p. 131. In common usage, at any rate, specialness need not be bilateral. Russia, for example, is now said to have a "special relationship" with NATO.

42. Lily Gardner Feldman, *The Special Relationship between West Germany and Israel* (Boston: George Allen and Unwin, 1984), pp. 261–88.

43. For similar treatments see John Baylis, "The Anglo-American Relationship and Alliance Theory," *International Relations*, 8 (1985), 368–79; Raymond Dawson and Richard Rosecrance, "Theory and Reality in the Anglo-American Alliance," *World Politics*, 19 (1966), 21–51.

44. Henry Kissinger, "Reflections on a Partnership," *International Affairs*, 58 (1982), 571–87.

45. Ben-Zevi, *United States and Israel*, pp. 15–16.

46. Ben-Zevi, *United States and Israel*, p. 24; Camille Mansour, *Beyond Alliance* (New York: Columbia University Press, 1994); Martin Wight, *Power Politics* (London: Penguin, 1986), p. 123. Wight continues: "Thus the British imagine their relationship to be with the United States (rather more generally than Americans imagine their relationship with England)."

47. See Alex Danchev, "Waltzing with Winston," *War in History*, 2 (1995), 202–30.

48. Wight, *Power Politics*, p. 123; Churchill to Roosevelt (unsent first draft), 5 Feb. 1942, PREM 4/17/3, PRO.

49. George Orwell, "As I Please," *Tribune*, 3 Dec. 1943, in Sonia Orwell and Ian Angus, eds., *The Collected Essays, Journalism and Letters of George Orwell*, vol. 3 (London: Penguin, 1970), p. 73.

50. Angela Carter, *Expletives Deleted* (London: Vintage, 1992), p. 5.

51. John Sloan Dickey, *Canada and the American Presence* (New York: New York University Press, 1975), p. 189.

52. For a résumé, see Alex Danchev, "Being Friends," in Lawrence Freedman *et al.*, eds., *War, Strategy and International Politics* (Oxford: Clarendon Press, 1992), pp. 195–210.

53. Churchill to Roosevelt (unsent drafts), 5 Feb. 1942 and 4 July 1944, PREM 4/17/3 and FO 954/17A, PRO.

54. This was Churchill's parable of the Tehran Conference of 1943. Lady Asquith, interviewed by Kenneth Harris, *The Listener*, 17 Aug. 1967. The anthropomorphism varied: after Yalta it was an elephant, a bear, and a lion. Colville diary, 24 Feb. 1945, in John Colville, *The Fringes of Power*, vol. 2 (London: Sceptre, 1987), p. 204.

55. James Gould Cozzens, *Guard of Honour* (New York: Harcourt, Brace and World, 1948), p. 394. Cozzens borrowed here from Rudyard Kipling's "Recessional," marking Queen Victoria's Jubilee in 1897. There is one recorded outburst. "What do you want me to do?", asked Churchill at one point in the Quebec Conference of 1944. "Get on my hind legs and beg like Fala [the President's dog]?" Quoted in *Foreign Relations of the United States, Conference at Quebec 1944* (Washington: GPO, 1972), p. 348.

56. Chamberlain to Hilda Chamberlain [his sister], 17 Dec. 1937, Chamberlain Papers, NC18/1/1032, Birmingham University Library.

57. Kinna to Gilbert, 10 Oct. 1984, quoted in Gilbert, *Churchill*, p. 28. Patrick Kinna was Churchill's regular shorthand writer and a member of his Private Office staff. This is probably the most reliable version of an apocryphal story. Cf. Robert E. Sherwood, *The White House Papers of Harry L. Hopkins*, vol. 1 (London: Eyre and Spottiswoode, 1948), p. 446.

The Federal Republic's Ostpolitik and the United States: Initiatives and Constraints

Gottfried Niedhart

In March 1971, Willy Brandt wrote a long letter to John McCloy, one of the founding fathers of the Federal Republic of Germany and known for his sceptical attitude towards Ostpolitik.[1] Brandt emphasized that his Ostpolitik was embedded in the general Western policy *vis-à-vis* the East. Ostpolitik did not ignore the conflict "between communism and democracy." The conflict would go on but military force must necessarily be avoided. This did not mean, however, that the military power of NATO and the political cohesion of the West could be disposed of. Brandt stressed his government's significant contributions in both of these fields. He also pointed out that the process of European integration had been pushed forward recently. "I cannot share your anxiousness," he wrote, "that the Soviet Union will reach her goals[2] without giving something in return and that her influence in Western Europe will increase." Brandt continued with a criticism of the old policy and a vision of what the new Ostpolitik might achieve. The old policy of confrontation had not been able to prevent the Berlin Wall and the division of Europe. The existence of the German Democratic Republic as a state could not be disputed even if the government in East Berlin was dependent on the presence of the Red Army. In the existing situation, it was of the utmost importance that the allegedly hostile Federal Republic could no longer be used by Moscow and East Berlin as an excuse to discipline the member states of the Warsaw Pact. It would serve Western interests if Ostpolitik removed the enemy image of the Federal Republic. Thereby, a change in East–West relations to the advantage of the West might be possible. Brandt alluded to "interesting information" as to the effects of Ostpolitik. However, he observed, it would not be wise to put this down in writing.

Brandt's letter summarized the main assumptions of Ostpolitik as well as American attitudes and reactions to it. Basically, Ostpolitik meant a decisive turn in dealing with the German question and the post-war status quo. By accepting the existing European borders and, consequently, by improving East–West relations, the financial burdens and military dangers of the confrontation between East and West were to be reduced. As to the supposed implications of Ostpolitik, the Bonn government had to react to fears and suspicions which were uttered in public in the United States and were shared to a certain extent by the Nixon administration. Accordingly, Brandt dealt with these fears. Furthermore, he indicated his long-term expectations. Through *détente*, and through Ostpolitik in particular, the Eastern bloc and the conflict-oriented behavior of the Soviet Union might change. Recognizing the status quo could be the first step to its transformation.

It is interesting that Brandt did not mention explicitly that Ostpolitik – after the failure of Adenauer's revisionism – was a new kind of revisionism. The German question was still regarded as open. This was realized at once in East Berlin (though, apparently, not immediately in Moscow), and also in Washington. It goes without saying that this caused some American uneasiness and suspicion. Furthermore, Brandt did not refer to West German perceptions of the United States and the European security system. He was silent about the impact which, in his view, the Vietnam War and America's over-commitment in world politics might have on the future role of the United States in Europe and of Europe as an actor in international affairs.

When Brandt wrote his letter, the treaties with Moscow and Warsaw were signed but not yet ratified. The ratification by the German Bundestag depended on a satisfactory agreement on Berlin. Any American doubts over the usefulness of Ostpolitik had to be removed in order to get the full support not only of the U.S. government but also of public opinion. Hence Brandt's efforts to convince the "old protectors of Germany McCloy and Clay." Apparently, he succeeded when he met them in New York on 17 June 1971, on the occasion of his speech to the American Council on Germany.[3] Two days earlier, Brandt had talked to President Nixon. At a press conference, he was able to tell journalists that there was "complete agreement" on the issues of Berlin and Ostpolitik.[4] Brandt and the members of his cabinet regarded American support for Ostpolitik as a vital precondition for its success. This chapter deals with the efforts to insure it, mainly between 1969, when the Brandt government took office, and 1971, when the agreement on Berlin was signed by the Four Powers.

For Willy Brandt, an ardent anti-communist and strict adherent to the Western alliance, it was not easy to understand the scepticism and even opposition he initially encountered in Washington. Brandt had visions but he was no dreamer. This was also true, for example, in the case of Defense Minister Helmut Schmidt who, in contrast to Brandt, had never been a left-winger in his political life and, therefore, could not be under any suspicion of being disloyal to the Western cause. In his memoirs, Schmidt describes the initial distrust by parts of the Nixon administration as "unfounded."[5] The German self-perception and the American perception of Bonn's Ostpolitik differed at times. But these differences were a matter of perception, not of actual policy.

What worried Washington, and especially Kissinger, most was the self-consciousness and independence of the new government in Bonn when formulating the guidelines of Ostpolitik. This was done between 1966 and 1969, when Brandt was Foreign Minister in a Grand Coalition government formed by the Christian Democrats (CDU) and the Social Democrats (SPD). During these years, the planning staff of the Auswärtiges Amt (Foreign Office), directed by Egon Bahr, who had been Brandt's close confidant for many years, dealt with the possibilities and options of a more active Ostpolitik. Bahr emerged not as the only but as the principal architect of Ostpolitik on the intellectual as well as the operational level.[6] Throughout the period under consideration here, he emphasized both the necessity for change in East–West relations and for continuity in the Federal Republic's relations with its partners in NATO. Security for the Federal Republic, he was certain, was only conceivable as security provided by the United States.[7]

Although the CDU/SPD government started the first phase of a new Ostpolitik, there was no real breakthrough. Chancellor Kurt Georg Kiesinger, the leader of the CDU, was more reluctant than Brandt to launch a new policy based on accepting post-war realities in Europe. At the same time, the FDP, the small Liberal Party which was in opposition, advocated a more radical departure in Ostpolitik, very much on the lines of the views of the SPD and Bahr's planning staff.[8] In October 1969, after the elections for the Bundestag, both parties formed a new coalition government. Ostpolitik and foreign policy in general was the essential link between the otherwise often conflicting views of Social Democrats and Liberals.

Henry Kissinger clearly understood that the new government would pursue not only a new Ostpolitik but also a much more independent course in foreign affairs, and this seemed to indicate the end of the post-war period. The Federal Republic, in theory, was still a semi-sovereign country and had to keep in mind the constraints which stemmed from the rights of the Four Powers, not to mention the constraints which had to do with strict and faithful allegiance to the European Community and to NATO. But *within* these constraints, Bonn took initiatives of its own and did not ask for permission beforehand. Both Brandt and Kissinger later agreed on this point.[9]

When beginning its initiatives towards the East, the Bonn government followed the general American lead. The Germans could refer, for instance, to the beginnings of détente during the presidency of John F. Kennedy. In fact, this had provided the background to Brandt's reorientation towards the concept of détente in the early 1960s, when he was mayor of West Berlin and had to realize that the U.S. government was willing to accept the status quo. Later, the Germans were encouraged by President Johnson. Brandt met Johnson and Secretary of State Rusk in February 1967. Both emphasized the necessity of improving relations with the East. Rusk expressed his readiness to assist wherever help was needed.[10] A few months later, Johnson told two German journalists who played a prominent role as supporters of a new Ostpolitik that the German government did not need to ask permission for any initiative. In Johnson's view, German bridge-building towards the East was highly useful. He had no anxieties with regard to German reliability within the Western alliance, and no distrust of Willy Brandt.[11] The President felt reassured, as he regarded himself as undisputed leader in the process of bridge-building. Apparently, Johnson saw the Germans as firmly subject to U.S. guidance.[12] It is interesting, however, that reports reached Bonn in which the German government was asked to be on its guard and to avoid any inconsistencies in its policy which might follow from the overlap of NATO membership, European integration, and Ostpolitik.[13]

There was no change in the American reaction to Ostpolitik when Richard Nixon entered the White House with Henry Kissinger as his National Security Advisor. Ostpolitik was not to be blocked. But there was widespread disquiet over its wider implications. At least in the beginning, Kissinger had "grave reservations."[14] They were shared[15] by the Pentagon and by some sections of the State Department, although the U.S. embassy in Bonn gave full support. Opposition to Ostpolitik also came from conservative Congressmen and, as mentioned above, from people such as John McCloy, Lucius Clay, Dean Acheson, and George Ball, who had shaped the post-war policy towards and in Germany. Satirically, Denis Healey, British Defence Minister between 1964 and 1970, called them "distinguished American dinosaurs from the occupation age." They "clearly find it difficult," he noted, "to come to terms with a world so different from that in which they were able to determine the policies not only of the U.S. but of Germany too."[16]

As membership of NATO was not questioned for one moment by the Brandt government or by West German society as a whole, American perceptions of Ostpolitik were influenced principally by the legacy of German nationalism[17] and by the self-conscious way in which Ostpolitik was implemented. Kissinger did not fear that the new government in Bonn would do anything to endanger "Germany's Western association" deliberately.[18] But would the West Germans resist Soviet temptations for ever? Moscow could conceivably offer something which might lead to unification if the Federal Republic turned to neutralism. In Kissinger's view, Brandt "possessed neither the stamina nor the intellectual apparatus to manage the forces he had unleashed."[19] On the one hand, this was a gross misperception of Brandt's abilities and politics. On the other, it has to be taken into account when dealing with U.S. reactions to Ostpolitik.

The government in Bonn made its own contribution to Kissinger's reservations, as the U.S. government was not really consulted on Ostpolitik, but only informed. Willy Brandt insisted, in his memoirs, that his Ostpolitik did more than echo American initiatives. It had its own roots and logical basis.[20] As early as March 1969, Brandt warned of overrating the role of the Federal Republic as an independent actor in East–West relations.[21] But he was equally sure that Bonn should not underestimate its role "as a partner of the Soviet Union."[22] Without any publicity, a period of intense talks between Bonn and Moscow had just started.[23] The Social Democratic–Liberal government in Bonn wanted to accept the post-war realities in Europe as results of the war. This was in accordance with the expectations of Germany's NATO partners, the U.S. included.[24] At the same time, Brandt and his Foreign Minister, Walter Scheel, wanted to win some freedom of action. Their strategy of overcoming the status quo by first accepting it in the end conflicted with the post-war order. Other Western governments, which at times felt uneasy about the possible consequences of Ostpolitik, also had this conflict in mind.

Brandt's critics deplored the advantages the Soviet Union got by Ostpolitik. But Brandt expected to get something in return for recognizing the territorial status quo. In the medium term, he and Bahr looked forward to a transformation of the Eastern bloc. Instead of turning to neutrality, as feared by many observers in the West, they wanted to play a more active role in European and world politics. Their wish was to emancipate the Federal Republic from its postwar supervision by the Western powers. Konrad Adenauer had been the model pupil of the West (although time and again he had complained about U.S. policy).[25] Brandt, and even more so Scheel, wanted to leave school and enter normal life. They consequently questioned one of the central elements of the post-war European architecture, namely the containment of the Federal Republic by the Western alliance.[26] Twenty-five years after the end of the war, a new democratic and Westernized Germany wanted to be accepted as an equal partner. Ostpolitik has to be seen in this wider context (it is revealing that Brandt spoke of "legitimate national interests").[27]

When dealing with the Soviet Union, the Bonn government was fully aware of the above-mentioned constraints. Egon Bahr even emphasized them in his talks with Gromyko, held early in 1970, when he referred to the rights of the Four Powers in "Germany as a whole." He was, thereby, able to reject certain suggestions made by the Soviet Foreign Minister. Also, Bonn did not fail to keep its allies, and especially the United States, informed. Even before he was elected Federal Chancellor, Brandt asked the U.S. government to receive Bahr as his special envoy. The first contact between the White House and the SPD leadership after the election of 28 September was on 1 October 1969. Henry Kissinger talked to Bahr on the phone and apologized for President Nixon's earlier call to Kiesinger, the leader of the CDU and then still Chancellor. Immediately after the election, Nixon had congratulated Kiesinger, who headed the poll but had no majority in the Bundestag. Now Kissinger told Bahr he was looking forward to cooperation with the Brandt government. He agreed upon an early meeting. In a note to Brandt, Bahr commented: "That sounds good."[28]

Kissinger and Bahr had met before. But their meeting on 13 October 1969 began a series of talks and other communications between these two men at the center of power. After the elections, Bahr moved to the Federal Chancellery, where he was in charge of Ostpolitik. He now tried to implement the various steps which had earlier been envisaged by the planning staff of the Foreign Office. According to Bahr's notes, three issues were on the agenda in his conversation with Kissinger. The first was the way in which both governments should relate to each other. Bahr announced a greater degree of independence. The new government in Bonn wished to think for itself. Alluding to the peculiarities of American–German relations in the post-war period, Bahr added that Bonn would not ask every two months whether the American ally "still loves us" (Kissinger's reaction was: "Thank God!"). Second, Bahr dealt with the Non-Proliferation Treaty. Bonn was willing to sign it. But before doing so, certain clarifications by the Soviet Union would be needed, although for Bahr they were of minor relevance. "Absolutely central," he believed, "was the German–American relationship and the alliance." Concluding this point, both Bahr and Kissinger "moaned about the Russians in a moderate way." The third point was Ostpolitik. Bahr explained his ideas and concentrated on two aspects: the essential continuity of German foreign policy and the renunciation of force in German-Soviet relations. Kissinger's advice was to start negotiations as soon as possible. He concluded: "Your success will be our success."[29]

Whether Ostpolitik would be a success or not was an open question. Kissinger did not say so, but there is no doubt that he was more sceptical than Bahr. Whatever their expectations might have been, Bahr and Kissinger not only arranged to stay in touch, but Kissinger proposed to establish a back channel between the White House and the Chancellery in Bonn.[30] This enabled them to communicate directly and without interference from the bureaucracies of the respective foreign ministries. As a result, Bahr's contacts with the State Department were only of secondary importance.[31] Within a few days, this channel was used. On 23 October, Bahr received information that the Soviet government had suggested beginning the Strategic Arms Limitation Talks on 17 November. Washington wanted to accept this.[32] Bonn also kept the White House informed over Brandt's letter of 19 November 1969 to Kosygin. In this, Brandt suggested bilateral talks on the basis of the existing commitments of both sides to their security systems.[33] Washington's backing was expressed by Secretary of State William Rogers when he came to see Brandt in Bonn on 6 December 1969.[34] Later that month, Kissinger was informed about the imminent talks between the Germans and Russians to be held in Moscow.[35]

The first two rounds of these talks between Bahr and Gromyko had been completed when Chancellor Brandt himself travelled to Washington in April 1970. The White House did not give any special advice on the negotiations with the Soviet Union, nor did it voice specific objections to Ostpolitik.[36] Nevertheless, Henry Kissinger felt deep-seated reservations concerning both the new government in Bonn and its foreign policy. In June, he told Paul Frank, the new Staatssekretär in the German Foreign Office: "I tell you! If a course of détente is to be pursued, we do it."[37] Kissinger's claims to leadership must be seen in the context of his fears that the Soviet Union might be successful in pursuing "selective détente," improving relations with European countries while remaining tough towards the United States.[38] Although the NATO meeting in December 1969 had strengthened Bonn's position for its negotiations with the Soviet Union, while at the same time imposing some constraints,[39] and in spite of the intense exchange of information between Bonn and Washington, Kissinger still remained nervous about the dangers of German nationalism and the possibility that Ostpolitik could weaken the NATO alliance.[40] As Ostpolitik was officially backed by Washington, any doubts concerning the reliability of the West Germans could only be spread in the form of rumor. When such rumors reached Bonn, Bahr, in a letter to Kissinger, did not attach much importance to them. He reminded Kissinger of their mutual trust and added: "Who ever has a question or feels any cause for concern should express it frankly."[41]

Kissinger's doubts over the reliability of the Germans were shared by the French President, Georges Pompidou.[42] The British Prime Ministers Harold Wilson and (since June 1970) Edward Heath endorsed Ostpolitik, although Heath did not hide his anxiety that the Soviet Union wanted to test "the solidarity of the Western Alliance." In Western European perceptions of the Federal Republic, there was still a big question mark. How solid was the attachment of the West Germans to NATO? Had they really become an integral part of the Western world? Or was the containment of Germany still necessary? Heath wanted Brandt to remain "very conscious of the pitfalls on the way . . . I am confident that the Alliance can stand the strains of détente as it has survived the test of the Cold War. But in a climate of relaxation we shall have to be, and indeed more, on our guard."[43]

Kissinger's attitude was much more patronizing, at least as it is shown in his memoirs. He consoled himself with the thought that the Federal Republic did not have the means to pursue its Ostpolitik independently "on a purely national basis."[44] Bonn was not Paris, and Brandt was not de Gaulle. The problem of West Berlin could only be solved in cooperation with the Four Powers. In his memoirs, Kissinger, in great detail and almost crowing with pleasure, demonstrated the constraints of Ostpolitik which followed from the postwar settlement in Germany: "The linkage to Berlin was our ace in the hole."[45] Since Bonn wanted to develop a linkage policy as well, there was no disagreement in substance. There was disagreement, however, with respect to the speed of Western-Soviet talks on Berlin. Bonn wished for some early progress. Only the Western allies could put pressure on Moscow in order to improve the situation of West Berlin. Bonn insisted on Soviet recognition of the special links between the Federal Republic and West Berlin.[46] The success of Ostpolitik was dependent on progress in Berlin, and progress in Berlin was not only a matter of Soviet but also of U.S. policy.[47] In contrast to Brandt, Kissinger was not in a hurry.[48] For him, the Berlin problem was only one issue in his linkage strategy which included a wide range of questions such as SALT and Vietnam. Consequently, the speed of the German–Soviet *rapprochement* seemed to be too high. Why not wait for the results of the German–Soviet encounter?

The first result was the Treaty of Moscow, signed on 12 August 1970.

Immediately after the ceremony, which he had watched on TV in his summer retreat, Helmut Schmidt sent a remarkable handwritten letter to Brandt. In Schmidt's view, the treaty was a "great step" forward. There was every reason to believe that a "new era" had begun in East–West relations. Yet, almost in the same breath, Schmidt warned of "euphoric propaganda" which might shed doubts on the West German position in the Western camp. Euphoria would be counterproductive with respect to East Germany, the Western allies, and the forthcoming debate in the Federal Republic. Washington, London, and Paris ought to be informed immediately. Schmidt's impression was that the White House was frowning at the speed of Ostpolitik.[49]

Only five days after the signature in Moscow, Bahr arrived in Washington. Kissinger seemed to be impressed with the Russo-German agreement. The Federal Republic had been successful in realizing what it had earlier proposed in public and in the confidential talks in Washington. Kissinger expressed the wish to continue "our close relationship." Bonn, he advised, should not believe in rumours. The Nixon administration gave its full support to Ostpolitik. Time and again, Franz-Josef Strauss, the mighty leader of the Bavarian branch of the Christian Democrats, had been on the phone. But Kissinger only listened to him and did not encourage him in his opposition to Ostpolitik. It may be that Kissinger's trust in Bahr had increased by August 1970. But it is revealing that he wanted to know how Bahr perceived the motives of the Soviet Union. Assistant Secretary of State Hillenbrand also wanted to know whether the Soviet Union was hoping to undermine the Western alliance. In responding, Bahr pointed to the Soviet interest in economic cooperation with the West. As to American fears with regard to NATO, he took the contrary line, contending that the Soviet Union wanted to preserve the existing bloc structures, including the Federal Republic's NATO membership. Otherwise, the Soviet grip on the Warsaw Pact states would be in danger.[50]

Bahr did not only want to give information about the German–Soviet Treaty. He also urged Kissinger to speed up the Berlin negotiations.[51] In October 1970, Chancellor Brandt asked for consultations on the part of the "four Western governments" (including the Federal Republic) over Berlin. Difficulties between the United States and the Soviet Union should be solved, he argued, by improving the means of communication. "Whether the Soviet Union is really interested in a détente in Central Europe," he wrote to Nixon, "what I assume, will be proved in the test case of Berlin . . . We should not be discouraged by setbacks which are common practice in Soviet tactics."[52] Brandt was impatient and also critical of the American handling of the Berlin problem.[53] Bonn felt under enormous pressure of time. It was concerned that the frustrated government in East Berlin might, as a result of delay, regain some influence with Moscow.

During the autumn of 1970, the Federal Government in Bonn also took action to deal with public opinion in the United States. U.S. reactions in general towards Ostpolitik still seemed mixed. Hans Apel, deputy floor leader of the SPD in the Bundestag, reported home from Washington that he had found "odd ideas" about the aims of Ostpolitik among many members of the administration, Congressmen, and journalists.[54] Defense Secretary Melvin Laird also appeared concerned that certain sections of the SPD might harbor "illusions about the Soviet Union."[55]

In Bonn, it was realized that something had to be done. One strategy was to employ a public relations company in New York.[56] Another was to use any contacts with American politicians or institutions in order to work on those who remained sceptical about Ostpolitik.[57] Although the attitude of the Social Democrats towards the United States had changed during the 1960s, becoming at the same time more pragmatic and more positive,[58] not many Social Democrats had first-hand knowledge of American politics and society.[59] One outstanding exception was Horst Ehmke, a professor of law before he entered politics and, eventually, became Head of the Chancellery under Willy Brandt. After the German–Soviet Treaty of August 1970, he travelled twice to the United States. The first trip, in late September, was to influence American public opinion. Ehmke met not only journalists but also representatives of the trade unions and the Jewish community, two important segments of public opinion which were known to be highly pessimistic about the implications of Ostpolitik. He also held talks in the State Department, where he asked for quicker negotiations on Berlin. Ehmke discovered that people in New York or Washington had a much broader view of the Soviet Union. The United States, unlike West Germany, confronted Soviet power and ambitions on a global scale. Some Americans complained about Soviet activities in Cuba and the Middle East. American Jews wanted to know whether Bonn's relations with Israel were likely to change, given the anti-Israel stance of the Soviet Union. The AFL/CIO (trade union) officials did not oppose détente on principle, but rejected any closer relations between German and Soviet trade unions. Because of the allegedly "socialist" element in the Social Democratic–Liberal government in Bonn, Ehmke was faced with anxious questioning – from both his AFL/CIO interlocutors and members of the State Department – on whether the Federal Republic would move to the left. He was able to give reassurance on this point. In general, Ehmke found that Ostpolitik was being received in an open-minded way, although Americans had some questions and a number of reservations.[60]

At the start of his trip, Ehmke had been briefed by the public relations company in New York working for the government in Bonn:

> Today Germany is a full-fledged economic and political partner of the U.S., and its power in both those areas is respected and perhaps a little feared by Americans. The public relations status has entered a new phase which, for want of a better term, could be called the equality phase. The new Germany's coming of age has coincided in time with a period of great political, racial and economic stress in the U.S.

Under these circumstances, Bonn should not ignore the strictly anti-communist stance of the AFL/CIO and of big business as well. Occasionally, the company mentioned, the Federal Republic was depicted as a "workshop of the Reds." The main advice it offered was to organize a new "German clique in the U.S." which would be a substitute for the old one headed by McCloy and Clay: "Unfortunately no real attempt has been made to form a new and liberally oriented group to serve the same purposes as the old group."[61] Ehmke fully endorsed this recommendation. Contacts in America, he believed, had to be intensified. In particular, Karl Schiller, Minister for Economic Affairs, should go to Washington to try and improve the relations of the SPD with business and finance in the United States. In Ehmke's view, no such relations currently existed. This might be easily explained, but was at the same time deplorable: "This group, being not on close terms with the Social Democrats, is very close to the Republican government."[62]

Within a very short time, Ehmke made a second trip. In December 1970, just before Christmas, he hurried off to see Kissinger in order to find out definitely what the White House had in mind with regard to Berlin and Ostpolitik in general. Again, Bonn had received reports announcing "a storm mounting in the American right wing on the subject of Germany's Eastern politics."[63] Shepard Stone, who was in favour of Ostpolitik, advised taking such objections to Ostpolitik seriously.[64] This more or less normal American accompaniment to Ostpolitik might, however, have caused no particular alarm in Bonn had it not been for more dramatic developments. On 16 December, Russell Fessenden, from the U.S. embassy in Bonn, talked to Ulrich Sahm from the Chancellery and, three days later, also to Bahr and Ehmke. The White House and the Pentagon, he warned, were not happy with the speed of Ostpolitik. In Washington, the Soviet Union was still regarded as an expansionist power active in many parts of the world.[65]

From the German point of view, any slowing down of détente meant a delay in the solution of the Berlin question. The matter was urgent enough for Ehmke to telephone the White House. Kissinger was asked for a meeting, which took place on 21 December. He seemed completely surprised when informed about Fessenden's warnings. Ehmke's impression was that Kissinger's reaction was honest and not merely for show. But he could not find out on whose orders Fessenden had been acting. Hillenbrand and Sonnenfeld, when they joined in, were also either unwilling or simply not able to disclose the secret. With respect to Berlin, Ehmke repeated what the Germans had said before. Since the Soviet ambassador, Zarapkin, had hinted to Brandt that Moscow was interested in a Berlin settlement in order to get the Treaty of Moscow ratified, he argued that the Americans should not hesitate. Ehmke agreed that the Soviet Union still pursued a policy of confrontation in other parts of the world. But this did not justify risking a standstill in Berlin as well. Kissinger's response was typical. The United States, he asserted, was interested in a Berlin settlement. The main interest, however, was on the part of the Federal Republic. He added that President Nixon wanted to decrease tensions with the Russians. The Europeans should continue their policy of détente also, providing the Western allies were not played off against each other. As Ehmke shared this concern – Kissinger's principal obsession[66] – there was full agreement. Security and détente had to go hand in hand. Ehmke also took the opportunity to explain that any American concern about economic and technological cooperation with the Soviet Union was unfounded. One should not overestimate, he maintained, the importance of trade with the East.[67]

It is difficult to say whether Ehmke's fleeting visit achieved very much or, indeed, changed anything in American policy. The story of the meeting with the Americans is perhaps mostly revealing with respect to the anxieties on both sides. The well-known American misgivings notwithstanding, Bahr was quite happy with the kind of communications that were taking place between Bonn and Washington.[68] In January 1971, a German journalist reported home from Washington that "tiresome talk" about Ostpolitik had apparently come to an end.[69] In the final resort, Ostpolitik was perceived as what it had been all the time: an integral part of Western détente. When Brandt and Nixon met in June 1971, Ostpolitik was no longer on the agenda. The issues of China and relations between the United States and Europe had proved themselves more interesting.[70]

In the end, a Four-Power Agreement was reached in September 1971. Bonn was involved in the negotiations when, at a crucial point, secret talks took place. Its participants were two of the Four Powers, represented by ambassadors Kenneth Rush and Valentin Falin – and Bahr. Times had changed: Bonn had become part of a system of back channels in the triangle Washington–Bonn–Moscow.[71] Kissinger pointed out to Bahr that nobody outside the White House knew anything about the "Rush–Falin–Bahr meetings, or your channel to me."[72] The new situation did not alter the dependency of the Federal Republic on the United States. But the impact of the Federal Republic on inter-allied relations and on the conduct of East–West relations was now evident. This was confirmed when Brandt went to see Brezhnev in Oreanda, in the Crimea, roughly two weeks after the signature of the Berlin Agreement. Brandt was convinced that both sides had entered a phase of normality. They "know where they agree," he commented, "where a *rapprochement* is conceivable, where they have differences." According to Brandt's notes, both sides demonstrated "strict loyalty to their respective allies."[73] The Federal Republic was not in danger of neutralism. Instead, it was successful in undercutting German–Soviet enmity by starting a process of confidence-building. Former enemies, Brandt and his government believed, should become normal opponents. If approached in the proper way, Ostpolitik – as an integral part of the Western policy of détente – might influence Soviet politics for the better.

This was one of the key arguments put forward by Brandt when he met President Nixon in Key Biscayne in December 1971.[74] The meeting was part of a series of talks the President had before going to Peking and Moscow. Nixon naturally consulted the British Prime Minister Edward Heath and the French President Georges Pompidou. But Brandt was a must, too. Apart from the good personal relationship between Nixon and Brandt and the increasing weight of the Federal Republic within the Western alliance, Brandt's government had been a driving force of détente. Also, Nixon had no personal knowledge of Brezhnev and was as keen as Brezhnev had been in Oreanda three months earlier to gain reliable information about his opposite number. It is interesting that both Brandt and Nixon gave assurances of their loyalty to NATO. Ostpolitik – as an independent German approach to détente – was simply not conceivable without close cooperation within the alliance. Nixon, on his part, ruled out any idea of a bilateral understanding between the superpowers which might be detrimental to the interests of America's allies. Nixon asked about Brandt's perceptions of Soviet policy. Brandt believed he saw an opportunity for more political communication and economic exchanges and even, though this proved wrong, for a reduction in Soviet armaments. At the same time, he warned against illusions. The West must remain on guard. It would never know for how long the Soviet Union was prepared to respect Western interests.

Most reassuring of all for Brandt was that Nixon stressed the inter-relationship of Ostpolitik, the agreement on Berlin, and a breakthrough in American–Soviet relations. Instead of fearing a German move towards the East, Nixon acknowledged the achievements of Bonn's Ostpolitik, which had smoothed the way for better East–West relations. Consequently, he was interested in having the German–Soviet Treaty ratified by the Bundestag before his own meeting with Brezhnev. But he emphasized that it was Bonn's decision to make. The Federal Republic, as an "independent power," should have "every room of manoeuvre."

The Federal Republic seemed to have become established as an equal actor on the world stage. Ostpolitik was approved of "everywhere in the world," as Defence Minister Helmut Schmidt noted on a trip to Asia, Australia, and New Zealand. It was also important, he thought, that it was regarded as an independent German initiative.[75] For Bonn, the feeling of independence and the support of its allies, in particular the United States, were equally important. During the whole process of détente, German Ostpolitik and American approaches to the Soviet Union were mutually supportive. Among those who suffered from this growing concert between Washington and Bonn were the Federal Republic's Christian Democrats, who opposed Ostpolitik. They wanted to use American counter-arguments as a lever in the intra-German debate, which tended to be full of emotion and outright bitterness.[76]

Members or supporters of the Social Democratic–Liberal government tried it the other way round, happy when they could refer to American support for Ostpolitik. In the course of 1971, they gained the upper hand in the debate. Bahr himself was invited to give lectures at the universities of Harvard and Georgetown in April and June 1971. In the invitation he got from the Center for Strategic and International Studies in Georgetown, he was told that Ostpolitik "has not received a full hearing in Washington." Many speakers from a CDU background had had a chance to advance objections, with the consequence that "an imbalance of views on the Ostpolitik has emerged."[77] This was eventually corrected and, in March 1972, James Reston compared Brandt's Ostpolitik and Nixon's moves towards China. Both, he maintained, "are trying to dismantle the Cold War."[78] Even the American labor unions, whose attitude to Ostpolitik had been a continuous concern to the SPD,[79] seemed to be less negative.[80] At an official level, Bahr had the impression of an excellent working partnership. In March 1972, Kissinger proposed meetings every three months. "For the first time," Bahr noted, "the conversation with Kissinger could be described as cordial."[81]

There is no doubt that, during the period of Ostpolitik, the Federal Republic's foreign policy continued to rely on the United States. For the simple but vital reason of security, there was no alternative.[82] At the same time, as demonstrated above, there had been a change in the relationship between the American superpower and the semi-sovereign Federal Republic. The United States was still the cornerstone of the Western alliance, but the perception of the American role in international affairs had changed. The Cold War pattern had to alter, in part to serve the cause of peace, in part because U.S. resources were now clearly limited. Hence the vital German interest in improving the European security system. It was always assumed, however, that the United States would remain an essential part of that system. In particular, no European Security Conference – proposed by the Soviet Union and regarded as useful by the government in Bonn – was conceivable without the participation of the United States. Kissinger was not at all enthusiastic about the prospect of such a conference, but he did not prevent it either. Addressing a group of American and German parliamentarians in November 1971, he dismissed it as "superfluous."[83] Bonn, however, wanted the Harmel formula to be further developed. The existing balance, it believed, ought to be supplemented by additional moves towards confidence-building. This aim seemed attainable because the Soviet Union was currently behaving in a promising way. But it also seemed to be a necessity: "It is not Holy Writ," remarked Helmut Schmidt, "that U.S. forces will have to remain in Europe at present strength for ever and ever."[84]

In the overall assessment, there was no short-term alternative to the role of the United States in Europe. Though its responsibility for its own security was growing, Western Europe could not "substitute the balance of Soviet Union/United States" in the foreseeable future.[85] But the Federal Republic and the other European states had to be aware that the role of the United States might change. Given the isolationist voices in America and the never-ending rumours of a reduction of U.S. troops in Europe, given the impact of the Vietnam War on U.S. foreign policy and the financial strain caused by the American global overcommitment, a policy of détente seemed vital for the Federal Republic, which might find itself greatly disadvantaged by renewed tensions with the Soviet Union. In this different situation, the United States was regarded as an indispensable, if somewhat uncertain, ally. "Is the U.S. going to continue to be a great nation, number one?" – President Nixon's nervous question,[86] asked in August 1971 when the dollar was taken off the gold standard and a symbol of the post-war order disappeared – was answered by Willy Brandt in a simple and affirmative way. For him, there was no change in the American role as a Western world power.[87] But it seemed both highly probably and timely that the United States should adapt to new circumstances.

The accommodation to realities was a characteristic feature of international politics from the 1960s to the 1970s. The Federal Republic had to accept the territorial status quo as the result of the Second World War. The superpowers had to acknowledge that their resources were limited and that the days of the bipolar world had gone. More specifically, the United States had to come to terms with an integrating Europe and, at the same time, to realize that maintaining a military presence in Europe, rather than isolationism, was in its own best interest. For Moscow, the economic shortcomings of the Soviet system could only be overcome by a reduction of armaments and economic cooperation with the West. Western financial, economic, and technological aid was dependent on a Soviet willingness to accept realities in Europe, including the closer integration of Western Europe, the links of West Berlin with the Federal Republic, and the continuing presence of U.S. troops in Europe.

In the long run, the policy of détente proved profitable to the West and especially to the Federal Republic of Germany and its revisionism. From the outset, Ostpolitik disputed the Soviet view that frontiers in Europe were forever unalterable. Bonn accepted the status quo only in the sense of a *modus vivendi*. Bahr put it succinctly as early as 1968: "The Soviet goal is to legalize the status quo. Our goal is to overcome it. It is a real conflict of interest."[88] Of course, this could not be said openly. But there is enough evidence that the architects of Ostpolitik had in mind not only West Germany's reconciliation with the Soviet Union, but also a change in the postwar order. A policy of détente with its implications (better East–West communications, an increase of trade relations, etc.) might transform the Warsaw Pact. Contrary to Kissinger's early pessimistic anxiety that the Soviet Union might be the only winner,[89] Brandt and Bahr did not rule out the chance that it might be the loser. Or, to put it more precisely, the Soviet Union might be forced to accept peaceful change. Although they had no timetable in mind for the change they envisaged, their policy was not only directed towards the recognition of the status quo but also towards its transformation. At a later stage of Ostpolitik, Bahr disclosed their strategy to Kissinger. The expansion of trade with the East, he argued, would produce more and more friction within the communist countries. As a result, it would contribute to changing them.[90]

Notes

1. Brandt to McCloy, 24 Mar. 1971, Willy-Brandt-Archiv im Archiv der sozialen Demokratie der Friedrich-Ebert-Stiftung, Bonn (WBA), Aktengruppe Bundeskanzler und Bundesregierung 1969–1974 (BK), 43.
2. Namely the recognition of the post-war borders in Europe and of Soviet hegemony in Eastern Europe.
3. Willy Brandt, *Erinnerungen* (Frankfurt: Propyläen, 1989), p. 193.
4. "Berlin und Ostpolitik: Nahtlose Übereinstimmung," WBA, BK 92. See also Brandt, *Erinnerungen*, p. 191.
5. Helmut Schmidt, *Menschen und Mächte* (paperback ed., Berlin: Goldmann, 1991), p. 187.
6. See Andreas Vogtmeier, *Egon Bahr und die deutsche Frage: Zur Entwicklung der sozialdemokratischen Ost- und Deutschlandpolitik vom Kriegsende bis zur Vereinigung* (Bonn: Dietz, 1996).
7. Memorandum by Bahr for Brandt, 30 Jan. 1967, Archiv der sozialen Demokratie der Friedrich-Ebert-Stiftung, Bonn (AsD), Depositum (Dep.) Bahr 299/3.
8. Gottfried Niedhart, "Friedens- und Interessenwahrung: Zur Ostpolitik der FDP in Opposition und sozial-liberaler Regierung 1968–1970," *Jahrbuch zur Liberalismus-Forschung*, 7 (1995), 105–26.
9. Brandt, *Erinnerungen*, p. 189; Henry Kissinger, *White House Years* (Boston and Toronto: Little, Brown and Co., 1979), pp. 411, 530.
10. Notes by Brandt on his talks in Washington, 8 Feb. 1967, WBA, Aktengruppe Bundesminister des Auswärtigen (BMinA) 17.
11. Report by Henri Nannen and Theo Sommer, who were received by President Johnson on 8 July 1967, WBA, BMinA 7.
12. Frank Costigliola, "Lyndon B. Johnson, Germany and 'the End of the Cold War'," in Warren I. Cohen and Nancy Bernkopf Tucker, eds., *Lyndon Johnson Confronts the World: American Foreign Policy, 1963–1968* (Cambridge: Cambridge University Press, 1994), p. 197. See also Thomas Alan Schwartz, "Victories and Defeats in the Long Twilight Struggle: The United States and Westen Europe in the 1960s," in Diane B. Kunz, ed., *The Diplomacy of the Crucial Decade: American Foreign Relations during the 1960s* (New York: Columbia University Press, 1994), p. 137–38.
13. Report by Bernd von Staden (German embassy Washington), 18 July 1967, WBA, BMinA 1; note by the German journalist Georg Schröder on a conversation with R. S. Cline (U.S. embassy Bonn and Head of

the C.I.A. for Germany), 9 Apr. 1968, AsD, Dep. Helmut Schmidt 5202.

14. Henry Kissinger, *Diplomacy* (New York: Simon and Schuster, 1994), p. 735.

15. Willy Brandt, *Begegnungen und Einsichten: Die Jahre 1960–1975* (Hamburg: Hoffman und Campe, 1976), pp. 385–86. See also Clay Clemens, "Amerikanische Entspannungs- und deutsche Ostpolitik 1969–1975," in Wolfgang-Uwe Friedrich, ed., *Die USA und die Deutsche Frage 1945–1990* (Frankfurt and New York: Campus, 1991), p. 207; Dietrich Orlow, "Ambivalence and Attraction: The German Social Democrats and the United States, 1945–1974," in Reiner Pommerin, ed., *The American Impact on Postwar Germany* (Providence and Oxford: Berghahn, 1995), p. 46.

16. Denis Healey in a working paper "The Nixon Doctrine and the Future of Europe," presented to the twentieth Bilderberg Meeting at Woodstock, Vermont, 23–25 Apr. 1971, AsD, Dep. Bahr 301/4.

17. See, for example, Kissinger's comments on Bahr as an "old-fashioned German nationalist." Henry Kissinger, *Years of Upheaval* (London: Weidenfeld and Nicolson, 1982), p. 147. Although the impact of the Wilhelmine and Nazi periods on the image of Germany was still there in the 1960s, a more positive image of the Federal Republic as a loyal and trustworthy partner of the West had made progress in the United States. See Ernest May, "Das nationale Interesse der USA und die deutsche Frage 1966–1972," in Gottfried Niedhart, Detlef Junker, and Michael W. Richter, eds., *Deutschland in Europa: Nationale Interessen und internationale Ordnung im 20. Jahrhundert* (Mannheim: Palatium Verlag, 1997), p. 275. On the Johnson administration and its perceptions of Germany, see Costigliola, "Johnson," pp. 173–79 and 189–90.

18. Kissinger, *White House Years*, p. 408.

19. Kissinger, *Years of Upheaval*, p. 144. Raymond L. Garthoff, *Detente and Confrontation: American–Soviet Relations from Nixon to Reagan* (Washington: Brookings, 1985), p. 109, is right when he makes the point that Kissinger, in his memoirs, tries vainly to prove that he rescued Ostpolitik from failure.

20. Brandt, *Erinnerungen*, pp. 189–90.

21. He had been told by Rusk in August 1967 that the Europeans could not simply leave the American-Soviet conflict. Notes on talks with Rusk, 15–16 Aug. 1967, WBA, BMinA 17.

22. Brandt, addressing the parliamentary party of the SPD, 4 Mar. 1969, AsD, SPD-Fraktion, 5, Wahlperiode (WP) 119.

23. Brandt, *Erinnerungen*, p. 176. Summaries and positive assessments of the whole series of talks at government and party level were given by Brandt, Schmidt, and Wehner at a meeting of the party executive of the SPD, 25 Aug. 1969, AsD, Parteivorstandsprotokolle. Helmut Schmidt, at that time leader of the parliamentary party of the SPD in the Bundestag, had just returned from a trip to Moscow. In July 1969, Walter Scheel and two more FDP politicians travelled to Moscow, after having talks in Washington. Kissinger, *White House Years*, pp. 435, 440.

24. For details see Adrian W. Schertz, *Die Deutschlandpolitik Kennedys und Johnsons: Unterschiedliche Ansätze innerhalb der amerikanischen Regierung* (Cologne: Böhlau, 1992).

25. Klaus Schwabe, ed., *Adenauer und die USA* (Bonn: Bouvier, 1994).

26. Wolfram F. Hanrieder, "Deutschland und die USA: Partner im transatlantischen Bündnis der Nachkriegsära," in Jürgen Elvert and Michael Salewski, eds., *Deutschland und der Westen im 19. und 20. Jahrhundert: Teil 1: Transatlantische Beziehungen* (Stuttgart: Steiner Verlag, 1993), p. 131. See also Wolfram F. Hanrieder, *Deutschland, Europa, Amerika: Die Außenpolitik der Bundesrepublik Deutschland 1949–1994* (Paderborn: Schöningh, 2nd edn., 1995), pp. 25–30.

27. Brandt, *Erinnerungen*, p. 170.

28. Note by Bahr for Brandt, 1 Oct. 1969, WBA, Loses Material.

29. AsD, Dep. Bahr 439/2.

30. Note by Bahr for Brandt, 14 Oct. 1969, AsD, Dep. Bahr 439/2. See also Kissinger, *White House Years*, p. 411.

31. Author's interview with Bahr, 15 Mar. 1996.

32. AsD, Dep. Bahr 439/2.

33. *Ibid.*

34. AsD, Dep. Bahr 440/2. See also Ambassador Kenneth Rush to Brandt, 28 Oct. 1969, *ibid.* Rush's predecessor, George McGhee, had endorsed Ostpolitik too. George McGhee, *At the Creation of a New Germany – From Adenauer to Brandt: An Ambassador's Account* (New Haven and London: Yale University Press, 1989), p. 243.

35. Bahr to Kissinger, 30 Dec. 1969, AsD, Dep. Bahr 439/2.

36. Kissinger, *White House Years*, p. 423–24. Brandt, addressing the executive of the parliamentary party of the SPD in Bonn, 13 Apr. 1970: "Die Gespräche von Moskau, Warschau und Erfurt werden von den USA mit Sympathie betrachtet." AsD, SPD-Fraktion, 6. WP, 139.

37. Paul Frank, *Entschlüsselte Botschaft: Ein Diplomat macht Inventur* (Munich: dtv, 1985), p. 287.

38. Kissinger, *White House Years*, pp. 410, 528–29.

39. *Ibid.*, p. 412.

40. *Ibid.*, pp. 409-11. See also Kissinger's memorandum for President Nixon, 16 Feb. 1970, *ibid.*, pp. 529–30.

41. Bahr to Kissinger, 24 July 1970, AsD, Dep. Bahr 439/2.

42. Georges-Henri Soutou, "L'attitude de Georges Pompidou face à l'Allemagne," in Association Georges Pompidou, ed., *Georges Pompidou et l'Europe* (Brussels: Complexe, 1995), pp. 267–313.

43. Heath to Brandt, 27 Sept. 1971, WBA, BK 52.

44. Kissinger, *White House Years*, p. 410

45. *Ibid.*, p. 531.

46. Letters by Brandt to Washington, London, and Paris, 25 Feb. and 22 Mar. 1970, WBA, BK 51. See also Bahr to Kissinger, 25 May 1970, AsD, Dep. Bahr 439/2.

47. On the central importance of the "American-led negotiations on the Berlin problem," see also Frank Ninkovich, *Germany and the United States: The Transformation of the German Question since 1945* (Boston: Twayne, 1988), p. 153.

48. Kissinger, *White House Years*, p. 532.

49. Schmidt to Brandt, 13 Aug. 1970, WBA, BK 18. On 18 Aug. 1970, Schmidt asked the planning staff of the Defence Ministry for an analysis of the Treaty of Moscow. In a memorandum of 28 Aug. 1970, the main points, marked by Schmidt, were: the treaty did not remove the differences which existed between both sides; it leaves room to manoeuvre with respect to peaceful change of the status quo; it must not lead to an inappropriate feeling of security; the Federal Republic is in need of a solid safeguard in the West against any risks which might come up. AsD, Dep. Schmidt 1649 A.

50. Notes on Bahr's conversations with Kissinger and Hillenbrand, 17 and 18 Aug. 1970, AsD, Dep. Bahr 439/2 and 444/1.

51. *Ibid.* and Kissinger, *White House Years*, p. 533.

52. Brandt to Nixon, 14 Oct. 1970, WBA, BK 60.

53. Kissinger, *White House Years*, p. 800.

54. Apel to Wehner, 20 Aug. 1970, AsD, SPD-Fraktion, 6. WP, 322.

55. Peter Petersen, SPD member of the Bundestag, to Helmut Schmidt, 29 Sept. 1970, on a conversation with Laird, AsD, Dep. Schmidt 5493.

56. The company, Roy Blumenthal International Associates: Public Relations and Advertising, had a contract with the government in Bonn. AsD, Dep. Bahr 81.

57. Hans Eberhard Dingels, Head of the Department for International

Affairs of the SPD, to Karl Wienand and Kurt Mattick, 4 Nov. 1970, WBA, Aktengruppe Parteivorsitzender, 59. See also Martin J. Hillenbrand, "Die Vereinigten Staaten und Deutschland," in Wolfram F. Hanrieder and Hans Rühle, eds., *Im Spannungsfeld der Weltpolitik: 30 Jahre deutsche Außenpolitik (1949–1979)* (Stuttgart: Bonn Aktuell, 1981), pp. 144–45.

58. Orlow, "Ambivalence and Attraction," p. 44–46.

59. In 1974, a Social-Democratic study group on the United States, which was directed by Heinz Ruhnau, still complained about the prevailing attention paid by SPD parliamentarians to Eastern Europe at the expense of the United States. Meeting of 21 Jan. 1974, AsD, Dep. Schmidt 6240.

60. Ehmke's memorandum of 13 Oct. 1970 on his trip to the United States, which lasted from 27 Sept. to 3 Oct. 1970, AsD, Dep. Ehmke 286. In the same file, there are notes by the German consulate general in New York (6 Oct. 1970) and by Ulrich Sahm of the Federal Chancellery in Bonn, who accompanied Ehmke (20 Oct. 1970). See also Horst Ehmke, *Mittendrin. Von der Großen Koalition zur Deutschen Einheit* (Berlin: Rowohlt, 1994), p. 140; Ulrich Sahm, *"Diplomaten taugen nichts": Aus dem Leben eines Staatsdieners* (Düsseldorf: Droste, 1994), pp. 277–78. On 23 Oct. 1970, Ehmke had a conversation with Ray Cline who, after his time in Bonn (see above n. 13), had moved to the State Department. Cline had doubts concerning the Soviets' reliability. But the U.S. government did not wish to return to a policy of confrontation. Ehmke stressed that the German initiatives towards the East were possible only on the basis of a strong Western alliance. AsD, Dep. Ehmke 286.

61. Memorandum by Blumenthal for Ehmke, 10 Sept. 1970, AsD, Dep. Bahr 81 A/1.

62. Memorandum by Ehmke, 13 Oct. 1970 (see above n. 60).

63. Memorandum by Blumenthal for Ehmke, 10 Dec. 1970, AsD, Dep. Bahr 81/A 1.

64. Klaus Harpprecht, a journalist who was close to Brandt, on a conversation with Shepard Stone. Harpprecht to Brandt, 17 Dec. 1970, WBA, BK 8.

65. Note by Sahm, 16 Dec. 1970, AsD, Dep. Ehmke 286; Ehmke, *Mittendrin*, pp. 140–41.

66. Repeated frequently, for instance on 24 Apr. 1971, when Kissinger gave a speech at the Bilderberg conference. Kissinger's support for Ostpolitik was combined with a warning against "differentiated negotiations" with Moscow. In the event of a race of Western states

to Moscow, it was beyond any doubt who would win. Notes by Bahr, 28 Apr. 1971, AsD, Dep. Bahr 439/2.

67. Back in Bonn, Ehmke wrote a lengthy note on his talks in Washington on 21 Dec. 1970, AsD, Dep. Ehmke 286. Also see Ehmke, *Mittendrin*, pp. 141–42 – where Ehmke, however, gives a wrong date for his meeting with Kissinger.

68. Bahr to Blumenthal, 13 Jan. 1971, AsD, Dep. Bahr 81B/1.

69. Klaus Bölling to Helmut Schmidt, 24 Jan. 1971, AsD, Dep. Schmidt 5701.

70. Notes by Brandt on his talks in Washington, 15 and 16 June 1971, AsD, Dep. Bahr 440/2. See also Brandt, *Begegnungen*, p. 390.

71. Kissinger, *White House Years*, pp. 807-809; Valentin Falin, *Politische Erinnerungen* (Munich: Droemer Knaur, 1993), pp. 165–74; Werner Link, "Außen- und Deutschlandpolitik in der Ära Brandt 1969–1974," in Karl Dietrich Bracher, Wolfgang Jäger, and Werner Link, *Republik im Wandel 1969–1974: Die Ära Brandt* (Stuttgart and Mannheim: Deutsche Verlags-Anstalt/F.A. Brockhaus, 1986), p. 202.

72. Kissinger to Bahr, 24 May 1971, AsD, Dep. Bahr 439/2.

73. Notes taken by Brandt, 18 Sept. 1971, WBA, BK 92. Kissinger was informed by Bahr in a letter of 20 Sept. 1971, AsD, Dep. Bahr 439/2.

74. For a full account of the meeting on 28 and 29 Dec. 1971, see Brandt, *Begegnungen*, pp. 395–402. Also see Brandt, *Erinnerungen*, p. 193.

75. Schmidt, addressing the parliamentary party of the SPD, 14 Dec. 1971, AsD, SPD-Fraktion, 6. WP, 81.

76. A good example can be found in Kurt Birrenbach, *Meine Sondermissionen: Rückblick auf zwei Jahrzehnte bundesdeutscher Außenpolitik* (Düsseldorf and Vienna: Econ Verlag, 1984), pp. 324–43.

77. John M. Steeves to Bahr, 6 May 1971, AsD, Dep. Bahr 301/3. On the lecture at Harvard, *ibid.*, 440/1.

78. *New York Times*, 1 Mar. 1972, reported immediately by the German ambassador to Bonn, AsD, Dep. Schmidt 342.

79. Helmut Schmidt to George Meany, 18 Mar. 1971, AsD, Dep. Schmidt 5813; Schmidt to Brandt, 23 Apr. 1971, AsD, SPD-Fraktion, 6. WP, 310.

80. Ruhnau to Wehner, 14 Apr. 1972, AsD, SPD-Fraktion, 6. WP, 243. However, the relations of the German trade unions with the East were still criticized.

81. Notes by Bahr on a conversation with Kissinger, 28 Mar. 1972, AsD, Dep. Bahr 439/2.

82. Bahr stressed this point time and again. See, for instance, his memo-

randum, 18 Sept. 1969, and his letter to Brandt, 21 Sept. 1969, on the foreign policy guidelines of the Federal Republic: "The United States are our most important ally. Our security depends on the U.S." Vogtmeier, *Bahr*, p. 110.

83. Report by Heinz Ruhnau on the conference, 14–16 Nov. 1971, AsD, SPD-Fraktion, 6. WP, 211.

84. Helmut Schmidt, "Germany in the Era of Negotiations," *Foreign Affairs*, vol. 49, no. 1 (1970), 43. See also notes by Brandt in June 1970: "US bleiben, aber reduzieren," WBA, BK 91.

85. Undated notes by Brandt (Notizen für Krim September 1971), WBA, BK 92.

86. President Nixon, 13 Aug. 1971, H. R. Haldeman, *The Haldeman Diaries: Inside the Nixon White House* (New York: G.P. Putnam's Sons, 1994), p. 344.

87. Brandt, *Begegnungen*, p. 379. For his resentment of the way Washington acted, see *ibid.*, pp. 387, 395.

88. Memorandum by Bahr, 1 Oct. 1968, quoted in Vogtmeier, *Bahr*, p. 129.

89. Kissinger, *White House Years*, pp. 408–10, 533.

90. Bahr to Kissinger, 14 Apr. 1973: "Eine systematische, aber nicht wahllose Erweiterung der wirtschaftlichen Ost–West-Beziehungen wird die Widersprüche in den kommunistisch regierten Ländern steigern und zu weiteren Modifikationen des Systems beitragen." Vogtmeier, *Bahr*, p. 177.

Notes on Contributors

Kathleen Burk is Professor of Modern and Contemporary History at University College London. She is the author of a number of books, including *Britain, America and the Sinews of War 1914–1918* (1985) and (with Alec Cairncross) *'Goodbye, Great Britain': The 1976 IMF Crisis* (1992), and many articles. She is currently completing a life and history of A. J. P. Taylor and beginning a large project on the Marshall Plan from the European perspective.

Frank Costigliola is Professor of History at the University of Connecticut. He has written *Awkward Dominion: American Political Economic, and Cultural Relations with Europe, 1919-1933* (1984), and "'Unceasing Pressure for Penetration': Gender, Pathology, and Emotion in George Kennan's Formation of the Cold War," *The Journal of American History* (March 1997).

Alex Danchev is Professor of International Relations and Dean of Social Sciences at Keele University. His writings on Anglo-American relations include a collection of essays, *On Specialness* (1998), and biographical studies of Field Marshal Sir John Dill and Oliver Franks. His latest book is a biography of Basil Liddell Hart, *Alchemist of War* (1998).

Alan P. Dobson is a Reader in Politics at University of Wales, Swansea. His books include *Anglo-American Relations in the Twentieth Century* (1995); *Peaceful Air Warfare* (1991); and *Flying in the Face of Competition* (1995). He has edited *Deconstructing and Reconstructing the Cold War* (1999) and is currently completing two books, one co-authored, *US Foreign Policy*, and a monograph *US Economic Statecraft: Policies of Economic Warfare and Economic Embargo 1933–1990*. In 1997 he was a senior research fellow at the Norwegian Nobel Institute.

Lawrence Freedman is Professor of War Studies at King's College, London and currently official historian of the Falklands campaign. He has written extensively on nuclear strategy and contemporary conflicts.

John Gearson is a lecturer in War Studies at King's College, London. He is the author of *Harold Macmillan and the Berlin Wall Crisis 1958-62: The Limits of Interests and Force* (1998) and has written on various aspects of British foreign policy during the Cold War. He is currently researching a book on terrorism.

Beatrice Heuser is a Senior Lecturer at the Department of War Studies, King's College London. She holds a doctorate from Oxford and a *Habilitation* from the Philipps University at Marburg an der Lahn. Her major publications include *Nuclear Strategies and Forces for Europe, 1949–2000* (1997); *Nuclear Mentalities? Britain, France and the FRG* (1998); *Western 'Containment' Policies in the Cold War: the Yugoslav Case* (1989), and with Cyril Buffet (eds): *Haunted by History: Myths in International Relations* (1998). Her next book will be *The Bomb* in the Longman's series *Turning Points in History*.

Geir Lundestad is director of the Norwegian Nobel Institute and professor of history at the University of Oslo. His most recent books are *'Empire' by Integration: The United States and European Integration, 1945–1997* (1998), *No End to Alliance* (1998) and *East, West, North, South. Major Developments in International Politics since 1945* (1999).

James Edward Miller is the editor for Western Europe of the series *Foreign Relations of the United States*. He chairs the programs on Italy and Greece-Cyprus at the Department of State's Foreign Service Institute and teaches European history and politics at Georgetown University and the School of Advanced International Studies, Johns Hopkins University. Among his books are *The United States and Italy, 1940-1950, From Elite to Mass Politics*, and the forthcoming *Politics in a Museum*, a study of postwar Florence.

Gottfried Niedhart is Professor of Modern History at the University of Mannheim. He has published on English and German history, and on the history of international relations. Recent works are *Geschichte Englands im 19. und 20. Jahrhundert* (2nd edn. 1996); *Deutsche Geschichte 1918–1933* (2nd edn. 1996); *Internationale Beziehungen 1917–1947* (1989). Together with D. Junker and M. Richter he has edited *Deutschland in Europa. Nationale Interessen und internationale Ordnung im 20. Jahrhundert* (1997).

Klaus Schwabe is Professor Emeritus at the Historisches Institut, RWTH Aachen. He has written numerous books on international relations in the twentieth century and his most recent publications include "Germany's Peace Aims and the Domestic and International Constraints," in Manfred Boemke, Gerald D. Feldman, Elisabeth Glaser (eds), *The Treaty of Versailles. A reassessment after 75 years.*

Melvyn Stokes teaches American history at University College London, where he has been the principal organizer of the Commonwealth Fund Conference in American history since 1988. He is co-editor of *Race and Class in the American South Since 1890* (Berg, 1994), *The Market Revolution in America: Social, Political and Religious Expressions, 1800–1880* (Virginia, 1996), *American Movie Audiences: From the Turn of the Century to The Early Sound Era* and *Identifying Hollywood's Audiences* (both British Film Institute, 1999). He has also published numerous articles on American reform movements, historiography and film history.

Fiona Venn is a Senior Lecturer in United States history at the University of Essex. Her main areas of research are oil diplomacy and the New Deal. Her principal publications are *Oil Diplomacy in the Twentieth Century* (1986); *Franklin D Roosevelt* (1990) and *The New Deal* (1998). She is currently working on a book on the oil crises of the 1970s.

Pascaline Winand is Senior Lecturer at the Université Libre de Bruxelles and Senior Research Fellow at the Belgian National Fund for Scientific Research. Her publications include: *Eisenhower, Kennedy and the United States of Europe* (1994/1997) for which she received the Adolphe Bentinck Special Mention Prize. Her current research focuses on policy-making in US-EU relations, and lobbying and European integration.

Index

Index